P9-AFZ-436

# GOD, MAN & HOLLYWOOD

# GOD, MAN & HOLLYWOOD

Politically Incorrect Cinema
from *The Birth of a Nation* to *The Passion of the Christ*

MARK ROYDEN WINCHELL

WILMINGTON, DELAWARE

Winchell, Mark Royden, 1948–

God, man, and Hollywood : politically incorrect cinema from "The birth of a nation" to "The passion of the Christ" / Mark Winchell.—1st ed. —Wilmington, Del. : ISI Books, 2008.

p. ; cm.

ISBN: 978-1-933859-56-9

1. Motion pictures—Social aspects—United States. 2. Culture in motion pictures. 3. Motion pictures—Political aspects—United States. 4. Politics in motion pictures. 5. Conservatism—United States. 6. Popular culture—United States. I. Title.

PN1995.9.S6 W56 2008 2007941671
302.2343/0973—dc22 0805

ISI Books
Intercollegiate Studies Institute
Post Office Box 4431
Wilmington, DE 19807-0431
www.isibooks.org

Manufactured in the United States of America

# CONTENTS

## PART FOUR: ONE HUNDRED POLITICALLY INCORRECT FILMS

# FOREWORD

In 1949, Arthur M. Schlesinger Jr. published a book titled *The Vital Center: The Politics of Freedom*. Early postwar America, at the dawn of the nuclear age, was a time not unlike our own, the country wracked by racial and economic discontent and facing seemingly apocalyptic threats from abroad. In the space of a year the international crisis would deepen, as the Cold War then being waged between the United States and the Soviet Union would turn hot with the invasion of South Korea by its northern counterpart. Though he recognized that "Western man in the middle of the twentieth century [was] tense, uncertain, adrift," Schlesinger was no advocate of extremism in the defense of the nation's liberty. In *The Vital Center*, he celebrated instead the era's political liberalism, the consensus that was then emerging from the demonstrable failure of extreme policies on both the right and the left. Unyielding Republican advocates of free markets and minimal government regulation, so Schlesinger argued, had failed to protect democracy from suicidal economic inequality: "Terrified of change, lacking confidence and resolution, subject to spasms of panic and hysteria, the extreme right-wing elements keep the American business community in far too irresponsible a condition to work steadily for the national interest."

But the socialist wing of the Democratic Party had, Schlesinger wrote, misidentified private ownership as the root of all evil, fundamentally misunderstanding the nature of good government. Naïvely embracing social Pelagianism, the "belief that man is perfectible," socialists (such as the failed presidential aspirant Henry Wallace) found themselves committed to "the endless task of explaining why, in spite of history and in spite of rhetoric, he does not always behave that way."[1] To Schlesinger and many other intellectuals of his era, liberalism did not mean, as it now regrettably has come to do, an extreme leftist political and, especially, cultural outlook. It was instead a "spirit of radicalism" which is also "the spirit of the center—the spirit of human decency, opposing the extremes of tyranny." Such radicalism "dedicates itself to problems as they come, attacking them in terms which best advance the humane and libertarian values, which best secure the freedom and fulfillment of the individual."[2] This spirit prevailed through the Eisenhower and Kennedy presidencies, and it was not lacking even during Lyndon Johnson's more embattled administrations.

In its emphasis on individual freedom, and in its acknowledgement of the social contract (for what else are human values but those which advance our collective destiny?), this form of liberalism is a political philosophy which offers common ground to social conservatives like Mark Winchell and progressives such as myself. But to find this place beyond partisanship today, we must retreat nearly a half century to a time when the most dangerous international threat was totalitarianism (itself a movement in which the extreme left and right wings met, and hence a mirror image of the consensus liberalism that arose to oppose and, eventually, triumph over it). The task Schlesinger set for America, a "continuous and exacting commitment" to defend democratic ideals "against both right and left," has proven difficult for us to fulfill. It is high time that early-twenty-first-century America set about building the kind of consensus that served America so well five decades ago.

Unfortunately, developments in the national culture since the contentious 1960s have put an end to the postwar public sphere whose emergence Schlesinger rightly imagined as quintessentially American, and in which those on the right and on the left might speak respectfully to one another and to their mutual profit. A refusal to listen to or entertain the ideas of others, as well as a terror of the controversial or confrontational, now prevails. Mark Winchell condemns this atmosphere of political correctness, and I firmly share his sentiments. We agree that the First Amendment protects speech that some might find offensive and that the stifling of political expression is a vice. And Winchell is enough of a liberal (in Schlesinger's understanding of the term) to recognize that political correctness on the right is worthy of the same outright dismissal. Though it pays its respects to such contemporary conservative pundits as Michael Medved, Winchell's approach to Hollywood film is decidedly old-fashioned. It offers a rational, informed, and passionate critique of (and also tribute to) Hollywood filmmaking in the vein of William F. Buckley Jr.'s *God and Man at Yale* (1951), a text that this book honors. Buckley's polemic brought into sharp focus the position of the cultural conservative, who, in James Davison Hunter's useful formulation, is committed to "an external, definable, and transcendent authority." His opponent, the progressive, is inclined "to resymbolize historic faiths according to the prevailing assumptions of contemporary life."[3] Like Buckley, Winchell is an eloquent spokesman for the conservative position.

This book offers a self-avowedly tendentious analysis of a well-chosen body of American films of undoubted political and cultural importance, arguing that, from a socially conservative point of view, they can be seen as politically incorrect. To that end, Winchell does not preach to the choir, but instead offers carefully argued, intellectually sophisticated readings of these key and often controversial productions, paying appropriate attention to historical context. Winchell doubtless has fired a shot in that particular theater of the so-called "culture wars" in which the nature and functioning of the national film industry is at issue. But, I repeat, he does not write with the single-minded and ultimately unpersuasive fervor of the true believer. That makes this book compelling reading—even, perhaps especially, for those who, like me, do not share the author's political assumptions.

The virtues of this volume are its demonstrable intelligence and perspicacity. It is no mean trick, for example, to write about D. W. Griffith's *The Birth of a Nation* in a way that recontextualizes the film for students of the cinema, who are accustomed to praise the director's art as fervently as they condemn his politics. Winchell usefully reminds us that both Griffith's film and its source—two Thomas Dixon novels (and stage play versions of same)—should be understood within that ongoing battle over racial politics inaugurated by Harriet Beecher Stowe's *Uncle Tom's Cabin* more than fifty years earlier. Winchell is no apologist for the film's regrettable appeal to fears that the presence of free black men inherently threatens the sexual purity of white women, but he is right to point out that the power of Stowe's book stems in part from her indictment of slavery as an institution that destroys the white family from within, providing slave owners with irresistible temptations to sexual malfeasance.

I'm not sure, however, that *The Birth of a Nation* belongs in the category of politically incorrect films. Its incredible popularity with educated, wealthy white filmgoers all over the country suggests that its racial politics, like its views of Reconstruction, were widely shared. In fact, in my view it is the widespread appeal of Griffith's representations that make his film necessary viewing for any American interested in facing squarely up to early-twentieth-century racism. Griffith, like Dixon, has too often been demonized for expressing what were consensus views about American history and race, even if they were not shared by a growing minority within the intelligentsia. I crossed a picket line at New York University to view this film as a graduate student, and when I screened it myself in a course devoted to African-American film at Georgia State University in Atlanta in the early '90s, I was faced with a well-organized and respectful band of protesters who, invited to present their views, turned that class into a lively exchange about the virtues and discontents of showing the film. *Birth*, in short, has only become politically incorrect over time, demonstrating the dangers posed to free expression by an excessive sensitivity to what some might find offensive. Winchell and I agree that it is a central document in American cultural history. Though Winchell is more disposed than I to see *Birth* as a robust, perhaps justified defense of Southern values, I share his view that, despite its regrettable politics, the film is possessed of an extraordinary power.

Like the others in this continually surprising book, Winchell's chapter on Griffith's movie is filled with interesting insights, demonstrating the author's studious avoidance of a "talking points" approach to cultural questions. For example, he raises an issue of real embarrassment to the contemporary Republican Party, whose "base" is in the South, in complaining that Griffith's treatment of Lincoln is not faithful in the least to the great hatred felt by many Southerners for the man who raised an army of volunteers to oppose their ostensibly peaceful secession. We are inclined to forget that secession raised a series of legal questions that were never adjudicated after the war when Jefferson Davis was released from federal custody without being charged with a crime. No court of law ever established that Lincoln had the right to raise that initial army of volunteers. Furthermore, it is the party of Lincoln that becomes the villain in *Birth*, as the "bloody shirt" radicals seize control of the federal government after rejecting Andrew Johnson's more moderate approaches to the reestablishment of legitimate governments in the former Confederate states. As Winchell points out, the film's treatment of Lincoln offers further evidence that Griffith did not produce a film that was politically incorrect, but offered instead a series of quite conscious appeals to consensus values, avoiding what might prove unpopular to Northerners, among whom something like a Lincoln cult had long since developed.

In closing, let me, in the centrist spirit of Arthur Schlesinger, offer another perspective on the Hollywood history traced in the introduction. Here I find Winchell's account a bit overcommitted to the conspiratorially inclined mythologies of both the Left and the Right. Hollywood accepted both a production code written by a Catholic college professor (and priest) in 1930 and, in 1934, a Production Code Administration to oversee its enforcement. The code, it turns out, was easily accommodated by the studios because its underlying aesthetic, derived from mid-Victorian moralist approaches to literary practice and value, was already dominant in Hollywood production. And, perhaps more importantly, having the major industry players adopt a uniform moral approach created the kind of level playing field with regard to content that suited a heavily capitalized business in which cartelization rather than competition guaranteed better profits for all. Self-censorship meant that no studio could differentiate its products from the others by injecting them with more outrageous violence or titillating visuals. Furthermore, the code was ideally suited for a period of production in which every film was intended for a vast, general audience, both national and worldwide. Left-wing critics of the code, however, see the code only as an attempt to stifle artistic expression and keep American audiences from enjoying the pleasures of post-Enlightenment artistic production. Consider Gerald Gardner's ranting denunciation: "Behind closed doors, a group of men had the power to lay their hands on the creations of artists, to twist them this way and that, to satisfy the mandates and morals of a pious little group who feared for the souls of their fellow men. It was all done in the name of public morality and the greater good."[4]

In the course of three decades, however, as America underwent enormous transformations in social values and cultural practice, the code gradually lost touch with the tastes of filmgoers. Reflecting the same trend toward obsolescence, the Catholic Legion of Decency, which had been formed to keep motion pictures "decent," itself quickly faded from the scene, its film-rating functions eventually taken over in the 1960s by a less confrontational, more culturally liberal National Catholic Office on Motion Pictures. The failure of traditional Hollywood formulas with audiences in the 1960s, and the success of foreign films that pushed the envelope in terms of sexual themes, led to the establishment of the current ratings system in 1966. Like American society, the audience for films is now fragmented into several niches, even as the exhibition year consists of seasons in which, predominantly, different kinds of films are released. Michael Medved has famously demonstrated that "G" rated films stand a better chance of making a profit than those rated "R," but this data does not justify his conclusion that Hollywood should make only "G" productions. Such a decision would leave the tastes of many unaddressed, and it would be financially disastrous—as Medved himself, an industry insider, must surely know. The decision to adopt the code, like the decision to abandon it for the ratings system, came about in response to audience demand and pressure—and these decisions, in both cases, suited Hollywood's bottom line. Such are the virtues and discontents of the free market, which knows only the morality of corporate survival and profit.

We should no more blame Hollywood for reflecting back to American society its desires and beliefs than we should indict D. W. Griffith for giving powerful form to what most white people believed about American history in 1915. If the values that shape "R" productions conflict with those celebrated in "G" films, then our challenge, as Schlesinger advocates, is to "create a social framework where conflict issues, not in excessive anxiety, but in creativity."[5] As Mark Winchell advocates, we should not fall victim to the condemnatory pieties of either the Right or the Left. We have much to learn from one another.

R. BARTON PALMER
CLEMSON, SOUTH CAROLINA
OCTOBER 2007

# ACKNOWLEDGMENTS

Several people assisted me in the preparation of this book. A particular debt of thanks is owed to Jeremy Beer and his staff at ISI Books for believing in this project and seeing it through every step of the way. Bill Kauffman's careful and tactful editing made the finished product better than it otherwise would have been. Moreover, discussions with my old friend Richard Kuntz were particularly helpful in developing the list of films included in part 4. Finally, I thank Barton Palmer for his generous foreword.

The following chapters originated as lectures given before meetings of the Institute of Southern History and Culture: "Ride to the Rescue," "The Bourgeois Sentimentality of *Gone With the Wind*," "What a Beautiful Day," "Copperhead Cinema," and "The Cause of Us All." The chapter on *Intruder in the Dust* was initially published in R. Barton Palmer's *Twentieth-Century American Fiction on Screen* (Cambridge: Cambridge University Press, 2007). Everything else was written expressly for this book.

In addition to proofreading and critiquing this text, my wife Donna sustained me through the ordeal of writing, as she has through every other day of our marriage. I am also grateful beyond measure for the inspiration and support of my sons Jonathan and Matthew. As the world will soon realize, Jonathan is the real film critic in the family. He made more suggestions for this book (most of them helpful) than all other persons put together.

# THE VIEW FROM MAIN STREET

Social conservatives have traditionally been suspicious of popular entertainment. Those who are aesthetic elitists rail against the vulgarity of mass culture, while puritans (of whatever theological persuasion) shun graven images and anything that appeals to the pleasure principle—even in their own worship. Nevertheless, in the proverbial Golden Age of Hollywood (which is to say, prior to the great upheavals of the 1960s and later), there were few exclusively political conflicts between the American Right and the entertainment industry. The studios ruled Hollywood, and the studios themselves were ruled by businessmen (many of them second-generation Americans) who might not know much about art but did know what they and the American public wanted. That is no longer the case.

By the end of the sixties, it was apparent to anyone who attended a movie or turned on prime-time television that ordinary Americans occupied a different universe from the keepers of our national dream factory. This point was brought home in 1972, when Richard Nixon carried forty-nine of the fifty states, and yet the distinguished film critic Pauline Kael said that she couldn't understand how Nixon won because *no one she knew had voted for him*. As the gap between movie-made reality and the lives that most Americans lived grew ever wider, certain syndicated columnists and right-wing journals of opinion began commenting on the culture war. Then, in 1979, Ben Stein published a courageous and groundbreaking book called *The View from Sunset Boulevard: America as Brought to You by the People Who Make Television.*

Stein is that rarest of birds—a bona fide Hollywood insider who is also a political conservative. In his book he describes the Hollywood production community "as part of a small but extremely energetic and militant class." He goes on to say:

> The TV people see certain classes as their enemies from long ago. Moreover, they still see those people as enemies, except that now a sea change has occurred. Instead of having to work out of nothing to become something, the TV people are now in a position to dominate society. They can contend with the businessman class, with the military class, with small-town gentry, with *anyone* for the leadership role in society.[1]

In the decade following the publication of *The View from Sunset Boulevard*, a former Hollywood actor served as American president. One might have thought that the film community would have regarded this fact as a bestowal of legitimacy on its entire profession. No longer was the highest office in the land reserved for lawyers, retired generals, or (in the cases of Herbert Hoover and Jimmy Carter) civil engineers. But ideology trumped vocational pride. Because Ronald Reagan was a conservative, many in Hollywood regarded him as a civic embarrassment. More than a decade after Reagan left office and at a time when he was dying slowly of Alzheimer's disease, the heralded film critic Richard Schickel wrote a particularly nasty essay suggesting that Reagan lived in a seamless make-believe world as both actor and politician.[2]

One charge made against Reagan is that he tended to see world problems as replays of movie scripts. At various times in his film career, he played Brass Bancroft in a series of pictures called *Secret Service of the Air.* In the last of these, Brass must defend a device known as the Inertia Protector from enemy agents. Because this wonder weapon knocks enemy planes out of the sky from a distance of up to four miles, Schickel patronizingly compares it to Reagan's Strategic Defense Initiative, which he predictably refers to as Star Wars—apparently believing that two sarcastic Hollywood references are better than one. None of this is particularly original. These charges were made constantly during the time that Reagan was in office. But by the time that this essay was published in 2001, international experts as diverse as Margaret Thatcher and Mikhail Gorbachev were citing the role of the Strategic Defense Initiative in ending the Cold War and bringing down the Soviet Empire—without a shot being fired. Unfortunately, Richard Schickel, who can write with such sensitivity and nuance about the art of the cinema, preferred to remain in an ideological time warp.

If Reagan made the world a safer place in which to live and helped to restore economic growth to the country, there wasn't a whole lot he could do to change the state of American culture. (The bully pulpit has limited effectiveness when the church is empty or when you are preaching only to the choir.) If anything, the forces of moral iconoclasm felt particularly embattled and pugnacious during the Reagan years. With the poster boy of the Moral Majority in the White House, the culture war seemed to be the logical place for critics of traditional values to take their stand and score at least provisional victories.

By the time that Reagan's successor, George H. W. Bush, was running for reelection in 1992, the value assumptions of the media had become fodder for the campaign trail. When Murphy Brown, the title character of a popular CBS sitcom, decided to become a single mother, Vice President Dan Quayle decried the message that this choice would send to the viewing public. Rather than considering his argument at face value (and asking what effect the federal government could or should have on the matter), elite opinion makers regarded this as simply another gaffe on the part of the supposedly dim-witted Quayle.

As fate would have it, the Quayle flap materialized at about the same time that the film critic Michael Medved published his provocative book *Hollywood vs. America* (1992). At first glance, Medved would seem to be an unlikely candidate for what Hillary Clinton has called the "vast right-wing conspiracy." A member of the baby-boom generation, Medved had been reared in the mindset of the countercultural Left. By the early 1990s, he and Jeffrey Lyons were cohosts of the popular PBS show *Sneak Previews*. By this time, Medved had become a husband and father and had begun to rediscover the religious roots of his Jewish identity.[3] Not only did he find most of the movies he was paid to see personally offensive, he was convinced that a growing percentage of the American public agreed with him. Declining attendance at the box office tended to support this surmise.

Then in 1990, a film called *The Cook, The Thief, His Wife and Her Lover* began getting rave reviews. Medved didn't know which was worse—the fact that this loathsome tribute to sadomasochism was made in the first place or that reputable critics, many of whom he respected, were praising it as a work of art without considering its moral content. Medved's own denunciation of this film on *Sneak Previews* blew any cover he might have had as a disinterested or conventional film critic. Over the next few years, he repeatedly spoke and wrote about what he considered the corrosive moral effects of American popular culture. Not surprisingly, he was subjected to increasingly shrill denunciations from the cultural elite. Just as predictably, Medved was embraced by right-wing critics of that elite. When *Hollywood vs. America* became a nationwide best-seller, it was clear that Medved had hit a nerve with the reading public.

Beyond "Amen, Brother," I have little to add to what Stein, Medved, and others have had to say about the course that Hollywood has taken over the past half century. Just as we do not need another book informing us that there were a lot of poor people during the Depression or that Hitler was a very bad man, neither do we need yet another treatise belaboring the sins of Hollywood. If the defenders of the film industry are not exactly on the same level as Holocaust deniers, I gladly leave them to quarrel with the exceptionally well-documented arguments of Medved and company. What I propose is a complementary but different line of inquiry. Because even a stopped clock is right twice a day, there must be at least a few films that do not fit the dreary conformist mold of left-wing groupthink. In referring to such films, I have chosen to use the convenient shorthand "politically incorrect."

The concept of political correctness emerged in academia at some point in the late eighties or early nineties. This involves more than the fact that college professors (particularly in the liberal arts) are less inclined than auto mechanics or stockbrokers to vote Republican. Back in 1951, a young Yale alumnus named William F. Buckley Jr. wrote an exposé of the left-wing biases of his alma mater. Compared to the infantile ravings of a Ward Churchill, the views of the Yale faculty during the late forties and early fifties now seem positively tame and genteel. The

point that Buckley made in *God and Man at Yale*, however, remains valid. Any student entering college with a belief in God, the free market, traditional morality, and the superiority of Western civilization is more than likely to find those beliefs derided in the classroom. Regardless of what they believe personally, intellectually honest professors at least encourage a lively exchange of ideas. The politically correct do not.

Right-wing political correctness is not only conceivable; at certain times in history, it has prevailed. Galileo suffered from the dogmatic ignorance of the medieval church. Religious and political dissidents from the early Christians to the underground in more recent totalitarian dictatorships have given their very lives for freedom of belief and expression. In comparison, today's left-wing "political correctness" seems pretty effete. It is for that very reason that one is appalled by the fact that so many of its victims knuckle under without a fight.

In the older academy, a conservative professor might argue politics with a liberal colleague and then go out for a beer with him. In the politically correct academy, the denizens of ideological righteousness will not even speak to their benighted colleagues when they pass in the hall. The neoconservative critic Roger Kimball argues that the change took place when the erstwhile student radicals of the sixties managed to land academic positions and then rise through the ranks. Not surprisingly, Kimball called his book *Tenured Radicals*. Leslie Fiedler, who was the veteran of many ideological battles over a long academic career, has suggested that "Tenured Stalinists" would have been an even better title.[4]

## I

Although there are considerable differences between Hollywood and the university, both tend to be insular cultures where people think alike. It is not necessary to use coercion to produce the politically correct and morally vile films that so often earn an "R" rating. Given certain social and historical facts about Hollywood, the results are quite predictable. It is only when an irreverent and independent-minded filmmaker chooses to buck the trend that we have a "man-bites-dog" story. Even when the results have been produced by accident, the product is still worthy of note. But before considering the films that I have selected for analysis, we should probably ask how things got to be the way they are.

One of the most important differences between the old and the new Hollywood lies in corporate structure. Anyone who has read one of the bitter anti-Hollywood novels of the thirties through the fifties knows that the old Hollywood was a fiefdom run by vulgar, avaricious, semiliterate studio heads. With the occasional exception of a star big enough to write his or her own ticket, creative people were treated as serfs. Long-term contracts could stifle an actor's career by limiting his mobility or forcing him into unsuitable roles designed only to make a quick buck for the studios. The situation of the screenwriters was even worse. Lacking the visibility of actors, they were often used as interchangeable parts in what was by its very nature a collaborative medium. Jack Warner is said to have referred to them as "schmucks with Underwoods."[5]

The introduction of sound into motion pictures in the late twenties created an increased need for dialogue. Throughout the thirties, writers fled the Depression in the rest of the country for what seemed to be easy money in Hollywood. Among those who came west were some of the most accomplished writers of the day: William Faulkner, F. Scott Fitzgerald, Aldous Huxley, Nathanael West, and others. The image of the great writer prostituting his talent in Hollywood has become a fixture in our collective imagination, if only because the writers themselves possessed a talent for dramatizing their plight. It is no wonder that so many of them shared the Marxist dream of one day controlling the terms and fruits of their labor. It was among the writers that the Communist Party USA made its earliest and most substantial inroads.

The eventual demise of the studio system meant that the creative talent in Hollywood finally exercised greater control over its own work. As liberating as that may have been for the talent, it inevitably changed the kind of movies that were made. As incredible as it might seem, pursuit of the almighty dollar has always been a secondary concern among the creative folk who now run Hollywood. They are primarily interested in projecting what they consider an artistic vision, with validation coming not from the box office, but from the praise of equally alienated critics. In 1992, the Academy Award–winning director Sydney Pollack told the American Enterprise Institute, "You must remember that most of us who were doing this got into it for the romance, the glory, the applause, the chance to tell stories, even to learn, but rarely for the money."[6] The one factor left out of this equation is the public itself.

Even with greater control over the making of films, the creative community could have exercised internal constraint had it not scrapped the Production Code that had been in effect since 1920. From 1930 on, the bureaucracy that administered the code was known as the Hays Office after its first head, former postmaster general Will H. Hays. More lenient in practice than in precept, this effort at self-policing kept the threat of federal censorship at bay for more than four decades. During this time, Hollywood managed to make some interesting and challenging movies, even if the cartoon character Betty Boop did lose her cleavage and married couples were required to occupy separate beds. With the decline of the studio system that had supported the Production Code, the Hays Office soon became a thing of the past. Shortly after he became president of the Motion Picture Association of America in 1966, Jack Valenti replaced the old Production Code with a new multilayered ratings system.

The new code, which took effect in 1968, consisted of four categories. Persons under sixteen were not to be admitted to an X-rated movie. They could get into a film with an R (for restricted) rating but only if accompanied by an adult. (In 1970, the MPAA raised the minimum age for escort-less admission to R and X movies to seventeen.) Although all audiences were admitted to M (for mature) movies, potential patrons were admonished that the film might require parental discretion. Only movies rated G (for general audiences) were deemed suitable for everyone. In 1990, the X rating was replaced by NC-17 because porno houses were advertising their offerings as "Triple X," thus blurring the distinction between, say, *Deep Throat* and the more intellectually challenging tits-with-subtitles fare of the local art house. While the R and G categories remained intact, M was eventually subdivided into PG (advising parental guidance) and PG-13 (urging parents to exercise particular vigilance before allowing their preadolescent offspring through the turnstiles.) What initially seemed like a Solomonic compromise soon began to resemble nothing more than cutting a live baby in two.

Michael Medved argues persuasively that if Hollywood had simply paid attention to box-office receipts, it would have seen that G-rated movies outdrew all others and that R-rated pictures were least popular. Nevertheless, Hollywood filmmakers persisted in making a preponderance of R-rated pictures in order to see their personal fantasies enshrined on the screen.[7] It seems that, each year, those visions push the boundary just a bit farther. This is perhaps an example of a more general cultural phenomenon that the late Senator Daniel Patrick Moynihan called "defining deviancy down." In terms of motion pictures, this means that, after a while, R movies start resembling the old X product, while PG-13 films begin to contain elements previously found only in R works. Accordingly, the PG rating (which Medved quips must stand for "profanity guaranteed") is enough to scare off many parents. Only the G rating has managed to remain relatively safe—as well as immensely profitable.

Despite the protestations of the Religious Right, political bias and moral content are not one and the same. For years, Tipper Gore has campaigned for a ratings system for rock music based on its violent message and pornographic content. (This effort led Frank Zappa to label her a "cultural terrorist.") The late Senator Paul Simon of Illinois and Senator Joseph Lieberman of Connecticut (both as Democrats) have spearheaded efforts to clean up television. On the other side of the aisle, some of the most gratuitously violent films ever released for popular consumption were vehicles for the future Republican governor of California, Arnold Schwarzenegger. The political correctness and moral depravity that are all too common in Hollywood may seem to go hand in hand, but there is no direct logical connection.

For whatever reason, creative artists are at least as likely as liberal arts professors to buy into a hegemonic left-wing worldview. Beyond that, I am convinced that, half a century later, the Hollywood community is also doing penance for the blacklist of the 1950s. So much tendentious nonsense has been written about this period in history that an objective account may be next to impossible. At the very least, however, we need to try to put the so-called "Red Scare" into some kind of historical perspective.

In 1949, the nation was shocked to discover that Alger Hiss, a man of impeccable establishment credentials and a high-placed aide to President Franklin D. Roosevelt, had been an espionage agent for the Soviet

Union. Two years later, it was discovered that a couple of fairly low-level government employees, Julius and Ethel Rosenberg, were passing secrets to the Soviets that helped our Cold War adversary develop an atomic bomb. Hiss and the Rosenbergs were not innocent victims of some paranoid right-wing witch-hunt. They were traitors to their country. What was perhaps worse was the attempt by many American leftists to defend these individuals and malign their accusers. It did not require any particular neurosis to realize that the Soviets had agents in this country intent on undermining our way of life. The salient question, however, concerns Hollywood's role in all of this.

As early as the 1930s, the Communist Party USA had a concentrated following in Hollywood, particularly among screenwriters, who habitually cleaved to the left and liked to think of themselves as an exploited proletariat. Although the Moscow show trials of the thirties and the Hitler-Stalin Pact of 1939 turned many American leftists away from communism, support for the party remained unusually strong in the film capital through the 1930s. (The situation was complicated by the fact that the party also functioned through many innocent-seeming front organizations not officially connected with the party itself.) Then, in the 1940s, America found itself allied with the Soviet Union against the Axis forces of Germany, Japan, and Italy. Suddenly, the Soviets were seen as dear friends rather than as potential enemies. At times, it seemed that the only people opposing Stalin were the followers of Leon Trotsky, the charismatic rival whom Stalin exiled from Russia to Mexico, where he was eventually murdered with an ice pick to the back of his neck.

As Ronald and Allis Radosh have pointed out, the most egregiously pro-Soviet films churned out by Hollywood were wartime propaganda. The first of these was *North Star* (1943). With a script by Communist apologist Lillian Hellman and music by Aaron Copland, this film depicts a group of youth heading to Kiev on a camping trip. After the men leave to become guerilla fighters, invading German soldiers take blood from Russian children for the benefit of their wounded brethren in arms. The portrayal of the happy Ukrainians in this film neglects to note that four million inhabitants of this region died from a famine caused by Stalin's efforts at agricultural collectivization. Despite this minor oversight, *North Star* did well at the box office and garnered six Academy Award nominations.[8]

A second film, *Song of Russia* (1944), features Robert Taylor as an American conductor on a concert tour of the Soviet Union. He falls in love with a Russian girl, and the two are performing on radio when the Germans attack and destroy a thriving collective farm, which could exist only in the imagination of the most tendentious Soviet stooge. The script was written by party stalwarts Paul Jarrico and Richard Collins from a story coauthored by fellow Communist Guy Endore. Lyrics for the songs in the film were written by Communist composer E. Y. (Yip) Harburg. As film historian Robert Mayhew has noted, the movie was carefully vetted and approved by Lloyd Mellett at the Office of War Information. Mellet even went so far as to submit the script for suggestions and approval to the first secretary of the Soviet embassy.[9]

By far the most blatant and contemptible example of Soviet propaganda was the Warner Brothers production *Mission to Moscow* (1943). Based on a book by Joseph Davies, a remarkably gullible American ambassador to Russia, this film was written by the notoriously procommunist Howard Koch, who hired long-time party hack Jay Leyda as a technical adviser. No one involved with the project, however, was more favorably disposed toward the Soviets than Ambassador Davies himself. Incredible as it may seem, Davies insisted that the film depict the Russian invasion of Finland as a protective measure requested by the Finns! According to Ronald and Allis Radosh: "The most significant change made by Davies was the insertion of the prologue that opens the movie. Speaking directly to the theater audience, the real Davies intones that 'no leaders of a nation have been so misrepresented and misunderstood as those in the Soviet government during these critical years between the two world wars.' The film, he hopes, 'will help to correct that misunderstanding. . . .'"[10]

In contrast to *North Star* and *Song of Russia*, which simply purveyed an idyllic—and false—image of Soviet life, *Mission to Moscow* sought to glorify one of Stalin's most outrageous acts of oppression: the show trials of the late 1930s. The Radoshes describe the film's treatment of Nikolai Bukharin, one of the victims of those trials, as follows:

> [I]n the film, audiences see Bukharin confessing: "My hope is that this trial may be the last severe lesson in proving to the world the growing menace of Fascist aggression and the awareness and united strength of Rus-

> sia. . . . What matters is not the personal feelings of a repentant enemy, but the welfare and progress of our country." The Soviet state prosecutor, the vicious Andrei Vyshinsky, who told the court that "dogs gone mad should be shot," is portrayed not as a stooge of Stalin but as a benevolent, serious jurist. It is Vyshinsky who shames the defendants and gets them to confess. The court finds them guilty and orders each and every one of them to be shot. When fellow diplomats ask Davies what he thinks, he answers: "Based on twenty years' trial practice, I'd be inclined to believe these confessions."

The independent leftist Dwight Macdonald hardly overstated the case when he called this picture "the first totalitarian film to come out of Hollywood."[11]

When public sentiment turned violently against the Soviet Union after World War II, attitudes among many in Hollywood did not turn with it. As a result, in October 1947, the House Committee on Un-American Activities opened an investigation of communism in the film industry. It soon became evident, however, that the committee was less interested in analyzing subversive messages in celluloid than in exploring the past and present political affiliations of prominent figures in Hollywood.[12] In order to come away with a clean bill of health, a witness would not only need to confess his own past sins and resolve to walk the straight and narrow, he also had to be willing to reveal the names of anyone he might have seen at a meeting sponsored by the party or one of its many fronts. Those unwilling to "name names" could be considered in contempt of Congress. In 1950, ten individuals were actually sent to jail for this offense. Two hundred people who avoided imprisonment were nevertheless listed by HUAC as security risks. The private blacklist that the studios maintained of those "guilty by association" was even longer. As a result, more than a few innocent people suffered because of collusion between frightened studios and opportunistic politicians.

Perhaps the most sensible description of the blacklist was offered by the libertarian economist Milton Friedman in his book *Capitalism and Freedom* (1962): "One may believe, as I do, that communism would destroy all of our freedoms, one may be opposed to it as firmly and as strongly as possible, and yet, at the same time, also believe that in a free society it is intolerable for a man to be prevented from making voluntary arrangements with others that are mutually attractive because he believes in or is trying to promote communism. Freedom also, of course, includes the freedom of others not to deal with him under those circumstances."[13] It is curious that liberals who applaud boycotting the merchants of an entire state because of the conduct of that state's legislature (e.g., failing to pass the Equal Rights Amendment or choosing to display the Confederate flag on the statehouse grounds) act as if the failure of Hollywood studios to do business with Stalinists was tantamount to imposing the Third Reich in America.

It is not necessary to defend the excesses of the blacklist to see that its most far-reaching impact has been the opposite of what was intended. After the initial chilling effect, survivors of that era and their successors vowed never again to knuckle under to government pressure. Feature films and documentaries were made lauding those who stood up to HUAC (particularly the heroic ten) and trashing those rats who agreed to name names. When the Academy of Motion Picture Arts and Sciences decided, nearly half a century later, to give a lifetime achievement award to one such friendly witness, the uproar against the aging Elia Kazan might have led one to believe that the blacklist had never gone away.[14] In any event, every stridently anti-American film subsequently made in Hollywood can be seen as atonement for the blacklist.

## II

The orthodox history of Hollywood under the old Production Code holds that it was a period of right-wing repression during which only the most conservative values could be affirmed. As we have seen, the relatively comfortable position of left-wing artists (including members of the Communist Party) and the presence of Soviet propaganda in the films of the thirties and forties suggests that the actual situation was more complex. Moreover, when we consider the informal censorship that existed during Hollywood's Golden Age, it is clear that not all of it came from the Right. At the time of the cinema's very beginning, left-wing pressure groups tried to suppress D. W. Griffith's *The Birth of a*

*Nation* (1915). (As we shall see, they did not achieve substantial success until the 1980s.) These efforts had a chilling effect on subsequent movies dealing with the Reconstruction era in American history. The most notable of these was David O. Selznick's film of Margaret Mitchell's *Gone With the Wind* (1939).

Published two decades after the release of *The Birth of a Nation*, Mitchell's novel was an instant best-seller whose potential for success on the big screen seemed even greater. At the same time, the NAACP and much of the black press were apprehensive that Mitchell's views of the Old South, which resembled those of Griffith in substance if not in tone, would set back the cause of black advancement. Although the most successful black actors in Hollywood were a well-paid aristocracy, black intellectuals were often critical of the subservient roles they were forced to play. Not only was *Gone With the Wind* replete with such stereotypes, it also glorified the Ku Klux Klan and used the offensive word "nigger." The pressure to tone down Mitchell's depiction of race relations in the South became so intense that, by 1937, Selznick had created a clerical file called "The Negro Problem."

According to Leonard J. Leff, Lloyd Brown, the secretary of Pittsburgh's Negro Youth Congress, wrote Selznick on January 21, 1937, to denounce *Gone With the Wind* and to threaten boycotts and pickets if the movie were ever made. In addition to summoning the one thousand members of his own organization, Brown vowed to "elicit support from churches, liberal institutions, and 'especially the Jewish people.'"[15] This last threat was particularly telling, given that Selznick was a Jew who also considered himself a social liberal.

Initially, Selznick was more interested in convincing African Americans that his film was inoffensive than in making substantive changes to what Margaret Mitchell had written. Eventually, however, changes were made. When Scarlett's second husband, Frank Kennedy, is killed, the novel makes it clear that he is attending a Klan rally, whereas the film simply has him at a "political meeting." In fact, all references to the Klan are surgically deleted. Although Selznick held out for as long as he could to keep a few uses of the word "nigger," political pressure and the displeasure of the Production Code finally forced a total capitulation. Selznick felt it more important to go to the mat for Rhett Butler's final line: "Frankly, my dear, I don't give a damn."

A host of other changes softened the racial politics of Mitchell's novel without obscuring her pro-Confederate sympathies or those of her black characters. Without these changes, it is conceivable that *Gone With the Wind* would not have been the beloved movie it turned out to be but would have been marginalized the way that *The Birth of a Nation* has been. The point, however, is that liberal pressure groups, not reactionary studio moguls, materially reshaped the most popular movie of all time before it was even made.

If this could happen to *Gone With the Wind*, one can only imagine the fate of lesser films. As a case in point, Bill Kauffman cites an innocuous effort by MGM to produce a film biography of President Andrew Johnson in 1943. Whenever establishment historians rate our presidents, Johnson is usually toward the bottom of the list. His immediate predecessor is considered our greatest chief executive for having started a war that resulted in at least 650,000 deaths. All Johnson did was to try vainly to bind up the wounds of that war. For his trouble, he was impeached by radical abolitionists intent on extracting a pound of flesh from the conquered provinces. Originally titled *The Man on America's Conscience*, this film was too politically incorrect to be accepted by the Hollywood and Washington elite, even in the 1940s. The script, by John L. Balderston and Wells Root, portrayed Johnson as a valiant warrior for constitutional liberty and cast the South-hating Pennsylvania congressman Thaddeus Stevens as the villain of the piece.

NAACP secretary Walter White, who had played a major role in the controversies surrounding *The Birth of a Nation* and *Gone With the Wind*, was irate that MGM was making an anti-Reconstruction film. Rather than complaining to the studio, however, he took his grievance to Lowell Mellett, director of the Bureau of Motion Pictures of the Office of War Information. Upon viewing the completed film, which bore the title *Tennessee Johnson*, Mellett and White demanded that substantial revisions be made. The character of Stevens was made more endearing, and the role of his mulatto housekeeper and mistress was eliminated altogether. But not even that was enough for some. According to Kauffman: "Despite the changes, a gang of Hollywood liberals—Ben Hecht, Zero Mostel, Vincent Price—petitioned the OWI to destroy the picture, in best fascist fashion, in the cause of national unity."[16]

Although the movie was not destroyed, the fact that so many of its original intentions were reversed by an agency of the United States government is far more ominous than a studio simply caving in to pressure from either the Left or the Right. By this point in American history, only the most benign view of Reconstruction was tolerated in our popular culture. As George Orwell would vividly demonstrate only a few years later, those who would control the present must also control the past. This means not only writing the history that students read but creating the images we receive from even our most casual entertainment.

## III

Obviously, the political incorrectness of a given film must be measured against the resistance of the prevailing ethos. For that reason, despite the examples cited above, a film espousing conservative values would be a more noteworthy achievement in the sixties and later than during Hollywood's earlier Golden Age. Accordingly, most of the films I have selected for detailed analysis come from this later period—five were produced between 1962 and 1978 and another seven between 1989 and 2004. I might have left it at that except that the phenomenon of political incorrectness in recent cinema cannot be properly understood apart from a historical context. The roots of these more recent films can be found in pictures that were made during the Golden Age. I have selected six of these—made between 1915 and 1959—as a foreground for what comes later.

As fate would have it, the history of the American cinema begins with what is probably its most controversial film. As we have noted, *The Birth of a Nation* was greeted with protests before it was ever screened and continues to be pilloried by would-be censors appalled by D. W. Griffith's cultural politics. Because of the undeniable historical importance of this film, it is frequently taught as a technical achievement in academic courses with all appropriate disclaimers for its message. The only problem is that the power of the film—the end that all of its technical achievements serve—is inseparable from its message. One does not need to buy into the myth of a glorious antebellum South or the far more invidious myth of white supremacy to realize that the appeal of

*The Birth of a Nation* is its depiction of a people being rescued by friends from the clutches of strangers. Griffith (like the novelist Thomas Dixon before him) told that story in terms of the struggle against Reconstruction. Given his background and ideology, that was understandable, but other versions are possible.

In 1996, for example, Joel Schumacher directed a film version of John Grisham's best-selling novel *A Time to Kill.* This story is almost a reverse mirror image of *The Birth of a Nation.* Two white rednecks, with the obligatory Confederate battle flag on their pickup truck, rape a ten-year-old black girl. Fearing that these cretins might walk, her father (played by Samuel L. Jackson) shoots up the courthouse, killing the two attackers and inadvertently maiming an innocent bystander. Although the racial identities have been changed, we still have the highly charged themes of interracial rape and vigilante justice. Unfortunately, the dramatic intensity is blunted by the fact that it requires a court trial to vindicate Jackson. In Griffith's film, the rightness of the vigilantes is taken for granted.

Despite David O Selznick's efforts to make *Gone With the Wind* more palatable to a biracial audience, it is also the sort of picture that isn't made anymore. Even in its cautious self-censored form, the film reflects racial attitudes that Michael Medved finds "unfortunate" and that more liberal critics have denounced in stronger terms.[17] But even if this film had not glorified the South or portrayed racial stereotypes, it did something far more dangerous—it showed characters either growing up emotionally or suffering the consequences of not doing so. The adolescent sensibility sees middle-class values as the ultimate enemy of the spirit, and in the years since *Gone With the Wind* was made, Hollywood has increasingly become the land of perpetual adolescence.

A scenario in which a Walt Disney movie is so offensive that it has to be returned indefinitely to the famous Disney vault sounds like the stuff of satire or outright farce. No, the vertically challenged did not protest against *Snow White and the Seven Dwarfs.* Instead, civil-rights groups became incensed that a film called *Song of the South* (1946) portrayed amicable relations between a white family in the South and their old black retainer, Uncle Remus. This particular black man projected an image of servility that African Americans were desperately trying to shed. The fact that he is probably the most independent and thoroughly admirable character in the movie counted for little with the protesters. In the land of political correctness, even the charge of racism is often enough to convict people with the most benign intentions of a thought crime.

At first glance, the strangest inclusion in this account of politically incorrect films would probably be *Intruder in the Dust* (1949). Here we have a black man, Lucas Beauchamp, who is wrongly accused of having killed a white man. (In movie-made America, actual black murderers are rare as hen's teeth.) The redneck family of the man who was killed wants to lynch Lucas, but the sheriff is intent on keeping his jail impregnable. In the meantime, Chick Mallison, a white adolescent who has bonded with Lucas, enlists his lawyer uncle to defend the black man. Add an eccentric old woman who loves playing detective, and you have the makings of an earnest liberal tract against the evils of lynching and the general uncouthness of white trash.

When we look at the film more closely, however, we find that it is not your grandpa's *To Kill a Mockingbird.* For one thing, Lucas's ancestral pride has nothing to do with his African heritage. He boasts, instead, of being the direct lineal heir of the white slave owner Carothers McCaslin. Moreover, his white supporters are influenced by personal motivations that have little to do with establishing a general climate of racial equality. In the William Faulkner novel from which this movie was adapted, the lawyer Gavin Stevens is an articulate, even obsessive, advocate of local control of local institutions. The book would seem to argue that well-intentioned Southern whites can handle racial problems without interference from the federal government. For this reason, the novel was panned by some liberal critics. Although this issue is not raised explicitly in the film, it is implicit in the action. *Intruder in the Dust* is therefore an ideologically subversive film.

In *Ben-Hur*, we see Hollywood making a blockbuster from a popular novel that had enjoyed considerable success on stage. In fact, *Ben-Hur* was good for two classic films—a silent epic in 1926 and an even more spectacular sound production in 1959. Far from being controversial, both movies have been cited for their artistry, particularly by professional filmmakers. Surprisingly, however, admiration has not taken the form of imitation. To be sure, one can see the technical influence of *Ben-Hur* in George Lucas's *Star Wars: Episode One* (1999) and in Ridley

Scott's *Gladiator* (2000). But the genre that *Ben-Hur* exemplifies—the Christological or quasi-Christological epic—effectively disappeared from the motion-picture screen with George Stevens's *The Greatest Story Ever Told* in 1965. Today, a Hollywood movie about Jesus is likely to show him as an all-too-human wretch (as in Martin Scorcese's *The Last Temptation of Christ* [1985]) or the butt of satire (as in *Monty Python's Life of Brian* [1979]). The reason why movies such as *Ben-Hur* are not made any more tells us a lot about the religious, or irreligious, mindset of Hollywood filmmakers.

Given the wealth and diversity of cinema produced during Hollywood's Golden Age, I might have selected an entirely different list of pictures to discuss. My choices have been made primarily to establish continuity with what follows in parts 2 and 3. If you do not see your favorite politically incorrect film in any of these sections, perhaps it is included in part 4, which includes brief summaries of one hundred additional movies. And if it's not there, I can only respond as Samuel Johnson did when an irate reader asked him to account for an incorrect definition in his dictionary. "Ignorance," Dr. Johnson replied, "pure ignorance."

# PART ONE

# BEFORE THE CULTURE WARS

# ONE

# RIDE TO THE RESCUE

## D. W. GRIFFITH'S *THE BIRTH OF A NATION* (1915)

As we came to the end of both a century and a millennium a few years ago, professional experts and amateur buffs alike compiled lists of the most influential figures in various fields. The name of David Wark Griffith appeared at or near the top of every list of filmmakers. As such, Griffith was one of the great artists of the twentieth century. In the entire history of civilization, there have been few radical innovations in the way that songs and stories can be transmitted. The development of written language was one of them. This made it possible to preserve literature that had previously existed only in the memory of a few designated bards, who could forget part of the text or change it at will. (A friend of mine who teaches classics at the University of Wisconsin at Milwaukee believes that the great intellectual achievements of the ancient Greeks resulted from their possessing an alphabet complex enough to render human experience but simple enough to be mastered by people of ordinary intelligence.)[1] The next great leap forward came when Gutenberg invented movable type in the fifteenth century. This gave rise to the mass production of literature, thus taking it out of the court and salon and making it accessible to a general audience. Then, in the late nineteenth century, Thomas Edison developed a technology for telling stories with moving pictures. All that was needed was an artist capable of developing the creative possibilities of this new medium.

When Griffith's *The Birth of a Nation* premiered at the Liberty Theater in New York on March 3, 1915, it was the first important feature film ever produced. And, at 202 minutes, it is still one of the longest. In addition to being the first director to tell a complex and coherent story on film, Griffith also developed such cinematic techniques as the close-up, the long shot, the flashback, and the fade-out. (His predecessors had done little more than train a camera on what were essentially static theatrical productions.) In the more than nine decades since its first release, this movie has come to be regarded as the most influential film of all time. Over the past quarter century, however, public screenings of Griffith's masterpiece have become exceedingly rare. In an age when soft-core pornography is readily available on cable television, *The Birth of a Nation* has been effectively banned because of its inflammatory presentation of race relations.

David Wark Griffith was born on January 22, 1875, to a rural Kentucky family still suffering economically from the ravages of the War Between the States. His ancestors had come to America from Wales before the Revolutionary War and had settled in Virginia. (His great-grandfather had fought the British in 1776.) Young David's father, Jacob Griffith, had briefly studied medicine before going off to fight in the Mexican War under General Zachary Taylor. In 1850, he escorted a wagon train from Missouri to California during the final days of the Gold Rush. He later returned to Kentucky, where he owned a small farm and served for a term in the Kentucky legislature. When the War Between the States broke out, Jake Griffith enlisted in the Confederate Army and served as a colonel under Stonewall Jackson. Young David's earliest memories were of his father's stories of wartime adventure. The elder Griffith's Southern loyalties and his flair for the theatrical left an indelible impression on his son. Because of the primitive treatment he received for his war wounds, "Thunder Jake" Griffith died in 1882, when his son was only seven.

Although he dreamed of becoming a playwright and made a precarious living as a traveling actor, D. W. Griffith was not destined for a conventional theatrical or literary career. Ever since he had seen a magic lantern show as a schoolboy in Kentucky, Griffith had been fascinated with the artistic possibilities of moving pictures. In 1908, he began a five-year directorial apprenticeship with the Biograph Company. During that period, he developed the techniques that would mark his later career and influence the style of other great directors, including the revolutionary Russian filmmaker Sergey Eisenstein. If Griffith's work at Biograph could be said to have any social vision, it was decidedly progressive. He championed the rights of American Indians against white oppression in *The Redman's View* (1909) and *Ramona* (1910). In *A Corner in Wheat* (1909), he attacked wealth and power as forthrightly as any contemporaneous muckraker. He exposed the horrors of urban poverty in *What Shall We Do with Our Old?* (1910) and *The Musketeers of Pig Alley* (1912) and even presented the Ku Klux Klan in an unfavorable light in *The Rose of Kentucky* (1911)! After starting his own independent company in 1913, Griffith continued to produce films with righteous liberal sentiments. There can be little question that he considered *The Birth of a Nation* to be in this tradition. Griffith believed that he was making a strong statement against the brutality of war as his father had experienced it, while championing the underdog South against Northern oppression.[2]

The image of the South in American culture during the second half of the nineteenth century was largely shaped by the seemingly ubiquitous theatrical versions of Harriet Beecher Stowe's *Uncle Tom's Cabin*. Because of the role of Stowe's novel in bringing about the War Between the States, we sometimes overlook the fact that the various plays based on that novel reached an even larger audience for nearly four decades after the war was over. Although the plantation novels of Thomas Nelson Page and the Uncle Remus stories of Joel Chandler Harris presented a more positive view of the antebellum South, no form of popular entertainment had been able to counter the effect of the Uncle Tom plays. Then, one night around the turn of the century, a minister and temperance lecturer from North Carolina attended one of these infamous productions. Angered by what he considered an injustice to the South, it was all that Thomas Dixon Jr. could do to keep from leaping to his feet and denouncing the drama. When the performance was over, he rose with tears in his eyes—vowing not to rest until he had told the true story of the South. In a five-year period, he produced a trilogy of novels—*The Leopard's Spots* (1902), *The Clansman* (1905), and *The Traitor* (1907)—which sold millions of copies and provided the first effective challenge to the powerful myth embodied in *Uncle Tom's Cabin*.

Unlike more genteel apologists for the Confederate South, Dixon seemed intent on beating Mrs. Stowe at her own game. In *Uncle Tom's Cabin*, the most powerful argument against slavery is not that it violates individual human rights but that it threatens middle-class family values and the sanctity of the home. The ultimate embodiment of that threat was the nightmare image of interracial rape.[3] Well before Mrs. Stowe put pen to paper, abolitionist propaganda had painted lurid pictures of Southern slave owners violating their female chattel and then selling the mulatto babies away from their grieving mothers. If the indigenous Southerners in *Uncle Tom's Cabin* rarely go that far, Stowe's most loathsome slave owner, the Vermont-born Simon Legree, is the very incarnation of sadism and lust. By equating slavery with miscegenetic rape, Harriet Beecher Stowe appealed to the most visceral fears of her readers.

The success of this appeal required a kind of imaginative empathy on the part of Stowe's readers, almost all of whom were free white people, whose condition was far removed from that of the victimized slave women. To assure the effectiveness of her propaganda, Stowe enters the novel in certain key scenes and directly asks the reader to imagine herself subjected to such inhumane treatment. (It was just such an act of empathy that prompted the writing of the novel in the first place; when one of Stowe's own sons died of a childhood illness, she felt an immediate kinship with slave women separated from their offspring.) Dixon does not resort to such narrative hectoring because the distance between his characters and his readers is considerably narrower. Like Stowe—and unlike so many male novelists, who celebrate the flight from home and domestic entanglements—Dixon believed in the sanctity of the family. Also, like Stowe, he saw interracial rape as the ultimate threat to the stability of home life. The crucial difference is that his victims were white Southerners suffering from the ravages of Reconstruction, while his villains were freed blacks intent on ravishing the sisters, wives, and daughters of their former masters. If appeals to reason had failed to make the case for the South, perhaps evoking people's most troubled dreams would do the trick.

Because social, racial, and gender equality are unchallenged ideals in our own age, it is often difficult to appreciate the governing assumptions of an earlier time. Throughout most of recorded history, men of the highest social class have considered women of a lower order to be fair game. It was only with the rise of the middle class that women began demanding marriage as payment for their sexual favors. Samuel Richardson's *Pamela* (1740), often cited as the first novel in English, tells the tale of a servant girl who finally extorts a proposal of marriage from the predatory young squire who has been pursuing her for several hundred pages. (The subtitle, *Virtue Rewarded*, tells us all we need to know about the game that Pamela is playing.) But when the threat of forcible seduction comes from a social inferior, what is at stake is not just a single woman's chastity but the order of society itself.

Born in Shelby, North Carolina, in 1864, Thomas Dixon graduated at age nineteen from Wake Forest College with a master of arts and the highest honors ever awarded by that institution, after which he did a year of graduate work at Johns Hopkins—where he formed a lifelong friendship with his classmate Woodrow Wilson. Prior to embarking on his career as a novelist, Dixon was a lawyer, an actor, and a popular lecturer against strong drink and other vices. Although he was an ordained Baptist minister, he left that church to form his own interdenominational congregation in New York City. Like the early D. W. Griffith, Dixon was on the liberal side of most political and economic issues. In fact, as late as 1896, he had publicly thanked God "that there is not to-day the clang of a single slave's chain on this continent," because "democracy is the destiny of the race, because all men are bound together in the bonds of fraternal equality with one common love." Dixon seems to have changed his views on race not because of any lingering prejudices from his Southern upbringing but as a reaction to American foreign policy. Our imperialist war against Spain resulted in American control of several Pacific and Caribbean populations. Believing that these dark-skinned peoples had proved incapable of self-government, Dixon concluded that all non-Aryans shared a genetic tendency toward barbarism. Although such views have been discredited in our own age, they were held by many reputable anthropologists in Dixon's own time.[4]

## I

*The Clansman* is the story of two families—the Camerons of South Carolina and the Stonemans of Pennsylvania.[5] Although Ben Cameron and

Phil Stoneman fought on opposite sides in the War Between the States, they are willing to forget regional differences in a spirit of healing under the benevolent leadership of Abraham Lincoln, who is considered by North and South alike to be the "Great Heart." Unfortunately, Lincoln is assassinated, and radical forces within his own party (led by Phil's father Austin Stoneman) are intent on bringing the conquered South under the heel of black despotism. As the story opens, Stoneman's saintly daughter Elsie is playing the banjo for wounded soldiers from both sides in a makeshift hospital set up in the U.S. Patent Office. Ben Cameron, who is recovering from war wounds and facing trumped-up charges for guerilla activity, immediately falls in love with the Northern girl. With Elsie's help, Ben's mother secures a presidential pardon for her son and escapes with him to South Carolina before Lincoln's murder incites a reign of recrimination in the nation's capital. Except for a dramatic account of the impeachment and trial of Andrew Johnson, the rest of the action takes place in the Piedmont region of South Carolina.

In the public realm, we see radical white Reconstructionists using the newly freed black slaves to terrorize their former masters. At a personal level, romantic passion is bringing the Cameron and Stoneman children closer together. Not only is Ben Cameron smitten with Elsie Stoneman, but Elsie's brother Phil has also fallen in love with Ben's sister Margaret. In the meantime, Austin Stoneman (who has moved to the warmer climate of South Carolina for his health) is growing increasingly fond of individual Southerners, even as he doggedly pursues his vengeful political agenda.

In what Dixon implies is the inevitable consequence of emancipation, Ben Cameron's former sweetheart, Marion Lenoir, is raped by a bestial former slave named Gus. (Having been irreparably polluted, both Marion and her mother throw themselves off a nearby cliff.) At this point, the Invisible Empire of the Ku Klux Klan materializes to avenge the violated damsel. Shortly thereafter, several thousand federal troops are summoned to quell the insurrection threatened by this show of vigilante justice. In the incendiary atmosphere, Phil Stoneman kills a black who has behaved in an uppity manner toward Margaret Cameron. Once again, Margaret's hard-luck brother Ben is suspected of a crime he has not committed and sentenced to death. After Phil replaces his look-alike friend in the death cell, the Klan rides to the rescue. Phil is saved, Old Austin Stoneman is chastened, and the Klan wins the victory over federal intervention that had previously eluded the more conventional forces of the Confederacy.

With its combination of sex, violence, and unabashed sentimentality, *The Clansman* was an even bigger success than its immediate predecessor, *The Leopard's Spots*. (Richard Schickel tells us that when Dixon submitted the manuscript of that earlier novel to his old friend Walter Hines Page, the redoubtable New South liberal stayed up all night reading it. Setting forth in search of breakfast the next morning and continuing to read while he walked, Page was promptly struck by a streetcar, with the blood from his cuts staining Dixon's text.) But no mere novel or pair of novels, no matter how popular, could undo the damage that *Uncle Tom's Cabin* had wrought, both in print and on stage, for over half a century. Fired by both ambition and greed, Dixon combined the most sensational elements of both his anti–Uncle Tom books in a play he also called *The Clansman*, which began touring the nation in 1905.

Dixon's play, like the novels on which it was based, was panned by professional critics and public moralists, even as ordinary people fought for seats in crowded theaters while police stood ready with fire hoses to drive back those still trying to get in. Although one of the main actors had great difficulty learning his lines and the horses bearing the Klansmen always seemed on the verge of leaping over the footlights into the audience, the opening night and subsequent performances came off without mishap. When Dixon first heard the applause for his play, he thought, "What a tame thing [is] a book compared to this! There I saw, felt, heard, and touched the hands of my readers and their united heart beat lifted me to the heights." He believed that, even if his novel eventually sold five million copies, a successful play could reach ten million with an emotional power ten times as great as cold type. In the first week alone, the play recouped all its production cost and earned a profit of fifty thousand dollars. After touring the South and Midwest for four months, *The Clansman* opened in New York on January 8, 1906.[6]

Although the New York critics and ideologues were even more antagonistic toward Dixon's play than their counterparts in the provinces had been, the theater continued to be packed night after night. This remained true when the show went on the road in other Northern cities. No doubt, the popularity of *The Clansman* was due in part to the spectacle of the production. Seeing white-robed Klansmen riding across the stage was even more thrilling than watching a runaway slave be pursued by bloodhounds in *Uncle Tom's Cabin*. But the racial politics of the play must also have been congenial to Yankee audiences. Anti-black sentiment was particularly strong among recent immigrants, who competed with African Americans for low-paying jobs. (At the Atlanta Exposition of 1900, Booker T. Washington had taken an anti-immigrant stance on the grounds that blacks had been in this country first and had proved themselves to be reliable workers.) If Northern playgoers were not exactly forgetting *Uncle Tom's Cabin*, racial solidarity was beginning to trump sectional animosity.

Just as Dixon had become frustrated with the limitations of print when he transferred his story to the stage, he eventually came to realize that stage drama itself was a dying genre. His new dream was to produce a version of his story in the emerging medium of motion pictures. In 1911, he tried unsuccessfully to form his own company for that purpose. After two years of having the door slammed in his face by established producers, Dixon approached the small-time entrepreneur Harry E. Aitken in 1913. Aitken had just hired D. W. Griffith away from Biograph, and the two were looking for a more ambitious project than the one-reel films Griffith had been used to turning out. Because of his own Southern background, Griffith felt an immediate affinity with Dixon's story. Moreover, as a director he was impressed with the visual possibilities for the film. He recalls that, when he first looked into *The Clansman*, he "skipped quickly through the book until I got to the part about the Klansmen, who, according to no less than Woodrow Wilson, ran to the rescue of the downtrodden South after the Civil War. I could see these Klansmen in a movie with their robes flying." What he envisioned was a ride to the rescue that would outdo anything previously attempted on stage or screen. "Instead of saving one poor Little Nell of the Plains," he said, "this ride would be to save a nation."[7]

Although Griffith's version of *The Clansman* was more faithful to Dixon's novel than many movies are to their sources, he made several crucial changes that rendered the narrative more effective.[8] He starts the film well before Reconstruction with a scene of a Puritan clergyman praying over a slave market. (The subtitle reads: "The bringing of the African to America sows the first seeds of disunion.") The very next scene is of a nineteenth-century abolitionist meeting. The same Puritan types who had blessed the original slave trade are now agitating for an end to the peculiar institution. Through this visual juxtaposition, Griffith exploits the stereotype of Puritans as cold-blooded hypocrites. Shortly thereafter, we see the two Stoneman boys visiting their boarding school chums the Camerons in South Carolina. (Griffith has supplied Phil Stoneman with a younger brother, while giving Ben two younger brothers and an additional sister.) In contrast to Puritan New England, life in the South is filled with grace, laughter, and a sense of joy large enough to include both races—the black slaves sing and dance during their two-hour lunch break. That such a life depends on social and racial hierarchy is emphasized visually by another pair of consecutive scenes. As a wagon full of jovial disorderly blacks passes in the street, a couple of "pickaninnies" fall out and are retrieved with a playful pat on the rear. Immediately thereafter, a carriage of well-dressed aristocratic whites passes in the opposite direction.

Because Griffith begins prior to the war, he is able to broaden his epic by showing us scenes of battle. The scope and realism of these scenes was unprecedented in the American cinema. Also, because World War I had already begun in Europe, Griffith's condemnation of armed conflict was particularly timely. He quickly kills off the two younger brothers he has provided for Ben Cameron and shows the gallant Ben succoring a fallen foe. (This scene is described in a conversation after the fact in the novel.) Only then do we see the angelic Elsie Stoneman ministering to Ben and the other wounded soldiers in the patent office.

With a kind of dramatic economy, Griffith has the black predator Gus pursue the additional younger sister he has given Ben, thus dispensing altogether with the character of Marion Lenoir. Rather than depicting an actual rape—which occurs off the page in Dixon's novel, anyway—he has the little sister leap off the cliff in order to avoid what would otherwise be a fate worse than death. Also, in the film the Klan rescues Elsie Stoneman rather than her brother Phil. Her calamity is the prospect of a forced marriage with the mulatto lieutenant governor of South Carolina, Silas Lynch. In the end, however, the happy outcome is the same as in the novel—the Klan is triumphant, the blacks suppressed, and the Reconstructionists on the run. After the film's first showing, in a private screening at Clune's Auditorium in Los Angeles in February 1915, Thomas Dixon was so moved by the spectacle that he told Griffith that *The Clansman* was "too tame a title for so powerful a story." Instead, it must be called *The Birth of a Nation*.

If Thomas Dixon Jr. had hoped that his novel and play would replace *Uncle Tom's Cabin* in the American consciousness, he was to be sadly disappointed. Nearly every American has at least heard of *Uncle Tom's Cabin*, and tens of millions of people who have never read the novel or seen an Uncle Tom play can identify characters and scenes from Stowe's story. After their obligatory fifteen minutes of fame, Dixon and *The Clansman* were soon forgotten. (Dixon's work is included in no anthology of American or Southern literature, and most of the standard reference books in the field fail even to mention his name.) Nevertheless, Dixon's vision continues to live in the first great film of the American cinema.[9]

## II

For many years, *The Birth of a Nation* was the most widely distributed and highest-grossing movie ever. Even if those distinctions have now been eclipsed by more recent films (particularly *Gone With the Wind*, which it influenced), Griffith's masterpiece has enjoyed remarkable longevity. Despite persistent efforts at suppression by political foes from the Communist Party to the NAACP, *The Birth of a Nation* continued for decades to be shown in revival houses specializing in classic films. Unfortunately, this practice came to a virtual end in 1980, when a lily-white group of Berkeley radicals stormed a San Francisco theater showing the movie. After they vandalized the building, destroyed projection equipment, and burned the print of the film, most other theaters owners became too scared to show the movie. But no amount of intimidation or censorship can completely banish myths and dreams. If Griffith's consummate artistry is responsible for the technical excellence of *The Birth of a Nation*, the much-maligned hack writer Thomas Dixon gave him two of the film's most memorable and disturbing images—the black rapist attacking his white victim, and the Klan riding to the rescue. It is perhaps for this reason, Leslie Fiedler argues, that Griffith "for all his talent never again was able to project archetypes that have refused to fade from the mind of the world."[10]

These two images, much more than the Jim Crow stereotypes shown earlier in the film, are really what the fuss is all about. What are we to make of these images? How should we as enlightened twenty-first-century Americans respond to the controversy they have spawned? In considering the specter of interracial rape, we should probably acknowledge the fact that it was the abolitionists—particularly Harriet Beecher Stowe—who introduced this image into the debate over race relations. What is perhaps more telling, however, is not the convoluted genealogy of this image but the way in which it has been used in the nine decades since the filming of *The Birth of a Nation*. If Uncle Tom is the prototypical "Good Nigger," then Gus is the equally prototypical bad one. In our own day and age, the worst thing you can possibly call a black male is an "Uncle Tom." The Gus prototype, however, has fared much better.

The protagonist of Richard Wright's *Native Son* (1940), the first great American novel by a black writer, achieves a sense of manhood and spiritual fulfillment when he convinces himself that he has raped and murdered a white girl—although he, like Gus in the movie, is technically innocent of both crimes. When the white Southern liberal William Styron wrote a historical novel about Nat Turner in 1967, he had the leader of this famous slave rebellion murder a white girl for whom he had secretly lusted. In *Soul on Ice* (1968), the black radical Eldridge Cleaver speaks of rape as a revolutionary act. He would begin by practicing on black women in his own neighborhood and then move to the white side of town when he got good enough at his craft. If miscegenetic rape has become an image of black power in the minds of some who are sympathetic to the cause of civil rights and black aspirations, it seems a bit disingenuous to blame Thomas Dixon and D. W. Griffith for being the first artists to plant this image in the American imagination.

The glorification of the Klan, however, is far more troubling than worrying about predators in the woodpile. Wright, Styron, and Cleaver notwithstanding, most decent people disapprove of sexual assault. But they would also add that such matters are properly handled by the police and the courts. The Klan, especially as we know it today, is more a terrorist organization than a fraternity of white knights. (It is true that reputable historians such as Woodrow Wilson once saw the original Klan as a necessary response to radical Reconstruction. Griffith's film is filled with quotes from Tom Dixon's old classmate, who was president in 1915. After a screening of *The Birth of a Nation* in the White House, Wilson said: "It is like writing history with lightning. And my only regret is that it is all so terribly true.")

But an even more basic point needs to be made. When people are in distress, the last thing they are likely to do is demand a background check of those willing to help them. In countless B Westerns, seemingly acceptable to those who decry *The Birth of a Nation*, the cavalry rides to the rescue of helpless whites under siege by dark-skinned Native Americans. In the Tarzan movies, the potential victims are invariably white and the attackers black savages. (Even if the savior does swing from a vine, he is still a British lord.) Finally, in Hitler's favorite movie, *King Kong* (1933), the entire technology of civilized mankind is directed against the African beast who is climbing the Empire State Building with blonde Fay Wray in hand. Back when ethnic profiling was still allowed, the orders were to shoot Kong on sight.

When white leftists, such as the ones who vandalized the revival house in Berkeley, seek to suppress *The Birth of a Nation*, I am reminded of the scene in *Hamlet* in which the prince says, "Methinks the lady doth protest too much." In an essay on Dixon and Griffith, Leslie Fiedler writes: "I myself once saw . . . the members of a left-wing ciné club in Athens, believers all in the equality of the races and the unmitigated evil of the Klan, rise to their feet at ten o'clock in the morning (the year was 1960, two wars and innumerable revolutions after the making of the film) to scream with bloodlust and approval equal to that of the racist first-nighters of 1915 as white womanhood was once more delivered from the threat of black rape."[11]

The scenario that Dixon and Griffith depicted so memorably seems to have been *discovered* rather than *created* by them. Consider, for example, a poem called "The Pipes of Lucknow: An Incident of the Sepoy Mutiny," written in 1858. The scene is India, where a group of Scottish women and children are besieged by an uprising of fearsome brown-skinned natives. Early in the poem, the dire scene is set:

Day by day the Indian Tiger
Louder yelled, and nearer crept;
Round and round the jungle serpent
Near and nearer circles swept.
"Pray for rescue wives and mothers—
Pray to-day!" the soldier said;
"To-morrow, death's between us
And the wrong and shame we dread."

At the moment when danger is greatest and all hope seems lost, one of the women hears a familiar sound in the distance. A silence falls on the group as the sound grows progressively louder.

Oh, they listened dumb and breathless,
And they caught the sound at last;
Faint and far beyond the Goomtee
Rose and fell the piper's blast!
Then a burst of wild thanksgiving
Mingled woman's voice and man's;
"God be praised!—the march of Havelock!
The piping of the clans!"

Louder, nearer, fierce as vengeance,
Sharp and shrill as swords at strife,
Came the wild MacGregor's clan-call,
Stinging all the air to life.
But when the far-off dust-cloud
To plaided legions grew,
Full tenderly and blithesomely
The pipes of rescue blew!

Round the silver domes of Lucknow,
Moslem mosque and Pagan shrine,
Breathed the air to Britons dearest,
The air of Auld Lang Syne.
O'er the cruel roll of war-drums
Rose that sweet and homelike strain;
And the tartan clove the turban,
As the Goomtee cleaves the plain . . .[12]

This poem was not written by a Southern defender of slavery or even by a Northern copperhead. It couldn't have been written by Rudyard Kipling, who wasn't born until 1865. The author of "The Pipes of Lucknow" was none other than the righteous Quaker abolitionist John Greenleaf Whittier.

Even if *The Birth of a Nation* is a powerful work of art capable of exposing liberal hypocrisy, its depiction of the South, and hence of America, is incomplete. For that reason, it finally falls short of the total social vision that we demand of the greatest art. Ironically, the fact that Dixon and Griffith were both racists results in their undercutting the more principled rationale for secession. *The Birth of a Nation* is an accurate title for a film that so insistently depicts the reconciliation of North and South. In terms of the fictional story line, that reconciliation is symbolized by the double wedding that joins the Stoneman and Cameron families at the end of the movie. (Austin Stoneman, who is loosely based on the radical Reconstructionist Thaddeus Stevens, apparently realizes the error of his ways when his mulatto protégé seeks to marry Stoneman's own daughter.) Should we miss the larger historical point he is making, Griffith ends his film with Daniel Webster's statement, "Liberty and Union, now and forever, one and inseparable." This is not just a plea for national healing but an implicit admission that the South had been wrong to secede from the inseparable union, which is now being reconstituted on the principle of *white supremacy*.

In order to maintain a unionist perspective and still denounce the horrors of Reconstruction, it is necessary for Dixon and Griffith to buy into the Great Heart fraud. If only the saintly and compassionate Lincoln had not been murdered, Reconstruction would have been a joy rather than an agony. No literary or historical gushmeister from Walt Whitman to James Agee has given us a more saccharine view of Lincoln than the one we get in *The Birth of a Nation.* When the news of the assassination reaches Piedmont, South Carolina, old Colonel Cameron laments: "Our best friend is gone. What will become of us now?" Before the war, the same Colonel Cameron had read a newspaper headline saying: "If the North Carries the Election, the South Will Secede." This is of course historical nonsense. It was the election of *Lincoln* that prompted secession. Had the Northerner Stephen A. Douglas won the election, the South would have stayed in the union. But Griffith would rather rewrite history than suggest that there was anything more than a temporary disagreement separating Lincoln from the South. It is deplorable that Dixon and Griffith would rather celebrate the lynching of African Americans than denounce the documented excesses of the Great Emancipator.[13]

Finally, another aspect of the question of race cannot be ignored. Even if *The Birth of a Nation* tells a hard and bitter truth, it is finally only a partial truth. In places, Griffith gives us what he no doubt considered to be a positive view of African Americans. The house servants of the Cameron family (who seem not to have heard about the Emancipation Proclamation) remain loyal and submissive. When the little sister plummets to her death, we see a shot of the servants' quarters and the subtitle "None grieved more than these." But no positive portrayal of a black character attains the mythic resonance we find in the image of Gus. Not only is there no counterpart to Uncle Tom in *The Birth of a Nation*, neither is there an equivalent to William Faulkner's Dilsey or Margaret Mitchell's Mammy. The absence of such characters is far more troubling than the presence of Gus.

Despite these limitations, the power of *The Birth of a Nation* has never been more evident than it is today. In recent years, we have been repeatedly told that America is a different country since the events of September 11, 2001. That particular day of infamy reminded us of our individual and collective vulnerability. It also taught us that tolerance and goodwill do not constitute an effective defense against real enemies. Tribal loyalty inevitably seems less of a vice when the tribe is under attack. These are views that D. W. Griffith instinctively affirmed nearly a century ago. For that reason, his great film continues to strike a responsive chord in us—whether we like it or not.

# THE BOURGEOIS SENTIMENTALITY OF *GONE WITH THE WIND*

## DAVID O. SELZNICK'S *GONE WITH THE WIND* (1939)

While appearing on William F. Buckley Jr.'s *Firing Line* on November 15, 1974, the iconoclastic literary critic Leslie Fiedler observed: "I attended a conference a couple of weeks ago at which people were talking about the literature of the Thirties and there were a lot of survivors of the Thirties being very nostalgic about how great it was back in the days of the Depression. And what they were talking about were the so-called proletarian novels which were published in 1500 copies and sold 400 of them. . . . The rest molded in somebody's basement. . . . These were the books that seemed to them worth memorializing[,] and I said 'Look, there is one book which was written in the middle of the Thirties images from which, scenes and situations from which, language from which is in everybody's mind, and that's *Gone With the Wind*."[1]

Although most ordinary people would not hesitate to consider *Gone With the Wind* a great American novel, the certified intellectuals with whom Fiedler was conferring had not even thought to include it in their discussion. At least since the early twentieth century, there has been a growing divide between the songs and stories enjoyed by the masses and the literature that scholars and critics consider worthy of reverence. Margaret Mitchell's *Gone With the Wind* is simply an extreme example of this phenomenon.

The very popularity of Mitchell's novel makes it suspect in elitist circles. Although it appeared during the depths of the Depression, *Gone With the Wind* sold a million copies in its first year of publication, and it has seldom sold fewer than forty thousand *hardback* copies in any subsequent year. It has been translated into at least twenty-seven languages and is nearly as popular in Germany and Japan as it is in Atlanta, Georgia. It is true that mere popularity does not guarantee literary excellence, but *Gone With the Wind* is no seasonal blockbuster, which generates a flurry of attention and then goes out of print, never to be revived and scarcely even remembered. In the more than seven decades since Margaret Mitchell's masterpiece was first published, tens of thousands of trashy romance novels have come and gone. If her book were no different from any of them, why has it survived while the others have perished? Ever since the literary critic Longinus wrote in the first century A.D., even the most demanding highbrows have conceded that great works of art are those that please many and please long. Compared to the three-thousand-year run of Homer's epic poetry or even the four hundred years that Shakespeare has been around, a mere seven decades must seem like the blink of an eye. Nevertheless, no other book written in the twentieth century is as widely known and as instantly recognizable as *Gone With the Wind*. For that reason, it is not only an important American novel but also a classic of world literature.

Nevertheless, much of the popularity of *Gone With the Wind* is due to David O. Selznick's unforgettable motion-picture version of the novel. Although the book has sold more than thirty million copies and still sells 350,000 copies per year, even more people have seen the movie—an audience that exceeds the total population of the United States. When it was first shown on television in 1976, it drew 110 million viewers, making the occasion a national event more akin to a Super Bowl than the screening of a film that had been playing in movie houses for nearly forty years.[2] If we adjust for inflation, *Gone With the Wind* has made more money than any other movie ever filmed. Rather than detracting from Mitchell's achievement, it seems to me that the appeal of the film is a further testament to her ability to please many and please long.

Great as the motion picture might be, its appeal does not seem to lie in any *exclusively* cinematic qualities. Because film is by its very nature a collaborative medium, it is not always easy to assign creative responsibility for a movie's success or failure. More often than not, the director is considered the central creative intelligence. But this generalization cannot be usefully applied to *Gone With the Wind*. Victor Fleming is given final screen credit; however, he replaced the original director, George Cukor, after much of the film had already been shot. Although Sidney Howard was the principal author of the script, several other screenwriters (including F. Scott Fitzgerald) contributed to the project. As excellent as the acting might have been, this movie was more than a mere vehicle for a towering Hollywood personality. Neither before nor after did any of the leading players deliver as memorable a performance. That includes Clark Gable, who was the only genuine star to appear in the film. In what is considered by many to have been the greatest motion picture of all time, nothing was finally more important than the tale itself.

A story that possesses true mythic power almost always transcends the genre in which it was originally rendered. Great poetry can be read as print on a page or heard as recited verse. (Some of the greatest poetry began in the oral tradition before the invention of print.) The dramas of Sophocles and Shakespeare can be performed in the imagination of an isolated reader or on the stage of a crowded theater. Like *The Clansman* and *Ben-Hur*, some works that began as novels have actually reached their widest audiences as popular entertainment. In this respect, *Gone With the Wind* most nearly resembles *Uncle Tom's Cabin*. It is not known whether Margaret Mitchell ever read Mrs. Stowe's novel; however, she was clearly aware of its notorious reputation in the South.

At one point in *Gone With the Wind*, Mitchell writes:

> Accepting *Uncle Tom's Cabin* as revelation second only to the Bible, the Yankee women all wanted to know about the bloodhounds which every Southerner kept to track down runaway slaves. And they never believed her when she told them she had only seen one bloodhound in all her life and it was a small mild dog and not a huge ferocious mastiff. They wanted to know about the dreadful branding irons which planters used to mark the faces of their slaves and the cat-o'-nine-tails with which they beat them to death, and they evidenced what Scarlett felt was a very nasty and ill-bred interest in slave concubinage.

> Especially did she resent this in view of the enormous increase in mulatto babies in Atlanta since the Yankee soldiers had settled in the town.[3]

Although Lincoln was certainly overstating the case when he called Mrs. Stowe "the little lady who started the big war," the abolitionist sentiment that was brought to a fever pitch by *Uncle Tom's Cabin* helped to hasten the war. What is perhaps even more significant is the degree to which that abolitionist sentiment determined the later interpretation of the war in American culture. To this day, countless people who ought to know better believe that the War Between the States was nothing but a holy crusade to free the slaves. The continuing popularity of the various stage versions of *Uncle Tom's Cabin* throughout the second half of the nineteenth century certainly contributed to this widely held misperception. Having lost the war in the 1860s and the peace during Reconstruction, the South was in danger of also losing control of its own history in the consciousness of the reunited nation.

Literary responses to *Uncle Tom's Cabin* proliferated in the decade after the publication of Stowe's novel. (In his 1985 book *Uncle Tom's Cabin and American Culture*, Thomas F. Gossett lists no fewer than twenty-seven anti-Tom books published between 1852 and 1861.) Some, such as William Gilmore Simms's *Woodcraft* and William J. Grayson's *The Hireling and the Slave*, were works of genuine literary merit. Others, such as Mary Eastman's *Aunt Phillis's Cabin* or William L. G. Smith's *Uncle Tom's Cabin as It Is*, had little immediate impact and were quickly forgotten. As we have seen, it was not until the turn of the century that Thomas Dixon Jr. would make significant headway in countering the appeal of Stowe's novel and its even more popular theatrical vulgarizations.

If Thomas Dixon and D. W. Griffith made a strong case for the South in the public imagination, Margaret Mitchell was destined to write the novel that would eclipse *Uncle Tom's Cabin.* In terms of their political ideology, sectional loyalties, and views of race, two books could scarcely seem more different than *Gone With the Wind* and *Uncle Tom's Cabin.* Nevertheless, the novels are remarkably similar in their understanding of human happiness. It is precisely because of this fact that the great popular acceptance enjoyed by Stowe and Mitchell has been matched by the disfavor of elitist literary critics.

It is no secret that for many years the intellectual establishment in this country has formed what Lionel Trilling called an "adversary culture." This involves a contempt for the free market, middle-class values, religious piety, and instinctive patriotism. Not surprisingly, the books most revered by certified intellectuals also depict home life and family bonds as a form of despotism. (In the first great American short story, "Rip Van Winkle," Washington Irving coined the evocative phrase "petticoat government.") Homer may have created one of the great archetypal heroes of Western civilization in the figure of Odysseus, whose mythic quest is the struggle to return home after the Trojan War, but the canonical *American* hero achieves personal fulfillment by running away from home. Whether his name is Rip Van Winkle, Hawkeye, Ishmael, Huckleberry Finn, Nick Adams, or Ike McCaslin, the typical hero of the highbrow American novel finds Home to be Hell on Earth. Place names such as "Winesburg, Ohio" and "Main Street" have come to represent everything that is small-minded and repressive in American life. To affirm a countervision of Home as Heaven is to open oneself to the charge of bourgeois sentimentality. More often than not, it has been women novelists who have challenged this critical orthodoxy. None have done so more successfully than Stowe and Mitchell.

No doubt Stowe shared the general abolitionist belief that slavery was a violation of individual human rights, but the emotional force of her narrative lay in its depiction of sundered families and of slaves sold away from their native homes. The humble structure that provides the title of her novel is the closest approximation of paradise that Uncle Tom is likely to find this side of his Heavenly Home. Like the Religious Right of our own time, Harriet Beecher Stowe was an evangelical Christian who entered the political arena in order to affirm family values. It is significant that most of the slave owners depicted in her novel share those values and behave benevolently toward their slaves. But the system itself creates the possibility that a master might fall into serious debt or die unexpectedly. The first contingency separates Uncle Tom from his wife and children. The second delivers him into the hands of the truly demonic Simon Legree. Not only did the pathos of Uncle Tom's loss of home move readers of the novel and viewers of the play, it also inspired several of Stephen Foster's best-known songs—most obviously "My Old Kentucky Home."

In Margaret Mitchell's novel, it is war and Reconstruction that deprive her characters of their home and their familiar way of life. Although a few black freedmen profited from emancipation, the most important black characters in *Gone With the Wind* also suffer from the deracination and social upheaval created by the Northern invasion. This includes Gerald O'Hara's faithful valet Pork, Aunt Pittypat's fussy coachman Uncle Peter, and Scarlett's indomitable Mammy. When Uncle Peter explains to Scarlett what a blockade office is, he says, "Dey's awfisses whar furriners stays dat buy us Confedruts' cotton an' ship it outer Chas'ton and Wilmin'ton an' ship us back gunpowder." Uncle Peter's use of the first-person plural leaves no doubt where his sympathies lie. For her part, Mammy is openly contemptuous of white trash, who are too poor to own many slaves, and of "free-issue Niggers," who don't know their proper place in society.[4]

It is easy to denounce such characterizations as patronizing and racist, but servants who have enjoyed even limited status within a hierarchical society are often more reluctant than their masters to see the hierarchy destroyed. The most socially conservative character in Anton Chekhov's *The Cherry Orchard* (1904) is the aged servant Firs. The same is true of Hudson, the butler in the long-running British soap opera *Upstairs, Downstairs,* and Stevens, the protagonist of the novel and film *Remains of the Day.* Whether we are dealing with the plantation South, feudal Russia, or Edwardian England, the welfare of the household help is bound to the fate of those they serve. This is never more true than in times of change.

Charles Darwin was certainly correct in maintaining that a species survives only if it is able to adapt to changing circumstances. If anything, the burden of adaptation is greater for those who regard men as moral and spiritual beings because they have more to preserve than those who seek mere brute survival. In this effort, the various institutions and traditions of civilized society are of inestimable value. Rather than facing change with only our own ingenuity to guide us, we have the accumulated wisdom of the ages as it has become manifest in culture. The catastrophe faced by the characters in *Gone With the Wind* and the Southern people they represent is that their civilization, as well as much of their material well-being, was destroyed by an enemy waging total war and bent on total victory. When Islamic terrorists flew airplanes into the World Trade Center and the Pentagon on September 11, 2001, many well-meaning but historically ignorant people expressed disbelief that anyone could be so implacably evil as to target a civilian population in order to achieve a political objective. Anyone who had read Margaret Mitchell's description of the burning of Atlanta or seen that event depicted on the movie screen would know that such evil was not invented by Osama bin Laden. Terrorism is as old as Original Sin and as American as William Tecumseh Sherman.

We now know that the twentieth century was the century of totalitarianism. When *Gone With the Wind* was published in 1936, the world was just becoming aware that Hitler and Stalin and the ideologies they espoused were fundamentally different from even the vilest forms of authoritarianism that had plagued earlier ages of history. It was not enough for totalitarians to achieve temporal power; they must also control the hearts and minds of their subjects. In the Moscow show trials, Stalin extorted false confessions from his enemies before executing them. In George Orwell's *1984* (published in 1949), it was not enough to obey Big Brother; one must also *love* him. Even though the ravages of Reconstruction fell far short of the horrors of Auschwitz or the Gulag Archipelago, the Northern invaders were fired by the same kind of apocalyptic zeal that turned our own age into the bloodiest nightmare in human history. Is it a mere accident that *Gone With the Wind* played in London throughout the entirety of World War II or that the great popularity of the novel and film coincided with the worst totalitarian excesses the world has ever known? Leslie Fiedler recalls once seeing the movie in a fishing village in Yugoslavia. He tells us that it was "dubbed into French and subtitled in Croatian—but so immediately apprehensible in terms of its images that no one seemed dismayed even when, from time to time, the sound track sputtered and died."[5]

## I

Scarlett O'Hara is a compelling protagonist at least in part because she is so obviously a flawed human being. She begins the novel with the same contempt for home that we find in the rebellious young men of our more critically acclaimed novels. If they are the Good Bad Boys of American fiction, she is the Good Bad Girl.[6] Although she may worship her saintly and seemingly virginal mother, Ellen, Scarlett is more like her plainspoken and fiery-tempered father, Gerald. Even her desire to marry Ashley Wilkes is an assault on convention, since he is engaged to another woman. Nevertheless, hers is a safe and limited rebellion which never threatens the foundations of a social order she assumes will last forever. In fact, at the outset of the novel, virtually no one in her community entertains the thought of radical change. To be sure, there will be a war. But that will be a lark, which will be over in a few months when the Yankees see what great warriors the Southerners are. Ashley does suspect that things may be a bit more difficult than anyone is willing to admit, but only the outcast Rhett Butler is impertinent enough to suggest that the lack of an industrial base will doom the South to defeat.

Any romance novel worthy of the name must feature a love triangle. If the woman is at the apex of the triangle, she typically must choose between Apollo and Dionysus. In Emily Brontë's *Wuthering Heights* (1847), Cathy is torn between the respectable but effete Linton and the primitive, half-mad Heathcliff. The title character of Hardy's *Tess of the D'Urbervilles* (1891) loves the priggish, otherworldly Angel Clare after having been ravished by the predatory Alec D'Urberville. For her part, Scarlett dreams of the Apollonian Ashley, even as she is drawn to the Dionysian Rhett. It takes her more than a thousand pages in the novel and nearly four hours in the movie to realize something that most of the rest of us knew from the outset—that her love for Ashley is built on monumental self-delusion. When she witnesses his helplessness in the wake of Melanie's death, Scarlett tells herself: "He never really existed at all, except in my imagination. . . . I loved something I made up, something that is just as dead as Melly is. I made a pretty suit of clothes and fell in love with it. And when Ashley came along, so handsome, so different, I put that suit on him and made him wear it whether it fitted him or not. . . . I kept on loving the pretty clothes—and not him at all."[7]

I suspect that Scarlett's delusions about Ashley would have vanished much more quickly had the war not intervened. Despite her irritation with some of the more hidebound conventions of her upbringing and her impatience with the political disputes that prompted the war, Scarlett's vision of happiness is rooted in the culture she has known throughout her girlhood. Unlike Huck Finn, she is not ready to "light out for the territory"; she simply wants to call the shots in a familiar world. With the coming of the war, the only part of that world with which she is left is her dream of Ashley. To his credit, Ashley realizes that the war has brought irreversible change. When he is home on leave, he tells Scarlett:

> And so when I lie on my blanket and look up at the stars and say "What am I fighting for?" I think of States' Rights and cotton and the darkies and the Yankees whom we have been bred to hate, and I know that none of these is the reason why I am fighting. Instead, I see Twelve Oaks and remember how the moonlight slants across the white columns, and the unearthly way the magnolias look, opening under the moon, and how the climbing roses make the side porch shady even at the hottest noon. And I see Mother sewing there, as she did when I was a little boy. And I hear the darkies coming home across the fields at dusk, tired and singing and ready for supper, and the sound of the windlass as the bucket goes down into the cool well. And there's the long view down the road to the . . . bottom lands in the twilight. And that is why I am here who have no love of death or misery or glory and no hatred for anyone. . . . I am fighting for the old days, the old ways I love so much but which, I fear, are now gone forever, no matter how the die may fall. For, win or lose, we lose just the same.

After the war, when Scarlett comes across Ashley splitting rails (he himself makes the obvious comparison to Abe Lincoln), she asks him what will become of the South. Ashley replies: "In the end what will happen will be what has happened whenever a civilization breaks up. The people who have brains and courage come through and the ones who haven't are winnowed out. At least, it has been interesting, if not comfortable, to witness a *Gotterdammerung*."[8] Although he does not explicitly refer to Darwin, Ashley is saying quite candidly that only the fit survive and that he and his kind are dinosaurs, marked for extinction in the brave new world of Reconstruction.

If Ashley cannot provide an adequate model for adaptation and survival in the postbellum world, perhaps Scarlett's example is the only reasonable alternative. In order to make the money she needs to survive in a hostile environment, she marries a man she can barely tolerate, trades with carpetbaggers and scalawags, works prison labor, and thumbs her nose at the dying vestiges of the old order. But as James Boatwright, one of the severest critics of the novel, has pointed out, Scarlett is not a true rebel.[9] In her twisted mind, all of her pragmatic behavior is simply a means to restore things to what they used to be. In practical terms, this means saving Tara. It also means keeping alive the hope of winning Ashley's love. One of the supreme ironies of the novel is that the dreamy and anachronistic Ashley actually has a more realistic view of the world as it actually is than does the hardheaded and ruthless Scarlett.

Read simply as the story of Scarlett and Ashley, *Gone With the Wind* would seem to be a Darwinian parable of the New South. With the old illusions swept away, it is now necessary to make one's way in the modern world. If this were the case, however, one would think that Scarlett would feel a sense of vindication and liberation upon finally getting what she thinks she wants. Instead, she loses most of what she truly values. Not only does her dream of Ashley vanish in the mist, but she soon realizes that it is too late to save her marriage to Rhett. More than anything else, it is his love that might have offered her a happiness she has not found as either a conniving belle or a soulless businesswoman.

As most fans of the novel and the movie would readily agree, Rhett is an attractive figure. He may scandalize polite society with his misbehavior, but his essential virtue is never in doubt. He is the opposite of a hypocrite—he is better than he seems to be. Rhett might have fallen out of favor with the bluenosed moralists of Charleston after taking a young lady riding one afternoon and then refusing to marry her when weather prevents them from returning before dark, but not even the most straitlaced readers of 1936 were likely to hold that against him. Some jealous citizens of Atlanta might think him an unscrupulous speculator, but others see him as a hero whose exploits are essential to the survival of the South.

To erase any doubt where his true loyalties lie, Mitchell has Rhett abandon Scarlett on the road to Tara so that he can enlist in the Confederate army during the darkest days of the war. (This flowering of patriotism may be a bit much, in that Mitchell has not previously had Rhett express even grudging admiration for the gallantry of the troops.) Then, after the war, in a gesture that could have come right out of a Thomas Dixon novel, Rhett is imprisoned by the Yankees and faces a possible sentence of death for killing a black man who has insulted a Southern lady. After his marriage to Scarlett, he courts the matrons of Atlanta society on behalf of his daughter Bonnie. Finally, when he leaves Scarlett, it is to return to his native Charleston to repair relations with his family.

James Boatwright is certainly correct in arguing that Scarlett and Rhett (and presumably Margaret Mitchell herself) were really conservatives at heart, figures only playing at rebellion or—worse yet—going through a phase. For critics from the adversary culture, that fact represents a damning flaw in the novel. For readers who do not regard rebellion as the highest human virtue, it might mean that the two principal characters in the novel have finally grown up. It is all the more remarkable that they have done so in the ruins of a civilization they had earlier seemed to scorn. But Mitchell will not let them—or us—off with an unambiguously happy ending. If Scarlett and Rhett have both found the path to maturity, they will not travel that path together.

The very fact that they are so much alike is itself a source of conflict. When they are not clashing with each other, they seem to be dangerously self-absorbed. They are perhaps closest—emotionally as well as physically—on the night that a drunken Rhett takes Scarlett by force. In an unforgettable scene in both print and film, he carries his wife up the stairs in their home in Atlanta for a night of passion. (In the book, the descriptions of that night remind us why romance novels are often called "bodice rippers," while the movie simply cuts to a shot of Scarlett sitting up in bed the next morning with a look of utter contentment on her face.) Unfortunately, whenever either character reaches out to the other, circumstances always intervene to prevent true communion. The cheerless ending of their marriage contradicts the charge that *Gone With the Wind* is a simplistic or optimistic tale. If tomorrow is another day, it will not necessarily be better than today—only another desperate opportunity to get things right.

If there is one character who always does seem to get things right, it is Melanie. Even if she were not a moral norm, her presence would be necessary if only to complicate the romantic configuration of the novel. Like Scarlett, Ashley is at the apex of a love triangle. His choice is between the female equivalents of Apollo and Dionysus. Melanie is the pale, virtuous, seemingly asexual snow maiden whom he marries, while Scarlett is the fiery, passionate dark lady he secretly desires. In remaining technically faithful to Melanie, Ashley makes the choice that is morally correct but dramatically less interesting. If the Wilkeses and Hamiltons have weakened their stock biologically through constant intermarriage, the mating of Ashley and Melanie is also a kind of mythic incest, which matches the Good Good Boy with the Good Good Girl. We are tempted to conclude that neither character possesses the vitality to survive. But such a conclusion would sell Melanie short. Ashley belongs to an extinct species, while his wife merely dies.

Melanie is an extraordinary character in several respects. To begin with, as a Good Good Girl, she should never have made it to adulthood. The sentimental novels of the nineteenth century are filled with angelic females who are dispatched from this fallen world before the onset of puberty. This allows the author to preserve their symbolic innocence, while titillating his (or more often her) audience with tear-jerking deathbed scenes. Melanie, however, has turned the seemingly impossible trick of being a *totally innocent* wife and mother; her innocence always strikes us as the most convincing thing about her. Because of her narrow hips and the difficulty she experiences in giving birth, Melanie and Ashley remain celibate for long stretches of their marriage. Even when this is not the case, it is easier to imagine their discussing the relative merits of Dickens and Thackeray than indulging in the erotic abandon of Rhett and Scarlett. When Melanie does defy doctor's orders and bears a second child, she dies in the process. Thus, her mythic maidenhood, if not her literal maidenhead, remains intact.

If Mitchell were interested in connecting all the dots among her major characters, she would no doubt have contrived some chemistry between Melanie and Rhett. It is, after all, the traditional role of the Good Good Girl to redeem the Good Bad Boy. As she brings him into the confines of society without breaking his spirit or completely taming his mischief, he puts her in touch with the wild side she has kept under wraps. (Think of Mark Twain's Tom Sawyer and Becky Thatcher, or Professor Harold Hill and Marian the Librarian in Meredith Willson's *The Music Man.)* Although the plot does not develop in such a way in *Gone With the Wind*, the utterly platonic relationship between Rhett and Melanie suggests that in many respects these are the two wisest characters in the novel.

It is significant that Rhett and Melanie are the only characters who instinctively see each other for their true worth. When the bluebloods of Atlanta shun Rhett, Melanie insists on receiving him at Aunt Pittypat's house. For her, his service as a blockade runner and his many private kindnesses outweigh rumors of scandal.

If anything, Melanie has a more independent mind than Scarlett. She challenges propriety on the basis of principle rather than convenience, as she does when she approves the auctioning of dances to raise money for the Confederacy and even contributes her wedding ring to the cause. For his part, Rhett regards Melanie as the only true lady he has ever known and redeems her ring. When he places himself in danger to rescue Ashley after the raid on Shantytown, it is for Melanie's benefit, not Scarlett's. Toward the end of the novel, when Rhett is driven mad by the death of Bonnie, Melanie is the only one who can bring him back to sanity and return him to the human community. Finally, on her deathbed, the last thing she says to Scarlett is, "Captain Butler—be kind to him. He—loves you so."[10]

Because there is so little closure at the end of the tale, Scarlett experiences neither tragic catharsis nor comic resolution. *Gone With the Wind* ends as it began—*in medias res.* For that reason, readers and viewers have speculated about what Scarlett might do with the wisdom she seems to have acquired at such a great price. Getting Rhett back, however, is truly a task for another day. Her immediate goal is to return to Tara and begin life anew with whatever is left of a largely vanished civilization. That she will not be alone in that task is something that only a Southerner of Margaret Mitchell's vision could have known. On the final page of the novel, we read that Scarlett "stood for a moment remembering small things, the avenue of dark cedars leading to Tara, the banks of cape jessamine bushes, vivid green against the white walls, the fluttering white curtains. And Mammy would be there. Suddenly she wanted Mammy desperately, as she had wanted her when she was a little girl, wanted the broad bosom on which to lay her head, the gnarled black hand on her hair. Mammy, the last link with the old days."[11] As Faulkner had already told us, it is the women—particularly the black women—who endure.

Politically correct critics have scorned the image of Mammy and other instances of what they regard as racial stereotyping in *Gone With the Wind*. (They tend to patronize the success of this classic tale while celebrating the fact that such a story wouldn't be told today.) Race, however, seems to me to be a red herring. It is not the color of Mammy's skin but the content of her character that they find ultimately offensive—and that Rhett, for one, finds worthy of unconditional admiration. Her sense of propriety and love of home are too credible to be endured. They are aspects of the pervasive bourgeois sentimentality that underlies both the novel and the film. None of the characters *grows* in a way that a critic from the adversary culture would approve. Margaret Mitchell's profoundly conservative (and hence subversive) message would seem to be that, in every sense of the word, you not only can but *must* go home again.

# WHAT A BEAUTIFUL DAY!

## WALT DISNEY'S *SONG OF THE SOUTH* (1946)

A small rural town in middle Georgia, Eatonton is decidedly off the beaten path. My family and I pass through there a couple of times each year on our way from Clemson, South Carolina, to St. Petersburg, Florida, but that is only because we can never seem to get off in time to beat the rush-hour traffic in Atlanta. So we leave Interstate 85 at Commerce, Georgia, and follow a circuitous route of state roads until we reach Interstate 75 in Macon. In recent years, highway engineers have even constructed a "business route" that will allow travelers in a hurry to bypass the lower speed limits in Eatonton proper. As tiny and insignificant as this town might seem, it has produced two of the most prominent writers of the American South—Joel Chandler Harris and Alice Walker. To understand Harris's current status among literary intellectuals, one could hardly do better than to begin with what Walker has to say about him.

In a talk she delivered to the Atlanta Historical Society in 1981, Walker began by blaming her own inability to write about folklore on the painful and depressing legacy of Joel Chandler Harris. By way of explanation, she quotes extensively from the biographical introduction that Harris's daughter-in-law, Julia Collier Harris, wrote for an edition of her famous kinsman's letters. Walker is particularly troubled by the assumption that personal affection often united black and white people in the plantation South. (When Harris's mentor Joseph Addison Turner would hear of slaves running away or rising up against their masters, he would simply laugh and say that "people who treat their negroes right have nothing to fear from them.") Julia Harris describes Uncle Remus himself as having "nothing but pleasant memories of the discipline of slavery."[1] Walker finds it curious that, despite the biracial paradise depicted in the narrative frame to the Uncle Remus tales, Harris himself would never agree to read the stories aloud, either to his own or other people's children.

Walker has less difficulty with the stories Uncle Remus tells. For the most part, they are authentic folk tales passed down to her by her own parents and relatives, none of whom had ever read Joel Chandler Harris. Nevertheless, the fact that a white man became rich and famous by writing these stories spoiled them for Walker. In her depiction, Harris comes off as a nineteenth-century Elvis Presley who enjoyed a phenomenally successful career stealing the black man's culture. The final indignity was seeing another white man, Walt Disney, reaping further profits from Uncle Remus's persona in the film *Song of the South*, which Walker and her playmates first saw in a segregated theater. At least part of the problem is that Walker recognized too much of her own parents and other adult blacks she knew in the servile image of Uncle Remus singing "Zip-a-dee Doo Dah" as he frolicked down a red dirt road with a procession of mostly white children and cartoon animals.[2] Not too far from the theater that showed *Song of the South*, Walker can remember an Uncle Remus restaurant, which featured a dummy of a wooly-haired darkie sitting in a rocking chair on the porch of an establishment blacks were forbidden to enter.

Reputations in the world of literature are hard enough to maintain from generation to generation without having to withstand the kind of political assault mounted by Alice Walker. The fact that relatively few people have heard her lecture or read it in its published form is beside the point. Her indictment of Joel Chandler Harris is widely shared by the sort of folks who design undergraduate curricula and graduate reading lists in our nation's universities. If Harris made Alice Walker and others like her feel ashamed of their own cultural heritage, these same victims seem intent on making white people feel ashamed of both Joel Chandler Harris and Walt Disney.

One of the problems with appreciating, or even understanding, Harris is that the world he lived in was different from our own but finally not remote enough for him to seem a truly historical figure. Joel Chandler Harris was born on December 8, 1848, and died on July 3, 1908. This made him just old enough to have some recollection of antebellum life while living the bulk of his years during Reconstruction and its immediate aftermath. Even though he is seen as a defender of the plantation system, Harris was the illegitimate son of an Irish railway worker and a local girl, whom her lover abandoned shortly after Joel's birth. At the age of fifteen, Harris went to work for Joseph Turner on the Turnwold Plantation near Eatonton. In this situation Harris benefited from the paternalism of a Southern planter, whom he sometimes fantasized was his real father.

If his fictionalized autobiography, *On the Plantation* (1892), is any indication, Harris also empathized with the free blacks who lived and worked with him at Turnwold. Not only does his protagonist and alter ego, Joe Maxwell, mingle easily with his black coworkers, there is even some evidence to suggest that he helps sabotage the hunt for a runaway slave. At one point, Joe observes a bateau floating along a stream and sitting low in the water. Although he correctly surmises that it contains the runaway, he says nothing. Even if this episode is pure fiction, it shows where Harris's sympathies lay. As Louis D. Rubin Jr. points out, this incident could have come right out of Mark Twain's *Adventures of Huckleberry Finn*, which had been published seven years earlier.[3]

At Turnwold, Harris worked as an apprentice on Turner's weekly literary newspaper, the *Countryman*. Not only did he learn to set type, he also began contributing items to the paper. Although he had no formal education, he did have unfettered access to Joe Turner's library. It was here that the creator of Uncle Remus first read *Uncle Tom's Cabin*. He later recalled that that book "made a more vivid impression on my mind than anything I have ever read since." Shortly after Sherman's infamous march to the sea, Harris witnessed an incident that made an equally indelible impression on his memory. Coming upon an old black woman shivering and moaning, he noticed an old black man lying nearby, his shoulders covered with a ragged shawl. In *On the Plantation*, Harris describes the incident as follows:

> "Who is that lying there?" asked Joe.
> "It my ole man, suh."
> What is the matter with him?"
> "He dead, suh! But, bless God, he died free!"[4]

The man who remembered this scene and preserved it for posterity was no simpleminded defender of slavery.

Shortly after the war, the *Countryman* ceased publication, and Harris took a job as a printer on the *Macon Telegraph.* This was followed by similar positions on the *Monroe Advertiser* in Forsyth, Georgia, and on the *Savannah Morning News.* The latter job was a considerable professional advancement and paid the substantial salary of forty dollars a week. In each situation, Harris wrote editorials and contributed humorous sketches in addition to helping produce the paper itself. Having met and married the daughter of a French Canadian sea captain in 1873, Harris might have remained in Savannah indefinitely had a yellow-fever epidemic in 1876 not persuaded him to seek higher ground for himself and his family. Harris ended up in Atlanta as an editor on the *Atlanta Constitution*, where he worked side-by-side with the New South progressive Henry W. Grady.

On the surface, Grady and Harris would seem to represent opposite views of the South. Grady was a chamber-of-commerce type who wanted to bring business and industry to the region. He believed in looking to the future and discarding any remnants of Southern culture that seemed to be reactionary and un-American. Harris, on the other hand, told romantic tales of an older precapitalist South, in which black and white lived in a kind of pastoral harmony. If Grady had been one of today's civic boosters, he might have seen Harris's stories as a regional embarrassment. In fact, Grady and Harris were good friends, who saw themselves as engaged in a common venture—to bring the South back into the union.

Harris's contribution to this goal is described by Paul M. Gaston, who writes: "By convincing Northern readers that relations between the races were kindly and mutually beneficial, a principal obstacle in the way of sectional harmony was removed. The North had doubted this point, but on the authority of Harris and others it came to accept the [S]outhern point of view." At a time when stage plays based on *Uncle Tom's Cabin* were being performed everywhere in the nation, it was Harris's task to create a powerful countermyth of race relations in the South. If Uncle Remus seemed to be a more mirthful and secular version of Uncle Tom, the way in which these legendary slaves were treated by their white masters differed radically. As Louis Rubin points out: "Mrs. Stowe showed Uncle Tom as mocked, beaten, starved, his humanity denied, his virtue unrewarded. Harris showed Uncle Remus as honored, pampered, respected, his simplicity and gentleness cherished by his grateful and indulgent white patrons."[5] Far too many commentators, judging Harris's intentions according to contemporary political standards, assume that he is trying to glorify or at least sugarcoat the institution of slavery. Any suggestion of amicable relations between the races would call into question the righteousness of the recent war and the necessity of continuing Reconstruction. Or so the argument goes. Unfortunately for Harris's detractors, his work will simply not justify their moral outrage.

It is not my intention to make Joel Chandler Harris into some kind of self-hating Southern liberal. Neither the facts of his life nor the evidence of his work will support such an absurd characterization. But neither will a knowledge of his life and work support the equally absurd view that he saw the Old South as a biracial utopia. Despite the presence of humanoid beasts in his fiction, Harris was a social realist who could appreciate the complexity of actual life. And he saw it with the clear, unsentimental eyes of one born on the wrong side of the tracks. He knew what it was like to be poor and to be dependent on aristocratic patronage for his well-being. It is perhaps for this reason that the godfather of American realism, Mark Twain, believed that the most valuable part of the Uncle Remus saga was not the folklore but rather, as Kenneth S. Lynn writes,

> the part that Harris had contributed—the "frame," which dramatized the relationship between Uncle Remus and the little boy who comes to listen to his stories. . . . Seeking for a quality of experience they could not find in their white lives, both [Twain and Harris] sent their boy-heroes in search of the companionship and understanding of the black man. He was a mythical figure, this Negro of Twain's and Harris's, a figure out of a dream, passionate, loyal, immensely dignified—a Black Christ, in sum,

> but with a very human sense of humor, that Mrs. Stowe's great prototype notably lacked. In Uncle Remus's cabin, or spinning down the big river at night with Nigger Jim, there were beauty, and mystery, and laughter.[6]

I

An American mythmaker who surely ranks with Mark Twain and Joel Chandler Harris was born in Chicago on December 5, 1901. Walter Elias Disney was the fourth of five children born to Elias and Flora Call Disney. Although the Disneys were not destitute, they faced a struggle keeping a roof over their heads and food on their table. When Elias Disney worked as a newspaper-route manager in Kansas City, Walt and his older brother Roy had to rise at three a.m. to help deliver papers. Years later, Walt recalled: "The papers had to be stuck behind the storm doors. You couldn't just toss them on the porch. And in the winters, there'd be as much as three feet of snow. I was a little guy and I'd be up to my nose in the snow. I still have nightmares about it."[7] Although this early experience honed Disney's work ethic, it also caused him to miss so many classes that he eventually dropped out of high school and enrolled in the Kansas City Art Institute at age fourteen. Two years later, Disney entered the Red Cross Ambulance Corps and served as a driver in France during the final year of World War I. Returning to Kansas City after the war, he got his first job as an artist with a commercial art studio. After holding several such jobs, Disney started his own animation firm, Laugh-O-Grams. From then until his death on December 15, 1966, he would be his own boss.

After he moved his operations to Los Angeles, one of Disney's early projects was a series of films called *Alice's Wonderland*. Although primitive by contemporary standards, these films featured a combination of live action and animation that would later be one of his professional trademarks. The rest of the story is well known. After selling a series of cartoons starring a character named Oswald the Lucky Rabbit to Universal in New York, Disney sketched an entirely new animated creature on the train trip back to the West Coast. This miniature rodent, Mickey Mouse, would soon be one of the biggest stars in Hollywood.

Disney had the luck—or ingenuity—to be just ahead of several of the most lucrative trends in entertainment history. When Mickey Mouse appeared in "Plane Crazy" (1928), it was the first cartoon to use sound. A decade later, when most movies were still being made in black and white, Disney used Technicolor for the first full-length animated film ever produced, *Snow White and the Seven Dwarfs* (1937). Later, he would prove to be a pioneer in television and an innovator in the development of amusement parks. For our purposes, however, Disney's most important contribution to American culture was one of his oldest techniques—the mixture of live action and animation.

After pioneering this technique with the *Alice's Wonderland* series, he improved upon it in *The Reluctant Dragon* (1941), an entertainment film featuring the humorist Robert Benchley, which also served as an instructional video on how cartoons are made. Two years later, a goodwill tour to Latin America sponsored by the State Department resulted in a combination cartoon/travelogue called *Saludos Amigos*. Then, in 1945, Disney released *The Three Caballeros*, which was based on that same trip to Latin America. All of these efforts served as a lead-in to what would inadvertently prove to be the most controversial film that Disney ever produced—*Song of the South* (1946).

In *Song of the South*, a man brings his wife and son Johnny down from Atlanta to the old plantation where he had listened to Uncle Remus during his own boyhood. Although the father returns to Atlanta, mother and son remain on the plantation. (The reason is apparently marital discord.) Because the mother's obsessive protectiveness poses a psychological barrier that Johnny must overcome, Uncle Remus takes the place of the boy's absent father and uses the tales of Brer Rabbit to provide him with a useful model of ingenuity. The boy soon makes friends with a little girl from a local poor white family and tangles a couple of times with her pugnacious brothers.

As Johnny grows wiser and more independent under Uncle Remus's tutelage, his mother becomes increasingly distressed. After she tells Uncle Remus to stay away from her son, the disconsolate old retainer packs his belongings and points a carriage in the direction of Atlanta. When the boy tries to stop him by cutting across a field where a bull is grazing, he is knocked unconscious. Although Johnny's father is summoned, not even his presence can bring the lad out of his delirium.

Only Uncle Remus can do that. After the old black man has worked his magic, the lad is restored to normal, and his parents are reconciled. In the movie's final scene (as described by Leonard Maltin), Johnny, his prepubescent girlfriend Ginny, and a little black boy who seems to belong to the place sing "Zip-a-dee Doo-Dah" as they conjure up the cartoon animals that "previously only Uncle Remus had been able to bring to life." Unable to believe his eyes, Remus runs to catch up with them at the crest of the hill "as they all join hands and walk into the sunset on what is *truly* a beautiful day."[8]

Reacting to the happy ending that is typical Disney fare, the critics found this film to be overly sentimental. Also, the superior charm of the animated segments featuring Brers Rabbit, Fox, and Bear was so much more captivating than the live-action story that many observers thought Disney should have done an all-cartoon version of the film. (The animated sequences constitute less than a third of the movie.) The severest criticism, however, had to do with Disney's idyllic depiction of race relations in the Old South.

This fatal flaw troubled the predictable cadre of activists almost from the very beginning. In 1950, a mere four years after the release of *Song of the South*, the distinguished African-American critic Sterling Brown wrote that "'Uncle Remus and his Brer Rabbit tales [no longer] stood for the Negro folk and their lore.' Instead, *Song of the South* had revealed that Uncle Remus 'belonged to white people rather than to Negroes.'" Should there be any doubt that Brown was placing the blame for this situation on Disney rather than Harris, consider the fact that, prior to 1946, he had described Harris's Uncle Remus as "one of the best characters in American fiction." Brown was hardly alone in this earlier belief. The prominent black novelist and poet James Weldon Johnson said in 1922 that "the Uncle Remus stories constitute the greatest body of folk lore that America has produced." W. E. B. Dubois, founder of the NAACP, praised Harris as "the deft and singularly successful translator" of black folklore to a white audience. And Alain Locke, a major figure of the Harlem Renaissance, believed that Harris had "rendered as much poetic justice to the Negro as an orthodox Southerner could."[9]

One can discern at least three separate positions taken in opposition to Uncle Remus. One option was to hold onto the tales themselves but to condemn the white men (principally Harris and Disney) who had profited from them. Yet another group of critics argued that the Remus stories were acceptable when told by Harris but had been irredeemably vulgarized by Disney. The most extreme stance was to reject the entire body of folk material as a painful reminder of a racist past.

The chorus of protest seemed to increase with each passing year. In 1973, Bernard Wolfe, who had once written favorably about the tales, described Remus as "an 'Uncle Tom' Negro telling amusing stories for the little white boy, son of the plantation owners, . . . [thus constituting] a painful reminder of slavery times in which a grown Negro man is depicted as the playmate or nursemaid of a 'boy.'" Two years later, Robert Bone noted that "Joel Chandler Harris is in bad odor among the younger generation of literary men. The blacks, who tend to equate Uncle Remus with Uncle Tom—sometimes, one suspects, without having read either Harris or Stowe—reject the Uncle Remus books out of hand. And sympathetic whites, who hope thereby to ingratiate themselves with the black militants, are fond of giving Harris a gratuitous kick in the shins." Peggy A. Russo is quick to point out that "if Uncle Remus is equated with Uncle Tom by critics who have not read the text, the equation surely comes from familiarity with the Disney image."[10] This situation was exacerbated by the fact that older texts of the Uncle Remus tales were being replaced by the Golden Book edition of the Disney version of those same tales.

By the 1980s, those who wished to retain the folk tales without what they regarded as the problematical frame narrative had become more vocal. In fact, Peggy Russo notes:

> The latest trend in publishing is to translate the [dialectical] language into a facsimile of standard English, and to remove the frame completely, thereby erasing from the tales any "taint" of slavery. Two such editions appeared in the late eighties: *Jump! The Adventures of Brer Rabbit*, adapted by Van Dyke Parks and Malcolm Jones, and Julius Lester's *The Tales of Uncle Remus: The Adventures of Brer Rabbit*. . . . Lester apologetically tells us that he cannot include Uncle Remus in his book despite his statement that "there are no inaccuracies in Harris's characteriza-

> tion. . . . [because Uncle Remus] became a stereotype and therefore negative." Indeed, he *became* a stereotype—in a film called *Song of the South*.[11]

June Jordan speaks for those who believe that Lester did not go far enough, that nothing short of eradicating the folk tales themselves will rid our collective imagination of the hideous specter of Uncle Remus. "How shall anyone salvage 'The Tales of Uncle Remus,'" she writes in the *New York Times Book Review*, "and yet hope to escape the implications of that mythical, that garrulous ol' slave whom Joel Chandler Harris used to narrate his stories?"[12] Apparently, for Jordan, the distinction between Disney and Harris (and perhaps Lester himself) is without a significant difference.

The Disney Company's own response to the racial furor raised by *Song of the South* was to try subtly to deemphasize the controversial content of the film. When it was first released in 1946, animated characters could hardly be seen above the title in the theatrical poster. With each subsequent release, however, these characters assumed an increasingly larger share of the poster. Jason Sperb notes that by 1986, the fortieth anniversary of the film's release, "Brer Rabbit was the main attraction. . . . Uncle Remus and the children were barely visible above the title, even though *Song of the South* was still the same *Gone With the Wind*-esque Southern melodrama that it had been forty years earlier."[13]

A year after the 1986 release of *Song of the South*, the Disney Company broke ground at Disney World for a spectacular new attraction based on the film. Splash Mountain was an eighty-million-dollar log-flume ride. As the riders descend Splash Mountain in a cascade of water, they are serenaded by various voices, including those of cartoon characters telling tales ostensibly from *Song of the South*. Not only is the voice of Uncle Remus silenced, but the controversial story of the Tar Baby has been replaced by a more innocuous saga of a beehive of honey that entraps Brer Rabbit. Jason Isaac Mauro may be right when he says that this slight but crucial alteration is a tacit admission on the part of the Disney Company that it has "structured the entire multimillion-dollar ride around a narrative that they regard as fundamentally racist."[14] I suspect, however, that this disingenuous transformation was nothing more than an example of a large corporation heading off potential controversy.

One thing Uncle Remus was right about is that you can't run away from trouble. If his presence as narrator of his tales sparked protests, his absence caused the same protesters to cry foul for different reasons. He seems like nothing so much as the proverbial nobody who won't go away. Unfortunately, discourse about Uncle Remus often begins with the assumption that his manner and milieu are cause for collective shame on the part of both races. The fact that he is the most admirable character in Disney's film seems to get lost in the shouting. He is more of a parent to young Johnny than the lad's own self-absorbed mother and father. When he is insulted, he doesn't shuck and jive. Instead, he prepares to leave the plantation—a gesture of independence for which the PC police give him (and Disney) no credit. So what if the story seems too good to be true? The same could be said of scores of other Disney movies. If there is a fatal flaw in *Song of the South*, it has nothing to do with Uncle Remus's lack of militancy. It is rather the failure of the film to probe the pathos that is at the heart of the frame narrative on which the picture is based. Uncle Remus is victimized less by racial oppression than by that mortal enemy of us all—the passage of time.

## II

If the stories Uncle Remus tells tend to be set pieces, which can stand by themselves and be told in any conceivable order, the narrative frame reflects a definite change in the world that Uncle Remus inhabits. Although the New South journalist Joel Chandler Harris helped to create that world, his black alter ego regards it with a jaundiced eye. Like so many lifelong servants, Uncle Remus is more threatened by change in society than are the rich and powerful, who are better able to adjust to new conditions. In an essay written in 1948, Donald Davidson argues that "the Negro, so far as he has not been corrupted into heresy by modern education, was the most traditional of Southerners, the mirror which faithfully and lovingly reflected the traits that Southerners once all but unanimously professed." In Davidson's opinion, the vision of the good life most loyally adhered to by traditional Southern blacks consisted of equal amounts of hunting, dancing, singing, talking, eating, praying, and lovemaking. Rather than being a sign of indolence, this sense of life's priorities is one of the supreme virtues of African-

American and Southern-American culture. Two decades earlier, when he learned that Robert Penn Warren was to write an essay about black folk for the Agrarian manifesto *I'll Take My Stand* (1930), Davidson enthusiastically wrote to Warren: "It's up to you, Red, to prove that negroes are country folks 'bawn and bred in a briar patch.'"[15]

Uncle Remus has little use for the city that his creator called home. He refers to Atlanta as "Lantatantarum," as if to emphasize the urban bedlam that characterizes the place. As the little boy to whom he tells his stories becomes ever more citified, Uncle Remus deliberately paints the rural world of the past as a kind of lost Eden. Even if it was literally far from being an earthly paradise, the alchemy of memory can make it so, especially in contrast to the impersonal culture that replaced it. This becomes particularly evident by the time we get to the final book in the Uncle Remus series—*Told by Uncle Remus*, published in 1905. Harris appears to be using a black *doppelganger* to express his own fondness for a bygone era. That is not exactly the same as arguing for a repeal of the Emancipation Proclamation.

In the first two Remus books—*Uncle Remus: His Songs and Sayings* (1880) and *Nights with Uncle Remus* (1883)—the setting of the narrative frame is an old plantation not unlike Turnwold, and the listener is a white child young enough to believe anything Uncle Remus tells him. Lucinda MacKethan suspects that the sheltering love this lad receives from the older black man represents much that Harris's own childhood lacked.[16] Whether or not this is the case, the bonding of the white boy and the colored man is a persistent theme in American literature from Twain's *Huckleberry Finn* (1884) to Faulkner's *The Bear* (1942). In the tradition of the noble savage, the man of color possesses a primitive wisdom and an instinctive sense of freedom that is largely absent from the overcivilized white world.

As early as *Nights with Uncle Remus*, the narrative frame ceases to be a perfunctory excuse for getting into the animal fables and becomes a series of detailed dramas, which involve friendly competition among Uncle Remus and three other storytellers, as well as the ongoing courtship of two young slaves on the plantation. The view that we get of antebellum life is not from the perspective of the white overlords but from the slaves themselves. (If Harris shared the race of the plantation owners, he was tied by class to the servants in the slave quarters.) Already, Uncle Remus realizes that the canker is in the rose. "Dey ain't no dancin' deze days," he complains; "folks shoes too tight, en dey ain't got dey limbersomeness in de hips w'at dey uster is."[17]

By the time we get to *Uncle Remus and His Friends* in 1892, the little boy is beginning to grow up. With maturity comes skepticism and a corresponding loss of innocence. Uncle Remus is clearly upset when the lad demands logical explanations for points that must be accepted on faith or not at all. In a sense, the boy's growing lack of credulity becomes a measure of how far the world itself has come since the simple times of the recent past. Uncle Remus and, one assumes, Harris himself blame the situation on an excessive love of the almighty dollar. "Hit's money, honey, de worl' over," Remus declares. "Go whar you will . . . en you'll fin' folks huntin' atter money—mornin' en evenin', day en night."[18] Because Harris suspected that such a world might no longer be interested in rural folklore, he intended this third book to be his last. But the reading public would not let Uncle Remus fade away. Perhaps, like Harris, it too needed a reminder of how things used to be.

In *Told by Uncle Remus* (1905)—the last major book of the cycle and the one on which the frame story of *Song of the South* is based—the little boy who had originally listened to Uncle Remus's tales has grown up, married, and moved to Atlanta. His mother, the aging Miss Sally, continues to preside over the plantation that Uncle Remus had long known as home. Disliking city life with the Atlanta couple, Uncle Remus is granted permission to return to the old homestead. There, in a crucial element of the plot jettisoned by Disney, he discovers that the values he and Miss Sally share because of their advancing age are stronger than any differences that may separate them. Bruce Bickley writes:

> [P]rimarily it is their mutual old age that seems to break down the barriers between black and white, and between lower and higher social station. Remus and Sally share a quiet sympathy; the two talk of feeling useless, and at times a gesture or glance is sufficient to express their sense of helplessness. In his mutually reflecting portraits of Sally and Uncle Remus, Harris is also suggesting that survivors of the Old South, those remaining patrons of former times, can only turn to each other for support

> and understanding; for the new postwar generation has a different system of values and a different cultural and social orientation.[19]

In an age of cultural separatism the broad and enduring appeal of the Uncle Remus stories may well be the equivalent of a political thought crime. This is because that appeal is based on the subversive notion that there were happy times and interracial friendships during slavery and Reconstruction. If Harris and Disney, like Stephen Foster before them, give us only one side of the picture, their vision is finally no more distorted than are the sadomasochistic fantasies of Alex Haley's *Roots* (1976). Neither black self-esteem nor racial reconciliation is advanced by a wholesale condemnation of the Old South. Understanding the full complexity of race relations in that society may be a prerequisite for building a more harmonious future. In that effort, a wise old black man, an eager-eyed young white boy, and a mischievous rabbit can help to lead the way.

# THE KEEPER OF OUR CONSCIENCE

## CLARENCE BROWN'S *INTRUDER IN THE DUST* (1949)

When *Intruder in the Dust* was published in 1948, it was William Faulkner's first book to appear since *Go Down, Moses* in 1942. During that six-year period, Faulkner's literary reputation had experienced a remarkable reversal of fortune. Although he had been held in high critical esteem throughout the 1930s and had even graced the cover of *Time* magazine on January 23, 1939, his books began going out of print in the early to mid 1940s. In some cases, the very plates on which those books were printed had been melted down for war material. Then, in 1946, the general reading public rediscovered the Mississippi novelist with the publication of Malcolm Cowley's *The Portable Faulkner*—a selection of fiction set in the author's mythical Yoknapatawpha County. In editing this volume, Cowley paid scant attention to the formal distinction between stories and excerpts from novels. Believing that Faulkner was less the careful craftsman than the grand mythmaker, Cowley arranged the contents of his book according to narrative chronology, giving us a history of Yoknapatawpha County over a period of two centuries.

Faulkner's newly acquired fame (which included his receiving the Nobel Prize for Literature in 1950) coincided with the birth of the postwar civil-rights movement in America. Two months before *Intruder in the Dust* was published, the Democratic National Convention in Philadelphia had split over the party's stand on race. At the urging of the fiery young mayor of Minneapolis, Hubert Humphrey, the convention committed the party to support strong federal action on behalf of civil rights. As a result, delegates from several Southern states walked out. When the smoke had cleared, the dissident Southerners had formed the States' Rights (or Dixiecrat) Party and had nominated Strom Thurmond of South Carolina for president and Fielding Wright of Faulkner's home state of Mississippi for vice president. Because Faulkner was a Southern novelist who had written with sensitivity about race, the intellectual community was curious to see what, if anything, his new novel had to say about the controversy over civil rights. Not surprisingly, there was enough in *Intruder in the Dust* to intrigue and infuriate just about everybody.

The general action of Faulkner's new novel was congenial to Northern liberal sensibilities. A proud black man is accused of a murder he didn't commit. While he is in danger of being lynched for his uppity ways, the black is defended by a white lawyer, a boy still too young to have been completely tainted by racial bigotry, and an independent old spinster, who has always behaved decently toward African Americans. By defying community sentiment, this trio proves the black man's innocence and forces the mob to back down. Make the lawyer a bit more idealistic and (a decade and a half later) you have Atticus Finch in Harper Lee's *To Kill a Mockingbird* (1960). Faulkner is clearly on the side of the liberal angels. Or is he? The closer we look at the lawyer, Gavin Stevens, the more flaws he seems to have as both an attorney and a man. Without even speaking to his client, he assumes the man's guilt and plans only to seek a change of venue in the hope of copping a plea and sparing his life. What is even worse, Stevens is constantly lecturing his nephew on the evils of federal intervention and the need to allow the South to solve the race problem in its own way and in its own time. Critics began to suspect that Faulkner was posing as a liberal in order to make the same old conservative argument for local autonomy.

The critics who were troubled by what they considered to be Faulkner's political stance included several of his more discerning admirers. Malcolm Cowley thought that *Intruder in the Dust* should have been either less political or more politically correct. Writing in the *New Republic*, he concluded that "the tragedy of intelligent Southerners like

Faulkner is that their two fundamental beliefs, in human equality and in Southern independence[,] are now in violent conflict." In an even stronger statement in *Partisan Review*, Elizabeth Hardwick argued that Faulkner's "states rights pamphlet . . . falsifies and degrades his fine comprehension of the moral dilemma of the decent guilt-ridden Southerner." But the most extended discussion of the author's political transgressions came in Edmund Wilson's review in the October 23, 1948, issue of the *New Yorker.* While finding much to admire in the novel, Wilson believed that it ultimately descended to the level of a tract whenever Gavin Stevens opened his mouth. In an ingenious twist of logic, Wilson contended that, all arguments to the contrary notwithstanding, Southerners do respond to outside pressures regarding race. Otherwise, Faulkner (the Southerner) would never have written such an overtly political book as *Intruder in the Dust.*[1]

The problem with this analysis is not that it is inaccurate but that it is insufficient. Even if Faulkner has written a social-protest novel or novel of ideas, it is still a novel, and the statements made within that context ought not to be read as if they appeared in an essay or interview, although he did express similar views in more than one public forum. (This is a less obvious version of the error made by people who rip a speech made by Polonius or Falstasff out of context and preface it with the words "Shakespeare believes.") In *The Well Wrought Urn* (published the year before *Intruder in the Dust*), Cleanth Brooks maintained that "a poem does not *state* ideas but rather *tests* ideas." If we extend this generalization to prose fiction, then any given statement that Faulkner's novel makes about race must be seen not in isolation but as part of the larger dramatic action of the story.

Not surprisingly, Brooks himself interprets Gavin Stevens's political observations in precisely that light in his own analysis of *Intruder in the Dust*. According to Brooks, *Intruder* is essentially a tale of initiation, in which young Chick Mallison finds his place in the community to which he has been born. "Gavin is the person who would naturally talk to the boy about the problems that are disturbing him," Brooks writes, "and the adult's notions about the community, the Negro, and the nature of the law and justice represent for the boy at once a resource and an impediment. It is against these that his own developing notions must contend and it is these views which he must accept, repudiate, or transcend."[2]

What, then, does *Intruder in the Dust*, as a novel, say about race in the American South? The fact that young Chick Mallison is Faulkner's primary center of consciousness is an important part of the answer to that question. Although Chick is not a first-person narrator, his relationship to Lucas Beauchamp is not unlike the situation of the peripheral observer in any number of modern novels. Such an eyewitness (Conrad's Marlow, Fitzgerald's Nick Carraway, and even Melville's Ishmael) observes another person's story and seeks to understand that person through what Robert Scholes and Robert Kellogg call "an imaginative sharing of his experience." Contending that "this has been a very fruitful device in modern fiction," Scholes and Kellogg note that "the story of the protagonist becomes the outward sign or symbol of the inward story of the narrator, who learns from his imaginative participation in the other's experience." Consequently, "the factual or empirical aspect of the protagonist's life becomes subordinated to the narrator's understanding of it." Thus, "not what really happened but the meaning of what the narrator believes to have happened becomes the central preoccupation."[3] If you substitute the word "observer" for "narrator," you have a fairly accurate description of Faulkner's technique in *Intruder in the Dust*.

Chick's first encounter with Lucas comes when the young white boy, who is out hunting, falls into an icy pond on the old Negro's property. When Lucas takes him in and provides him with both warm clothes and supper, Chick does not know how to respond. Lucas's proud rejection of payment for these services suggests a kind of social equality that Chick finds unsettling. Every time he tries to reestablish a position of superiority by sending Lucas a gift, Chick receives a gift of equal or greater value in return. (This game ends only when Lucas is plunged into grief by the death of his wife.) As Chick indignantly observes: "*We got to make him be a nigger first. He's got to admit he's a nigger. Then maybe we will accept him as he seems to intend to be accepted.*"[4] Clearly, "being a nigger" is more a matter of social construction than of biology. If Lucas is too obstinate or proud to play his assigned racial role, it is up to the white folks of the community to put him in his place. Even in the most earnest propaganda novel, Chick would start out believing such things, if only so that he could unlearn them as he matures morally.

If Lucas has no intention of being a nigger, he is no conventional crusader for civil rights, either. This became evident in an encounter he had had with some white working men at a crossroads grocery store three years before the present action of the novel had even begun. Taking exception to his swagger and his indifference to their presence as he purchases and starts to eat a package of ginger snaps, one of the white men jumps up and accosts Lucas, saying, "You goddamn biggity stiffnecked stinking burrheaded Edmonds sonofabitch." Showing what he most objects to in this diatribe, Lucas replies: "I aint a Edmonds. I dont belong to these new folks. I belongs to the old lot. I'm a McCaslin." Readers of *Go Down, Moses* will know what Lucas is talking about. He is the grandson of a wealthy local planter, who is patriarch to a line of black and white descendants. Lucas's racial pride derives not from any notion that black is beautiful but from his heritage as a *male* McCaslin. (The bulk of the McCaslin inheritance is now owned by the Edmonds family, a white clan descended from a McCaslin *daughter*.) Unlike Malcolm X, Lucas has not "learned to hate every drop of that white rapist's blood that is in me."[5] To compound the irony, Carothers McCaslin had represented everything that was most loathsome about race relations in the antebellum South.

The black McCaslin progeny are yet another reminder of how difficult it is to find a biologically "pure" African in the South or, indeed, in all of America. At one time, the racial caste system stigmatized anyone with the slightest taint of African ancestry. As a consequence, the tragic mulatto became a stock figure in our literature, while the phenomenon of "passing through" both racial worlds became the subject of novels as diverse as Mark Twain's *The Tragedy of Puddn'head Wilson* (1894) and James Weldon Johnson's *The Autobiography of an Ex-Coloured Man* (1912). In the figure of Lucas Beauchamp, Faulkner demonstrates even further ambiguities of race and class. In antebellum times, slaves who were owned by an aristocratic family often felt socially superior to free white trash. (Consider Mammy and Uncle Peter in Margaret Mitchell's *Gone With the Wind*.) If Lucas is capable of condescending to the Edmondses because they represent a distaff line of the McCaslin family, one can only imagine the contempt that he feels for the decidedly non-aristocratic whites he encounters in the crossroads grocery. Not only does Lucas refuse to act like a nigger, he puts on the airs of an aristocratic white man.

Even if he is neither heroic enough nor victimized enough to be the sacrificial Negro of Northern liberal mythology, Lucas's plight does test some indigenous Southern approaches to the race problem. One is the lynch mentality represented by Crawford Gowrie and many of the townspeople. Another is the ostrich-like indifference of Chick's parents. A third is the much-maligned gradualism of Gavin Stevens. A fourth is exemplified by the rustic professionalism of Sheriff Hampton. A fifth and final paradigm is provided by Miss Eunice Habersham. It is from these various white role models that Chick must learn how to deal with the enigmatic Lucas and, in the process, find his own place in the community of Yoknapatawpha County.

No serious observer believes that Faulkner is advocating lynch law. His entire canon disparages the knee-jerk white supremacy that has all too often dehumanized American blacks. Nor can he be accused of ignoring the situation. Although some of the most accomplished Southern literature is monochromatic in content, Faulkner's work does not fall into that category. What is perhaps more to the point, Chick is never tempted to join the mob and refuses to let sloth or cowardice dissuade him from helping Lucas. If his Uncle Gavin and Sheriff Hampton seem to be more plausible role models, each leaves much to be desired. Unlike Gavin, Chick is genuinely interested in the question of Lucas's guilt or innocence. The sheriff may be an exemplar of courage and decency in protecting Lucas from the mob, but he does not think to examine the bullet in Vinson Gowrie's body until after Chick, his black friend Aleck Sander, and Miss Habersham have dug up the grave in which Vinson was presumed to be lying.

Miss Habersham is the one character in the novel who believes unwaveringly in Lucas's innocence. She also leads the exhumation party to the empty grave and holds Crawford Gowrie and the mob at bay merely with the moral force of her presence. It may be naïve, even sentimental, to build a political platform on Miss Habersham's example, but she is clearly the moral center of Faulkner's novel. If Gavin Stevens can be said to speak for the public Faulkner, Miss Habersham is closer to the author's most deeply held intuition when she says to Chick: "Lucas knew it would take a child—or an old woman like me: someone not concerned with probability, with evidence. Men like your uncle and Mr. Hampton have had to be men too long, busy too long."[6]

For all of the male bonding in Faulkner's fiction (and Lucas and Chick are surely an example of that phenomenon), it is invariably the women who show the way in Yoknapatawpha County. Consider, for example, the title narrative of *Go Down, Moses*, a story which immediately preceded *Intruder in the Dust* in the Faulkner canon and included some of the same characters. In this tale, Gavin Stevens represents both the possibilities and limits of what a later public figure would call "compassionate conservatism." He raises money among the white people of Jefferson so that the body of Lucas and Mollie Beauchamp's grandson can be returned home. (Butch Beauchamp was a career criminal who had been executed for murder in Chicago.) Nevertheless, for all his good intentions, Gavin indulges the elitist notion that he knows what is best for the Beauchamp family and is decidedly uncomfortable in the presence of Mollie's overt emotionalism.

If Gavin's sincere concern is accompanied by incomplete understanding, a more elemental bond unites Mollie with her long-time white friend Miss Belle Worsham. (As Arthur Mizener points out, "Miss Worsham speak[s] quite unconsciously of the grief, which is primarily her Negro sister Mollie's, as 'our grief.'") Although elderly black women (such as Dilsey in *The Sound and the Fury* and Mollie in *Go Down, Moses*) may be Faulkner's primary moral exemplars, it is encouraging that a white woman such as Miss Worsham can occasionally achieve an empathy that crosses racial lines. It is perhaps because both Miss Worsham and Miss Habersham are said to have grown up with Mollie Beauchamp that the critic Edmund L. Volpe is convinced that the two white women were meant to be one and the same and that Faulkner had simply forgotten the character's name in the six years between his two books.[7]

## I

Although it is possible to consider *Intruder in the Dust* as a self-contained literary artifact, it is neither necessary nor particularly desirable to do so. As I have tried to suggest, placing it within the larger context of Faulkner's Yoknapatawpha fiction sheds useful light on recurring characters and recurring themes. But there is another sense in which the novelistic version of *Intruder in the Dust* lacks a fully independent existence. Two months before the novel was even published, Bennett Cerf of Random House negotiated a $50,000 deal for film rights to the story. In a sense, *Intruder* was a potential movie before it was an actual book.

*Intruder in the Dust* lent itself to film adaptation in a way that some of Faulkner's more obviously literary novels did not. The author's initial intention was to write "a blood-and-thunder mystery novel which would sell." Although he eventually did more than that, *Intruder* became his best-selling novel since *Sanctuary* in 1931. We are so accustomed to thinking of Faulkner as a difficult high modernist that we sometimes forget that the journal in which he published most frequently was the *Saturday Evening Post*, the magazine that Leslie Fiedler supposes was "most likely to be picked up by the common man when he had seen all the movies in town." Although Faulkner was capable of doing hack work for much-needed money, some of his best fiction was written for a popular audience. While textual scholars have created a cottage industry by publishing "restored editions" that track every stray comma in his original manuscripts, Faulkner himself frequently agreed to publish truncated versions of his work. As early as 1948, he tried to secure a magazine serialization of *Intruder in the Dust* that would have completely excluded chapter 9.[8]

By the time the movie was released in 1949, Faulkner's tale of a young white boy's initiation into manhood had been transformed into a character study of an eccentric old black man's near-fatal refusal to be a "nigger." Not your usual cinematic adaptation, the film version of *Intruder* was made with Faulkner's approval and assistance. Ninety percent of the movie was shot in Oxford, Mississippi, with townspeople used as extras and cast in small speaking roles. Perhaps even more important was the fact that the film was produced and directed by Clarence Brown. By 1949, Brown had been directing films for nearly three decades. In addition to being a highly respected craftsman, he was also a specialist in literary adaptation.

Brown's second film (released in 1920) was a silent version of *The Last of the Mohicans*. While there have been at least three subsequent adaptations of James Fenimore Cooper's classic novel, Brown's is most faithful to the original text. Over the next twenty-seven years, Brown brought more than forty literary works to the screen. Although most of his sources are eminently forgettable, they also include such undeniable classics as Eugene O'Neill's *Anna Christie* (1930) and *Ah, Wilderness!* (1935), Leo Tolstoy's *Anna Karenina* (1935), Robert E. Sherwood's *Idiot's Delight* (1939), William Saroyan's *The Human Comedy* (1943), and Marjorie Kinnan Rawlings's *The Yearling* (1946). Like Faulkner, Brown was a Southerner with his own distinctive artistic and moral vision. When a reporter asked the author if he believed the movie was true to his book, Faulkner replied: "I do. Of course you can't say the same thing with a picture as you can with a book any more than you can express with paint what you can with plaster. The mediums are different. Mr. Brown knows his medium and he's made a fine picture. I wish I had made it."[9]

Faulkner had reason to be pleased with the film version of his novel. While staying remarkably faithful to the original text, Brown and screenwriter Ben Maddow made several changes that rendered the action more coherent. When Chick, Aleck Sander, and Miss Habersham dig up the purported grave of Vincent Gowrie in the novel, they discover the body of an extraneous character who had witnessed the murder and was blackmailing Crawford Gowrie. By the time Sheriff Hampton has the grave officially reopened, Crawford has dug up and disposed of the body of his second victim and filled in an empty grave. (Cleanth Brooks finds this bit of tomfoolery to be one of the most egregious flaws in the novel.)[10] Brown and Maddow wisely dispose of the blackmailer and leave the grave empty to begin with. In another gesture toward narrative economy, the film has Vinson Gowrie (rather than an unidentified white man) attack Lucas in the crossroads grocery store. This makes it more plausible for the townspeople to believe that Lucas killed Vinson out of revenge.

Technically speaking, both the novel and film begin *in medias res* with the captured Lucas being brought into town on Sunday morning. After ten lines, however, Faulkner moves into a flashback that depicts Chick's first encounter with Lucas. In contrast, Brown introduces the community of Jefferson with shots of men in the barbershop and of families singing a hymn in church. (Because there is no artificial soundtrack, all of the background noises are an integral and literal part of the plot.) If our view of the church service is meant to emphasize the sanctimoniousness of the townspeople, the scene in the barbershop serves an expository function. As the center of male gossip, it is the place where Lucas's plight would naturally be discussed. Moreover, the absence of the shine boy is an indication of how the frightened blacks of the community are lying low. Then, when the sheriff's car crosses a temporarily empty town square, we notice that he is driving with a flat tire. Whether or not this is meant to symbolize a malfunctioning system of justice, the flat raises suspicions of sabotage and thus increases the general sense of foreboding in the scene.

After the opening sequences in the town, which are climaxed by Lucas's request that Chick summon his uncle, the lad returns home for Sunday dinner. Disturbed by Lucas's situation and irritated by his parents' treatment of him as a child, Chick abruptly leaves the dinner table and heads for his room. His uncle (called *John* Stevens in the film) immediately follows him in an effort to console and gently reprove the high-strung adolescent. Visually, this action suggests a bond between uncle and nephew. That fact is further emphasized when Stevens enters the room and finds Chick desultorily tossing a baseball in the air. Wordlessly, the two throw the ball back and forth, as Stevens's calm demeanor clashes markedly with Chick's growing agitation. It is only then that Chick reveals to his uncle (and to us) the circumstances of his first meeting with Lucas and of the altercation he had witnessed in the grocery store. Not only does this delayed exposition increase the narrative tension, it also gives us a cinematic equivalent of an interior monologue. Because Stevens is a perfectly logical audience for these recollections, Brown avoids the clunky artifice of having Chick address the audience directly or speak to no one in particular.

One could go through this film scene by scene demonstrating the formal aptness of the choices made by Clarence Brown. The very decision to shoot the picture in black and white, ultimately bleeding into shades of gray, accentuates the atmosphere of stark realism. So, too, does the setting of Oxford and the participation of so many of its citizens. Although the movie is not a documentary, there is an aura of danger in some of the crowd scenes which could not have been obtained in a Hollywood studio with a cast of professional extras. When Lucas is brought from the sheriff's car to the steps of the jail and, again, when Crawford Gowrie runs that same gauntlet, the camera moves with them rather than cutting back and forth to close-ups of the crowd. If Faulkner was never able to capture the grammar and poetry of film in his own screenwriting career, he could recognize it when he saw it in the work of Clarence Brown.

The fact that Brown has created a film that is remarkably faithful to its source should not delude us into thinking that his vision is identical to Faulkner's. To begin with, there is a difference in point of view. The kind of peripheral narration that Scholes and Kellogg describe has never been successfully translated onto the screen. When a good movie is made from a novel that employs this technique, the moral education of the observing character is inevitably reduced in significance as the enigmatic protagonist takes center stage. Remove the narrator Jack Burden from Robert Penn Warren's *All the King's Men* (1946), and you are left with a political melodrama. In adapting Warren's novel for the screen, Robert Rossen did essentially that. Although Burden (as played by John Ireland) remains a vestigial figure in the film, he is completely overshadowed by Broderick Crawford's performance as Willie Stark. By the same token, Chick Mallison is not so much the protagonist of Clarence Brown's film as he is a transparency through which the audience sees Lucas Beauchamp. This is accomplished at least in part by reducing the cautionary rhetoric of Chick's uncle Stevens. Thus, there is no compelling *middle way* between Chick's bonding with Lucas and his joining the mob. Although Chick comes of age in the film, he does so with less dramatic complexity than in the novel.

In the film, as in the novel, Lucas is an example of what Pauline Kael calls "the maddening Negro. . . . He refuses to accept condescension or patronage, he insists on his right to be no better than a white man, and what is truly intolerable—he acts as if he *were* white."[11] But, of course, the novel makes the point that Lucas not only *is* part white but is of aristocratic descent as well. Faulkner emphasizes that fact in the confrontation at the crossroads grocery. In Brown's rendering of that same scene, Lucas's white ancestry is never mentioned. If there is any racial ambiguity, it lies in the fact that the part of Lucas is being played by a Puerto Rican actor, Juano Hernandez. The poor whites in the grocery and the lynch mob (dominated by Gowries in both cases) are attacking a man of color, not a McCaslin who haughtily refuses to act like a nigger.

Whereas Faulkner merely assumes that lynching is a bad thing and proceeds from there, Brown was more intent on filming an anti-lynching polemic. Ben Maddow explained the director's intentions as follows: "He had witnessed when he was a young man of perhaps sixteen or seventeen, a so-called 'race riot' in which blacks were shot down on the streets and piled onto a flatcar at the railway station, and then dumped in the woods miles away from the scene of the slaughter. To him the film was a kind of payment of his conscience."[12] Without lawyer Stevens's pleas to allow the South to solve the racial problem in its own way, the viewer of the film might be more apt to conclude that outside action is necessary—although that particular argument is never explicitly made. Clarence Brown, however, is no self-loathing white Southerner. Lucas is freed not by some fast-talking civil-rights attorney from Chicago but by the combined efforts of Chick, Aleck Sander, and Miss Habersham, with the assistance of lawyer Stevens and Sheriff Hampton. These people are all as much Southerners as the Gowries, who are themselves not even uniformly despicable. Nub Gowrie genuinely mourns the death of his son and refuses to make Lucas a scapegoat after his innocence is demonstrated. Moreover, Brown's Southerners are finally apolitical, in that they speak neither for nor against federal civil-rights legislation.

In the penultimate scene of the film (which corresponds to the final scene of the novel), Lucas shows up at Stevens's office to insist on paying what he owes. Stevens deflects this gesture by saying that Lucas's debt is really to Chick and Miss Habersham. He advises his "client" to thank the old lady by buying her some flowers but not to pay Chick anything for fear that the boy will be charged with practicing law without a license. Finally, the exasperated and bemused Stevens agrees to accept two dollars to repair the pipe he had dropped in Lucas's jail cell. Lucas counts out the money, the last fifty cents of which is in pennies, and then asks for a receipt. This legalistic charade is surely recognized as a joke by the people involved. Faulkner's point would seem to be that no balance scale will ever determine what black and white Southerners owe to each other. Lucas himself had emphatically made that point when he refused Chick's payment for his hospitality at the beginning of the story.

Although the novel ends with this farcical accounting, the film continues with some additional dialogue. Chick and Stevens watch Lucas as he leaves the law office and crosses the town square. "Proud, stubborn—insufferable: but there he goes," Stevens says: "the keeper of my conscience." To which Chick quickly adds: "Our conscience, Uncle John." These lines were supplied by Dore Schary, the liberal MGM executive who persuaded Louis B. Mayer to make the picture. Critics who dismiss this exchange as an overly sententious way of driving home the film's message assume that Schary is tacking on a homily about the race problem being a universal *American* obligation.[13] If, however, Chick's reference is to the South (or perhaps only to Yoknapatawpha County), he is making a point that rises naturally from the action of the story, which is insistently local in scope. In that case, Chick has become part of a truly promising *Southern* community. If Lucas is indeed the keeper of its conscience, that community may well be capable of finding its own way. At least in the late 1940s, that seemed a distinct possibility to William Faulkner and Clarence Brown.

# RACING FOR GLORY

## FRED NIBLO'S *BEN-HUR* (1926) AND WILLIAM WYLER'S *BEN-HUR* (1959)

If *Uncle Tom's Cabin* was the most popular American story for most of the last half of the nineteenth century, it was eventually supplanted by an even more spectacular tale with which it bears striking similarities and differences. In 1880, Lew Wallace, a retired general of the Union Army, published a romance novel called *Ben-Hur: A Tale of the Christ.* The two-hundred-thousand-word book sold reasonably well from the beginning but picked up momentum as readers sang its praises. Lee Scott Theisen tells the story of its phenomenal success:

> From November 1880 to March 3, 1883, Harpers printed only 16,000 copies and paid royalties of about $2,800. In its third year, however, *Ben-Hur* began selling at the rate of 750 copies a month. By the end of February 1885, total sales stood at 48,245, with almost half that number sold during the previous year. Sales averaged seventy-five copies a day. Sales in the second six months of 1885 brought in royalties of $3,295.12 for almost 15,000 copies, a rate of better than 4,500 a month and combined royalties rose to over $11,000 a year. Through 1889, nearly 400,000 copies had been sold. The General's royalties ran as high as $27,000 a year during the next decade and the end seemed nowhere in sight.[1]

By 1893, *Ben-Hur* had surpassed *Uncle Tom's Cabin* to become the best-selling American novel of all time.

The story of *Ben-Hur* began forming in Wallace's mind as early as 1875. At the time, he was a religious skeptic who decided to write a quasi-biblical romance simply because he figured that at least some of the vast multitude who read the Bible might pick up his book. After writing an opening sequence involving the visit of the wise men to the baby Jesus, Wallace was stumped as to how to proceed. Then, one night in 1876, he encountered the famed agnostic Colonel Robert Ingersoll on a Pullman car moving toward Indianapolis. The men had a heated discussion concerning religion, particularly the divinity of Christ. Confounded by his own ignorance, Wallace resolved to make his uncompleted novel into a powerful testimony on behalf of Christ. This experience may well be considered the equivalent of the moment when Harriet Beecher Stowe realized that she could make something good out of the death of her son if she wrote a novel that would end slavery. At the very least, it sent General Wallace on the road to belief and *Ben-Hur* on the road to completion.

Strictly speaking, *Ben-Hur* is not a "tale of the Christ" in the sense of being a modern version of the Gospels. The title character—Judah Ben-Hur—is a young Hebrew seeking to remove first-century Palestine from the yoke of Roman oppression. At the beginning of his story, which follows the visit of the wise men to Bethlehem, Judah is reunited with his childhood friend, the young Roman Messala. Unfortunately, Messala is so sold on the idea of Roman hegemony that he tries to recruit Judah as a collaborator. This leads to their permanent estrangement. Shortly thereafter, when a loose tile from the roof of Judah's house gives way under his hand and strikes a Roman official riding in a parade below, the young Jew is wrongfully accused of having hurled the tile. Without the protection of his former friend Messala, this incident leads to a lifetime sentence as a galley slave.

Unlike so many other prisoners, Judah seems to thrive physically in the galleys. During a sea battle, he manages to escape and to rescue a Roman officer who had taken an interest in him. The officer first befriends and later adopts Judah, who becomes a proficient charioteer in his leisure time. After the death of his foster father, Judah wins permission to return to Palestine with the new Roman governor, Pontius

Pilate. Once there, he engages his old adversary Messala in a harrowing chariot race. His victory climaxes one line of action in the novel, while providing a spectacle for later adaptations on both stage and screen. Having dispatched Messala, Judah searches for his long-lost mother and sister, who have contracted leprosy in prison. He discovers that they have been released to a leper colony and almost certain death. As grace would have it, however, the two women are cured by Jesus on his way to the cross. This is enough to convince them that this new rabbi is the real deal, and they are converted to a life of Christian devotion. The story ends two years later, when they persuade Judah to join them in the faith.

Wallace experienced several advantages in writing his book this way. By focusing on an imaginary character, he could include elements of romance and revenge completely foreign to the Son of God. (One can hardly see Jesus engaging Satan in a chariot race.) Also, new plot elements save the author from having to rework familiar elements from the Bible. After the initial visit of the wise men, which is taken more from legend than from scripture anyway, the only places where Wallace's text crosses with the Bible are the Sermon on the Mount and certain events of Holy Week—specifically the crucifixion. Judah Ben-Hur, in effect, becomes our surrogate for encountering the Christ. By having it both ways, Wallace gets the best of both the sacred and the secular worlds.

In addition to considering aggregate numbers, one might ask what sort of people read *Ben-Hur.* In an intriguing essay, Paul Gutjahr argues that Wallace was writing for a conservative Protestant audience not predisposed to reading novels or even approving of them.[2] According to this argument, the religious subject matter (not to mention the subtitle) was enough to bring the latter-day Puritans around. Although Gutjahr has a point, it is interesting to note that, as a genre, the novel's origin in English literature was as an instrument of moral instruction.

The first English narrative to approximate a novel was John Bunyan's *Pilgrim's Progress* (1678–84), a book that from the time of the nation's founding was commonly found in American Protestant households next to the Bible. (Huckleberry Finn found a copy in the Grangerford parlor.) And Samuel Richardson was certainly intent on giving moral instruction in *Pamela,* the subtitle of which is "Virtue Rewarded," and later in *Clarissa*. Because novels were composed with words, latter-day Puritans could not claim that they were graven images. If by Wallace's time Protestants had become wary of prose fiction, that might be because they saw it as having become more secularized, along with society itself. Nevertheless, they were willing to make an exception for a religiously motivated blockbuster such as *Uncle Tom's Cabin*. Perhaps Wallace was simply bringing them the rest of the way with his "Tale of the Christ."

Evangelical Christians (who constituted about 30 percent of church members in nineteenth-century America) not only accepted *Ben-Hur*, they also made it a principal instrument of witness for their faith. This reflected a deliberate intention on Wallace's part. In his autobiography, he stressed "the importance to a writer of first discerning a body of readers possible of capture and then addressing himself to their tastes, [which] was a matter of instinct with me." Much later, he explained that such an audience "would not have tolerated a novel with Jesus Christ as its hero."[3] Thus, the character of Ben-Hur became a theological necessity as well as a literary asset.

If bringing Protestant readers back to the novel was the principal accomplishment of *Ben-Hur* in the nineteenth century, Wallace's work took a different path in the twentieth. Like *Uncle Tom's Cabin* and other classics of the popular imagination, Wallace's tale moved from one medium to another without loss of meaning or appeal. The first such transformation took place on November 29, 1899, when a stage adaptation of *Ben-Hur* opened at the Broadway Theater in New York City. Wallace had been reluctant to allow a stage version of his novel because of the difficulties in portraying both Christ and the chariot race. Fortunately, the producers, Marc Klaw and Abraham Erlanger, found a solution to both problems. Rather than have an actor portray Jesus, the character's presence was indicated by a 25,000-candlepower light.

Depicting the chariot race involved running eight trained horses and two chariots on treadmills on the stage floor. Background scenery was installed on a cyclorama, which moved behind the racing chariots to give the impression that the chariots and horses were actually moving forward. The stage race was so ingeniously done that it was featured in a cover story in *Scientific American*, which diagrammed and explained the stage mechanics. The part of Ben-Hur was originally played by

Edward Morgan, who was later replaced by William Farnum. Messala was played by the future cowboy star William S. Hart.[4]

After a successful New York engagement, the play toured on three continents. It opened in Australia in 1901 and the following year played at the Drury Lane in London, which was the only theater in England large enough to handle the production. The play earned $23,000 a week in London and $32,000 a week in San Francisco. Railway companies chartered special trains for performances in various cities. *Ben-Hur* played to standing-room audiences in everything from circus tents to fancy theaters. It was performed six thousand times before nearly twenty million people and grossed $10 million. (Should conservative Protestants feel leery about entering a playhouse, William Jennings Bryan proclaimed *Ben-Hur* "the greatest play on the stage when measured by its religious tone and moral effect," while Billy Sunday wished that one hundred million people could see the play.)[5] If *Ben-Hur* did not run as long as *Uncle Tom's Cabin* on the stage, that was only because the new art of motion pictures was crowding out live theatrical productions.

I

The first attempt to put the story of *Ben-Hur* on screen came in 1907, when the Kalem Company produced a thirteen-minute short based on Wallace's novel and advertised it as "positively the most superb moving picture spectacle ever made in America." Because movies were so new at the time, there was not yet a settled body of copyright law. Moreover, all sorts of items were being sold with the *Ben-Hur* logo without any royalty payment to the Wallace family or anyone else. These included the Ben-Hur bicycle, the Ben-Hur cigar, various spices and herbs, baking powder, coffee and tea, gasoline, toys, perfume, tobacco, a red Ben-Hur rose, Ben-Hur candy made by the Wunderle Candy Company of Philadelphia, a Ben-Hur store in Houston, an insurance company, and the town of Ben-Hur, Texas. Nevertheless, General Wallace's son and heir, Henry, sensed that a film version of the novel (even one so short and tawdry) posed a greater threat to product integrity than all of these commodity rip-offs put together.

Henry Wallace, along with Harper & Brothers publishers and the theatrical producers Klaw and Erlanger, collectively brought suit against Kalem for infringing the copyright on the book *Ben-Hur* and for cutting into the potential profitability of the play. Kalem responded by arguing that the film would be good publicity for both the book and the play. According to at least one film theoretician, the issue came down to whether the Kalem film more nearly resembled a dramatic "adaptation" of *Ben-Hur* or a candy bar using the novel's title. The case eventually ended up in the United States Supreme Court, which found in favor of the plaintiffs in a historic decision announced on November 13, 1911. Kalem was ordered to pay $25,000 in damages, which probably exceeded the cost of producing the film.[6]

Stung by this experience and holding the entire cinema in low esteem, Henry Wallace was reluctant to sell the rights to his father's works at any price. But in 1915, he saw *The Birth of a Nation* and realized what could be accomplished on celluloid. He set the price for *Ben-Hur* at a prohibitive one million dollars. When he finally came down to $600,000, a group headed by Abraham Erlanger purchased the rights to the film and headed to Italy to shoot it on location. George Walsh was cast in the title role with Francis X. Bushman as Messala. The movie was to be distributed by Goldwyn Films.

It seemed that everything that could possibly go wrong on the set did. Mussolini had risen to power in Italy, and the strife between the Fascist and anti-Fascist forces produced labor shortages and other delays. Back at home, Goldwyn Pictures had merged with the Metro-Mayer company headed by Louis B. Mayer. The reputation and future of the newly incorporated Metro-Goldwyn-Mayer studio rested with the success of *Ben-Hur.* Irving Thalberg, who was the head producer at MGM and right-hand man of studio head Louis B. Mayer, put veteran director Fred Niblo in charge of the troubled picture and replaced George Walsh with the young Mexican-American actor Ramon Novarro. But the main problem was not so much personnel as location. When a fiery sea battle came close to producing fatalities, Thalberg packed up the entire production and brought it back to be filmed in Los Angeles.

Bringing the film home required building a three-thousand-foot-long stadium in downtown Los Angeles and finding enough extras to fill it. When even that did not seem sufficient, Niblo created a dummy section of seats with mannequins, which could be photographed to look like another layer of spectators at the chariot race. The *Ben-Hur* set soon came to be the place to be in Hollywood, with the ranks of extras including such luminaries as Douglas Fairbanks, Mary Pickford, Harold Lloyd, and Lillian Gish, along with an obscure nineteen-year-old named Myrna Loy. The film cost what was then an unprecedented sum of $5 million. The enthusiastic critical and popular reception that greeted the picture when it premiered in December 1925 made the investment pay off. Not only did the film eventually show a substantial profit, it established Metro-Goldwyn-Mayer as an important Hollywood studio.

Although full-color motion pictures were more than a decade away, some scenes were tinted, which made the film look even more technologically advanced. (Sound was added in a 1931 reissue.) But the crowning achievement of the movie was the chariot race between Messala and Ben-Hur. In order to add some collateral excitement to the main competition, the producers offered prize money to the wranglers and rodeo cowboys who drove the other chariots. Consequently, much of the race was deadly serious—almost literally so when one pileup caught on screen endangered the lives of several horses and men.

The film also had a religious resonance that the stage version notably lacked. As Marcia L. Pentz-Harris, Linda Seger, and R. Barton Palmer have noted:

> Niblo depicts in detail the arrival of Mary into Bethlehem, demonstrating her holiness through reaction shots of those who assemble to honor her child. Well-known events from the life of Christ, such as the crowd's stoning a prostitute and his arrival in Jerusalem, find a place in the film. Niblo even stages the Last Supper in what was to become its best-known screen rendition. Because these scenes develop in more depth the events of Jesus's life, they build credibility for Ben-Hur's conversion, framing the worldly events with those of timeless religious import.[7]

As singular an achievement as this film might have been, it was not produced in a vacuum. During the same decade, Cecil B. DeMille directed two notable biblical classics—*The Ten Commandments* (1923) and *The King of Kings* (1927). If no film of *Ben-Hur* had ever been made, the biblical epic would still have been a hot property in Hollywood. Apparently, the straitlaced religious audience was finally no more resistant to motion pictures than it had been to novels and plays—so long as the subject matter was sacred and the treatment sufficiently tasteful. One challenge, however, was to craft a picture with the broadest possible appeal. This meant making a film that was acceptable to Jews as well as Christians.

Most Jews had no objections to a dramatization of the Christian gospel. (Irving Thalberg, Louis B. Mayer, and others involved with *Ben-Hur*—including an assistant director named William Wyler—were themselves Jewish.) Over many centuries, however, various passion plays in Europe had depicted the Jews as Christ-killers. This, in turn, had led to an ugly history of anti-Semitic violence. When Cecil B. DeMille (who was himself part Jewish on his mother's side) made *The King of Kings*, he felt compelled to open the film with the following prologue: "The events portrayed in this picture occurred in Palestine nineteen centuries ago, when the Jews were under the complete subjection of Rome—even their own High Priest being appointed by the Roman procurator."[8] Perhaps DeMille hoped that this disclaimer would cause people not to notice that the High Priest in his film was the vilest anti-Semitic stereotype imaginable.

The story of *Ben-Hur* provided a way around this conundrum. Because the main character is a Jew, the audience is invited to empathize with a heroic young Hebrew. Moreover, the resistance to Roman occupation becomes a central theme rather than something the audience needs to be reminded of in a prologue. The point that is fudged, however, is the final identity of Christ. We know that he is a rabbi with a message of peace and reconciliation and a ministry of healing. Because the film of *Ben-Hur* ends with the crucifixion, we are allowed to assume that Christianity flourished simply because people such as Judah Ben-Hur followed the example of this remarkable man. Christians, if they like, can choose to believe much more. In contrast, those viewing DeMille's *King of Kings* are confronted with the empty tomb and with a post-Resurrection appearance to the disciples. Audiences for that film are meant to exit the theater muttering: "Surely, this was the Son of God."

## II

Thirty-four years after the premiere of Fred Niblo's *Ben-Hur*, MGM issued a remake of the film that had saved the studio back in its infancy. Although MGM was in no danger of going under in the late 1950s, all Hollywood was feeling competition from the new medium of television. Why buy tickets to a movie theater and pay a babysitter when the whole family could enjoy an evening of free entertainment at home? In response to this challenge in an age before big-screen TV sets and the wide availability of color television, the movie industry began producing ever bigger and more spectacular pictures.

In an early venture in virtual reality, Lowell Thomas produced a series of novelty films in a technique called "Cinerama." (Because this required special alterations in the theater, it never really caught on, but its memory survives as a measure of Hollywood's desperation.) This was also a time when 3-D movies, requiring only special glasses to be fully appreciated, were introduced to the viewing public. In 1956, Cecil B. DeMille produced a remake of his silent classic *The Ten Commandments*, featuring the parting of the Red Sea on what, to my eight-year-old eyes, seemed like a screen as big as a city block. That same year, Mike Todd brought out an equally spectacular screen version of Jules Verne's *Around the World in Eighty Days*, with a mysterious process he called Todd A-O. These pictures were more like a theatrical event than an afternoon serial at the Bijou. Even if they cost a mint to make, they usually showed a profit, and even more important, they established the technical superiority of the Hollywood product over anything that one could get at home. Because *Ben-Hur* was, as if by definition, a theatrical spectacle, it seemed to be a natural project for a struggling studio to undertake in the late '50s.

For a variety of reasons, the biblical epic was one of Hollywood's most popular genres throughout the 1950s. According to Melani McAlister, "for six of the twelve years from 1950 to 1962, a religious historical epic was the year's number-one box office moneymaker."[9] If one considers the social milieu of the 1950s, it is easy to see why that was true. Several commentators have surmised that, in the era of the blacklist, biblical material offered a safe, politically neutral subject matter for Hollywood. However, a look beneath the surface at some of the biblical epics suggests that they were meant, at least in part, to be historical parables for contemporary political events.

Cecil B. DeMille, in particular, made this point by appearing in person in a prologue to his already lengthy remake of *The Ten Commandments*. "The theme of this picture," he opined, "is whether man should be ruled by God's law, or by the whims of a dictator like Rameses. Are men the property of the state, or are they free souls under God? This same struggle is going on today."[10] It took little ingenuity to realize that DeMille was equating the ancient Hebrews with the Free World and their Egyptian persecutors with the Soviet Empire. This equation gave DeMille's film a kind of political relevance, while arming the forces of anticommunism with biblical righteousness.

It was also appropriate that the biblical epics were historically set in the Middle East. Then, as now, this was a scene of international turmoil involving the state of Israel and its many enemies. In the Old Testament, the Jews are God's chosen people. As such, they are the good guys in any conflict—whether it be against the Canaanites, the Egyptians, the Philistines, the Babylonians, or the Romans. In any such conflict in the mid-twentieth century, the Israelis were America's chosen people. (That there might be legitimate Arab interests is a possibility which had not yet made it on to our diplomatic radar screen.) Even if that were not the geopolitical reality of the time, the sort of conservative Protestant most likely to attend a biblical epic could be counted on as a supporter of both the old and the new Israel. Although evangelical millennialism had not yet achieved the pervasive acceptance that it has today, our public religion (what Justice William O. Douglas aptly characterized as a kind of "ceremonial deism") was Judeo-Christian. Public service announcements on local television would admonish viewers to "attend the church or synagogue of your choice." Not only were mosques not included, no one thought to ask why.

Out of biblical materials, the screen epics construct what can be considered historical fictions. By this term I mean stories that create a usable paradigm for the purpose of commenting on the present. (At the very time that the biblical epics were playing in movie houses, the scourge of McCarthyism was being symbolically denounced on Broadway by Arthur Miller in *The Crucible* [1953] and Jerome Lawrence and Robert E. Lee in *Inherit the Wind* [1955].) Melani McAlister suggests that the biblical epics followed a generic pattern: "The plots invariably expose the totalitarian nature of an older imperial form, be it Roman or Egyptian or other; they suggest that the old empire is in decline; and construct an alternative: a Hebrew/Christian nationalism, individualistic in its emphases, which is politically, morally, and sexually superior to the old order it will displace. Through a powerful set of parallels, overlaps, and re-figurations, the ancient histories claimed by the films are recuperated as a useable past, suitable for imaging 'America' at the moment of European decline."[11] As critics were quick to note, the Hebrews in these films were invariably played by American actors, whereas British thespians portrayed members of the occupying force.

One unique aspect of *Ben-Hur* is that it features a prominent Arab character. A strictly Zionist text would have had Sheik Ilderim cast as a villain simply because various Arab states are the enemies of modern-day Israel. But in the story of *Ben-Hur*, the sheik is less a historical Arab than he is a symbolic player in the historical fiction. Even if he comes across as something of an oaf (he is played in brown-face by the Welsh actor Hugh Griffith), his primary role is to serve as an enabler for Judah Ben-Hur in his revenge plot against Messala. It may be reading too much into the casting to find significance in the nationality of Hugh Griffith; however, as a Welshman, he is part of the United Kingdom without actually being an Englishman. As such, he is more colonial than colonizer. Or perhaps it is better to say that he exists in a no-man's-land and so can be used to signify either camp.

The significance of casting goes beyond national identity. By the time that Charlton Heston landed the role of Ben-Hur, he had already become identified as a formidable Hebrew political leader by virtue of having played Moses in DeMille's recent remake of *The Ten Commandments*. (The fact that Heston is a Gentile simply makes the identification more universal.) Consequently, anyone who had seen him in that earlier role would have had no difficulty in regarding him as a Hebrew nationalist seeking to throw off the manacles of oppression. What we are finally asked to accept is that he would renounce this lifelong commitment in order to follow the spiritual example of Jesus.

One thing that director William Wyler (himself a Jew) inadvertently accomplished with his remake of *Ben-Hur* was to complete a task that Lew Wallace had begun eight decades earlier—to create a distinctively

Protestant iconography. Because Christianity (like Judaism) is an officially patriarchal religion, it would seem to be relatively easy to establish male images of reverence. In point of fact, Christianity has constantly been subject to feminizing influences. In Roman Catholicism, and to a lesser extent in Eastern Orthodoxy, the female principle has been honored in the veneration of the Virgin Mary. This trend went much farther in culture than in theology. In the Catholic Mediterranean countries, Leslie Fiedler has observed, the trinity of Father, Son, and Holy Ghost was enshrined in dogma, even as the baroque trinity of cuckold, mother, and son was worshipped in art.[12]

In its rejection of anything smacking of popery, Protestantism has condemned the cult of Mary as a form of idolatry. That, however, has not freed Protestants of the need for a feminizing influence in their faith. For that reason, images of Jesus—particularly as a child—became over time increasingly androgynous. Robert K. Johnston notes that "although Protestants removed statues and icons from their churches long ago, on the walls of their parents' homes and in their Sunday School classrooms was hung Warner Stallman's sentimental portrait of the 'Head of Christ.' (It has been reprinted an inconceivable 500 million times.)"[13]

At the same time, the virtues that were celebrated as most Christian (meekness, compassion, forbearance ) were those most naturally associated with women. In *Uncle Tom's Cabin*, almost all of the Christlike characters are female. (In contrast, the truly Satanic figures are all males, who practice the characteristic male vices of drinking, gambling, and lechery.) The one notable exception to this dichotomy is the title character, who is so neutered that the term "Uncle Tom" has now come to be seen as an insult to black manhood. If *Uncle Tom's Cabin* helped to restore the respectability of the novel in the eyes of Protestant readers, it also helped to confirm the uneasy feeling that Protestant Christianity was a religion for women and epicene males.

In the figure of Judah Ben-Hur, Lew Wallace sought to remasculinize Christianity, not by making the Savior into a man's man, but by creating a first-century Christian whom any red-blooded American male would admire and want to emulate. This essential aim was stressed even more when Wallace's "Tale of the Christ" was first translated into popular culture. In commenting on the stage play, Pentz-Harris, Seger, and Palmer note that "male relationships become paramount, and they clearly partake of emerging muscular Christian emphases on male physicality and beauty. . . . While Wallace sought to marry manliness and godliness, [the playwright William] Young privileges manliness over godliness."[14]

Part of the masculinity of Wyler's Ben-Hur lies in the fervor of his Jewish nationalism. Ben-Hur was looking for a political leader and would not have followed a Messiah who could counsel nothing more than turning the other cheek. In their two brief encounters in the film, Jesus (or as much as we are allowed to see of him) radiates an unearthly power. When he gives water to a thirsting Judah, we are struck not so much by his compassion as by the failure of the Roman soldiers to restrain him. This speaks volumes about his mere presence. Even his absence can prove compelling. When Judah's leprous mother and sister are driven into a cave for trying to approach Jesus on the way to Calvary, a thunderstorm brings his dying blood to them. In the words of countless Protestant hymns, they are literally washed clean by that precious blood.

Wyler also does something that Tennessee Williams had made possible in *A Streetcar Named Desire* (1947)—he eroticizes the male body. As Pentz-Harris, Seger, and Palmer have noted, Fred Niblo had eroticized the female body in his version of *Ben-Hur* "in order to depict the moral dangers and decadence of Roman culture, but Wyler prefers shots of Heston's well-oiled massive torso, thick arms straining at the oar."[15] Moreover, when there seemed to be insufficient motivation in the relationship of Messala and Judah early in the film, one of the screenwriters, Gore Vidal, suggested that there be the hint of an earlier homosexual affair between the two young men.

According to this subtext, Messala becomes irate when Judah refuses to pick up where things had left off. Since the Production Code was still ostensibly in effect, all of this had to remain implicit. Nevertheless, Vidal confidently told a reporter that "among the thundering hooves and clichés of the last (to date) 'Ben-Hur,' there is something odd and authentic in one unstated relationship."[16] If we assume that Vidal is correct, then Wyler has done something that would cause outrage among gay activists were it done today—in Messala he has made a villain out of a pagan bisexual! At the same time, the director has emphasized the heterosexual romance between Judah and his girlfriend Esther far more than had been done in earlier versions of the tale.

What makes the story of *Ben-Hur* truly anachronistic, however, is its insistence on making Judah's conversion the triumphal climax of the movie. More recent Hollywood films that have dealt with Christ (e.g., *Jesus Christ, Superstar* [1973], Monty Python's *Life of Brian* [1979], and *The Last Temptation of Christ* [1988]) have portrayed the Savior as an equivocal figure rather than an unambiguous object of reverence. The only question in *Ben-Hur* is how long it will take Judah to convert, not whether he is devoting himself to a sacred fraud. But that was the 1950s, when a kind of generic Protestantism was still our true civic religion.

# PART TWO

# IN THE BELLY OF THE BEAST

# CACTUS ROSE

## JOHN FORD'S *THE MAN WHO SHOT LIBERTY VALANCE* (1962)

Few films have met with the wide range of critical responses elicited by John Ford's *The Man Who Shot Liberty Valance* (1962). When the movie was first released, several reviewers considered it to be a pale reflection of Ford's earlier Westerns. A. H. Weiler of the *New York Times* found it "creaky," while the reviewer for *Daily Variety* thought it lacked "sophistication." Brenden Gill of the *New Yorker* declared it "a parody of Mr. Ford's best work." The highly regarded critic Judith Crist dismissed it as a "yeoman-like western." But perhaps the most damning comments came from Bosley Crowther, the lead film critic for the *New York Times*, who thought the film to be "strangely synthetic . . . an almost slapdash sort of entertainment that is a sort of baffling oddity." Not only did Crowther find the story's moral values to be "as disconcertingly confused as its two or three styles of storytelling," but he also declared *Liberty Valance* to be "a sinister little fable," which could be regarded as "baleful evidence of a creeping fatigue in Hollywood."[1]

The response in England was much more positive. The reviewer for the *London Observer* thought that the film was "bathed in Ford's talent and affection," while the critic in the *London Times* believed that its "violence had an offhand good humor." Probably the most influential praise for the movie came from two Americans—the critic Andrew Sarris and the director Peter Bogdanovich. Sarris considered *Liberty*

*Valance* to be one of Ford's "major works," and indeed one of the crowning achievements of the American cinema. "Along with *Lola Montez* and *Citizen Kane*," he wrote, "*The Man Who Shot Liberty Valance* must be ranked as one of the enduring masterpieces of that cinema which has chosen to focus on the mystical processes of time." Bogdanovich, who organized a festival featuring fourteen of Ford's films at Dan Talbot's New Yorker Theater in 1963, characterized *Liberty Valance* as "perhaps [the director's] most deeply felt personal statement."[2]

I suspect that the critics who praised the movie did so because they accepted its elegiac intent, whereas those who slammed it were expecting a more conventional Western. Both Sarris and Bogdanovich subscribe to the auteur theory of film criticism. Simply put, this approach argues that, despite its collaborative nature, a single artistic consciousness shapes a film just as surely as it does other works of the imagination. A strong producer or a marketable star can sometimes make a picture his own. As we have seen in the case of *Gone With the Wind*, the story itself is sometimes so powerful that it is the determining force in the completed film.

More often than not, however, the director is the auteur. This is particularly true in the case of John Ford, who could manipulate both producers and stars and who changed stories at will. Ford's career lasted nearly half a century, from *The Tornado* in 1917 to *Seven Women* in 1966, from the silent black-and-white era to a time when movies were made in Technicolor and stereophonic sound. Throughout this expanse of time, it is possible to speak of an entire corpus of work, just as literary critics can speak of the canon of Shakespeare or Faulkner.[3] One of the many themes that fascinated Ford from first to last was the effort to civilize the American frontier. Prior to *Liberty Valance,* we can see that theme at the center of *Stagecoach* (1939), *My Darling Clementine* (1946), and *The Searchers* (1956).

Although Ford had worked with John Wayne in silent pictures, *Stagecoach* was their first joint effort in the sound medium. The story is not so much a formula Western as a rendition of the "ship of fools" motif in a Western setting. This involves a disparate group of characters, from varying social backgrounds, being joined together in a journey that reveals their true souls. (As Ford noted, the film owes less to its ostensible source, Ernest Haycox's pulp story "Stage to Lordsburg," than to

Guy de Maupassant's "Suet Pudding.")[4] In the course of this particular stagecoach journey, the most socially prominent character—a banker who, it turns out, has embezzled a large sum of money—is revealed to be the least admirable. A drunken doctor—played by Thomas Mitchell—redeems himself by sobering up in time to deliver a baby to an army wife. A slightly disreputable whiskey salesman gains a kind of mock-heroic status by taking an Apache arrow, while both the army wife and the chivalrous Southern gambler who defends her honor seem to claim a dignity and deference they do not entirely merit. The other two passengers on the coach—an escaped convict played by Wayne and a prostitute played by Claire Trevor—turn out to be the most heroic characters in the film.

In his role as the Ringo Kid, Wayne is not a hardened criminal but an avenger seeking frontier justice for ravages on his family. Trevor's prostitute is the typical whore with a heart of gold. She is run out of the town of Tonto by a group of crusading women, who represent a cramped and hypocritical image of civilization. (The fact that the banker's wife is one of these harridans is about the only thing that elicits our sympathy for him.) The Kid is manacled, presumably to be delivered to the authorities in Lordsburg, while the whore is simply drifting from one town to the next. During the course of the journey, the two fall in love with each other. When the whore shows her better side by helping to deliver and care for the army wife's baby, and the Kid enhances his stock by fighting bravely against an onslaught of Apaches, the marshal charged with maintaining order contrives their escape. He puts the Kid and the whore on a buckboard and tosses rocks at the horses to make them run away, even as he takes his badge off and offers to buy the doctor a drink. As they ride off, Doc Boone remarks: "Well, they're saved from the blessings of civilization."

This line expresses the romantic vision implicit in the film as a whole. At this point in his career, Ford seemed to subscribe to Jean-Jacques Rousseau's view that society is a corrupting force. True virtue, or at least true authenticity, is to be found in the noble savage—such as the man brave enough to avenge his family (in Lordsburg, Ringo gets rid of the rest of the gang he has been stalking) or the whore benevolent enough to cradle a newborn infant in her arms. In his later films, Ford's vision would be far more ambivalent.

In 1946, seven years after *Stagecoach*, Ford again used the Western as a vehicle for exploring the competing claims of the wilderness and civilization. At the beginning of *My Darling Clementine*, Wyatt Earp (played by Henry Fonda) and his brothers approach the Western town of Tombstone. There they run into the Clanton family, who try to buy their cattle. Once in town, Wyatt's attempt to reintegrate himself into civilization with a shave at the local barbershop is thwarted by the rampage of a drunken Indian. After running the Indian out of town, Wyatt goes back to the barbershop but rejects the offer to become town marshal. Upon returning to his campsite to find the cattle stolen and their guardian (the youngest Earp brother) murdered, Wyatt decides to put on the lawman's badge after all. Later in the movie, two other important characters enter town. One is Doc Holliday (played by Victor Mature), who is a physician turned gunslinger. The other is Holliday's former nurse, Clementine Carter (played by Cathy Downs), who has searched for him across the country. Doc is killed in the climactic gunfight between the Earps and the Clantons at the OK Corral, while Clementine returns to the East with the slightest hint that she might bring her civilizing influence back west at a later time.

In this film, there is little vestige of the noble savage. Pa Clanton (played by Walter Brennan) and his brood are as irredeemably evil as Liberty Valance will later prove to be. (Like Liberty, Pa uses a bullwhip as his weapon of choice.) On the other hand, Clementine is both virtuous and endearing in her embodiment of civilized values. If anything, she seems a trifle naïve in insisting that Doc (who is both a consumptive and an alcoholic) can simply resume his medical practice and become a respectable member of the community. In what is probably the film's most famous scene, Earp dances with her at a celebration for the building of the town's first church. If the idea of the church abstractly symbolizes the coming of order to the frontier, the dance is a concrete embodiment of the same phenomenon. At the end of the movie, Wyatt Earp is caught between the wilderness and civilization. It is a story whose last chapter has yet to be written.

In *The Searchers*, one of Ford's most highly regarded films, the focus is on a man who functions as a savage within what passes for civilization. Ethan Edwards (played by John Wayne) is a former Confederate officer and latter-day drifter who has yet to make peace with either the Yankees or with civilization in general. He reserves his greatest hatred, however, for the Indians. At the beginning of the film, Ethan is summoned from his brother's ranch to join a contingent of Texas Rangers pursuing suspected cattle rustlers. (There are strong visual indications that he and his sister-in-law are secretly in love with each other.) Upon arriving at the Jorgenson place, forty miles distant, they find the cattle slain but not stolen. This diversionary tactic has allowed the Comanches time to carry out a raid on the Edwards ranch. When the white men return to that ranch, they find evidence of murder and rape. The only family member not accounted for is the child Debbie. Ethan spends the next six years looking for her, less concerned that she has been physically harmed than that she might have freely joined the Indian tribe both socially and sexually.

In the fifth year of his search, Ethan's worst fears are confirmed—Debbie has willingly become one of the wives of the Indian chief. When the Indians attack Ethan and his companion Martin Pauley (played by Jeffrey Hunter), Ethan is wounded and Martin nurses him back to health. The two return to the Jorgenson ranch just in time for Martin to prevent his neglected girlfriend, Laurie Jorgenson, from marrying another man. As the movie draws to a close, the cavalry rides up to the Jorgenson home with information that the Comanches are camped nearby. Martin rides off to rescue Debbie, who he fears will be killed by the cavalry. After Martin kills the Indian chief, Ethan scalps the chief and gathers Debbie in his arms. At first, he holds her over his head, as if he were ready to destroy something contaminated, then cradles her as he would a child. Debbie now agrees to return to white civilization, Martin and Laurie prepare to marry, and Ethan walks away—a loner to the end.

Although he sees himself as upholding some of the most revered values of civilization (particularly the sanctity of the white race), Ethan is a deeply alienated character. He has fought for the losing side in the War Between the States, and the woman he loves is the wife of his own brother. Although he is technically successful in rescuing Debbie, he has done the right thing for the wrong reason. The one bond he seems to have forged in the film is with Martin, whom Ethan originally derides for his one-eighth Indian blood and whom he subsequently loses to Laurie Jorgenson.

Garry Wills describes Ethan's isolation in classical terms, noting that "Aristotle said that a man without a polis [i.e., society] is either a god or beast, above or below the compromised and accommodating world of interdependent creatures. Ethan is both above and below that plane, divine and bestial in the scale and ferocity of his willpower. . . . In his distinct, brighter, more intense world, he is a god we can watch go by, without power to affect or assuage or save him. He is the West, 'our' West. The West that is no longer ours."[5]

## I

Unlike John Ford, many observers wrongly assume that the Western genre is an unambiguous celebration of American individualism. Our mythic Western heroes do tend to be lone males who face down the forces of evil with little or no help. The prototypical example of such a tale is the film *High Noon* (1952), in which Gary Cooper plays Marshal Will Kane. When news reaches town that Frank Miller, a criminal whom Kane had sent to jail, is now free and gunning for the marshal, no one is willing to assist in apprehending him. This forces the lawman to delay his wedding to a Quaker lady (played by Grace Kelly) in order to complete one last piece of unfinished business. He then crushes his badge into the dust of the street and rides off with his new bride. (At the time, his rejection of a corrupt society was seen as, at least in part, a response to McCarthyism.)

This movie would seem to make several points about both the Western myth and the broader heroic ideal that stands behind it. First, it stresses the isolation of the hero. Although some of our legendary figures are allowed a male companion, in a tradition that stretches back in ancient times to Achilles and his fellow warrior Patroclus, marriage and family life are incompatible with the heroic ideal. (Because a fear of miscegenation has also been part of the myth of the American frontier, at least from the time of James Fenimore Cooper, Kane's romantic liaison with a Mexican woman, played by Katy Jarado, cannot result in domesticity.)[6] Even if Will Kane wanted to continue his career as a lawman, the myth would not allow him to do so. If anything, his wife's pacifist leanings simply force the point. It is possible for the same man to be both a traditional hero and a family man—but not at the same time. In *The Man Who Shot Liberty Valance*, both Ransom Stoddard and Tom Doniphon are forced to choose between two ways of life—if it is not history itself that does the deciding for them.

The conflict between the libertarian ethos of the traditional frontier hero and the demands of social order is a common theme in Western fiction. One thinks, for example, of Stephen Crane's classic story "The Bride Comes to Yellow Sky" (1898). Here, the town lawman, Jack Potter, returns to Yellow Sky with bride in tow. Realizing that he is violating an unbroken rule, he has told no one about his nuptials. Moreover, like Ransom and Hallie Stoddard at the beginning of *The Man Who Shot Liberty Valance*, the couple arrives in town by train. The Stoddards, however, have long since left the frontier to live in the civilized East. Jack Potter must confront one remaining desperado, even if that confrontation turns out to be more farce than high drama.

The disturber of the peace in Yellow Sky is an old drunk named Scratchy Wilson. He is described by a knowledgeable citizen of the town as "about the last one of the old gang who used to hang out along the river here."[7] Scratchy is apparently harmless enough when sober but a public nuisance when drunk. He is in the latter condition when Jack Potter returns with his bride to Yellow Sky. When he faces Scratchy down, Potter is not wearing a gun and makes that fact clear to his adversary. With visions of the Pullman car still in his memory, Potter informs Scratchy that he is now married. "'Well I 'low it's off, Jack' said Wilson. He was looking at the ground. 'Married!' He was not a student of chivalry; it was merely that in the presence of this foreign condition he was a simple child of the earlier plains. He picked up his starboard revolver, and, placing both weapons in his holsters, he went away. His feet made funnel-shaped tracks in the heavy sand."[8]

In his response to Potter's announcement of his new status, Scratchy reveals that their confrontations have long since been reduced to friendly charades. For Scratchy, the notion that Potter might be married is virtually incomprehensible. Crane, however, has already hinted that Scratchy himself may no longer be the outlaw he once was. Not only is he no longer part of the gang that used to hang around the river, his dress is also strangely synthetic. As he approaches Potter, Scratchy is described as "a man in a maroon-colored flannel shirt, which had been purchased for purposes of decoration, and made principally by some

Jewish women on the East Side of New York . . . [and whose] boots had red tops with gilded imprints, of the kind beloved in winter by little sledding boys on the hillsides of New England."[9]

As M. E. Bradford has noted, the literature of the actual American West, as opposed to an eastern dream of the West, has frequently been a tale of socialization. Perhaps because America, unlike the nations of Europe, is a huge country with a brief history, we have tended to mythologize our experience in terms of space rather than time. New Englanders developed the Puritan myth of a "shining city on a hill," while their Southern brethren adopted a very different, antimillennialist, agrarian myth. In contrast, the middle colonies tended to define themselves in terms of a commercial ethic. The inhabitants of each of these three regions, Bradford notes, "felt about the West, as the West . . . in pretty much the same terms. To be unbounded in space and beyond the definition of familiar institutions was both exhilarating and frightening. Or rather, first exhilarating and then frightening, once one had a taste of 'nature unimproved.'"[10]

No matter how attractive the anarchic virtues of the frontier might seem, civilization is not possible until those virtues have given way to the disciplines of corporate life. Throughout our literature, runaway males (and males they have invariably been) have fled civilization by heading west. In 1893, however, the historian Frederick Jackson Turner noted that, for all intents and purposes, the frontier had disappeared as the defining reality of American life. For more than a century the persecuted male hero had fled from what Washington Irving called the horrors of "petticoat government," only to find those horrors catching up with him as the Pullman car finally pulled into Yellow Sky.[11] The fact that the hero often fetched the bride there himself simply tells us that the attractions of civilization were frequently stronger than the pleasures of perpetual adolescence. One who tried to hang on to those pleasures was likely to end up a hopeless buffoon like Scratchy Wilson.

Perhaps one of the reasons that some critics have had difficulty with *Liberty Valance* is that the film is finally more symbolic than realistic. It was anachronistically photographed on a sound stage in black and white. Moreover, the bulk of the film is conveyed through the memory of Ransom Stoddard, a character whose reputation is built on a lie. Because it is a memory film, *The Man Who Shot Liberty Valance* probably bears as much resemblance to a play such as Tennessee Williams's *Glass Menagerie* (1944) as it does to a conventional cinematic Western.[12] Consequently, our response to the story is shaped to a large extent by our opinion of Ransom Stoddard. According to all objective standards, Stoddard is a fraud who takes credit for what another man has done while stealing that man's girl. In the story by Dorothy M. Johnson on which the film is loosely based, this character has no redeeming virtues whatsoever.

The character whom Ford calls Ransom Stoddard is named Ransom Foster in Johnson's story. The note of falseness suggested by the last name proves more than warranted. (The major vice of Ford's character is a kind of prissy stodginess.) While Ford's protagonist arrives in the West by way of stagecoach and incites the wrath of Liberty Valance by defending the honor of a woman passenger whom Valance robs, Foster is simply the victim of random violence on the prairie. In both versions of the story, "Ranse" is rescued by a more resourceful and hard-bitten native of the region. Johnson calls him "Bert Barricune," while Ford renames him "Tom Doniphon." Although Stoddard soon ingratiates himself with most of the community, Foster is the kind of whining nerd who thinks himself better than everyone around him.

When Liberty Valance comes gunning for Foster, it is simply to finish up what he started on the prairie. In the movie version, however, Valance is also the hired gun of the cattle interests, whom Stoddard opposes. In both versions, the Good Samaritan of the frontier (Barricune in the story, Doniphon in the film) ambushes Valance during his apparent showdown with his tenderfoot victim, thus making it possible for the tenderfoot to rise in politics and win the hand of Miss Hallie, who had originally been the Good Samaritan's girl. Both Johnson and Ford present these long-ago events in flashback when the tenderfoot (now a United States senator) and his wife return for the funeral of the Good Samaritan, who has long since become a nonentity—perhaps even of the Scratchy Wilson variety. In the story, when a young reporter asks the senator why he has come, he merely says, "Bert Barricune was my friend for more than thirty years."[13] In the film, the same query leads to a full revelation of the truth.

Even a cursory comparison of the two versions of *The Man Who Shot Liberty Valance* indicates that Ford has done more than just expand the materials of a short story for the needs of a feature-length film. He has fundamentally altered the meaning of the tale and has thus made it his own. For one thing, the tenderfoot becomes a much more sympathetic character. By 1962, James Stewart had become identified in the public mind as the quintessential "nice guy." Moreover, his defining Western role came in *Destry Rides Again* (1939), in which he plays a lawman intent on taming a wild Western town without the use of a gun. (This film was made the same year as *Stagecoach*.) Although Stewart had recently played the antihero in a series of five Westerns directed by Anthony Mann in the 1950s, Ford has him do something more complex—he commits some objectively questionable acts while still seeming to be a fundamentally decent human being. Ford suggests that the triumph of Ransom Stoddard is a historical inevitability, which we should celebrate, even as we regret the sacrifices that that triumph required. At the end of the film, one suspects that Ransom Stoddard (as played by Stewart) possesses a keen sense of the tension between the celebration and the sacrifice.

It seems to me that, along with such matters as camera angles and lighting, the issue of casting is an essential element of film criticism. Although a fair number of movies have been remade over the years, the vast majority have not been. Unlike plays, which are meant to be performed by a theoretically infinite number of casts, most motion pictures exist in a single incarnation. Thus, film actors tend to be more closely identified with the roles they play. Over a career, a particular actor can even take on a screen persona. It is simply wrongheaded for critics to write about the character of Ransom Stoddard without taking into account the fact that that character is played by Jimmy Stewart.

Noting the degree to which the main action of the film is shaped by the Stewart persona, Garry Wills writes: "The snarls of Valance, the condescension of Wayne, the heroine's motherly solicitude all are seen from Stewart's vantage point. He has set up this contrast by his expansive politician's way of dominating the conversation in the opening episode before the flashback. We see into Stewart's soul, into the cost *he* paid for success, the loss of Hallie's love to a dream he had to surrender but still cherishes. There is a delicacy here of unstated disappointments in the life of Hallie and Ranse that is like the unstated emotions in the Edwards family as *The Searchers* opens."[14]

By the same token, the full resonance of the figure of Tom Doniphon would be diminished were the part played by someone other than John Wayne. Perhaps because he is so deeply committed to auteur criticism, Andrew Sarris calls our attention to the fact that, in *The Man Who Shot Liberty Valance,* "the man in the coffin is John Wayne, the John Wayne of *Stagecoach, The Long Voyage Home, They Were Expendable, Fort Apache, She Wore a Yellow Ribbon, Rio Grande, Three Godfathers, The Quiet Man, The Searchers,* and *Wings of Eagles.*"[15] Even before the first word has been committed to paper or the first scene shot, the screen personae of Stewart and Wayne represent the most compelling embodiments of the respective values of civil society and the Western frontier.

## II

The reminiscence of Ransom Stoddard is also a kind of confession, with the unintended role of confessor being played by a young newspaper reporter eager for a scoop. Certainly by the end of the film, we realize how desperately Stoddard has wanted to get this guilty secret off his conscience. Much has been made of the fact that the editor of the *Shinbone Star* refuses to allow the confession to be printed. The irony, of course, is that the confession has been filmed in a motion picture intended for nationwide distribution. This is just one of the many instances of conflict between fact and fiction, legend and history, memory and experience that make *The Man Who Shot Liberty Valance* such a richly textured film.

It is worth noting that, when Stoddard decides to reveal all, the visual aid that launches him into his confession is an old stagecoach, which he identifies as the one that brought him to Shinbone, and which has apparently been preserved as a kind of museum artifact. Whether or not we are to accept this improbable assertion as literal truth, the stagecoach is a useful symbol. It contrasts with the train that brings the senator and his wife to town at the beginning of the film and then takes them back east at the end. It is only proper that the director of *Stagecoach* should have this vehicle play such a prominent role in his final, and in some ways definitive, Western film.[16]

If the stagecoach brings Stoddard and other tenderfoots from the East to the West, it cannot finally guarantee their safety. Liberty Valance, with his gang of ruffians, waylays the stage, robs a widow of her last physical remembrance of her husband, tears pages out of Stoddard's law books, and then practically beats him to death with a whip. The savagery of Liberty Valance (portrayed with appropriate menace by Lee Marvin) seems to be particularly evoked by the threat of civil order that Stoddard represents. Even though it is initially an inconsequential threat, Valance reacts with an instinctive revulsion.

Valance can be said to embody Hobbes's view of man in a brutish state of nature. (He is certainly a rebuke to Rousseau's concept of the noble savage.) What sort of social contract could possibly hold him in check? Stoddard may have "the law" on his side, but the most visible representative of the law in Shinbone is the ineffectual town marshal Link Appleyard. As played by Andy Devine, this character may provide a kind of Falstaffian comic relief, but he is no adequate match for Liberty Valance.[17] The one ad hoc solution has been to counter Valance with a more civilized opponent who can beat him at his own game. If Tom Doniphon doesn't officially represent the law, he is the only force for civil order that Shinbone has known prior to Stoddard's own unpromising arrival.

Stoddard's commitment to the *forms* of civilization is so deep that, for much of the flashback, he is nearly as opposed to Doniphon as he is to Valance. While regaining consciousness (after Doniphon has literally saved his life), Stoddard says of Valance: "I don't want to kill him. I want to put him in jail." When Doniphon responds, "Out here a man solves his own problems," Stoddard responds self-righteously: "You're as bad as he is! What kind of community have I come to here?" The answer, of course, is that it is a pragmatic community which does its best to keep the beast at bay—even if the means for doing so are unconventional by Eastern standards.

When Stoddard begins working at Pete and Nora's restaurant, he wears an apron, which symbolizes the feminized role to which he has been assigned. But we must remember that, in terms of the frontier myth, the bearer of civilization is, by definition, female—the representative of petticoat government. Rather than arming himself, Stoddard pores over his law books to find some pretext that would give Link Appleyard the authority to arrest Liberty Valance. It is here that Stoddard's pedantry and lack of realism both reach their zenith.

In the only direct conflict we see between Doniphon and Valance, the desperado enters the café and trips Stoddard, who is bringing Doniphon a steak. When it looks as if Doniphon will shoot Valance if he does not pick up the steak, Stoddard picks it up and declares a plague on both sides for being "kill crazy." The lesson is not lost on him, however; it was Doniphon's gun, not his own law books and certainly not the presence of Link Appleyard, that has kept Valance and his underlings in check. (Doniphon is backed by his faithful black retainer Pompey, about whom more later.)

If the entire scene would appear to be a triumph for Doniphon and his values, it was preceded by a significant encounter between Stoddard and Hallie. When Stoddard discovered the legal loophole that would have given Appleyard the authority to arrest Valance, he also stumbled over the embarrassing fact that Hallie had never learned how to read. Although this initially reveals some distance between the two, it also creates an opportunity for Stoddard when he offers to teach Hallie to read. (Although Doniphon can read, he has apparently never made a similar offer to his fiancée.) This prospect opens up an entire new world for Hallie. The symbolic contrast between that new world and the one she currently inhabits is emphasized when Doniphon brings her a cactus rose from the prairie. "Hallie, did you ever see a real rose?" Stoddard asks.

The scene immediately following the skirmish in the café occurs a few weeks later. Stoddard, who has put his law shingle outside the *Shinbone Star*, arrives by carriage, praises the paper's editor, Dutton Peabody, for his courageous editorial supporting statehood, and enters an adjoining room, where he proceeds to conduct class. That class includes everyone from small children (most of whom seem to be the offspring of Appleyard and his Hispanic wife) to adult ranch hands. If Stoddard appears to be completely in control (and perhaps a trifle sententious), one believes for a fleeting moment that he can actually bring civilization to the frontier. The credo he has written on the blackboard reads: "Education is the basis of law and order."

If we are apt to forget that, on the frontier, the role of educator is traditionally assigned to the weaker sex, the spell is quickly broken when Tom Doniphon enters the room and takes charge. He orders Pompey back to the ranch and tells Peabody that his support for statehood might well result in his being killed by Liberty Valance, hired gun of the cattlemen, who wish to maintain territorial status.[18] A disheartened Stoddard instructs Hallie to dismiss the class and proceeds to erase the blackboard. When Hallie asks how he can give up without a fight, Stoddard replies: "You heard what Tom said: 'When force threatens, talk's no good anymore.'"

This scene occurs at the precise center of the film. Immediately thereafter, Stoddard rides away, and Hallie learns from Peabody that the young lawyer has borrowed a gun so he can practice shooting in case Liberty Valance returns. We hear Hallie calling for Doniphon and in the very next scene see him overtaking Stoddard's buckboard on horseback. (Not only is it unnecessary for us to overhear her asking Tom to protect Ranse, such a scene would also violate the integrity of Stoddard's point of view.) In the ensuing scene at Doniphon's ranch, Stoddard is humiliated by having a can of paint shot from a post just above his head, with the contents spilling all over his suit. When he knocks Doniphon down out of indignation, it is clear that his ineptitude with a gun is matched only by his feistiness. Such a combination could prove fatal when facing Liberty Valance.

The next scene is set in the saloon, where the people of Shinbone will elect two representatives to the territorial convention in Capital City. In deference to the role that he has long played in the community, Stoddard nominates Tom Doniphon to be one of those representatives. Not surprisingly, Doniphon declines, citing other "personal plans." As Ford biographer Tag Gallagher observes: "This is Doniphon's curious nature; he provides the muscle to get things done and yet stubbornly declines responsibility. While this suggests democracy's tragedy, that those who are strong and good are often reluctant to assume duty, it is Doniphon's adhesion to his concept of personal freedom that makes him act as he does. His world and Stoddard's are mutually exclusive and belong to different ages. Stoddard is from the East, Doniphon probably from Texas. The triumph of one will entail the eclipse of the other, just as only one of them will get Hallie."[19]

Although Valance's attempt to bully the town into naming him one of the delegates is rejected by strength of numbers, he remains a lurking menace to the two delegates who are elected—Ransom Stoddard and Dutton Peabody. Valance brutally beats the drunken Peabody, and his cohorts trash the editor's office and shoot up Stoddard's sign reading "Attorney at Law." All that is left is a showdown with the attorney, the result of which seems a foregone conclusion. Although Pompey and Peter both urge Ranse to get out of town while he still can, he is too incensed by the beating of Peabody to do anything but take his stand. In his showdown with Valance, Stoddard is wounded in the arm, but Valance falls dead in the street, presumably killed by the tenderfoot. When Doniphon comes upon Hallie weeping over Ranse in Peter's kitchen, he realizes that he has lost his girl and beats a hasty retreat. After an altercation with several of Valance's lackeys in the saloon, a drunken Doniphon rides out to his ranch, sets fire to the room that he has built for Hallie, and falls into a corner in apparent indifference to his own safety. It is left to Pompey to drag him out.

We then cut to the territorial convention in Capital City. Stoddard arrives with his arm in a sling and Peabody cradling his ubiquitous jug. In a persistently wrongheaded discussion of *The Man Who Shot Liberty Valance*, Cheyney Ryan identifies Major Cassius Starbuckle as "Ranse's adversary in the election for representative [to Congress]."[20] In fact, Ranse's opponent is Custis "Buck" Langhorne, grinning instrument of the cattle interests, who sports a cutaway coat and a Windsor tie. Although Langhorne says nothing, a cowboy rides into the convention hall, mounts the stage, and proceeds to spin a lasso around the candidate.

Although this is meant to imply that Langhorne is a legitimate cowboy, we suspect that he belongs to a post-frontier charade, along with the dime novel and other trappings of cultural exploitation. (The lasso may also inadvertently indicate the extent to which he is bound to the cattlemen.) The opposition at the convention, then, is between a fake image of the past and a genuine embodiment of the future. Starbuckle (as played by John Carradine) is more appropriately contrasted with Dutton Peabody, in that Starbuckle gives the nominating speech for Langhorne, while Peabody nominates Stoddard. Although both men are given to bombastic oratory, Peabody's plea for statehood contains far more substance and sincerity than Starbuckle's empty rhetoric.

The one charge that nearly drives Stoddard out of the race is that his only claim to fame is that he killed a man. When he exits the convention in shame, Doniphon appears to tell him that, in fact, he was not the man who shot Liberty Valance. We then see the fatal confrontation from Doniphon's perspective. He had been lurking in the shadows across the street and had shot Valance—presumably as a favor to Hallie, who did not want to see Stoddard harmed. (As we recall, it was only moments later that Doniphon realized that, in so doing, he had delivered the girl to his rival.) After hearing the truth, Stoddard practically stumbles back into the convention. What would seem to be an act of crass opportunism on the part of most individuals comes off here as a virtual force of nature. Not only does Stoddard not seem to be moving entirely under his own power, he is also being propelled by the forces of history, even as those same forces consign Doniphon to a kind of obsolescence that he ironically shares with the cattle barons and their hired gun.

The move for statehood was the path to civilization. It has been Stoddard's destiny from the very beginning to advance this cause, just as holding civilization at bay worked to Doniphon's advantage. As long as Valance was alive, with the cattle barons calling the shots and Doniphon holding Valance in check, statehood and civilization were futile causes. But now that the historical momentum has shifted, it is possible—even necessary—for the "man who shot Liberty Valance" to bring civil order to the frontier. The price of doing so, however, is to spend the rest of his career living a lie.

One of the ironies of Stoddard's confession is that it does not result in absolution. The editor, who has been listening to the senator's story, simply crumples up his notes and remarks: "This is the West. When the legend becomes fact, you print the legend." One might well object that no newspaperman would pass up such a story, particularly on such metaphysical grounds. But this gesture simply heightens the pervasive symbolism of the film. If Ransom Stoddard did not literally kill Liberty Valance, he represents a system of values that could not have triumphed until Valance and his values were safely out of the way. Nor would Doniphon have been prompted to gun Valance down had Stoddard not been out in the street facing him. Both Doniphon and Stoddard play roles that are largely determined by their mythic identities. As appealing as he may be personally, Doniphon represents the dying old order. As Hallie notes on the train ride back east, it was Stoddard's destiny to turn the wilderness into a garden.

In an unusually perceptive essay on this film, David F. Courson writes:

> [W]hat is not so well understood about *Liberty Valance* is its awareness of the fact that the modern world is not simply a betrayal of what preceded it, that the flow of history is organic, the present an expression of the past. Ultimately, Ford professes faith in neither wilderness nor garden; he has considerable affection for the past, but no real belief in the viability of a society based on untrammeled individualism. Thus he undercuts his celebration of the mythic past with a corrosive revisionism that, far more than any lines of quotable dialogue, demonstrates his commitment to confronting and scrutinising, rather than simply printing, the legend that is the subject of *The Man Who Shot Liberty Valance.*[21]

In the frame of the story, several of the prominent characters in the flashback are transformed. Andy Devine's Link Appleyard has ceased being a buffoon and has instead become a character of quiet dignity. He instinctively knows where Hallie wants to go and takes her out to the charred ruins of Doniphon's ranch in his buckboard. It is there that she picks a cactus rose, which she places in an empty hatbox she has brought west with her. By the time that Stoddard is done with his confession, the cactus rose has appeared on top of the pine box that contains the mortal remains of Tom Doniphon. (Despite the many differences between the film and the story, the cactus flower appears in both versions of the tale.) Obviously, there is a part of Hallie that has never stopped loving Tom or the stark western simplicity represented by the cactus rose. This, after all, was a flower that bloomed in the desert before that desert became a man-made garden. When Ranse suggests that they come back to settle down in Shinbone, it is not surprising that Hallie declares her *roots* to be there.

Doniphon's loyal black servant Pompey is another grief-stricken specter from the past. Although Cheyney Ryan calls him "an offensive and cartoon-like character," Pompey is actually a more substantial figure than this description would imply.[22] Had the film focused more on Doniphon rather than being largely trapped in Stoddard's memory, we might have had a closer glimpse of the relationship between Doniphon and Pompey. From what little we do see, their friendship seems to belong to the great tradition of interethnic male bonding in American culture. Pompey is present to cover Doniphon with his rifle when he seems to be outgunned by Valance and his men in Pete's restaurant. Later, he is the one who tosses Doniphon the rifle with which he kills Liberty Valance. He seems almost literally to be Doniphon's third arm. Moreover, when the bartender tries to evict Pompey from the saloon because of his race, Doniphon insists that he remain.

Finally, Pompey may very well have played a role in a scene that is only implied rather than depicted. The only serious breach in Stoddard's point of view is the scene where Doniphon sets fire to his house. (Although he also has failed to witness the fracas in the saloon after Valance is shot, there were plenty of witnesses who could have supplied him with the details.) The only surviving witness to Doniphon's climactic and self-destructive act is Pompey. As such, he is Stoddard's only possible source for this information. That fact alone gives him a tragic dimension that defies Ryan's notion that he is a mere cartoon darkie.

Although Stoddard as a distinguished senator seems to hold the same values that motivated him as a young lawyer, he is now far more self-assured. Whether Hallie's sullenness is simply the result of Tom's death and the traumatic return to Shinbone is unclear. Cheyney Ryan assumes on scant evidence that her marriage has been a loveless and barren disaster.[23] It is, however, to Stoddard's credit that he senses that his wife wishes to return permanently to her old hometown. His evident desire to return there as well suggests that he and Hallie are not as estranged as some critics assume. Of course, the Shinbone to which they will return is very different from the one that they left.

Tom Doniphon is the character who is most changed. This goes beyond the obvious fact that he is now dead. He has gone from being one of the most prominent members of the community to someone whose name does not even register with the newspaper editor. Although it is not clear whether he had been reduced to the status of a Scratchy Wilson, that is not an unreasonable surmise. The world in which he flourished is forever gone, and he helped to kill it by shooting Liberty Valance. As long as a desperado such as Valance was loose, Tom Doniphon was an essential figure in the community. Now he is being buried without his boots because the undertaker figured he could make some money by selling them. (Civilization has its darker elements as well as its blessings.)

When Stoddard insists that both his boots and his gun belt be restored, Appleyard ruefully observes that Tom had not worn a gun in years. Apparently, the need was gone. If John Wayne is lying in that pine box, he is now a pale vestige of the traditional Western hero. And *The Man Who Shot Liberty Valance* is itself John Ford's valedictory to the Western genre and the myth that it embodied.

# SEVEN

# THE UNIVERSAL SOLDIER
## FRANKLIN SCHAFFNER'S *PATTON* (1970)

*Patton* would have been a remarkable film whenever it was released. The fact that it won popular and critical acclaim in 1970 is nothing short of amazing. At this point in our nation's history, a significant segment of the population was hostile to the military values that Patton represented. It had been six years since Lyndon Johnson had been elected president promising not to send American boys to fight a war that Asian boys should be fighting. Because of the unpopularity of that war, Johnson had declined to run for another term in 1968, and most of the men seeking to replace him promised to get America out of Vietnam. The successful candidate (Richard Nixon) said that he had a secret plan to do just that. Now, more than a year into Nixon's term in office, the conflict in Vietnam had become the longest war in American history, and there seemed to be no end in sight.

In addition to becoming an increasingly difficult war to sell, the Vietnam conflict faced two impediments not known in previous wars—an unusually large population of men subject to the military draft, and the presence of television on the battlefield. Because they were subject to conscription, the sons of the post–World War II baby boom took a hard cold look at the Vietnam War. Although some signed on to fight, others burned their draft cards, fled to Canada, or went to prison rather than risk life and limb in what seemed a dubious battle. Countless others (myself included) avoided service through every legal means available. It was not surprising that many people who opposed the war began to see the American military itself as a hostile and malignant force.

In addition to its ambiguous and protracted nature, Vietnam also suffered from being our first fully televised war. (The medium was in its infancy during the Korean conflict.) If television was not able to distinguish winners from losers or good guys from bad guys, it possessed enormous power to depict the carnage and suffering of the battlefield. (George Will was surely correct when he said that if there had been television cameras at Gettysburg, we would probably have customs officers on the Mason-Dixon Line today.) As a consequence, the Tet Offensive, which was a clear military defeat for the enemy, actually diminished support for the war among the American people!

When *Patton* was released in the spring of 1970, protests were erupting on the nation's campuses over Nixon's decision to extend the war from Vietnam into Cambodia, where enemy troops were being resupplied and (as it was later revealed) we had already been fighting for more than a year. (Nixon actually made the decision to invade Cambodia while watching *Patton*.) With the exception of John Wayne's *Green Berets* (1968), there was little positive treatment of the Vietnam War in Hollywood, and the military itself had become the object of denunciation and ridicule in American popular culture.

We began to witness what Norman Podhoretz calls the "'Vietnamization' of World War II."[1] Joseph Heller's *Catch-22* (1961) and Kurt Vonnegut's *Slaughterhouse-Five* (1969)—a pair of black comic novels denigrating what was (and is) generally regarded as America's "good war"—became cult classics of the anti-Vietnam crowd and were subsequently made into major motion pictures. Not surprisingly, perceptions of the Korean War were also affected by attitudes toward Vietnam. Moviegoers who did not think that we should be fighting Communists in Southeast Asia in the late 1960s applauded Robert Altman's *M*A*S*H*, a macabre version of our earlier crusade against Red Orientals. *M*A*S*H* was released the same year as *Patton*.

It is doubtful that a movie such as *Patton* would have been conceived in the late 1960s had Twentieth Century–Fox not acquired rights to film the general's life as far back as 1952. A decade later, the studio actually commissioned a young screenwriter named Francis Ford Coppola to write the script for such a movie. Not wanting to glorify Patton's militarism but leery of making the story into an antiwar parable, Coppola produced the sort of script that partisans of both camps could identify as their own. Unfortunately, the executives at Fox did not like a scene in which Patton harangued his troops while standing in front of a giant American flag. As the opening scene of the film, this seemed confusing and, if anything, too powerful. The studio paid young Coppola and promptly replaced him with the veteran screenwriter Edmund North. In the spring of 1971, when Coppola was on the verge of being fired as director of *The Godfather* (1972), he won an Academy Award for the script of *Patton*. Not only did the award honor his work as a screenwriter, it probably saved his job as *auteur* of what turned out to be one of the great films of all time.

The secret to *Patton*'s bipartisan (almost bipolar) appeal lay in its portrayal of the general as a maverick. If only some of the opponents of the Vietnam War were pacifists, almost all were rebels of one sort or another. Patton was yet another example of that familiar American hero—the loner who bucks authority. In this case, the authority was that of the military hierarchy. Patton was convinced that he was a better warrior than any of his colleagues or opponents, and he was proved right often enough to become a living legend. The source of his self-confidence was his belief in reincarnation. Having been a soldier in all his previous lives, Patton had been schooled in the great battles of history. It may be that his quirky mysticism also made him a more appealing figure to the rebellious youth of the counterculture.

The film presents Patton as an epic hero in an age in which the epic consciousness has disappeared. Because an epic expresses a nation's imaginative understanding of itself, it requires a sense of nationhood. Geographically and culturally, America is simply too diverse to be a nation in the sense that England and France are nations. It can be argued that one of the forces we were fighting in World War II was an excessive sense of nationalism on the part of Germany, Italy, and Japan. One even senses that Nazism and fascism were attempts to manufacture an ersatz nationalism, which was defied by the indigenous resistance against Hitler and Mussolini. The closest thing to a Nazi epic was probably Leni Riefenstahl's documentary film *The Triumph of the Will* (1935), while the closest to a fascist one was Ezra Pound's *Pisan Cantos*

(1948). Although Japanese nationalism reached a white-hot intensity during World War II, it seems to have dissipated rapidly thereafter.[2]

What has taken the place of the epic in America are the familiar genres of popular culture. Because they are immediately recognizable to persons of all races, classes, and levels of literacy, these genres have a power to unite us in a way that a great national poem (or even the great American novel) cannot. If Patton's belief in reincarnation removed him from the mundane reality of American life, his sense of himself as a heroic individualist put him in the mainstream of American mythology. It also helped to identify a common thread binding the mythologies of different countries at different times. When the movie was playing in the town where I went to college, I was taking a survey course in early British literature. My teacher, himself a veteran of the civil-rights and antiwar movements, announced to the class: "Go see *Patton*, and you'll understand *Beowulf*."

## I

Although George Smith Patton Jr. was born in San Gabriel, California (on November 11, 1885), and spent summers in Hamilton, Massachusetts, he was spiritually a son of the Old South. His grandfather, the original George Smith Patton, was born in Fredericksburg, Virginia, in 1833, graduated from the Virginia Military Institute in 1852, served in the Twenty-Second Infantry of the Confederate States of America, and died in the Third Battle of Winchester. His son, George William Patton, also graduated from VMI before taking up a career as a lawyer. A frequent guest in the Patton home during the future general's childhood was the legendary "grey ghost" of the Confederacy, Colonel John Singleton Mosby. Although he had spent time in prison for killing a fellow student at the University of Virginia and was now making his living as an attorney for the railroad, Mosby was a romantic figure to young Georgie Patton. Patton's sister once stated that until her brother was fifteen, "'Georgie' thought that the steel statues of Robert E. Lee and Stonewall Jackson in their house were those of God and Jesus Christ, respectively."[3]

George Patton followed in the footsteps of his father and grandfather by entering VMI in the fall of 1903 but transferred to West Point after one year. Although he had an extraordinary memory and was exposed to both literature and history in his home, he did not learn to read (indeed, did not *try* to read) until he started school at twelve. It is thought that he suffered from a variety of learning disabilities (ranging from dyslexia to a mild form of autism) that were essentially unknown at the time. Paradoxically, these deficiencies may be connected with the general's unquestioned gifts. The research psychologist Thomas G. West notes that some individuals are "so much in touch with their visual-spatial, non-verbal, right-hemisphere modes of thought that they have had difficulty doing orderly, sequential, verbal-mathematical, left-hemisphere tasks in a culture where left-hemisphere capabilities are so highly valued."[4] Probably because of this condition, Patton did not pass mathematics on his first attempt at West Point and eventually took five years to graduate.

Despite his academic deficiencies, Patton was a good athlete who made up for a lack of natural talent with a fierce competitive spirit. When the future general was eleven, Baron Pierre de Coubertin revived the ancient Olympic Games by persuading nine nations to send one hundred participants to Athens to participate in the first competition of the modern era. In 1912, George Patton represented the United States in the fifth modern Olympiad. His sport was the pentathlon, which included swimming three hundred meters, shooting pistols on a twenty-five meter range, running a four-thousand-meter course, fencing, and riding a five-thousand-meter steeplechase.

Although he was generally an excellent marksman, Patton turned in his worst performance in the shooting competition. When one of his bullet holes could not be located in the target, he argued that it must have passed though a hole from an earlier round. Unfortunately, when the bullet could not be found, the judges had no choice but to penalize Patton, who ended up an embarrassing twenty-first in the competition. On the second day, he finished sixth in the swimming event but was so exhausted that he had to be helped from the pool with a boat hook. In fencing, riding, and running, he did better, finishing third in each of the three events. In typical fashion, Patton began the four-thousand meter cross-country run by sprinting. By the time he got to the last fifty meters, he could barely walk and was passed by two runners who had paced themselves. As respectable as his performance may have been, Patton was completely overshadowed by the achievements of another American—Jim Thorpe, whose gold medals were eventually stripped when the Olympic Committee discovered that he had once played semipro baseball.[5]

In 1916, Patton served with Brigadier General John J. Pershing in his pursuit of the legendary Mexican bandit Pancho Villa. Along with ten soldiers of the Sixth Infantry Regiment, Patton killed Villa's personal bodyguard, Julio Cardenas. Impressed by the young soldier whom he called his "bandito," Pershing promoted Patton to the rank of captain when the United States entered World War I. Assigned to the newly formed United States Tank Corps, Patton began his lifelong infatuation with this new armored vehicle. In large part because of his success in organizing a training school for American tankers in Langres, France, he was promoted to major and later lieutenant colonel. As commander of the tank corps, Patton fought in the Battle of Saint Mihiel in September 1918 and was wounded in the upper thigh by machine-gun fire as he sought assistance for tanks mired in the mud. According to one source, "[F]or years afterwards, when Patton was tipsy at social events, he would drop his pants to show his wound and call himself a 'half-assed general.'"[6]

During the years between the two world wars, Patton unsuccessfully lobbied Congress to provide more funding for military preparedness in general and tanks in particular. He also formed a fast friendship with another rising young officer—Dwight D. Eisenhower. When the two men first met in the mid-1920s, Patton was Eisenhower's senior and one of the army's chief figures in tank warfare. Throughout the '30s, Patton was promoted more quickly than Eisenhower. By 1940, Patton was already a brigadier general. Eisenhower, who was still a lieutenant colonel, sought an appointment as tank corps commander from his friend and superior. A far more politic officer than Patton, Eisenhower was promoted to colonel and then to brigadier general in a period of six months in 1941. In 1942, Eisenhower was promoted first to major general and later to lieutenant general, thus outranking Patton for the first time. When the Allies invaded North Africa in 1942, Patton was now under the command of his former subordinate. As Patton would discover to his chagrin, strategic intelligence and valor on the battlefield were not enough. The coalition fighting the Axis powers would require a measure of tact and diplomacy never before seen in the annals of warfare.

## II

It is evident from the opening scene of the film that tact and diplomacy were not Patton's strong suits. The image of him addressing his troops, which Fox executives had once found so problematic, turns out to be a perfect introduction. Not only does it give us a sense of Patton's mentality, it also reveals the "flaw" that would later derail his career. In his memoir *A Soldier's Story* (1951), General Omar Bradley candidly admits that "it was this unhappy talent of Patton's for highly quotable crises that caused me to tighten the screws on press censorship at the time he joined my command."[7] Although the speech in the film is a composite of several different addresses, the words are all Patton's. Throughout the speech, he exhorts his men always to be on the offensive and assures them that all true Americans are fighters and killers by nature.

Interestingly enough, the movie does not include a significant passage from a speech Patton delivered to the Third Army in March 1945:

> I want to say a word to you about those low characters known as psychoneurotics. They are sons of bitches, bastards, and lice. In the last war they had "shell shock," and in the next war they will have some other kind of shock. But every one that quits means that more of a burden is thrown on you brave men who continue to fight. So if you have a man who thinks he is a psychoneurotic, make fun of him, kick his ass, and shake him out of it.[8]

As we shall see, it is significant that Patton would say such things about the psychological disability of soldiers as late as 1945. Even without this passage, he has probably achieved his objective of making his men more afraid of him than of the enemy.

The chronology of the film begins in the aftermath of a humiliating American defeat in Kasserine in 1943. After showing General Bradley surveying the carnage, the scene shifts to Morocco, where Patton is being decorated for leading a victorious landing against the Vichy government. It is clear that Patton enjoys the pomp and circumstance, which he tells the Moroccan minister is a combination of "the Bible and Hollywood." But he is obviously aching to get back into battle.

Shortly thereafter, when Bradley is taking him out to see the battlefield at Kasserine, Patton insists that the driver turn off the beaten path to visit the site of an older struggle, where the Romans defeated the Carthaginians. Not only was he familiar with this battle from his study of history, Patton was also convinced that he had actually been there in a previous life. He then proceeds to recite the first and twenty-second stanzas of one of his own poems:

> Through the travail of the ages
> Midst the pomp and toil of war
> Have I fought and strove and perished
> Countless times upon this star.
>
> So as through a glass and darkly
> The age long strife I see
> Where I fought in many guises,
> Many names—but always me.[9]

When one considers the various personae in Patton's verse, it is remarkable how many were on the losing side. In addition to having been with the Carthaginians, he fought with Napoleon's army when it nearly froze to death in Russia. And of course, his sympathies during the War Between the States were with his Confederate forebears. If it is true that the winners write the history of war and the losers its poetry, Patton may be considered one of the great bards of battle. As X. J. Kennedy has noted: "Next to him, other twentieth-century war poets, those mostly reluctant conscripts, seem dabbling amateurs. No other poet I know—not Wilfred Owen nor Keith Douglas, not Randall Jarrell nor Isaac Rosenberg, despite all the hideous evidence they bring to their case against war—knows war so intimately well, or leaves us in the end with a poorer opinion of it."[10]

As committed as he may have been to his country and as hungry as he was for victory, Patton also had an aesthetic appreciation of war that enabled him to admire a worthy opponent. When given command of the American troops that had previously been thwarted by the German field marshal Edwin Rommel, Patton read Rommel's book on tank warfare and told an aide, Captain Dick Jensen, that he would like to duel Rommel in the desert, each man in his own tank, with the outcome of the war in the balance. (He would even send Rommel an engraved invitation written in iambic pentameter.) "Too bad jousting's gone out of style," Jensen observed. "It's like your poetry, general. It isn't part of the twentieth century."[11]

## III

If Patton seemed out of place in the twentieth century, he would have fit in perfectly in the epic poetry of Homer. In *The Iliad*, Achilles is a warrior who knows that he is fated to live hard and die young. Other men might covet riches or the pleasures of domestic life, but Achilles knows that he will die on the battlefield. The only compensation for such a destiny is a glory that will outlive him. For modern men, war is at best a sad necessity. For the epic hero, it is the highest imaginable calling.

For that reason, the epic hero is expected to be flamboyant and egotistical. When Patton arrives at a new command standing in his tank, with sirens blaring, carrying a swagger stick, wearing leggings, and packing a pair of ivory-handled revolvers, he may seem to be a militant peacock. But he means to be an example to the lesser men under his command. When German bombs hit his headquarters one too many times, he leaps from his office window and fires his revolvers at the planes, daring them to hit him. Practically speaking, this is a foolhardy gesture, but one that is completely in character.

Audiences that might make poetic allowance for an Achilles can be understandably troubled by Patton. That is why moviegoers who disliked war (even good ones) could find their prejudices reinforced by the film *Patton*. Director Franklin J. Schaffner (whose previous credits included several live dramas during the golden age of television and the film *Planet of the Apes* [1968]) wisely avoids the kind of obvious irony that would have made *Patton* an overtly satirical film. Those who remember George C. Scott's portrayal of the buffoonish General Buck Turgidson in Stanley Kubrick's *Dr. Strangelove* (1963) might well be surprised and disappointed by Scott's sympathetic portrayal of Patton. But the very things that make Patton a modern Achilles are calculated to turn the stomachs of the antiwar crowd. This is particularly true of a couple of related incidents that almost cost Patton his command.

On August 3, 1943, after he had captured the public imagination with his daring march through Sicily, Patton visited the Fifteenth Evacuation Hospital outside Nicosia. In the midst of several severely wounded men, he came across Private Charles H. Kuhl, who seemed to have no visible injuries. When questioned, Kuhl admitted: "I guess I can't take it." Infuriated by what he considered an example of cowardice, Patton swore at Kuhl and ordered him out of the tent. When Kuhl did not respond, Patton became even more infuriated, slapped his face with a glove, grabbed him by the collar of the shirt, and forced him out of the tent with a kick in his rear.

A week later, on August 10, when Patton made an unannounced visit to the Ninety-Third Evacuation Hospital, it was as if history was repeating itself. After offering small talk and encouragement to several wounded men, Patton again encountered a soldier suffering from nervous exhaustion. This soldier, Private Paul G. Bennett, sobbed: "It's my nerves, I can't stand the shelling anymore." Patton ordered Bennett out of the tent, pulled his gun, and threatened to have the soldier shot for cowardice. The sight of Bennett crying so angered Patton that he slapped the soldier twice, the second time with such force that he knocked the private's helmet liner to the ground.

Even if Patton was correct in surmising that these men were malingerers (and there is no indication that that was the case), he violated the military code of conduct by striking them. Although Eisenhower, who was now commander of the Allied Forces, had no intention of removing Patton from his command, he could not ignore two such public instances of erratic and brutal behavior from one of his subordinates. (Those members of the public and the press who disliked Patton for his arrogance predictably screamed for his scalp.) At the same time, the Germans could not believe that one of America's most effective warriors should be in any trouble at all for what seemed to them a trivial offense. The irony of the situation was compounded by the fact that Patton may have acted from a form of battle fatigue himself. He was privately reprimanded by Eisenhower, who ordered him to apologize to the men in question and to all who witnessed the two incidents.[12]

For dramatic purposes, these two outbursts were collapsed into a single scene in the movie. We see Patton chatting with a Mexican-American soldier who has been hit in the chest. He then stops by the bedside of a man whose head is bandaged. Unable to speak because of an oxygen mask over his nose and mouth, this soldier is obviously in critical condition. Patton kneels by his bedside, whispers into his ear, and pins a medal on the man's pillow. Had the scene ended there, the general would have appeared to have been the soul of compassion. Instead, he sees a physically unmarked soldier sobbing from psychological distress. At this point, the character of Patton behaves exactly as the general had in real life.

No doubt the juxtaposition of this ostensibly "unharmed" soldier with brave men who had suffered obvious wounds triggered Patton's reaction. According to the enlightened standards of 1970 (or even 1943), his conduct was inexcusable. Nevertheless, many of his men and their parents were primitive enough to think that Patton had behaved properly. (The mail that the general received was overwhelmingly positive.) This was a time when many still believed that a slap in the face was an instant cure for hysteria. Furthermore, very few soldiers had not experienced some measure of fear, and it seemed wrong to allow some men to use that excuse to get a free ride. But Patton's real motivation for acting as he did may have been that battle fatigue was far too modern a concept to mean anything to a man who had fought with Hannibal, Napoleon, and Stonewall Jackson.

## IV

One of the most memorable scenes in the film occurs when Patton surveys the carnage of a battle in which both sides ran out of supplies and ammunition and were reduced to hand-to-hand combat. Ignoring the practical implications of this scene, the general tells his flustered aide about a dream he had had the previous night assuring him that he would have the Nazi army precisely where he wanted it. The prophecy seemed to be confirmed by the fact that carts he had seen in the dream were now on the battlefield in front of him. They reminded him of carts that Napoleon had used to transport supplies during his ill-fated invasion of Russia. Leaning over, Patton kisses the lone survivor of the battle. Then, overlooking the scene of utter desolation, he exclaims: "I love it. God help me, I do love it so. I love it more than my life."

This remark—a bit much even for admirers of the general—could be expected to bring gasps from moviegoers who hated war as much as Patton loved it. Unfortunately, both sides are apt to miss the context which gives specific meaning to these comments. It is not so much war itself as the primitive nature of hand-to-hand combat that moves Patton. As much as he may have been fascinated by tanks, his heart belonged to an earlier time when warriors could actually see the men they fought. The medieval era had brought the bow and arrow. Musket and cannon fire were introduced in the eighteenth century. By the First World War, we had aerial bombardment and poison gas. These advances in technology made war more deadly and more impersonal at the same time. There is more than a little truth to the notion that Patton would have been more comfortable with the sort of single-combat warfare that would have pitted him against Rommel or some other suitable adversary. The true warrior aspires to be an epic hero, not a bureaucratic drone.

With the war over, Patton is like a shark out of water. His impolitic statements predictably lead to his being relieved of command. But they also give us insight into his thinking and character. While riding a horse around an indoor track, he is interrogated by newspaper reporters eager for an off-the-cuff remark. "We've been told about these wonder weapons the Germans were working on," one observes. "Long-range rockets, push-button bombing, weapons that don't need soldiers." Responding in depression and exasperation, Patton sneers: "Wonder weapons! God, I can't see the wonder in them. Killing without heroics. Nothing is glorified, nothing is reaffirmed. No heroes, no cowards, no troops. . . . [pause in script] No generals. Only those who are left alive and those who are left . . . [pause] dead. I'm glad I won't live to see it."[13]

This last observation takes on a particular significance when seen in light of Patton's belief in reincarnation. In previous lives, he could expect to come back as an updated version of the soldier he had always been. Technological progress, however, threatens to make that soldier extinct. The consolation that he will not live to see this must surely be tempered by the realization that his next death will be fundamentally different from all previous ones. Viewers who are alert to this fact will detect an even greater level of profundity in the film's elegiac conclusion.

As he walks his dog Willy over a snow-covered field toward a windmill (which will remind most literate viewers of *Don Quixote*), we hear Patton in a voice-over:

> For over a thousand years, Roman conquerors returning from the wars enjoyed the honor of a triumph, a tumultuous parade. In the procession came trumpeters and musicians and strange animals from the conquered territories . . . [pause] together with carts laden with treasure and captured armaments. The conqueror rode in a triumphal chariot, the dazed prisoners walking in chains before him. Sometimes his children, robed in white, stood with him in the chariot, or rode the trace horses. . . . [pause] A slave stood behind the conqueror, holding a golden crown and whispering in his ear that all glory is fleeting.[14]

This passage confirms what alert viewers had already suspected—that the film is less an epic than a tragedy. Although classical norms insist that the tragic hero must possess a flaw, this flaw could just as easily be a virtue as a vice, just so long as it makes the hero's downfall inevitable. (If Oedipus were not so intent on saving Thebes by discovering the source of the plague afflicting his city, he might have died in blissful ignorance of the fact that he had killed his father and married his mother.) Patton's "flaw" would seem to be his rash insistence on living the life of an epic hero after that paradigm was no longer in fashion. Whether one sees him as closer to the earnest fool of Cervantes' novel or the noble idealist of *The Man of La Mancha* depends on one's perspective.

Anachronism that he was, Patton was still useful—even essential—to the Allied war effort. But one can hardly see him or his like making a similar contribution to any of America's subsequent (undeclared) wars. Douglas MacArthur was deemed too headstrong to be tolerated as commander in the Korean War. If one could imagine Rommel accepting an invitation to single-combat warfare, it is impossible to picture Ho Chi Minh doing the same. The first Gulf War, which seemed to many to resemble a high-tech video game, was the sort of conflict decried by the equestrian Patton. (Colin Powell, who rose to his position as a result of affirmative action, was a far more suitable politician-general.) In the War on Terror, where there have been no rules and far too little valor on either side, and where the shots are being called by civilians who have never been in harm's way, Patton would have been utterly lost. As my old teacher said, "See *Patton*, and you'll understand *Beowulf*."

# FIXING SIN

## STANLEY KUBRICK'S *A CLOCKWORK ORANGE* (1971)

The politics of Stanley Kubrick's *A Clockwork Orange* (1971) are hideously complicated. On the one hand, many moral traditionalists see the film as an example of the gratuitous sex and violence that has permeated the cinema since the Hays Office was replaced by the ratings system. Pauline Kael, who was hardly a blue-nosed moralist, said of the film: "At the movies, we are gradually being conditioned to accept violence as a sensual pleasure. The directors used to say they were showing us its real face and how ugly it was in order to sensitize us to its horrors. You don't have to be very keen to see that they are now in fact desensitizing us."[1]

Upon its initial release, *A Clockwork Orange* received a highly restrictive X rating. (The film was subsequently edited to allow reclassification as an R.) In England, however, a conservative group called Festival of Light agitated against the film being shown at all. As a result, by the end of 1972 the movie had been shown at only one theater in London. When an epidemic of youth violence in Britain was blamed on the picture, Kubrick had it withdrawn from circulation there. Although it remained widely available in the United States, the film was not shown again in Great Britain until after Kubrick's death in 1989.

The problem with leaving the matter there is that Kubrick remained remarkably faithful to the moral vision of Anthony Burgess's *A Clock-*

*work Orange* (1962), the novel on which the movie is based. Although he left the Roman Catholic Church while still an adolescent in the 1930s, Burgess was in many respects more conservative morally and theologically than those who remained in the fold and accepted the reforms of Vatican II. In particular, Burgess believed that much of the modern world was succumbing to the heresy of Pelagianism. Named for the fourth-century British monk Pelagius, this heresy holds that human nature is basically good and can be made perfect through an enlightened act of the will. When we speak of Original Sin, according to Pelagius, we are speaking only of Adam's error and not of a taint that his descendants have inherited. But once we eliminate that inheritance, we also do away with the need for divine grace. Salvation becomes a do-it-yourself project. Although condemned by the church, a secularized version of this philosophy forms the basis of many social reform movements.

Contrast Pelagianism with the orthodox position of St. Augustine. According to Augustine, we are born with the sin of Adam, which we are utterly incapable of eradicating on our own. Romantics such as Rousseau might believe in primal goodness, but the evidence of history suggests otherwise. Only through Christ's sacrifice on the cross, the benefits of which are mediated by the sacraments of the church, can one be rid of Adam's curse. Not only was Augustine a "doctor" of the Roman Church, his view of human nature has persisted in the Protestant tradition through the influence of John Calvin. Although Burgess remained perpetually drawn to the figure of Jesus, the strongest vestige of his original Catholic faith lay in his Augustinian view of human nature.[2]

In many respects, Burgess's work seems to belong to a tradition of Catholic modernism begun in the nineteenth century by Barbey d'Aullevilly and continued in the twentieth century by such writers as François Mauriac, Evelyn Waugh, Muriel Spark, Flannery O'Connor, J. F. Powers, and Graham Greene. Collectively, these writers articulate what can be regarded as an Augustinian (or at least antihumanist) sensibility. In their novels, Martin Green points out, "human achievements and modes of being are consistently and triumphantly shown to be inadequate, egotistic, just in being themselves, in being human. Under stress all natural goodness breaks down; only grace-assisted goodness is valid, and grace-assisted badness is perhaps even better."[3]

If one finds examples of the grotesque in the fiction of a Catholic writer such as Flannery O'Connor, it is because she believes that "you have to make your vision apparent by shock—to the hard of hearing you shout, and for the almost-blind you draw large and startling pictures." The self-described "Christian pornographer" D. Keith Mano goes even farther. "For any serious Christian writer," he observes, "the obscene, the grotesque, the violent seem almost prerequisite." This is because such a writer finds it extremely difficult to convey the awesomeness of faith to an audience "which—more likely than not—doesn't share the sign language by which Christians communicate in shorthand with one another: the Cross, the Trinity, sacraments, Grace. And that enormous paradox: death into life. In a profane age, the profane must be taken unawares and in their own tongue."[4]

Even if one questions the presence of Christian grace in Burgess's work, his novels do satirize the attempt of progressives to achieve heaven on earth through social engineering. If the conflict between the Augustinian and the Pelagian visions is most schematically evident in his novel *The Wanting Seed* (1963), it reached its widest audience in *A Clockwork Orange*, largely because of the popularity of Kubrick's film. The stark question posed by both the novel and the movie is whether man's capacity to choose between good and evil should be altered for the benefit of society.

Although it is assumed that man is a uniquely rational creature, plants and animals live according to a pattern of reason that makes the frequent chaos of human life seem positively insane.[5] Throughout history, societies have used punishment as a means of controlling human behavior. Fear of adverse consequences has kept many a wrongdoer on the path of righteousness. At first glance, it would seem that positive reinforcement would be an even more humane way of assuring social peace. Why use the stick if equally effective carrots are on hand? In the twentieth century the best-known exponent of nonaversive social control was the behavioral psychologist B. F. Skinner.

Skinner first became a best-selling writer in 1948 with his utopian novel *Walden Two*. Extrapolating from advances in technology and the development of benign social control, Skinner depicted a community of minimal labor, equal benefits, and ample leisure time. The only thing that had to be sacrificed was the notion that individual freedom was the supreme social value. But this was hardly an assumption that the general public was willing to take lying down. If the Western world seemed preoccupied with the threat of tyranny from abroad when *Walden Two* was published in the late '40s, the civil-rights and antiwar movements of the '60s had produced a new wariness about the coercive powers of ostensibly democratic governments by the time *A Clockwork Orange* was released in 1971. That same year, B. F. Skinner created a stir with a new book defiantly titled *Beyond Freedom and Dignity*.

The question raised by Kubrick's film (and by Burgess's novel before it) is not the simplistic one of free will versus environmental control. Strictly speaking, neither freedom nor destiny can exist apart from the other. No one has ever made a choice in a vacuum, and no fate is ever enacted apart from individual human behavior. For centuries, the public has accepted rehabilitation as a legitimate and enlightened goal of penology. The question raised by *A Clockwork Orange* is whether rehabilitation should ever go so far as to destroy the human personality. Civilized societies hold that negative reinforcement should stop short of torture. But is there a point where positive reinforcement goes too far? This is the issue graphically raised by *A Clockwork Orange*.

## I

Like Burgess's novel, Kubrick's film is set in a future society shockingly similar to our own. The protagonist and narrator is Alex, leader of a group of young thugs who wear bowler hats, terrorize their fellow citizens, and speak a hybrid language. (Kubrick originally wanted Mick Jagger and the Rolling Stones to play the gang, but a scheduled tour prevented them from doing so.) The opening scene of the film finds the four young hoodlums sitting in a baroque milk bar, where fiberglass nudes dispense a drug-laced version of the advertised beverage. (A close-up shows one of Alex's eyes ringed with false eyelashes.) After the scene and characters are established with a panoramic shot of the milk bar, we move outside to an old drunk singing—what else?—an Irish ditty. Offended by the sight of the dirty vagrant, Alex and his cronies beat him mercilessly with their canes, even as he claims not to want to live in a world without law and order. Immediately thereafter, the droogs—as they are called in Burgess's slang—fight a rival gang that had been occupied with raping a young girl.

But the evening is not yet over. Driving a stolen car, Alex and company stop at an otherwise chic and modern dwelling that bears the garish sign "HOME." This residence is inhabited by an intellectual, who sits at his IBM typewriter, and the man's attractive wife. When Alex rings the doorbell and informs the wife that there has been a terrible wreck on the road and that they need to use a telephone, she is naturally suspicious. The man, however, instructs her to let the supplicant in. The house is immediately invaded by Alex and his trio of followers, wearing masks with grotesque phallic noses. Alex then proceeds to rape the woman in her husband's presence while chortling a chorus of "Singin' in the Rain." Back at the milk bar for a little rest and relaxation, the most retarded of Alex's droogs (the appropriately named "Dim") blows a raspberry when one of the more sophisticated patrons hums a few bars of Beethoven. The ever-sensitive Alex bangs his companion with a cane.

Back home after such an exhausting night of revelry, Alex checks on his pet snake and his cache of stolen valuables, puts on his own tape of Beethoven, and proceeds to masturbate as the camera focuses on four plastic bleeding Jesuses doing a tap dance. Understandably, Alex is too tired to go to school the next day. His feckless parents have no idea what he does at night, and his probation officer, Mr. Deltoid, seems more interested in hitting on him sexually than in setting him on the path of the straight and narrow.

His energy rekindled the next day, Alex—decked out like one of Cinderella's footmen—encounters a couple of underage girls sucking on phallus-shaped candy at a boutique called The Thieving Magpie. Before you know it, the three are back in Alex's bedroom doing the "old in-and-out" with the camera running at twelve times normal speed and the "William Tell Overture" playing in the background. (Obviously, Alex's parents don't know what he does during the day, either.) Back in the lobby, where classical murals are defaced with obscene drawings, Alex meets up with his droogs, who seem on the verge of rebellion over his high-handed ways and their failure to pull in more lucre. As the camera goes into slow motion, with notes of Beethoven drifting from a high window, Alex puts his mates in their place by pushing them into a marina and slashing one of them with his knife. Then, in an act of generosity, he accepts the suggestion that they visit a nearby health farm.

The sole dweller at this health farm is a middle-aged woman who lives with a bevy of cats in a home decorated with sexually explicit pictures and sculpture. Unlike Alex's previous victims, this woman refuses to open the door. So he enters from the second floor, playfully rocks a plaster penis and scrotum the size of a fireplug, and teases the woman: "Naughty, naughty, you filthy old sooker." When the cat lady makes the mistake of defending herself with a bust of Alex's beloved Beethoven, he attacks her with the phallic sculpture—fatally, as it turns out. Back outside, Alex is attacked by his own mates, one of whom smashes a bottle of milk against his head. They immediately run for safety as their former leader is nabbed by the police.

This succession of incidents establishes Alex as a ruthless thug who nevertheless possesses more intelligence and aesthetic sensitivity than his companions. Although a liberal viewer might think him capable of turning out better under different circumstances, he has as yet revealed little to make us feel sorry for him. At the same time, his victims inspire more pity than sympathetic identification. His parents seem incapable of providing him with any direction, and the one representative of the state is worse than useless. From this point on, the image of society becomes progressively more dismal.

By the time that Alex is arrested and falls totally into the clutches of the state, our conscious judgment of his character is profoundly negative. (Otherwise, what happens later in the film becomes trivial and manipulative.) At the same time, there are appealing aspects of his personality. Kubrick himself has put the matter as follows:

> The psychiatrists tell us the unconscious has no conscience—and perhaps in our unconscious we are all potential Alexes. . . . Perhaps this makes some people feel uncomfortable and partly explains some of the controversy which has arisen over the film. . . . I think you find much the same psychological phenomena at work in Shakespeare's *Richard III*. You should feel nothing but dislike for Richard, and yet when the role is well played, with a bit of humour and charm, you find yourself mak-

> ing a similar kind of identification with him. Not because you sympathize with Richard's ambition or his actions, or that you like him or think that people should behave like him but, as you watch the play, because he gradually works his way into your unconscious, and recognition occurs in the recesses of the mind.[6]

In Anglo-American culture, there has been a long tradition of attractive rogues, from Robin Hood to Bonnie and Clyde. Even when we step out of the realm of legend, it is often easier to sympathize with the prisoner on death row than to remember the victims of his crime. Our first view of Alex's incarceration is a helicopter shot of an enormous prison surrounded by green fields. His outlandish costumes gone, he appears in a coat and tie and is systematically disrobed. (American men of that era might well be reminded of their draft physical.) When offered a swing at him, his probation officer, Mr. Deltoid, spits in Alex's face and says: "I hope to God they torture you to madness." It is a wish that almost comes true.

On the surface, Alex seems to adjust well to prison life. (In the book, he kills a man while behind bars.) He becomes friends with the prison chaplain and manifests an interest in the Bible—although it turns out that he is captivated only by the violent and racier parts of Scripture, imagining himself a Roman soldier beating Christ or an Old Testament satryr eating grapes with bare-breasted young lovelies. His main interest, however, is in getting out of prison as quickly as possible. Rather than being reformed, Alex has learned how to play the system for all it's worth.

## II

Alex has heard of a new therapy that will allow prisoners to earn early release. The government has concluded that it is more efficient to cure ordinary criminals so that truly punitive measures can be reserved for political prisoners. Although the chaplain has theological reservations about a treatment that would appear to strip a man of his free will, Alex defines freedom as simply being out of jail. This situation, of course, raises the question of what constitutes true freedom. For the chaplain, a man in possession of his own soul is freer in prison than a lobotomized individual on the outside. Perhaps Alex would have agreed had he known how effective the treatment would prove to be.

The chaplain is an equivocal character, both a figure of satire and the closest thing to a moral norm to be found in *A Clockwork Orange*. Although a conventional Anglican cleric, he delivers a hellfire-and-brimstone sermon more appropriate to a fundamentalist preacher or the Jesuit priest in Joyce's *A Portrait of the Artist as a Young Man* (1916). (His captive congregation responds with belching and raspberries, thus inviting the shouted threats of a cartoonish prison guard.) It is also clear that Alex is using the man's genuine interest in him to manipulate the system to his own advantage. Still, the chaplain is the only person in the story to make the point that a person deprived of free will is incapable of *choosing* either good or evil. Indifferent to the state of Alex's soul, the government is interested only in regulating his behavior, even if it means turning him into a cross between a vegetable and an automaton—a clockwork orange.

Contrary to some critical opinions, the psychological torture to which Alex is subjected bears very little resemblance to the nonaversive stimulus advocated by B. F. Skinner. Instead, it more nearly resembles Antabuse, the treatment for alcoholics that triggers extreme nausea at the very taste of liquor. Alex is programmed to have a similar reaction to thoughts of sex and violence and, quite by accident, to the sound of Beethoven's music. Everything that gave him pleasure in his former life has become the source of agony.

As soon as Alex is released, he experiences a series of reversals that resemble what Norman Kagen calls a "fairy tale of retribution." It is a doubling that recalls the plot of "Goldilocks," "in which the little girl uses the bears' chairs, porridge, and beds, then the bears track her down through the living room, dining room, and bedroom. The first time around we're secretly pleased with Goldilocks' cleverness; the second time increasingly afraid for her. So with Alex; during the first encounters we're titillated by violence; the second time afraid for his life, and feeling guilty about our first response."[7]

Returning to his previously indulgent home, Alex finds that all of his belongings have been confiscated by the police to make restitution for his victims and that his pet snake has met with an "accident." To make matters worse, his place has been taken by a young male boarder who admonishes Alex for his unfilial treatment of his parents. Because the boarder has already paid next month's rent in advance, there is no room for Alex. (When he feels like slugging the priggish boarder, he is overcome with induced revulsion.) Leaving his former home, Alex gives some money to a panhandler who turns out to be the bum that he and his droogs beat in the second scene of the film. Recognizing him, the bum summons a group of his own companions to pummel Alex. At this point, Alex is rescued by two young bobbies who happen to be his former cronies. Still smarting over the brutal treatment they had received at his hands, one holds Alex's head under a watering trough while the other flails him with a billy club.

A thoroughly beaten Alex seeks port in the storm when he sees a small sign illuminated by two light globes reading "HOME." It is, in fact, the house of the writer whose wife he had raped. When the writer says "I know you," we immediately assume that he recognizes Alex from the earlier encounter. Instead, he merely recalls seeing an item in the paper that morning reporting the circumstances of the lad's release from prison. A staunch enemy of totalitarianism, the writer believes that Alex is a victim of the state and befriends him. This adds an additional element of irony to the film. Because Burgess and Kubrick are both opposed to the mind-control experiments to which Alex has been subjected, they are ostensibly on the same side of this issue as the writer. And yet, he is obviously a figure of ridicule—a weak-kneed liberal (in a wheelchair, no less) who instinctively embraces a criminal simply because he hates the government.

The writer's emotions are then completely reversed when he hears the strains of "Singin' in the Rain" coming from the tub where Alex is bathing. This moment of epiphany causes the writer to plot his personal revenge. The man fits Irving Kristol's definition of a neoconservative as a liberal who's been mugged by reality.

Summoning two friends to help him, the writer offers Alex some wine, which he has drugged with a sedative, and a plateful of spaghetti and meatballs. Soon Alex is unconscious and lying face forward in the pasta. When he awakes, he is in an attic room flooded with the sounds of Beethoven's Ninth. (We then see the writer downstairs turning up the volume.) Physically ill and mentally panicked, Alex opens a window and plunges to what he hopes is oblivion. Instead, he ends up in a hospital bed with both legs in traction. "I came back to life," he says, "after a long, long gap of what might have been a million years."

If his life since prison has been something of a punitive nightmare, Alex now begins to experience a sort of rebirth. First, his parents arrive on the scene, blame the government for all his problems, and promise that he will always have a home with them. When a psychiatrist arrives to ascertain what pops in his mind when shown various pictures, Alex begins to demonstrate his old feisty self. The next visitor is a government minister, who apologizes to Alex for all he has been through. Bad recommendations were followed, but an inquiry will assign responsibility. Shrewdly, the minister suggests that there were those who meant him harm and intended to fix blame on the government. (One of these culprits was a certain writer of subversive literature.) But the state will now make amends by providing Alex with an interesting job at a good salary. All that is needed is Alex's pledge to help restore the government to the good graces of the people. To this Alex readily agrees.

A dozen reporters rush into the room, cameras flashing, as the "Ode to Joy" plays in the background. Alex is a free man who is on the mend, and the government seems more than willing to reverse his "cure"—even if it means restoring him to something resembling the antisocial cretin he had been prior to being imprisoned. What follows is a dream image consisting of Victorian Londoners—one row of men dressed in top hats and another of women holding parasols. All applaud as Alex takes his pleasure with a blond dressed only in black silk stockings. The final shot shows him back in the hospital, gleefully announcing: "I was cured all right!!!"

## III

The term "cured" is fraught with irony. If man is essentially good, then sin can be seen as a treatable illness. This is essentially the position of Pelagianism and all its secular manifestations. But the government in *A Clockwork Orange* is not a therapeutic state. It is concerned only with the pragmatic task of reducing antisocial behavior by any means necessary. What we have, then, is not so much a cure as a fix—the sort of solution that is more appropriate to a broken machine than a sick human being. If we find this fix to be abhorrent, however, it should not be because we find Alex to be an admirable character. Kubrick emphasized this point in an interview with Michel Ciment:

> It is absolutely essential that Alex is seen to be guilty of a terrible violence against society, so that when he is eventually transformed by the State into a harmless zombie you can reach a meaningful conclusion about the relative rights and wrongs. If we did not see Alex first as a brutal and merciless thug it would be too easy to agree that the State is involved in a worse evil in depriving him of his freedom to choose between good and evil. It must be clear that it is wrong to turn even unforgivably vicious criminals into vegetables, otherwise the story would fall into the same logical trap as did the old, anti-lynching Hollywood Westerns which always nullified their theme by lynching an innocent person—but will they agree that it is just as bad to lynch a guilty person, perhaps even someone guilty of a horrible crime? And so it is with conditioning Alex.[8]

The issue that is never raised directly in the film is the purpose of penology. The conservative position has always been that prisons exists for the sake of punishment. If we no longer require an eye for an eye, there is at least the belief that criminals should be made to suffer for their crimes. Without this social consensus, victims (or their families and friends) would rightfully seek retribution on their own. Vigilante justice, after all, is better than no justice at all. The Irish drunk, Alex's former droogs, and the writer who helplessly watched as Alex raped his wife (who later died) all feel entitled to take revenge against the man who has wronged them. Although the state has not required him to pay a proper debt, it has inadvertently put him in the position where others can make him do so at will.

As harsh as retributive punishment might seem, it at least has a limit. Deterrence and rehabilitation, which may seem far more compassionate, often do not. If the purpose of incarceration is to persuade other people not to commit a certain crime, we need not be concerned about justice for the criminal. In fact, punishing an innocent scapegoat might be just as effective. Given the high rate of recidivism, we are also coming to realize that most prisoners are not rehabilitated when they have served their sentences. Ironically, Alex is an exception. The point may be that the only sure rehabilitation is a corrective lobotomy.

As misguided as the state might be in this film, Kubrick realizes the dilemma faced by any society seeking to maintain order. Addressing himself to this issue, he said: "I think that when Rousseau transferred the concept of original sin from man to society, he was responsible for a lot of misguided social thinking which followed. I don't think that man is what he is because of an imperfectly structured society, but rather that society is imperfectly structured because of the nature of man. No philosophy based on an incorrect view of the nature of man is likely to produce social good."[9] Prior to his arrest, Alex fits into the permissive and hedonistic society in which he lives. It is only after his operation and his release from prison that he becomes a misfit. The fact that he is victimized by the same sort of violence that he used to mete out simply shows how much society mirrors his former character and how far it would have to go to achieve true social peace.

Kubrick's earlier classic film *Dr. Strangelove* was considered prophetic at the time of its release. As things turned out, however, there would be no cataclysmic nuclear exchange between the United States and the Soviet Union. If anything, *A Clockwork Orange* is more prophetic in asking how far a government should go in protecting its citizens from each other. If a crime is sufficiently horrible, should we strip the criminal or the suspected criminal of traditional civil liberties? In a "post-9/11 world" that question is far from academic. Kubrick could see this dilemma as far back as the 1970s. At that time, he put the matter as follows:

> Certainly one of the most challenging and difficult social problems we face today is, how can the State maintain the necessary degree of control over society without becoming repressive, and how can it achieve this in the face of an increasingly impatient electorate who are beginning to regard legal and political solutions as too slow? The State sees the spectre looming ahead of *terrorism and anarchy*, and this increases the risk of its over-reaction and a reduction in our freedom. As with everything else in life, it is a matter of groping for the right balance, and a certain amount of luck.[10]

Anyone who thinks that *A Clockwork Orange* leaves us with a Hobson's choice between criminal anarchy and fascist authoritarianism has not paid close enough attention to the ending of the film. When the government minister offers Alex a job, we can be certain that the benefit does not accrue exclusively to Alex. As a freelance thug, he is a menace to the state. As a pathetic zombie, he is an embarrassment. The sort of symbiotic relationship that the minister alludes to might well involve harnessing Alex's propensity for violence to the advantage of the government. After all, in a police state, there is not that much difference in character between the criminal element and the enforcers of order. (Consider, for example, the fact that Alex's former droogs are now cops.) A cured, or fixed, Alex can indulge in socially sanctioned "ultra-violence." He might even be able to have the last laugh at the "subversive writer" who tried to drive him to suicide. The point has already been made that street muggers are a mere nuisance to this state; it is political criminals who pose the gravest threat to the powers that be.

If one had to define the politics of this film, the correct label would be "libertarian." That does not mean that Alex's earlier life of crime is endorsed—even as the lesser of two evils. If anything, that earlier life is a prelude to his likely future as a government goon. Strictly speaking, the state in this film is amoral. Even if Alex is technically free to choose between good and evil, his choice is always the course of action that serves his immediate self-interest. We may recognize this choice as evil; however, Alex is too morally blind to know the difference. He lives in a world that is beyond *both* Pelagianism and Augustinianism. There seems little hope that the moral will can be enlightened, and the grace of God is not present—even in the bizarre form that it takes in the fiction of Graham Greene and Flannery O'Connor. The chaplain knows how to talk the talk, but no one seems to be listening. We are left with the feeling that the world will end not with a bang or a whimper but with the artificial sound of breaking wind.

# THE MORAL VISION OF *STRAW DOGS*

## SAM PECKINPAH'S *STRAW DOGS* (1971)

If Sam Peckinpah's *Straw Dogs* is not the most controversial film of Hollywood's most controversial director, it certainly seemed to be when the picture was released in 1971. In a review that would set the tone for much of the commentary about this movie, Pauline Kael wrote:

> Sam Peckinpah, who is an artist, has, with *Straw Dogs*, made the first American film that is a fascist work of art. . . . [I]t gets at the roots of fantasies that men carry from earliest childhood. It confirms their secret fears and prejudices that women respect only brutes; it confirms the male insanity that there is no such thing as rape. The movie taps a sexual fascism—that is what machismo is—that is so much a part of folklore that it's on the underside of many an educated consciousness and is rampant among the uneducated. . . . Violence is erotic in the movie because a man's prowess is in fighting and in loving. The one earns him the right to the other.[1]

Although this interpretation can be challenged, the fact that it would have occurred to an intelligent critic suggests how far the vision of *Straw Dogs* diverged from elite opinion. Prior to this film, Peckinpah was known primarily as a director of Westerns, particularly the ultra-violent cult film *The Wild Bunch* (1969). The offspring of a multi-generation western family, he had gotten his start as a writer and director working in the seemingly ubiquitous genre of television Westerns during the 1950s. *Straw Dogs*, however, was different from anything that he had ever done before. It was set, not in the American West, but in England. None of the conventions that made the violence of the traditional Western tolerable, or at least familiar, were present in this unusual picture. If anything, it was an atavistic throwback to an age before conventions, when one either had to kill or be killed.

As Peckinpah's biographer David Weddle points out, however, the basic plot of *Straw Dogs* would not have been strange to veteran moviegoers. It is a familiar story: "the meek bookworm is finally pushed to the brink, his passive façade is cracked, and he turns on his tormentors with the wrath of a wild cat and emerges victorious." Although this is a stock plot device of the Western, it has also been used in gangster and boxing pictures and can even be found in the work of such comedians as Buster Keaton, Harold Lloyd, and Harry Langdon. "Moviegoers had seen it over and over again, but, like salted peanuts, they could never get enough of it."[2] (The most explicit treatment of this motif is probably in James Thurber and Elliot Nugent's play *The Male Animal* [1941].) The appeal of such a plot should be obvious. For every Charles Atlas in the movie audience, there are surely scores of ninety-pound weaklings who fantasize about throttling the bully. Movies such as *Straw Dogs* enable them to do so vicariously.

What made Peckinpah's film different, in addition to the extreme lengths to which it went, was the intellectual environment of the late '60s and early '70s. If soldiers and cowboys and other men of action were the heroes of an earlier era, this was a time when intellectual elites (as well as many stoned youth who were neither intellectual nor elite) believed in flower power and giving peace a chance. If the gallant Audie Murphy—the most decorated American soldier of World War II—was the image of our most popular conflict, many thought that the barbarous William Calley—the butcher of My Lai—seemed to exemplify the brutality of Vietnam. Whatever Peckinpah's actual politics might be, it was easy for critics such as Pauline Kael to think of him as essentially a fascist. Had the protagonist of *Straw Dogs* been a woman or a racial minority, all might have been forgiven. But Peckinpah was indiscreet enough to make his hero a white middle-class male. Moreover, as an academic, he was precisely the sort of person who should have known better.

The hero of *Straw Dogs* is an American mathematician named David Sumner (played by Dustin Hoffman). Armed with a research grant, he travels with his British wife Amy (played by Susan George) to the supposed peace of Cornwall for a year of study and reflection. Feeling neglected, Amy pouts, sabotages David's calculations by altering the elaborate equations he writes on his blackboard, and parades around town in clingy sweaters with no brassiere. Unfortunately, the male inhabitants of the town consist of horny louts who lust after Amy and ridicule the feckless David. (One of them is her former lover Charlie Venner.) Rather than prompting David to show greater interest in her or to stand up to his tormentors, Amy sees her husband becoming ever more of a wimp. Several men from the town (who are also working on his garage) invite the American on a hunting expedition and then abandon him as two of them circle back to his house to rape Amy.

The plot turns when David, driving home from a party at the local vicar's house, accidentally hits the village idiot with his car. The half-wit has inadvertently killed a teenage girl who was flirting with him and is being hunted down by a vigilante mob from the local pub. Determined to protect this hapless creature, David gives him refuge in his home and successfully fights off the mob that tries to seize him. In the process, he transforms himself from a pussycat into a tiger. His defense of his home is one of the most intense and sustained instances of carnage in the history of the cinema.

At one level, *Straw Dogs*—which is based on Gordon Williams's novel *The Siege of Trencher's Farm*—can be seen as a defense of property rights. That alone would have been enough to raise the ire of liberals, who speak as if such rights inhere to property rather than being the right of *people* to own and use property, not to mention that one of the oldest principles of British common law is the notion that a man's home is his castle. Significantly, at the time that Peckinpah was making this movie, he was reading two books by the playwright and amateur anthropologist Robert Ardrey—*African Genesis* (1961) and *The Territorial Imperative* (1966), the first of which was given to him by Strother Martin after the filming of *The Wild Bunch*.[3]

According to David Weddle, "Ardrey argued that man's voracious appetite for violence is not the product of a negative socioeconomic environment, as Karl Marx and other sociologists believed, nor the product of traumatic childhood experiences, as Freud contended, but was caused instead by powerful instinctual drives. . . . It was a good fight, the exquisite pleasure of murder that men lusted after more than sex, Ardrey explained—it was the control of territory, not women, that men battled for." Peckinpah later told an interviewer that "Ardrey's the only prophet alive today."[4]

Although David Sumner is an intellectual, Peckinpah resists the temptation to have him analyze the meaning of his experience. When he is taking the retarded Henry Niles home after fending off his attackers, Niles admits that he doesn't know his way home. "I don't, either," David confesses. One can interpret this remark in any number of ways. Clearly, David has experienced something of a rebirth. Like Hemingway's Francis Macomber, he is now living a new life as a result of the courage he has discovered in himself. Unlike Macomber's wife, however, Amy seems not to resent this change in her husband. If anything, it may be what she secretly desired. In any event, his "home" will now be different from what it had been. Trying to adjust himself to that difference will require an act of will and intellect rather than the spontaneous outpouring of impulse we have just witnessed. It is the sort of thing that will take some getting used to.

I

Perhaps because both *Straw Dogs* and *A Clockwork Orange* were notoriously violent movies made by American directors in England at approximately the same time, the two films have often been discussed together. The differences, however, are more instructive than the similarities. When we first meet Alex in Kubrick's film, he is committed to a life of gratuitous brutality. In contrast, David Sumner is committed only to his academic research. His wife even suggests that they fled to England because of his reluctance to take a stand back in America. (Although this point is never elaborated, Weddle notes that the late '60s and early '70s were times of great political turmoil on the nation's campuses.)[5] Alex is first deprived of his capacity for violence and then finds it returned in the custody of the state; David discovers a kind of personal liberation in taking violent command of his own life. If there are any characters in *Straw Dogs* who resemble Alex and his droogs, they are the town roughnecks.

Given our ethnic stereotypes, it is ironic that the most refined character in Peckinpah's film is an American, while the undeniable white trash are Brits. The fact that they behave in a totally predictable manner has led some critics to project their attitudes toward sex and violence onto Peckinpah. If Pauline Kael is the best-known critic to have done so, Molly Haskell was even more vehement in her pronouncements. According to Haskell, Amy "struts around like Daisy Mae before the briar patch yokels, and then gets it once, twice, and again for the little tease she is. The provocative, sex-obsessed bitch is one of the great male-chauvinist (and apparently territorialist) fantasies, along with the fantasy that she is constantly fantasizing rape."[6] If Haskell is correct, then the audience should cheer Charlie Venner and Norman Scutt when they rape Amy and mourn their demise at David's hands. In fact, just the opposite is the case. Amy does behave indiscreetly, and she may well wish to be dominated. But she hardly takes pleasure in being sexually attacked, and the domination she seeks is from her husband.

Doug McKinney argues that *Straw Dogs* is like a well-made play in that it can be divided into three acts.[7] The first of these introduces the characters of the story and focuses on the sexual dynamics both inside and outside the Sumner marriage. The film opens with an ominous scene of children playing in a church graveyard. We then see David and Amy in front of the village pub. Amy has purchased an ancient man-trap as a birthday present for David. Although it initially seems to be nothing more than an antique, we soon see Amy as something of a walking man-trap. When she tries to explain his research to Charlie Venner, David patronizingly cuts her off. In this and other scenes, David makes it abundantly clear that he is the intellectual in the family and that his wife's attempts to match him in this realm are nothing short of embarrassing.

As Michael Bliss points out, David's condescension toward Amy is also reflected in a game of chess they play in the bedroom. Lacking an instinctive feel for the game, Amy reads a book on chess and wears a pair of glasses that contrasts with her natural sensuality. "When Amy tries to decide on her next move, David distracts her by jiggling the chessboard from under the covers." He later pretends to lose a rook under the bed covers, "thus reducing the game piece to a sexual toy."[8] (One is reminded of the section called "A Game of Chess" in Eliot's *The Waste Land* [1922].) Although David does not appear to be inadequate sexually, Amy obviously feels that he takes her for granted.

The adolescent Janice Hedden is a counterpart to Amy. With raging hormones and a miniskirt, she tries unsuccessfully to flirt with David. (She and her prepubescent brother later witness the Sumners making love through their bedroom window.) For frivolous reasons, she soon turns her attention to the half-wit Henry Niles. She sees him as an easy mark without realizing the danger posed by his physical strength and lack of mental capacity. For his part, Henry receives no apparent treatment for his disability. When he inadvertently misbehaves, his brother John assumes that a good slap in the face is all that is needed to correct him.

The only man in the village with any intellectual attainment is the local vicar, with whom David is more than willing to trade wits. When David observes that "there's never been a kingdom so given to bloodshed as that of Christ," the clergyman responds: "That's Montesquieu, isn't it?" His wife then asks: "Who's that?" In a put-down worthy of Sumner, the vicar replies: "Somebody worth reading." It may be his sense of intellectual superiority that causes David to ignore the ridicule heaped upon him by the men in the pub. If he knows that he is better than they are, why be concerned with what they think of him?

His wife, however, is embarrassed for him and desperately wants him to stand up to these predators, who are much closer to her in intelligence and background. If anything, her sexually provocative behavior is a desperate attempt to get her husband to defend her honor. His response (telling her to wear a bra and draw the curtains) is the opposite of what she desires and produces nothing but greater frustration. The conflict suddenly turns violent when David discovers the couple's pet cat hanging in his closet. Amy interprets this as a sign that their antagonists can now get into their bedroom.

## II

The killing of the cat, which launches the second act of the film, is horrifying on several different levels. First, it represents gratuitous cruelty toward a household pet. Second, it suggests the lengths to which the roughnecks will go to get their way. Finally, the very suddenness with which it occurs hints at the escalating violence of the rest of the film. Amy's prime concern, however, is that David simply assert himself against their tormentors. When and where the cat was killed remains something of a mystery. It has been missing for some time, and Amy's attempts to locate it have been intermingled with other instances of violation. At one such point, the perpetually giggling rat catcher who is working on the garage shows Norman Scutt a pair of Amy's panties that he has stolen from the house. Scutt contemptuously growls: "Bugger your trophy. I want what was in them."

Rather than firing the workmen immediately upon discovering the dead cat, David promises to flush them out by inviting them in for beer and conversation. Knowing that her husband will fail in this effort, Amy contemptuously puts a saucer of milk on the same tray with the beer. Rather than catching the attackers off guard, David puts himself in an even more awkward position by agreeing to go hunting with them. In disgust, Amy writes DID I CATCH YOU OFFGUARD on his blackboard and places the saucer of milk in front of it.

It is not entirely clear what David has in mind when he agrees to join the local roughnecks in a hunting party. He has no idea how to use a gun and cannot reasonably expect that the louts who have been making him the butt of their humor will miraculously accept him as one of the lads. If he thinks that he is proving something to Amy or that this outing will give him an opportunity to confront his antagonists free of his wife's meddling, he is sadly mistaken. If anything, he simply reveals what a hopeless fall guy he is. Of course, that may be Peckinpah's motivation—the more ineffectual David appears prior to the climactic siege, the more dramatic his transformation will be.

Hunting for sport has become such an integral part of the American myth of masculinity that few viewers are prepared to question the extent of David's humiliation. Peckinpah, however, was brought up in a different ethic. His maternal grandfather, Denver Church, taught him to live off the land. This meant hunting only for food and not for entertainment.[9] The attitude that Venner, Scutt, and company take toward the shooting of animals is roughly the same as their view of sex—an act that is most gratifying to the extent that it is an assault on their victim. In this case, the victim is David Sumner, with the birds who are to be shot assuming a minor and purely instrumental role in the exercise.

The crosscutting between David's inability to handle the phallic rifle and the attack on his wife makes clear that it is he, at least as much as Amy, who is being raped. The only limit on his humiliation is the fact that he doesn't know what is happening to his wife, even though we suspect that his passive stupidity has allowed it to happen. Does this mean, as Pauline Kael and Molly Haskell have suggested, that Amy secretly wants to be raped—perhaps as a way of getting back at her husband? If so, it is a fantasy she soon regrets.

Although Charlie Venner was once her paramour, there is no indication that Amy wants to rekindle the affair. When he puts his arm around her in one of the early scenes of the movie, she tells him to remove it. Whatever their previous relationship may have been, it is now for her nothing more than a bitter memory. With David safely out in the bush, Charlie initially attempts to seduce Amy. When that fails, he returns her slap with one of his own and takes her by force. It is only at this point that she succumbs and seems almost to enjoy her violation.

Had the scene ended there, we might agree that Amy is essentially a slut who simply enjoys rough sex—or is being portrayed as such by a misogynistic director. But an even more brutal attack follows. We recall Norman Scutt's remark about wanting "what was in" Amy's panties. As Michael Bliss notes, this turns out to be a prophetic statement when Scutt proceeds to sodomize Amy. At no point in this attack does she seem to be enjoying herself. Even Venner appears horrified by what happens. He does not stop it, however, because Scutt has a gun and Charlie's own position is compromised by what he has just done. Although this proved to be a difficult scene for actress Susan George, David Weddle argues that "she had captured Amy in all her conflicted, tortured passion. . . . [A]nd when Peckinpah was through cutting it, it would become one of the most perversely erotic sequences in cinema history."[10]

If the rape scene does not present women in a particularly favorable light, it is hardly a celebration of male superiority. Venner and Scutt are both disgusting examples of humanity; David Sumner is, at best, an object of pity. The one symbol of religious authority (the Reverend Mr. Hood) is even more ludicrous than the chaplain in *A Clockwork Orange*. And the town magistrate, who represents civil law, is not much better. At this point, the only "man" who has yet to reveal serious character flaws is the pathetic half-wit Henry Niles. When Amy asks, at the beginning of the film, why Niles has not been committed to an asylum, Charlie tells her that the town knows how "to take care of its own." This turns out to be a cruelly ironic observation as *Straw Dogs* moves into its climactic third act.

## III

Far from being an endorsement of rape, or even unlicensed sexual passion, *Straw Dogs* could easily be read as a puritanical movie in which sex and death are closely linked. Even before the siege that brings the film to its harrowing conclusion, we have the sad fate of Janice Hedden and Henry Niles. As Michael Bliss notes, Peckinpah continually cuts back and forth between the church social and the tryst between Janice and Henry:

The equation of sex and violence is underscored when Janice asks Henry, "Would you like to kiss me?" The statement is followed by a shot at the church gathering showing Tom Hedden brutally throwing Henry's brother to the floor. The reverend then says to the assembly, "Will you all now please stand? The standing up acts as a corollary for Henry's rising sexual excitement; the almost holy delirium that Henry presumably experiences when he touches Janice's breast is ironically compared to the feeling of being in the presence of "God, the Blessed Virgin, and all the saints" to whom the reverend refers.[11]

Of course, we know that this can come to no good end. Henry's sex education has consisted of being told that erotic pleasure leads to punishment, while Janice identifies it with a kind of guilty adventure. It is no surprise that Henry will go to great lengths to keep himself and Janice from being discovered. Her death is almost a foregone conclusion. Bliss makes an illustrative comparison in finding this reminiscent of the scene in Steinbeck's *Of Mice and Men* (1937), "in which Lenny inadvertently breaks the necks of his pet mice, and later Curly's wife."[12]

Unfortunately, Bliss makes Henry's act part of a reductive feminist reading, in which the behavior of all the men in the film comes off as bestial.

Bliss goes so far as to argue that Janice's death is the indirect result of David's ignoring her and that his subsequent act of protecting Niles is simply "an example of one murderer's sheltering another."[13] To characterize Niles's accidental killing of Janice and David's defense of his home and family as "murders" is surely to pervert the meaning of the term. Janice is not the victim of Niles so much as she is of the town's ignorance and hubris. David Sumner has suffered enough from both these traits to want to protect an innocent victim from them. Even if that is not his *primary* motivation in defending his home, it certainly represents an honorable instinct on his part.

The siege of the Sumner house is a brilliant tour de force at least in part because it is played out at night within a severely constricted space. The editing of the film also heightens suspense. As violent as the action might be, our primary response is neither to celebrate nor to recoil from the brutality but to greet each development with mild surprise and breathless anticipation of what will come next. This is due in large part to the spontaneous and primitive acts of defense to which David is reduced. Such firepower as exists belongs exclusively to his attackers.

At first, it may seem incredible that David is so quickly transformed from a meek-spirited intellectual into a courageous defender of hearth and home. Unlike Dr. Jekyll, he takes no magic potion to reverse his personality. We should note, however, that his initial resolve to protect Henry Niles is very much in character with the sensibility he has shown us throughout the film. He tries reasoning with the men, telling them that they have no evidence that Niles is guilty of anything. Rather than resorting to violence, he first threatens to press legal charges if the marauders don't leave him alone. It is only after the magistrate is accidentally killed by Tom Hedden's gun that David is left to his own devices.

Emotionally, David is pushed over the edge when Amy wants to let Charlie into the house and to release Niles to the mob. At this point, David will either have to assert his authority as head of the house or forget about ever doing so. It is significant that he conducts himself here in a manner that Amy can understand—grabbing her by the hair and slapping her hard. Doug McKinney notes that "this is David's first act of violence, performed when there is no other course left open to him. To stress its effect on Amy, it is seen in the same slow motion as Charlie's earlier matching slap beginning the rape."[14] This is not to suggest that David is morally identical to Charlie. The situations are vastly different, and even in the midst of his violence, David patiently explains to his wife that surrender at this juncture will probably mean their deaths.

As vile as the townspeople are in their treatment of Henry Niles, Peckinpah resists the temptation to sentimentalize the half-wit, even to the extent that Steinbeck sentimentalizes Lenny in *Of Mice and Men*. By harboring Niles, David risks subjecting his wife to the same fate suffered by Janice Hedden. In fact, while he is fending off the mob, Niles does attack Amy. This prompts David to slap him, just as Henry's brother had done, and to shake his head in reproof. This combination of physical discipline and rational explanation is remarkably similar to his treatment of Amy. In a sense, both these individuals behave like children.

The only weapons that David has at his disposal—other than his own wits—are household items such as wire, a fire poker, and boiling oil. (The last of these reminds one of a medieval knight defending his castle.) And, of course, there is the antique man-trap that Amy has bought for David's birthday. It is both dramatically and symbolically appropriate that David fends Charlie off with the man-trap, which is eventually clamped around his rival's neck. Along with David, we breathe a sigh of relief, thinking that all of the foes have been subdued. Another attacker named Riddaway, however, arises—as if from the dead—and seems to have the best of David when Amy shoots him. This is the only use of high technology by the House of Sumner, and it comes from the distaff side.

## IV

The title of Peckinpah's movie comes from the Chinese philosopher Lao-Tse: "Heaven and earth are ruthless and treat the myriad creatures as straw dogs; the sage is ruthless and treats the people as straw dogs."

If we view this as a description of the human condition, it seems to bear some affinities with the pessimistic fatalism of the naturalist writers of the late nineteenth and early twentieth centuries. In the wake of Darwin's revolutionary theories, man went from being a little lower than the angels to being the most well-adapted creature in the animal world. There are times, however, when our adaptations fall short and we seem to be victims of a malevolent fate. The shipwrecked men in Stephen Crane's "The Open Boat" (1898) curse whatever gods may be for toying with them until they realize that they are too insignificant in the cosmic scheme even to be playthings of a higher power.

As we have seen in our discussion of *A Clockwork Orange*, choice and destiny are not absolute antitheses but exist in a kind of creative tension. Similarly, the characters in *Straw Dogs* are shaped not only by nature and nurture but also by the choices they make. The one exception to this generalization might be Henry Niles, who lacks sufficient mental capacity to be fully human. In a sense, Niles becomes the touchstone against which the other characters can be measured. When Charlie Venner declares that the town knows how to take care of its own, he inadvertently expresses the standard by which we are to judge him and everyone else in the film.

To call *Straw Dogs* a "fascist work of art" is surely to miss the point. In a truly fascist society, someone such as Henry Niles would not be institutionalized—he would simply be eliminated. If the town roughnecks are protofascists, David Sumner is an enlightened liberal. The problem faced by many critics of the early '70s, however, was the notion that an enlightened liberal would resort to routing his enemies with boiling oil or a medieval man-trap. But then, genuine fascism (not the movie critic's all-purpose term of opprobrium) was not subdued by the nonviolent tactics of Mahatma Gandhi or Martin Luther King Jr. George S. Patton would not have thought to hand Rommel a flower, nor would Beowulf have asked Grendel why we can't all get along. Even in the youth counterculture to which critics of *Straw Dogs* keep alluding, there was a split between pacifists and anarchists. Borrowing the tune of the former group's favorite anthem, the latter faction would sing: "All we are saying is 'Smash the State!'"

Sam Peckinpah is able to hold humanity to a high standard precisely because he knows us at our worst. Charlie Venner, Norman Scutt, and company are the scum of the earth. And Peckinpah does not make excuses for them. We sense that the choices they make to harass and violate other people need not be made. Unfortunately, there appear to be no positive role models in the community. When we see the Reverend Mr. Hood performing magic tricks for the town, the message seems to be that religion itself amounts to little else. Throughout most of the film, David is willing to close his eyes to the moral lethargy of the community—even when doing so threatens his marriage.

Although the territorial imperative is not the primary source of morality, it becomes the catalyst through which David Sumner discovers his responsibilities as a man. Had his home not been under assault, would he have protected Henry Niles from what amounted to a lynch mob? Would he ever have shown the commitment that his wife found so sorely lacking in his character? Probably not. It is for such reasons that the right to property is not a poor second cousin to freedom of speech or of the press. Because a man's home is his castle, he has both the right and the obligation to defend it. To argue otherwise is to renounce the concept of individual liberty in favor of such utopian delusions as pacifism and collectivism. The experience of the race and the wisdom of thinkers far more profound than Robert Ardrey tell us that such delusions are contrary to human nature. Because conservatism is the politics of human nature, *Straw Dogs* should be seen as a profoundly conservative work of art.

# RITES IN CONFLICT

## MICHAEL CIMINO'S *THE DEER HUNTER* (1978)

When Michael Cimino's *The Deer Hunter* was released in 1978, critics didn't know what to make of it. This was an undeniably powerful film by an aesthetically ambitious director. (His only previous directorial credit, for the Clint Eastwood vehicle *Thunderbolt and Lightfoot* four years earlier, had prepared no one for this emotionally overpowering movie.) Amid the praise—five Academy Awards, including the ones for best picture and best director—were reservations about certain narrative implausibilities and a suspicion that the film dissented from the view of the Vietnam War widely held in Hollywood. Some of the more discerning reviewers realized from the start that questions about the literal probability of the plot were beside the point because *The Deer Hunter* was not meant to be a conventionally realistic movie but should actually be viewed in symbolic terms.

The more virulent attacks on the film's political orthodoxy stemmed from its failure to depict the North Vietnamese and Viet Cong as morally superior to America's fighting men. (Jane Fonda denounced the picture as racist, even though she admitted to not having seen it.) Accepting the Academy Award for his blatantly procommunist documentary *Hearts and Minds* in 1974, the producer Bert Schneider had said, "It is ironic that we're here at a time just before Vietnam is about to be liberated," and then proceeded to read a statement by the Viet Cong.[1] Cimino's position seemed to be considerably more nuanced.

It may well be that *The Deer Hunter* is not staking out a position on the Vietnam War so much as using the war as a means for developing an older and broader theme in American culture. Like so many Westerns, Cimino's film is about the conflict between the heroism of the individual and the demands of the community.[2] With the frontier effectively settled by the end of the nineteenth century, this conflict has had to manifest itself in places other than the cow towns and prairies of a bygone era. In a sense, Vietnam can be seen as a new Wild West, where men test their courage. The real home for an American, however, is not over there but right here. For many Vietnam veterans, coming home involved a particularly difficult reintegration into society. Thus, Cimino has found a contemporary way of telling an old story.

Ernest Hemingway told a similar story in his tales about Nick Adams, an emotionally fragile veteran of World War I. Beginning with his first full-length book, *In Our Time* (1924), Hemingway juxtaposed positive images of hunting and fishing with harrowing scenes of warfare. In the final narrative of that book, "Big Two-Hearted River," Nick tries to regain the psychic balance that the war has shattered by returning to an old fishing site. Nick, however, is not reentering society so much as attempting to make what Hemingway calls a "separate peace." For the characters in *The Deer Hunter*, there is no such thing.

A more recent comparison of outdoorsmanship and warfare can be found in Norman Mailer's *Why Are We in Vietnam?* (1967). In this novel, a Texas adolescent named Ranald Jethroe, preparing to depart for Vietnam the next day, recalls an Alaskan bear hunt that he and his father Rusty had taken two years earlier. Rusty and two underlings who are along for the ride work for a major plastics manufacturer in Dallas. Unlike Ike McCaslin in Faulkner's "The Bear," which Mailer seems to be parodying, the grownups on this trip appear to be uninterested in either the hunt as ritual or their prey as noble adversary. They simply want to bag a suitable trophy by any means necessary. Toward this end, they throw fair play to the wind and employ helicopters in the pursuit of their game.

Filled with disillusionment, which is exacerbated by Rusty's taking credit for a kill that rightfully belongs to his son, young Jethroe and his best friend, Tex Hyde, imitate Ike McCaslin by venturing ever deeper into the wilderness without either weapons or compass. Spending a night under the aurora borealis, Jethroe and Hyde experience a psychosexual communion that stops just short of sodomy. (Here Mailer appears to be spoofing Leslie Fiedler's "Come Back to the Raft Ag'in, Huck Honey!") When they return to camp, they regard themselves as killer-brothers, which one assumes is a kind of primitivist sainthood. As the novel ends, Ranald Jethroe tells us that he and Tex are "off to see the wizard in Vietnam."[3]

Mailer's point seems obvious enough, even though some critics have accused him of covertly endorsing a war that he had consistently attacked in his writings and public conduct. Corporate America, as represented by Rusty Jethroe, believes in technological overkill, whether it be on a bear hunt or in an undeclared war. Rather than embracing pacifism, his son becomes a kind of macho throwback to the traditional American hero—an updated Natty Bumppo, Nick Adams, or Ike McCaslin. The fact that he and Tex are "off to see the wizard" in Southeast Asia is probably Mailer's way of telling us that the killing fields of Vietnam will be just as disappointing to them as the Emerald City was to L. Frank Baum's pilgrims. In the character of Michael Vronsky, Cimino gives us yet another American who recreates himself in the mold of the frontier hero. In *The Deer Hunter*, we see what the experience of Vietnam does to him.

## I

As Robin Wood points out, the geography of the film can be divided into five major sections. The first, third, and fifth sections occur in the fictional mill town of Clairton, Pennsylvania, while sections two and four occur in Vietnam. As in so many versions of the quest myth, from Homer's *Odyssey* on, the hero returns home, presumably changed by what he has experienced on his adventure. Cimino takes great care in showing us what home is for Michael (played by Robert DeNiro) and his two best friends, Nick and Steven (played by Christopher Walken and John Savage, respectively). It is neither the South of Faulkner's Yoknapatawpha County nor the upper Michigan of Hemingway's fishing idylls. Nor does it possess any of the obvious cultural advantages of a big city. It is a gritty and dirty environment in which the main recreations (for the men, anyway) seem to be drinking and hunting.

As engaging as those activities may be for Michael and his buddies, we also see the effects of drinking and violence on the women when Linda's alcoholic father assaults her for the crime of being female and thus, by definition, a bitch.

The film opens in the early morning, which means the end of the night shift at the local steel mill. The three major characters, along with their pals Axel and Stan, head straight to the bar run by a sixth friend, even though this is Steven's wedding day. As the men frolic (drinking beer, playing pool, and singing along with Frankie Valli on the jukebox), the young women slosh through the muddy streets in their bridesmaid's dresses, with Linda (played by Meryl Streep) sporting the black eye her father has given her. As if to suggest what these girls will look like in a few years, we also see old women in babushkas making preparations for the wedding. The fact that all might not be well in Eden is indicated by the distress of Steven's mother that her son is marrying Angela, a strange girl who is not even thin (which is to say that she is pregnant by another man). Although she expresses her concerns to her priest, we do not hear his counsel. In any event, the mother rousts her son from the bar so that he will be sober enough to go through with the ceremony later that day.

There is something almost medieval in the centrality of the church in this town. With its onion-shaped domes, stained glass, and ornate decorations, the Russian Orthodox church building stands in stark contrast to the tawdriness of the secular town. (Several shots, including one of a derelict drinking a bottle of liquor from a paper sack, show this magnificent edifice looming over the local grocery store where Linda works.) In the hands of a different *auteur* with a different sensibility, we might be asked to indict the church for lavishing luxuries on itself while the people it serves live in relative squalor. But the characters in the film register no complaint. If anything, the rituals of the church, which are beautifully depicted in the wedding ceremony, lend a kind of majesty to their lives. One cannot help noticing that John the bartender (played by George Dzundza) sings in the choir.

After the ceremony, we see a much longer ethnic sequence at the American Legion hall where the wedding reception takes place. People of all ages drink and dance, filled with either the joy of life or unquiet desperation. Unlike the wedding reception in *The Godfather*, to which Roger Ebert has compared this scene, there is no wealth to be opulently displayed nor any paparazzi to be kept at bay.[4] The entertainment is provided not by a Frank Sinatra clone but by Linda's boss at the grocery store. (It may call itself the Eagle "Supermarket," but it is clearly part of no chain.) Although more exotic fare is available on this special occasion, the drink of choice is still Rolling Rock beer. And the dance hall is dominated by three life-size high school pictures of Michael, Steven, and Nick, who will be leaving for Vietnam the next day.

In one ominous scene, Cimino's three musketeers retreat to the bar just off the dance floor. There they encounter a taciturn Green Beret. When they try to engage him in conversation about Vietnam, his cryptic response is "Fuck it." At the literary level, this would appear to be an inversion of the situation in Coleridge's *Rime of the Ancient Mariner* (1798), in which the garrulous mariner detains a reluctant wedding guest in order to unburden himself.[5] Here the Green Beret is anything but garrulous, and the wedding guests are eager to hear what he does not want to tell them. This is also the first hint in the film that the actual experience of Vietnam will be different from the patriotic adventure that Michael and company anticipate.

After the reception, Michael runs through town ahead of the wedding car, stripping as he goes. When he and Nick end up on a local playground, Nick declares his love for the town and begs Michael not to leave him "over there," indeed not to leave him at all. (This exchange turns out to be more significant than either realizes at the time.) The next morning all of the men (except for the newly married Steven) are in the nearby mountains on their last deer hunt prior to Vietnam. It is soon clear, however, that only Michael invests this occasion with anything resembling religious solemnity.

If the other men simply see the hunt as an opportunity for good times, Michael insists that everything be done right. When the lackadaisical and self-indulgent Stanley (played by John Cazale) forgets to bring his boots, Michael refuses on principle to lend him his own extra pair. Moreover, no one else knows quite what to make of Michael's insistence that the deer be brought down with "one shot." Nick is more enamored with "the way the trees are" than with the one-shot doctrine, and it is he who eventually loans Stan an extra pair of boots. If Michael is a throwback to Cooper's Natty Bumppo, he is out of place even among his own closest companions.

The night following the hunt, the men return to town with the deer that Michael has felled (with one shot) on the hood of his battered old Coupe DeVille. They run into John's bar shaking and spraying cans of beer in what Robin Wood sees as simulated orgasm.[6] Their raucous singing of "Drop-Kick Me Jesus through the Goalposts of Life" is then interrupted by a pensive John, who plays one of Chopin's Nocturnes on the piano. This brings the extended opening sequence in Clairton to a fitting end; the next sound that we hear is of helicopters in Vietnam.

## II

The first narrative block in Vietnam lasts around forty minutes (as opposed to over an hour for the immediately preceding block in Clairton). We see a Vietnamese soldier throw a hand grenade in a hut, killing an entire family. In righteous indignation, Michael machine-guns the perpetrator. Although we are left to assume that the villain is North Vietnamese or Viet Cong, Robin Wood points out that it is historically more plausible that he is South Vietnamese—that he is probably eliminating an enemy of the American cause.[7] Before we know it, Michael is reunited with Nick and Steven (or have they been together all along?) in captivity. The enemy sadistically insists that they play a game of Russian roulette or be confined to an underwater cage where rats will gnaw on their extremities. Steven is the first to be thrown in the cage when he nervously jerks the pistol away from his head, thus avoiding the bullet that would have killed him. Michael insists that they play with even more bullets, so that he will have enough ammunition to get the jump on their captors and escape. After that escape, we see the three men trying to climb a rope ladder to a helicopter that hovers above the river. Although Nick makes it, a debilitated Steven falls into the water below with the selfless Michael jumping in after him.

While plunging us into "history," the scenes set in Vietnam raise the most questions in terms of narrative realism. The fact that there is no record of the Vietnamese fascination with Russian roulette presents no real problem. As several critics have noted, it is a brilliant metaphor for the randomness and brutality of warfare. But, even granting this point, the Clairton boys turn out to be phenomenally lucky at this game. Putting more bullets in the gun could have ended in catastrophe rather than escape back on the river. Later, a completely disoriented Nick finds himself in a Saigon gambling den where crazed Orientals bet on Russian roulette for sport. (The game is run by a corrupt Frenchman who is apparently a hangover from the earlier colonialist period.) Nick picks up a gun, puts it to his head, and pulls the trigger. Saved by the clicking sound, he vanishes into the night—just beyond the reach of Michael, who happens to be in that particular establishment on that particular night. If this does not stretch one's credulity to the breaking point, Nick remains on the Russian roulette circuit for at least the next several months. How he managed to survive for that long in a lethal game of chance is beyond me.

What is far more credible is the image of Nick as a psychological basket case. (It may be significant that he has the same first name as Hemingway's shell-shocked veteran.) Before he becomes involved in the Russian roulette game, we see him seriously confused in a Saigon hospital. As he is being questioned by a doctor, he is fixated on the stumps of a black amputee. He cannot remember the birth dates of his parents, and when the doctor asks him if his name, Cevoterevitch, is Russian, Nick replies: "American." Although he tries to place a phone call to his fiancée Linda back in Clairton, he hangs up before the call can be completed. It is not surprising that he has turned to heroin and Russian roulette—only that he has lasted as long as he has.

When the film returns to Clairton, Michael's friends are gathered to welcome him home in the trailer he had shared with Nick. Unable to face them, Michael tells the cabdriver to keep going until he comes to a motel on the outskirts of town. The next day, he finds Linda cleaning up after the party that never materialized. Linda and Michael soon realize that they have only each other to remind them of the absent Nick. When Linda suggests that they go to bed to comfort each other, a romantic triangle appears to develop. What is not clear, however, is whether Michael and Nick are competing for Linda or whether Linda and Michael are using each other to feel closer to Nick.

In Tennessee Williams's *Cat on a Hot Tin Roof* (1957), the character of Maggie becomes a point of communion for her husband Brick and his friend Skipper, two men who share a sexually ambiguous friendship. At one point in the play, Skipper tries unsuccessfully to seduce Maggie—ostensibly to prove his masculinity. She suspects, however, that he is vicariously trying to establish an amorous bond with Brick. According to Leslie Fiedler, this sharing of women "is a kind of homosexuality once removed."[8]

Although there is no evidence of an overt homoerotic attraction between Michael and Nick, their bonding, like that of the biblical David and Jonathan, surpasses the love of women. Stan cannot comprehend Michael's refusal to pursue the many women he has fixed him up with and deprecates Michael's obsession with the hunt as a sign of his being a "faggot." When one considers that the frontier hero, from Natty Bumppo on, is a womanless male whose closest ties are with his fellow men, Michael seems to be playing the mythic role he has chosen for himself. It is significant that he is in no hurry to break out of that role by jumping into a romance with Linda.

The first time they do go to bed together, he is asleep (or pretends to be) by the time she gets there, and the second time, he slips out of bed to track Steven down in a nearby VA hospital. Now a triple amputee, Steven does not want to leave the security of the hospital to return to a wife he scarcely knows and to another man's child. During their encounter, he shows Michael a considerable amount of cash that keeps arriving every month. Assuming that this money comes from Nick, Michael decides to go back to Saigon to fulfill his promise not to leave his friend.

One other significant scene during the first return to Clairton is the film's second deer hunt. With Nick absent, this sojourn into nature is even more unsatisfactory than the first one. Although Michael has a clear shot at a deer, he fires his gun harmlessly in the air. Then, upon returning to the lodge where they are staying, he sees Stan playing around with a small pistol. In a fit of rage, he puts the gun to Stan's head and pulls the trigger in memory of the Russian roulette that he had been forced to play in Vietnam. Having symbolically forsaken his role as hunter, he has even less patience with Stan's frivolous simulation of violence. At this point, Michael might well have become a part of the community by bonding with Linda—except for the fact that Nick is still alive and in need of rescue.

## III

The sudden unexplained appearance of cash in Steven's hospital room might seem a thin pretext for Michael's assumption that he can find Nick. But this is a story in which plot is driven by character. Having forced Steven to return home, Michael returns to Saigon at the very time that the city is falling to the enemy. Amid the chaos, which is accentuated by actual news footage of the flight from South Vietnam, Michael finds the Frenchman who runs the Russian roulette game and issues a challenge to the American who is now reigning champion. Flashing cash, which may actually have been the winnings that Nick sent to Steven, Michael is finally reunited with his friend. By now, Nick is so strung out on heroin that he seems not to recognize Michael or to remember his own talk about the way the trees are. When Michael says, "I love you. You're my friend," Nick only spits on him. In a final effort to reach him, Michael does enter the Russian roulette competition and once again tells Nick that he loves him. Nick smiles in an apparent response, speaks the familiar words "one shot," puts the gun to his head, and blows his brains out.

To call this act suicide, as several critics have done, hardly seems tenable. Nick has no more reason to believe that this particular shot will be fatal than he had to believe that all of the ones he had taken during the preceding months would not be. If he has given up his will to live, that happened in the Saigon hospital when his mind was clearly gone and he was unable to call Linda, whose love might have restored him to sanity. Perhaps Michael could have reached him on the night that he became a professional Russian roulette player, but Nick is spirited away by the Frenchman before Michael can catch up with him. Nick's death scene tells us more about Michael than it does about Nick. The ironic repetition of the exhortation to make "one shot" suggests the ultimate consequence of Michael's earlier devotion to the frontier code. It is not just family life but also the fantasy of male bonding that falls before its indiscriminate violence.

The film that virtually began with a wedding concludes with a wake. We see Nick's casket being carried out of the church where Steven had been married, and Steven himself being carried out in his wheelchair. Then, after a brief ritual at the graveside, Nick's friends gather again back at John's bar. (The presence of Angela and Linda indicates that it is no longer an exclusive men's club.) As he is cooking eggs for the assembled mourners, John begins to sing "God Bless America." Linda and Michael join in, and soon everyone is singing. Michael then offers a toast to Nick and the film fades to the credits, beginning with the image of Christopher Walken as their departed friend.

This final scene is the one most reviled by members of the adversary culture. If the Vietnam War has taught these people anything, it is surely the unmitigated evil of a country that would send its young men off to fight in another country's civil war. To call God's blessing down on America reeks of unmitigated jingoism. Such an interpretation, however, fails to make a needed distinction between the policies of one's government and an affection for the place where one lives. Cimino does not analyze the reasons why the United States entered the Vietnam War; however, he shows the effects of that war on three men who left a town and a life they loved to serve God and country.

While Nick and Steven are casualties of the war, Michael has the opportunity to find healing by integrating himself that much more fully into the community to which he has returned. And it may be love for one's community rather than abstract rhetoric that is the final test of patriotism. Ernest Hemingway makes this argument in *A Farewell to Arms* (1929), when he has his war-weary alter ego Frederic Henry say: "I was always embarrassed by the words sacred, glorious, and sacrifice and the expression in vain. . . . I had seen nothing sacred, and the things that were glorious had no glory and the sacrifices were like the stockyards in Chicago if nothing were done with the meat except to bury it."

Rather than stopping there, with what might seem to be a declaration of pacifism, Henry goes on to say: "There were many words you could not stand to hear and finally only the names of places had dignity. Certain numbers were the same way and certain dates and these with the names of the places were all you could say and have them mean anything. Abstract words such as glory, honor, courage, or hallow were obscene beside the concrete names of villages, the numbers of roads, the names of rivers, the numbers of regiments and the dates."[9]

The singing of "God Bless America" is an affirmation of the communal life and a recognition that such a life is not possible without the benediction of a merciful God. (After viewing this scene, Roger Ebert wrote that "the lyrics of 'God Bless America' have never before seemed to me to contain such an infinity of possible meanings, some tragic, some unspeakably sad, some still defiantly hopeful.")[10] This is something quite different from a simplistic desire to bomb Vietnam back to the Stone Age.

In a superb essay on *The Deer Hunter*, Robert E. Bourdette Jr. notes that Cimino's tale resembles Homer's *Iliad* in ending with a funeral and a feast.[11] Although Bourdette establishes some superficial parallels between Hector and Nick, the most striking comparison (which he does not make) is probably between Michael and Achilles. Both men see themselves as warriors who are excluded from a conventional family life. Both establish an extraordinary bond with a male companion. And both exhibit superhuman power and courage in warfare. It should also be noted that, at the end of the *Iliad*, Achilles is humanized when he turns over Hector's body to a grieving Priam. We know from the *Odyssey* that Achilles returns to battle and is slain by Paris. Without a sequel to *The Deer Hunter*, we do not know what will happen to Michael.

The implication, however, is that his experience in Vietnam—especially Nick's death—has caused him to abandon the individualistic frontier ethic to join the community of Clairton. What we have is neither a prowar nor an antiwar message. Instead, Cimino shows us the effects of this particular war on three of its participants.

## IV

When *The Deer Hunter* was made in 1978, the Vietnam War was still so recent that it would have been difficult to craft an epic that memorialized the feelings of the American people about that war. The fact that the nation was divided about the conflict and that it ultimately ended in defeat for the United States made national closure virtually impossible. The plight of the boat people made apologists for the North Vietnamese look like naïve fools. But at the same time, the failure of the rest of Southeast Asia to fall like dominoes suggested that the initial rationale for the war was tragically flawed. Within fifteen years, the only dominoes to fall were the nations of the Soviet bloc.

Throughout the Vietnam War, it was widely assumed that the conservative position was ardently prowar. This assumption ignored the fact that our commitment to South Vietnam was escalated by the Cold War liberals John F. Kennedy and Lyndon B. Johnson against the warnings of conservatives such as Senator Richard Russell of Georgia. Prior to World War II, conservatives were so opposed to an interventionist foreign policy that they were branded as isolationists. Such sentiment abruptly ended when the Japanese bombed Pearl Harbor on December 7, 1941. After the war, conservatives had to decide whether they would return to their noninterventionist principles or join the Truman administration's war on communism. Despite the warnings of America's foremost conservative, Senator Robert A. Taft (R-OH), the crusade against communism initially drew broad bipartisan support. If anything, the American Right (whose ranks were bolstered by repentant ex-Communists) thought that America should liberate the captive nations rather than simply contain the Soviet Empire. After Taft's death in 1953, conservative noninterventionists were effectively marginalized and silenced.

Because of the lack of a visible critique of the Cold War on the American Right, opposition to the intervention in Vietnam was led by the New Left. Some of these people were patriots, but many were latter-day Stalinists who routinely cheered any Communist victory. Their ranks were eventually swelled by young men who did not want to fight in the war and ordinary Americans of all ages, who could see neither a purpose nor a satisfactory conclusion to this conflict. Nevertheless, even as late as 1972, the hard-line antiwar Democratic candidate George McGovern was defeated in a historic landslide by an incumbent president who advocated "peace with honor." By the time *The Deer Hunter* was released in 1978, many Americans had concluded that the Vietnam War was a mistake (either in concept or execution), but it is doubtful that very many potential moviegoers had adopted the stridently anti-American mindset represented by Bert Schneider and the members of the Motion Picture Academy who honored and cheered him.

If the American people felt a certain ambivalence about the Vietnam War in 1978, it is only fitting that that ambivalence be reflected in *The Deer Hunter.* The differences between this film and William Wyler's *The Best Years of Our Lives* (1946), to which it has been compared, are instructive.[12] The three World War II veterans in Wyler's film have clearly been changed by their service overseas, and each experiences some difficulty in returning to civilian life. The sailor Homer, who loses his hands in the war, might be considered a precursor of Steven. The most obvious difference is that Homer returns to a girl who has always been faithful to him and who helps him readjust to life back home. (It is Steven who must finally reach out in sympathy to the nearly catatonic Angela.)

Furthermore, in Wyler's film there is no question about the righteousness of the conflict from which the men return. When a nonveteran suggests that Homer has been a fool to join the military, a brawl ensues. (Despite the hostile reception encountered by many of the soldiers returned from Vietnam, there is no similar scene in *The Deer Hunter.*) Because Wyler could be certain that the overwhelming sympathies of his audience would be with Homer and against his antagonist, this confrontation scene is not the least bit problematic. Such a scene in *The Deer Hunter*, however, would have politicized that movie in a way that would have shifted its moral and emotional center of balance. We leave *The Best Years of Our Lives* certain that family life will be the salvation of all three veterans. In *The Deer Hunter* we can only *hope* that it will help to heal the two major characters who have survived.

If there is a political message in *The Deer Hunter*, it has nothing to do with the Vietnam War, about which persons of goodwill across the political spectrum can disagree. In fact, it is in its refusal to spout any of the familiar pieties about Vietnam that the film achieves a high degree of political incorrectness. (To confirm that notion, one need only consider the negative press it received from so many ideological critics.)[13] Whatever its diplomatic or military merits, the Vietnam War was a kind of boy's adventure for the three main characters in *The Deer Hunter.* This is particularly true for Michael, who so clearly influences his friends. Unless one is to live either above or below the level of humanity (as has been the fate of isolated heroes from Achilles to Natty Bumppo and beyond), it is necessary to find one's place in the corporate life of the community. To run away from home is every boy's dream. To return wiser for the experience is the final test of manhood.

# PART THREE

# TOWARD THE MILLENNIUM AND BEYOND

# THAT'S WHAT FRIENDS ARE FOR

## BRUCE BERESFORD'S *DRIVING MISS DAISY* (1989)

The topic of race relations has obsessed American culture almost from the very beginning. If, as D. W. Griffith asserted, "the bringing of the African to America sowed the first seeds of disunion," it also sowed the seeds of an unusual friendship. Although *Uncle Tom's Cabin* was remembered by Abraham Lincoln as the book that started the big war, it is cherished by many of its readers for its idyllic depiction of the love of an old black man and a little white girl. Evangeline St. Clare is the prototypical Good Good Girl of nineteenth-century fiction. Too pure to remain in this world, she must be dispatched to Heaven while still an unspotted child. At the same time, she has had a profound effect on the adults she has encountered in her short life. As her name would suggest, she has been an evangelist, spreading Christ's grace.

Although Uncle Tom is neither white nor female, he is the other figure in the novel whose presence is most like that of Little Eva and, hence, most like that of Christ. The fact that he is not only an adult but also a husband and a father does not seem to compromise his mythological innocence. In our memory, he remains the imaginary uncle. Throughout the novel that bears his name, he is altruistic in his conduct toward persons of both genders and all races. Harriet Beecher Stowe was writing not just as an abolitionist but also as an evangelical Christian. It is for this reason that her book has struck many readers as overly sentimental. If the black man could be freed only by a holy crusade followed by a militant civil-rights movement, the idea that simple human affection might do the job struck some as hopelessly naïve.

Nevertheless, the bonding of black and white characters has been a persistent motif in American literature. Beyond Uncle Tom and Little Eva, we have the frequent union of black and white males, as Leslie Fiedler has so ably demonstrated in his classic essay "Come Back to the Raft Ag'in, Huck Honey!" Particularly in Southern literature, we find African-American servants—whether bond or free—becoming part of the family circle. Uncle Remus was almost a surrogate father to the young white boys in Joel Chandler Harris's stories. In *Gone With the Wind*, Mammy was more of a maternal figure to Scarlett O'Hara than her distant mother could ever be. Moreover, Uncle Peter seemed more the patriarch than the lackey in Miss Pittypat's household. As Eliza R. L. McGraw points out, this relationship seems to prefigure the one we see in Bruce Beresford's film *Driving Miss Daisy* (1989).[1]

Based on Alfred Uhrey's play of the same name, this movie depicts both an interracial friendship and a quarter century of Southern life. It is also unusual in portraying the role of the Jewish bourgeoisie in the culture of the American South. The fictional Werthan family had been in the dry goods business in Atlanta since the late nineteenth century. It is now 1948, and the postwar South is undergoing an industrial boom under new-wave governors such as Georgia's Herman Talmadge. Unfortunately, the owner of the Werthan firm has a problem at home. Boolie Werthan's seventy-two-year-old mother Daisy has just wrecked her car and cannot secure insurance. At the same time, she is too proud to give up her license. Boolie's task is to hire (and persuade Daisy to accept) a chauffeur.

The next day, Hoke Coleburn shows up at the firm. Although he has been unemployed for five years, he has experience driving a milk truck and once worked for a local Jewish judge. (In the film, Hoke also endears himself to all concerned by helping a fellow black disentangle himself from an elevator malfunction.) Contrasting his experience working for both a Baptist and a Jewish employer, Hoke found that, contrary to ethnic stereotypes, the Jew was more generous and honest. Delighted with both his credentials and his attitude, Boolie hires Hoke for what proves to be a difficult task.

*Driving Miss Daisy* began as a three-character off-Broadway play in a theater that sat an audience of a little more than seventy. Originally scheduled to close after five weeks, the play's run was extended to ten weeks and then to twenty before the show was finally moved to Broadway. Despite rave reviews and a Pulitzer Prize for Uhrey, the play did not have obvious cinematic potential. Although Richard and Lili Zanuck believed in the project and sold it to Warner Brothers, they were operating on what would be considered a shoestring budget in Hollywood (an initial $12 million, finally cut to a little more than $7 million). Fortunately, everyone connected with the film was a consummate professional, and the studio made the most of location shooting in Atlanta.

Uhrey contributed an intelligent adaptation of his own work, and the Australian director Bruce Beresford again proved his ability to translate a story from stage to screen (he had previously made the successful films *Breaker Morant* [1979] and *Crimes of the Heart* [1986] from plays.) If Uhrey was exceptionally close to the material (the play was based on his own grandmother and her chauffeur), Beresford gave it the universal significance that comes with an international perspective. He opens the action up just enough to make a realistic film that loses little of the magic of a non-naturalistic stage production.

In his screen adaptation, Beresford includes characters who are only mentioned in the play. Patti LuPone as Boolie's social-climbing wife Florine, and Esther Rolle as Daisy's cook Idella, are perfectly cast. Each makes the most of the very little time she spends on screen. Boolie, who is the third character in the play, is brought to life in an understated way by Dan Aykroyd. Uhrey intends this to be a supporting role; Boolie has none of the memorable scenes or piquant lines given to Daisy and Hoke. For that reason, it is a challenging part and one to which Aykroyd rises in what is easily the best performance of his career.

Daisy and Hoke are roles of a lifetime, and lesser actors might have overplayed them. Not Jessica Tandy and Morgan Freeman. Although her screen career began in the 1930s, Tandy made an indelible mark on the American theater as Blanche DuBois in the original stage production of Tennessee Williams's *A Streetcar Named Desire* in 1947. Like so many Brits, she was able to speak with a convincing Southern accent. In her eighties when *Driving Miss Daisy* was made, she had to look both younger and older than her actual age. In all of these transitions, she is utterly convincing and fully deserved the Academy Award she received for best actress.

At least as good is Morgan Freeman, who created the role of Hoke on stage and made it live on screen. The manner in which he delivers his lines, his facial expressions, and his body language cause one to believe that he was born to play this part. But his incredible range of previous performances prompted Pauline Kael to ask whether Freeman is, in fact, "the greatest American actor." Roger Ebert, for one, believed that when one examines Freeman's performances as a vicious pimp in *Street Smart* (1987), a self-confident school principal in *Lean On Me* (1989), an ignorant gravedigger in *Glory* (1989), and Hoke in *Driving Miss Daisy*, the question is far from presumptuous.[2]

## I

The connection between blacks and Jews is a major subtext of *Driving Miss Daisy*'s story. As a historically persecuted people, Jews have typically felt affinity with other victims of discrimination. In America, this has meant that the fates of blacks and Jews have often been linked. It was probably not until the social upheavals of the 1960s that much attention was focused on the possible disharmonies of America's two most excluded peoples. Nevertheless, prescient observers had detected signals much earlier. In the Northeast, middle-class Jews had often seen the black proletariat as a dangerous rabble, just as the black underclass regarded Jewish landlords and shopkeepers as economic predators. In *Notes of a Native Son* (1955), James Baldwin pointed out the tensions that existed between blacks and Jews in Harlem. According to Baldwin: "[J]ust as society must have a scapegoat, so hatred must have a symbol. Georgia has the Negro. Harlem has the Jew."[3]

If Baldwin was exposing a dirty little secret in 1955, the conflict between blacks and Jews had long been an underground issue. Among lower-class blacks, it tended be a variation of the strain of white populism that sees the Jew as the prototypical white capitalist. Insofar as he is religious, or imagined to be such, the Jew is an affront to both the black Christian and the black Muslim. The former perceives the Jews as having both crucified Christ and heckled Simon of Cyrene when he helped carry the cross. The latter are "obsessed by the legend of the 'Evil Jacob,' Israel the Usurper—as well as Isaac before him doing poor Ishmael out of his heritage."[4] These latter images have been continually reinforced by the anti-Semitic rhetoric of Elijah Muhammad and Louis Farrakhan.

At a mythological level, the Jew is neither black nor white but a third race. He is Shem, the son of Noah, trying at various times to pass as his black brother, Ham, or his white brother, Japheth. To the extent that he is discriminated against by Japheth, Shem is allied with Ham; however, when he assimilates into Japheth's culture, it is frequently by baiting Ham. Furthermore, even many liberal Jews have had their faith in human equality challenged by the intractable reality of the black underclass. Jews have been punished by quotas because of their obvious superiority to the WASP majority, while blacks have benefited from quotas because of their alleged inferiority.

In the South, the conflict between blacks and Jews was defined largely in economic terms. Consider the first edition of W. E. B. Du Bois's *The Souls of Black Folk* (1903). "[O]ne of the fairest regions of the 'Oakey Woods' [in Georgia]," Dubois writes, "had been ruined and ravished into a red waste, out of which only a Yankee or a Jew could squeeze more blood from debt-cursed tenants." Later in the same book, Dubois writes that "nearly all the lands belong to Russian Jews. . . . The rents are high, and day-laborers and 'contract' hands abound. It is a keen, hard struggle for living here." According to Eliza McGraw, "Du Bois's first image of the South and its reprehensible treatment of African Americans casts Southern Jews as approximate slaveowners. Du Bois's first-edition Southern Jews are compassionless and destructive, forcing a life of hardship upon their disenfranchised African American sharecroppers."[5]

Fifty years later, Du Bois significantly revised those references. He changed the term "Russian Jew" to "foreigner" and wrote a brief afterword for the 1953 edition that was eventually omitted. In it, he admits: "As I read the passages again in the light of subsequent history, I see how I laid myself open to this misapprehension [of possible anti-Semitism]. . . . My inner sympathy with the Jewish people was expressed better in the last paragraph of p. 227 [in the essay 'Of Alexander Crummell']."[6] Du Bois's later sentiments no doubt grew out of a half century of Jewish support for the civil-rights movement.

The connection between Jews and blacks in the Atlanta region was determined for much of the twentieth century by a notorious murder case in 1913. Leo Frank, the Northern Jewish superintendent of an Atlanta pencil factory, swore that he was alone in his office when a fourteen-year-old white girl named Mary Fagan was found dead elsewhere in the building. On the testimony of a black employee, Frank was convicted of the murder and sentenced to death. Because of doubts about the case, Governor John Slaton commuted the sentence to life imprisonment, thus ruining his chances for political success in Georgia.

Frank's initial sentence was the first instance in which a white man had been convicted of a capital crime on the testimony of a black man in the state of Georgia. The sentiment against Frank, and Jews in general, was so intense that he was later kidnapped from prison and lynched for his crime. Although scholarly opinion continues to be divided about Frank's guilt, he was pardoned by Georgia governor Joe Frank Harris seventy years later and generally exonerated in American popular culture.[7]

At the time of this case, several local Jews made the case for both their ethnic and regional identity. The owner of the *New York Times*, a Southern Jew named Adolph Ochs, wrote an editorial on Frank's behalf, noting "that a regional loyalty . . . made him eager to prove that his fellow-Southerners were not anti-Semites." Frank's wife Lucille wrote to the *Augusta Chronicle*: "I am a Georgia girl, born in this state and educated in her schools. I am a Jewess, some will throw that in my face, I know, but I have no apologies to make for my religion. I am also a Georgian, an American, and I do not apologize for that either." Nevertheless, a widely popular song of the time concluded with the words: "The Christian doers of Heaven / Sent Leo Frank to Hell."[8]

Although Jews in Atlanta had previously felt safe in their assimilated identity as New South merchants and industrialists, after the Frank case they began to join (and in some cases replace) blacks as objects of persecution. Much of the case against Frank was made by the radical agrarian journalist Tom Watson. During the latter part of the nineteenth century, Watson had enjoyed considerable success as a founder of the Populist Party and had even run as William Jennings Bryan's running mate on the Populist ticket in 1896. At that time, he was preaching a gospel of racial harmony and class solidarity. By 1913, however, he had suffered some political setbacks and had turned both anti-black and anti-Jew. Although Daisy and Hoke never mention Watson or the Frank case, in the chronology of the film she would have been thirty-seven in 1913, and he would have been twenty-five—certainly old enough to be aware of the controversy.

The first time that the joint persecution of blacks and Jews comes up in the story occurs after Hoke has been driving Miss Daisy for ten years. One Saturday morning, when he is taking her to her weekly temple service, they are stopped by a traffic jam. Hoke soon learns that the reason for the tie-up is that someone has bombed the temple. When Daisy asks, "Who would do that?" Hoke responds: "You know as good as me. Always be the same ones." Hoke then tries to establish an affinity with Daisy by telling her a story from his youth:

> Back down there above Macon on the farm—I 'bout ten or 'leven years old and one day my frien' Porter, his Daddy hangin' from a tree. And the day befo', he laughin' and pitchin' horseshoes wid us. Talkin' bout how Porter and me gon' have strong good right arms like him and den he hangin' up yonder wid his hands tie behind his back an' the flies all over him. And I see'd it with my own eyes and I throw up right where I standin'. You go on and cry.[9]

Daisy, however, refuses to join the circle of oppression. At first, she expresses surprise that the bombers didn't strike a Conservative or Orthodox temple—as if redneck terrorists were well-versed in Jewish sectarianism. She explicitly denies that Hoke's story has any connection to the temple bombing and insists that the policeman who told Hoke about the bombing must have been mistaken. She resembles nothing so much as a Jew who came of age before the Leo Frank case and is desperately trying to insist on her primary identity as a respectable Southerner. Hoke is just enough younger to know the truth.

## II

Prior to the temple bombing, the Jewish identity of the Werthan family has no more significance for the film's story than it would for a standard-issue sitcom. Daisy represents the Jewish matriarch who is trying to cling to the old traditions, while Boolie is clearly a transitional figure who is trying to placate both his mother and his assimilationist wife Florine. For Florine, the sign of respectability is to socialize with Episcopalians and to have the biggest and gaudiest Christmas display on the block. Although blind to her own foibles, Daisy has no trouble identifying her daughter-in-law's hypocrisies. "If I had a nose like Florine," she says, "I wouldn't go around saying Merry Christmas to anybody." A bit later, she remarks: "Too much running around. The Garden Club this. The Junior League that! As if any one of them would give her the time of day! But she'd die before she'd fix a glass of ice tea for the Temple Sisterhood!"[10]

One of the early bonding moments in the story occurs when Daisy and Hoke are out at the Jewish cemetery decorating the grave of Daisy's husband Sig. (Despite a "perpetual care" contract, Daisy makes the trek three times a month, proving herself in Hoke's estimation to be the best widow in Georgia.) When Daisy asks Hoke to put some flowers on the grave of a friend named Leo Bauer, he hesitates and then admits that he is unable to read. At first, Daisy's experience as a middle-class schoolteacher causes her to disbelieve that any adult could be illiterate. "You just don't know you can read," she says. "I taught some of the stupidest children that God ever put on the face of this earth and all of them could read well enough to find a name on a tombstone."[11] She then gives Hoke enough of a lesson in phonics to enable him to find Leo Bauer's grave.

In the following scene, as they are disembarking at one of Florine's Christmas parties (where Daisy assures Hoke that he will be the only Christian present), the old schoolteacher gives her chauffeur a fifth-grade copy handwriting book. "I taught Mayor Hartsfield out of this same book," she tells him. Rather than feeling patronized, Hoke is genuinely moved. "It's not a Christmas present," Daisy assures him. "Jews don't have any business giving Christmas presents."[12]

Shortly thereafter, Daisy and Hoke take their first long car trip together. The excursion is to Mobile, Alabama, to celebrate the ninetieth birthday of her brother Walter. Boolie cannot accompany them because he must attend a convention in New York, and Florine had written away eight months earlier to get tickets to *My Fair Lady*. The trip brings back memories of the time that Daisy attended Walter's wedding when she was twelve in 1888:

> We were on the train. And I was so excited. I'd never been on a train. I'd never been in a wedding party and I'd never seen the ocean. Papa said it was the Gulf of Mexico and not the ocean, but it was all the same to me. I remember we were out at a picnic somewhere—somebody must have taken us bathing—and I asked Papa if it was all right to dip my hand in the water. He laughed because I was so timid. And then I tasted the salt on my fingers. Isn't it silly to remember that?[13]

Significantly, this is first time that Hoke has ever been out of Georgia.

If this trip helps Daisy to open up to Hoke, it does the same thing for him in a very different and embarrassing way. As they are driving late at night, Hoke feels the need to relieve his bladder. When Daisy admonishes him that he should have thought of that back at the Standard Oil station, he reminds her that "colored cain' use the toilet at no Standard Oil." Eager to arrive in Mobile and afraid of being abandoned, if only for a moment, on a dark road, Daisy orders him not to stop. But Hoke, like Jim on the raft, asserts his dignity. "I ain' no dog," he says, "and I ain' no chile and I ain' jes' a back of the neck you look at while you goin' wherever you want to go. I a man nearly seventy-two years old and I know when my bladder full and I gettin' out dis car and goin' off down de road like I've got to do. And I'm takin' de car key dis time. And that's de end of it."[14]

Beresford gives additional dramatic impact and social nuance to the film version of the trip when he has a couple of Alabama troopers question Hoke about where he got the car. (Conforming to the cracker stereotype, one of them calls the elderly Hoke "boy.") When Daisy tells the officers that the car is hers, they demand that she produce its registration and then proceed to mispronounce her name. It is clear that the two cops see the pair in the car as being out of place in a world considerably less cosmopolitan than Atlanta. As they drive away, one officer says to his partner: "An old nigger and an old Jew woman taking off down the road together. Now that is one sorry sight."

Commenting on this scene, Eliza McGraw writes: "The car bearing Daisy and Hoke constitutes a spectacle, reminding audiences of the tenuous position each bears in racial terms down a Southern road at mid-century. The audience, along with the police officers, watches them continue down the highway, considering whether this is indeed a pitiful image or one with its own power, embodied in the confidence each shares in the other as well as the tension between them."[15]

## III

Part of the charm of *Driving Miss* Daisy is the failure of the two principals to become immediate friends. When Daisy and Hoke first meet, both are well along in years and set in their ways. Hoke is more accommodating, if only because of his position as an employee. Even if he prefers Jewish employers, there are only so many liberties he feels comfortable taking. When he chides Daisy as a "fine rich Jewish lady" who shouldn't have to be going to the Piggly Wiggly on the trolley car, she is sensitive about putting on airs. Remembering her working-class upbringing "on Forsyth Street," she maintains an air of fierce independence. She may also be chafing against the stereotypes of Jews with money, which she fears that Boolie and Florine are flaunting even as they turn their back on the more genuine aspects of their heritage.

In not wanting to appear as rich as she actually is, Daisy separates herself from other Jews, whose chauffeurs park in front of the temple in an apparent display of wealth. She tells Hoke: "On Forsyth Street we only had meat once a week. We made a meal on grits and gravy. . . . I did without plenty of times, I can tell you." Hoke, who has probably known even more severe poverty in his life as a working-class black man, forswears the luxury of such poor-mouthing. "And now you doin' with," he says. "What so terrible in that? . . . [I]f I was ever to get ahold of what you got I be shakin' it around for everybody in the world to see."[16]

In one particularly tense scene, Daisy believes that she has evidence that Hoke has been stealing from her. Sounding a bit like Captain Queeg in *The Caine Mutiny* (1951), she calls Boolie one morning to tell him that she has discovered a thirty-three-cent can of tuna missing from her pantry and suspects Hoke of having eaten it. ("They all take things, you know.") Although he thinks this a trivial reason to miss his breakfast and be late for a meeting, Boolie promises to confront Hoke. When the black man arrives, however, he is carrying a can of tuna to replace the one he ate. The leftover pork chops Daisy had put out for him were "too stiff." Even a woman who prides herself in not being prejudiced is apparently capable of patronizing the black help. It is only after years of seeing each other as human beings that Daisy and Hoke begin to transcend their deeply held attitudes.

At first, Boolie sees Hoke as his surrogate, a way of taking care of his mother so that he won't have the bother. Eventually, however, Daisy and Hoke form a bond that effectively excludes Boolie. One morning during an ice storm, Daisy calls her son, who promises to come to her house as soon as the roads are passable. Before he can arrive, however, Hoke shows up with her morning cup of coffee from a convenience store. (Although it is not as good as the coffee that Daisy's late black cook used to make, she is touched by the gesture.) When Boolie calls back, Daisy informs him that he is not needed after all, because "Hoke is here with me. . . . He is very handy." More than a little amused, Boolie says: "Have I got the wrong number? I never heard you say loving things about Hoke before." To this, Daisy replies: "I didn't say I love him. I said he was handy."[17]

Nevertheless, there are certain boundaries that cannot be easily crossed. When the United Jewish Appeal invites Martin Luther King Jr. to speak at a benefit, Boolie declines Daisy's invitation to accompany her. Although he believes that King has done some fine things, he realizes that not all of his business colleagues agree. He has just been named Atlanta Businessman of the Year and doesn't want to jeopardize that status by being branded as a racial liberal. He now has to compete with a New York Jew who, by definition, is smarter than an Atlanta Jew. Cognizant of how far his company has come since his father started it seventy-two years earlier, he is not about to let the less enlightened members of the community label him Martin Luther Werthan. Ironically, in his speech that night King argues that the greatest impediment to racial progress in America is not the action of outright racists but the inaction of people of good intentions.

When Boolie suggests that Daisy invite Hoke to the King dinner, the limits of her tolerance are revealed. Although she believes in the abstract concept of racial equality, Hoke is still her subservient driver. She assumes that, as a member of the black community, he can hear King whenever he wants to by simply attending his church. (That King was almost always on the road at that time and that not all black people attend the same church are facts that seem not to have occurred to her.)

When she finally does broach Boolie's suggestion with Hoke, it is as a silly idea beyond consideration, even as she expresses her approval for the way things are changing. Unwilling to let her off quite so easily, Hoke observes: "Invitation to dis heah dinner come in the mail a mont' ago. Did you want me to go wid you, how come you wait till we in the car on the way to ask me? . . . [N]ext time you ask me someplace, ask me regular." Then, as he is letting her out of the car, he remarks: "Things changin', but they ain't change all dat much."[18] It is an observation Hoke probably wouldn't have made only a few years earlier and is itself evidence of the rising assertiveness of the black underclass.

The story comes to a denouement after Daisy reaches ninety and starts losing her mind. One morning she wakes up agitated that she cannot find the test papers she is to return to her students the next day. Convinced that she is still a schoolteacher, Daisy walks around with her hair undone. Hoke arrives in time to size up the situation. In the film, he follows Daisy to various rooms in the house, finally stopping in a room where we have never seen them before. Trying to bring her back to reality, Hoke admonishes her: "You rich, you well for your time and you got people care about what happen to you. . . . You want something to cry about, I take you to the state home, show you what layin' out dere in de halls." Later he says, "You keep dis up, I promise, Mist' Werthan call the doctor on you and just as sho' as you born, that doctor gon' have you in de insane asylum 'fore you know what hit you." Despite her dementia, Daisy soon says something to Hoke that has been a quarter century in coming: "You're my best friend."[19] This is no mawkish sentiment, but a vision earned. And one come nearly too late.

The story (on both stage and film) concludes with Boolie driving Hoke to the nursing home where Daisy now resides. It is 1973, and Boolie has decided finally to sell his mother's house. (In the film, the passage of time is subtly indicated by a jogger passing on the sidewalk.) Hoke is now eighty-five and wearing glasses so thick that we know he can no longer drive. The passage of time is further indicated by the fact that he has been driven to Daisy's house by his thirty-seven-year-old granddaughter, who teaches biology at the historically black Spelman College. In true aristocratic fashion, Boolie assures Hoke that his check will keep coming each week.

When Boolie and Hoke arrive at the nursing home, Daisy, now ninety-seven, is visibly older and initially uncommunicative. Her son's comments about her making jewelry several times a week draw no response. When he tells Hoke that he thought of him the other day when seeing an Avondale milk truck on the expressway, Daisy snaps, "Hoke came to see me, not you." Both men take this as a welcome sign of her old feisty self. All Boolie has to do is to remind Daisy that Florine is now a Republican national committeewoman for the old lady to tell him to "go charm the nurses."[20] Taking his cue, Boolie retreats as Hoke feeds Miss Daisy a piece of Thanksgiving pie, and an image of their old car passes over the screen.

## IV

In its decision to honor *Driving Miss Daisy* with the Academy Award for best picture of 1989, Hollywood seemed to put distance between itself and the cultural Left. Either that, or the PC crowd was too surprised by the success of this small-scale production to mount its guns before the damage could be done. After the fact, however, the usual suspects made up for lost time. Aaron McGruder, whose comic strip "The Boondocks" specializes in vitriolic assaults on insufficiently radical blacks, belittled Will Smith's portrayal of a legendary caddie in *The Legend of Bagger Vance* (2000) by calling it "Driving Matt Damon." (And he did not mean it in a complimentary sense.) In his essay "Blues for Atticus Finch" (1995), Eric Sundquist attacks what he considers the racial ambivalence of Harper Lee's *To Kill a Mockingbird* (1960) by characterizing it as "Driving Miss Scout."[21]

Even more to the point, in her book *Skin Trade* (1996), Ann DuCille defines "the *Driving Miss Daisy* syndrome" as "an intellectual sleight of hand that transforms power and race relations to make best friends out of driver and driven, master and slave, boss and servant, white boy and black man."[22] One could continue this dreary litany, but the point should be clear: Anyone who suggests the possibility of interracial friendships, particularly in the South, should expect abuse from certain quarters. Harriet Beecher Stowe discovered that. So did Stephen Foster, Joel Chandler Harris, and Margaret Mitchell. Not even Faulkner was exempt from the charge of white racism.

A more benign way of looking at the situation is to say that imperfect people living in what is unquestionably an imperfect society simply have to do the best they can. Like Uncle Tom, Hoke is a figure of infinite kindness and generosity. Like Uncle Remus, he also has a sense of humor. If Daisy does not conform to twenty-first-century standards of political correctness, it may be because she was born in the nineteenth century and came of age in a different world. All good fiction reveals a truth rather than an ideology. Although race, class, and ethnicity give *Driving Miss Daisy* a recognizable social texture, its true appeal is to the human heart, not to the ethics of victimization.

# NO GREATER LOVE

## RICHARD ATTENBOROUGH'S *SHADOWLANDS* (1993)

A major section of Michael Medved's *Hollywood vs. America* consists of a devastating counterattack against the dream factory's assault on religion. If the much-maligned Production Code of 1930 had forbade any derogatory or offensive depictions of religious faith, filmmakers liberated by the new rating system seemed eager to make up for lost time. One would never guess from our popular entertainment that we live in a country where millions of people regularly attend religious services and where an overwhelming majority profess a belief in God. Some of the Hollywood elite may be trying to compensate for what they believe was an oppressive religious upbringing; others are enthralled by New Age mysticism or Scientology; even larger groups are so indifferent to religion that it doesn't even show up on their radar screens. (Although the situation has changed slightly in recent years, there was a time when the only television family that regularly attended church was the Simpsons.) Medved is surely on target when he describes Hollywood as "a community in which Shirley MacLaine has more followers than Jesus or Moses."[1]

This situation was dramatically illustrated in 1988 when Universal Studios released Martin Scorsese's controversial film *The Last Temptation of Christ*. Based on Nikos Kanzantzakis's novel of the same name, this movie attempts to portray the human side of Jesus' dual nature.

A former Roman Catholic seminarian, Scorsese may have had serious theological intentions, but several graphic scenes deeply offended a wide cross section of Christians, including the National Council of Catholic Bishops, the National Catholic Council, the Southern Baptist Convention, the Eastern Orthodox Church of America, the Archbishop of Canterbury, the Archbishop of Paris, the Christian Democratic Party of Paris, some sympathetic Jews, and Mother Teresa of Calcutta. When 25,000 protesters showed up at Universal's gates with a petition against the movie signed by 135,000 Americans, no one at the studio would devote even ten minutes to receiving the document. In fact, the only response was to instruct the protesters to leave their petition at the gates so that it could be disposed of with the rest of the day's trash. As Medved notes, this was the same studio that had passed on the opportunity to produce a film version of Salman Rushdie's *The Satanic Verses.* Did Hollywood consider Muhammad more sacrosanct than Christ, or were the moguls simply more in awe of believers who issue fatwas instead of petitions?

The studio was certainly emboldened by the fact that the most vocal protesters were Christian evangelicals who had not seen the film (which had not yet been released) and who would probably not attend an R movie regardless of its content. According to Medved, many of the critics who saw the movie found it to be a tendentious bore but praised it publicly in order to be on the right (or politically correct) side of the controversy. Medved quotes one such critic as saying: "Look, I know the picture's a dog. . . . We both know that, and probably Scorsese knows it, too. But with all the Christian crazies shooting at him from every direction, I'm not going to knock him in public. If I slammed the picture too hard, then people would associate me with Falwell—and there's no way I'm ready for that."[2]

Beyond the merits or weaknesses of this particular film, the controversy surrounding *The Last Temptation of Christ* demonstrates the double standard that Hollywood employs for dealing with groups that might have a special interest in one of its products. Within three years of the release of Scorsese's epic blasphemy, Disney altered its adaptation of Jack London's *White Fang* (1991) because animal-rights activists thought that it presented wolves in a bad light. Screenwriter Jonathan F. Lawton modified his screenplay *Red Sneakers* (which apparently was never filmed) because the Gay and Lesbian Alliance thought that it did not present a sufficiently idyllic view of the homosexual life. And producer Robert Redford allowed religious leaders of the Hopi Indian tribe to review and suggest changes in the script for *Dark Wind* (1994). "Leaders of the motion picture business," Medved notes, "showed more concern with possible sacrilege against a single Hopi village than with certain offense to the faith of tens of millions of believing Christians; the prospect of being labeled 'anti-wolf' produced greater worry than being labeled 'anti-Christ.'"[3]

In the area of religion, as with so many other traditional values, the attitudes of the Hollywood elite cannot even be explained by corporate greed. If anything, this trend would seem to run counter to the commercial interests of the entertainment industry. Medved concludes that "the religion bashing that occurs in the popular culture is spontaneous and instinctive rather than calculated; it arises out of the personal prejudices and preferences of the people who create that culture."[4] Few persons of intellectual seriousness would want to ban the theme of religious hypocrisy from art or to deny that there are villains (including serial killers) who can quote large passages of Scripture from memory. (As he amply demonstrated when tempting Christ in the wilderness, even the devil can do that.) The daily headlines and an even passing knowledge of history remind us that religion is often used for malevolent purposes. But a sense of proportion tells us that something is wrong with any medium in which a clerical collar comes to mean what a black hat did in old-time Western films.

If the honorable exceptions to this generalization are few, they are all the more worthy of note. Medved cites *Chariots of Fire* (1981), *Places in the Heart* (1983), *Tender Mercies* (1983), *Witness* (1985), *The Trip to Bountiful* (1985), and *Rambling Rose* (1991), among the few mainstream films that present religion in a positive light. (All of these are discussed in section 4 of this book.) Medved also argues that, in *Driving Miss Daisy* (1989), religion helps to strengthen the friendship of the white Jewish matriarch with her black Christian chauffeur, and as we saw in the last chapter, there is much truth in this observation.

Had *Hollywood vs. America* come out a few years later, it almost certainly would have lauded Richard Attenborough's *Shadowlands* (1993). A dozen years before *Shadowlands*, Attenborough's *Gandhi* had scored big at both the box office and at the Academy Awards. At the time, some cynics might have suspected that this homage to a Hindu holy man showed more political than religious piety. (After all, Mahatma-worship had been a fad among certain upper-class Brits since at least the 1920s.) *Shadowlands*, however, was enough to disabuse the cynics. The story of the marriage of British intellectual C. S. Lewis and American poet Joy Davidman Gresham, this film is both an affecting love story and an unusually moving treatment of Christian faith.

## I

One of the most remarkable men of the twentieth century, Clive Staples Lewis distinguished himself in three separate vocations. An accomplished professor of literature at both Oxford and Cambridge universities, his scholarly and critical writing has proved indispensable to students for seven decades. *The Allegory of Love* (1936) is still the best available introduction to the topic of courtly love and the historical development of allegory. Almost as good are *An Experiment in Criticism* (1941), *A Preface to Paradise Lost* (1942), and *The Discarded Image* (1964). In these and other lesser-known works, Lewis performs the role of the public intellectual, writing with clarity and grace about philosophically demanding material for an audience of intelligent general readers. His discussions of literature remain in demand because few subsequent writers have tried to do what he did—and none have done it nearly so well.

When not expounding on serious adult topics, Lewis established himself as a singularly gifted writer of fantasies for children. Beginning with *The Lion, the Witch, and the Wardrobe* (1950), Lewis's Narnia Chronicles rank only behind the works of his friend J. R. R. Tolkien in popularity and mythic resonance. His science fiction romances *Out of the Silent Planet* (1938), *Perelandra* (1943), and *That Hideous Strength* (1945) are addressed to the entire family. If in these years narrative realism continued to reign supreme in America, a British highbrow could still take fantasy literature seriously with no loss of cultural status.

Students of his imaginative writing (including his adult masterpiece *Till We Have Faces* [1956]) realize that Lewis was primarily a Christian allegorist. Born in Belfast, Ireland, in 1898, "Jack" Lewis was raised a nominal Anglican, only to lose his faith at age thirteen. (The death of his mother when he was nine and his subsequent estrangement from his father led to an unhappy childhood.) After passing through a period of atheism, Lewis made his way back to a generic belief in God by 1929.

Over the next two years, his discussions with Tolkien and Hugo Dyson convinced Lewis intellectually that Christianity could be seen as the literal fulfillment of the best pagan myths. (He was also greatly influenced by George MacDonald's allegorical romance *Phantastes* [1858].) Then, one afternoon in 1931, while he was riding to the Whipsnade Zoo in the sidecar of his brother's motorcycle, the grace of God converted him to the Christian faith. Over the remaining three decades of his life, Lewis became one of the most influential lay theologians in the English-speaking world. His books on moral and theological issues include *The Case for Christianity* (1942), *Christian Behaviour* (1943), *Miracles: A Preliminary Study* (1947), *Mere Christianity* (1952), and *The Four Loves* (1960). One of his earliest and most popular books of Christian apologetics was *The Screwtape Letters* (1942), an epistolary novel in which the demon Screwtape advises his nephew Wormwood on how to manipulate human beings.

Lewis's allegorical novel *The Pilgrim's Regress* (1933), published two years after his conversion, led to an invitation to write a book on pain for the Christian Challenge series. The resulting work of theodicy—*The Problem of Pain* (1940)—established Lewis as an apostle to the intellectuals. At about the same time, he began delivering religious talks to the general public on radio and to soldiers and women's groups in person. *Shadowlands* treats the problem of pain and the reality of faith in Lewis's own life more than a decade later. While demonstrating the strength of his intellectual arguments, it also shows how experience necessarily altered and humanized those arguments at a time of personal crisis.

Strictly speaking, *Shadowlands* is not so much a literal account of Lewis's love affair and brief marriage to Joy Davidman Gresham as it is a historical fiction based on their relationship. What comes across, even to those who knew the principals well, is an emotional truth that transcends the factual inaccuracies.[5] Written by William Nicholson, *Shadowlands* first appeared as a television play in England in 1985 with Joss Ackland as Lewis and Claire Bloom as Joy. It was brought to the stage in New York in 1990 with Nigel Hawthorne and Jane Alexander playing the lead roles. In 1994, Attenborough filmed the story with Anthony Hopkins and Debra Winger.

As the movie opens, we see Lewis living the quiet and sedentary life of an Oxford don. His circle of acquaintances is exclusively male, ranging from an amiable Anglican cleric, Harry Harrington, to a thoroughly skeptical university colleague, Christopher Riley. (Lewis lives with his brother, Warnie, a retired major in the British army.) Gathering frequently for beer at a local pub, this group engages in the friendly banter and intellectual give-and-take one might expect from middle-aged academics. (Only Warnie, who is more interested in drinking than talking, seems out of place.) All that removes Jack from this comfortable life is his voluminous correspondence with readers in both England and America. One of these readers is a Jewish American named Joy Gresham. A married woman and a former Communist, Mrs. Gresham has converted to Christianity and is drawn to Lewis's writing. When she makes a trip to England, she asks if she can meet Lewis for tea at a hotel.

The scene at the hotel highlights the radical outward differences between the two. Whereas Lewis is studious and reserved, Joy is loud and brash. Nevertheless, there seems to be a meeting of the minds. When Joy and her son Douglas are next in Oxford, Jack entertains them at the home he shares with Warnie and invites them to come back for Christmas dinner. It is on that occasion that he takes Joy to a party to meet his male friends. Unlike Lewis, they are not charmed by her forthrightness (which was apparently even more pronounced and offensive in real life). It is during this Christmas visit that Joy reveals that her husband is an alcoholic and a womanizer who wants a divorce so that he can marry another woman. By now, it is evident to the audience—if not to Lewis—that Joy feels more than casual friendship for her British pen pal. But when she and Douglas return to America, he assumes that they are out of his life forever.

Early in the film (it is the first scene in the play), Lewis speaks to a women's group about suffering, particularly about why God permits human beings to experience pain and grief. He concludes that it is to stir us out of our sense of indifference and self-sufficiency. "To put it in another way," he says, "pain is God's megaphone to rouse a deaf world."[6] The second time he gives this talk (before another women's group in London), he sees Joy in the audience and tells her that he has been thinking of her. She is now divorced from her husband and living in England, where she is ostensibly looking for a publisher. Their acquaintance rekindled, Jack tries to make it clear to Joy that he is interested only in her friendship and has no romantic designs upon her. It is therefore surprising that one morning not long thereafter, Jack casually tells Warnie that he has agreed to marry Joy. It is, he assures his brother, only a technical arrangement to extend his citizenship to her so that she can remain in England.

Even though it is a wedding of convenience conducted by a civil magistrate, the marriage brings Jack and Joy closer together. During one outing at Oxford, Christopher Riley notices her wiping something off Lewis's mouth. It is the sort of gesture that a wife is most likely to make. Shortly thereafter, when Jack is showing her his rooms, she comments that people must think that they are unmarried and up to all sorts of mischief, when, in fact, they are married and up to nothing. It is a situation that she obviously finds more amusing (and infinitely more frustrating) than he does. At this point, it looks as if even their friendship may become frayed. Then one day, when she tries to answer the phone at her home in London, she falls over in pain. Jack is on the other end of the line, but Joy is not able to reach the receiver. Not only is this scene fraught with symbolism, it is also a turning point in the story.

## II

Although there is reason to believe that Lewis was romantically involved with Joy Gresham before she fell ill, it is dramatically more effective for him to discover his true feelings for her when it is almost too late for him to do anything about them. Immediately after Joy falls in pain, we see Lewis giving yet another version of his talk on why God lets bad things happen to good people. But now he speaks with less certainty: "Recently a friend of mine, a brave and Christian woman, collapsed in terrible pain. One minute she seemed fit and well. The next minute she was in agony. She is now in hospital, suffering from advanced bone cancer, and almost certainly dying. Why?" After giving his standard explanation for pain, he asks—as if to himself: "But after we have suffered so much, must we still suffer more?"[7] One senses that the answer he usually gives to this question may no longer suffice.

When he sees Joy on what he assumes is her deathbed, Jack realizes that he is about to lose something that he has never really had. In one of the most emotionally wrenching scenes in the film, Jack's well-meaning but feckless friend Harry Harrington tries to console him by reminding him that Joy is only a friend, not family. "Not my wife," Lewis replies. ". . . How could Joy be my wife? I'd have to love her, wouldn't I. I'd have to care more for her than for anyone else in the world. I'd have to suffer the torments of the damned at the prospect of losing her."[8] As Anthony Hopkins delivers this line, both Harrington and the audience realize that he means every word of it.

All that Lewis can do to make amends is to marry Joy in the eyes of God. In the film, this is a simple enough action. In real life and in the stage version of *Shadowlands*, however, there were ecclesiastical impediments. Although the Anglican Church began in part to enable Henry VIII to get rid of one wife and take another, the church later adopted severe strictures against divorce and remarriage. (We are reminded in the play that, at approximately the same time that Jack and Joy were seeking church approval for their nuptials, the archbishop of Canterbury forbade Princess Margaret from marrying a divorcé.)[9] Apparently, Attenborough determined that this was too arcane an issue for a film directed at an international audience in the mid-1990s. So an essentially anonymous priest presides over the bedside ceremony.

In a development that would have seemed wildly improbable were it not true, Joy's condition begins to improve within days of the marriage. Jack takes her and her son home with him and tries to live as if they have all the time in the world. Soon they are on a honeymoon to a particularly bucolic area of Herefordshire that seems to be paradise itself. Joy, however, realizes that she is not cured but only in temporary remission. The time that she and Jack have together is all the more precious because it is so short. Looking ahead to the time when she will be gone, she tells him that "pain, then, is part of the happiness now. That's the deal."[10] Although this may not be a specifically Christian notion, it is a statement of profound wisdom. As Wallace Stevens wrote in his great pagan poem "Sunday Morning," "Death is the mother of beauty."

One minor subplot in the film, which shows how Jack is changing in other aspects of his life during his relationship with Joy, involves his conduct toward a student named Whistler. This seemingly boorish young man sleeps during a class conducted before a handful of students in Lewis's rooms at Oxford. (There are few graver or more obvious insults to a teacher's vanity.) Whistler appears in an even worse light when Lewis observes him stealing a book from a local store. The young man then responds churlishly when Lewis appears at his lodgings and generously offers him a loan. It turns out, however, that Whistler possesses an aesthetic sensitivity that transcends the trivial mind games and witty repartee that characterize so much of life at Oxford. He sleeps in class because he often stays up all night reading. The lad's father, a humble schoolmaster, once told him, "We read to know that we are not alone." The tie-in with the main plot of the film is obvious when one considers the fact that Joy first came to "know" Jack from his writing.

Part of the appeal of the film lies in the seeming incompatibility of Jack and Joy. Although he is neither a prig nor a sissy, he is just stuffy enough to come close to being the Good Good Boy. Joy, in all her brashness, is clearly the Good Bad Girl. There is just enough conflict and chemistry to make for an interesting romance of the sort that sustained many a screwball comedy during the golden days of Hollywood. Over this comic subtext we have the serious theme of religious faith. The combination makes for a truly moving film.

If there is a tragic inevitability to Joy's death, it would have to be attributed to nothing more personal than the way of all flesh. Nothing that she or Jack has done can be said to have affected their fate. Strictly speaking, there is no tragic flaw in either character. But the point of classical tragedy is that what must happen will happen. The only thing that is really contingent is how the hero reacts. This is particularly important for Lewis because of his reputation as a committed Christian who has frequently written and spoken on the subject of suffering. The man who has spent much of his adult life justifying the ways of God to men must now justify them to himself.

The one character who seems to have been pushed out of the picture is Joy's son, Douglas. A fan of Lewis's children's books, he desperately wants to believe in the existence of magic in the world. At the same time, he is leery of discovering that there is none. When he sees an old wardrobe in Lewis's house, he pushes through the coats inside only to find an ordinary back, not an entrance to a magical land. If he takes his mother's recovery as a sign of supernatural intervention, her subsequent death seems to shatter his belief in just about everything. Jack is so consumed with his own grief that Warnie finally has to admonish him to talk to Douglas.

Jack remembers the traumatic experience of his own mother's death, when he was younger than Douglas is now. Although not yet the Christian that he would become, he had prayed for her recovery and then watched her die. When Douglas sees this as evidence that prayer doesn't "work," Lewis must agree with him. This does not mean that Lewis has ceased to pray or ceased to believe in prayer, only that he does not regard it as a magic incantation that forces God to give one whatever one wants. In fact, earlier he has said that he prays not because it changes God but because it changes himself. The change that seems most evident is a doubt in those things which had previously given his life meaning. One is reminded of the stoic in Samuel Johnson's *Rasselas* (1759). One day, the title character hears a stoic preach forbearance in the face of nature and the unavoidable ills of human life. When Prince Rasselas returns later, he finds this man inconsolable over the death of his young daughter. A philosophy that sounded good in the abstract has failed to heal a grieving heart. Is this also true of Jack Lewis's Christian faith?

## III

In the immediate aftermath of Joy's death, Harry Harrington becomes Lewis's foil. In a genuine effort to console his friend, Harry says all of the proper things about faith, only to find that Jack does not respond to these statements as he would have before being blindsided by experience. He is willing to admit that God knows what is best, but he is no longer certain that God cares. He is the creator, and we are but creatures—"rats in the cosmic laboratory." Although he is willing to concede that "the great experiment is for our own good . . . that still makes God the vivisectionist." These are harsh words, which might suggest to some that Lewis did lose his faith. They are, however, dramatically appropriate and historically accurate. As we will recall, Cleanth Brooks held that literature does not *state* ideas; it *tests* ideas.[11]

The seeming contrast between divine goodness and the problem of evil has been one of the most vexing religious conundrums since the time of Job. If Lewis had to go through his own dark night of the soul in dealing with this problem, his faith may have been stronger for that very fact. The available biographical information and his own memoir, *A Grief Observed* (1961), would seem to suggest that that was the case. In his biography of Lewis, A. N. Wilson writes, "Outside the Psalms and the Book of Job, there is not a book quite like *A Grief Observed*, a book by a man who still believes in God but cannot find evidence for his goodness."[12]

Perhaps because this was the most personal book that Lewis ever wrote, he initially chose to publish it under a pseudonym—N. W. Clerk. This enabled the author to be brutally frank without initially revealing his identity. As such, it is less a theological treatise than an account of the anguish of belief. The dualistic religions and philosophies of the world (particularly Manichaeanism) make room for a principle of evil equal to that of good. Christianity, however, asserts that all things work together for good, whether we recognize it as such or not.

If Christ on the cross could feel forsaken by the Father, what of ordinary mortals? In the midst of suffering that is all too real, one is apt to ask, "Where is God?" Pursuing this thought, Lewis writes:

> When you are happy, so happy that you see no sense of needing Him, so happy that you are tempted to feel His claims upon you as an interruption, if you remember yourself and turn to Him with gratitude and praise, you will be—or so it feels—welcomed with open arms. But go to Him when your need is desperate, when all other help is vain, and what do you find? A door slammed in your face, and a sound of bolting and double bolting on the inside. After that, silence.[13]

In a way, it would be more comforting, or at least make more sense, to regard God as a Cosmic Sadist. If He hurts us only for our own good, what use is there to plead for mercy? A cruel man can occasionally be bribed, but a surgeon, who is convinced that he is cutting on us for our own good, will continue to cut regardless of the agony he inflicts. If the tortures we experience "are unnecessary, then there is no God or a bad one. If there is a good God, then these tortures are necessary. For no even moderately good Being could possibly inflict or permit them if they weren't."[14]

If there is a solution to this quandary, it is suggested by the title of the film. The world in which we live is a land of shadows in comparison to the world that is to come. This is the message which Lewis has proclaimed in his theological talks and the one he is in danger of forgetting during his grief. In his last exchange with his stepfather, Douglas asks Jack whether he believes in heaven. When Lewis replies, "Yes," Douglas responds, "I don't believe in heaven," and Lewis says, "That's okay."[15] Lewis, it seems to me, is not telling Douglas that the existence of Heaven is a matter of no significance but rather is responding compassionately to the boy's confusion. His own belief in Heaven, however, makes all the difference.

In *The Four Loves*, Lewis writes:

> For the dream of finding our end, the thing we were made for, in a Heaven of purely human love could not be true unless our faith were wrong. We were made for God. Only by being in some respect like Him, only by being a manifestation of His beauty, lovingkindness, wisdom or goodness has any earthly Beloved excited our love. It is not that we have loved them too much, but that we do not quite understand why we were loving. It is not that we shall be asked to turn from them, so dearly familiar, to a Stranger. When we see the face of God we shall know that we have always known it. He has been a party to, has made, sustained and moved moment by moment within, all our earthly experiences of innocent love. All that was true love within them was, even on earth, far more His than ours, and ours only because His. In Heaven there will be no anguish and no duty of turning away from our earthly Beloveds. First, because we shall have turned already; from the portraits to the original; from the rivulets to the Fountain, from the creatures He made lovable to Love Himself. But secondly, because we shall find them all in Him. By loving Him more than we do them we shall love them more than we now do.
>
> But all that is far away in "the land of the Trinity," not here in exile, in the Weeping Valley.[16]

# THIRTEEN

# COPPERHEAD CINEMA

## ANG LEE'S *RIDE WITH THE DEVIL* (1999) AND MARTIN SCORSESE'S *GANGS OF NEW YORK* (2002)

One would be hard pressed to find a more versatile international filmmaker than Ang Lee. Born in Taiwan in 1954, Lee gained a solid reputation in the early '90s among the art-house crowd for three films in Mandarin with subtitles. After *Pushing Hands* (1992), *The Wedding Banquet* (1993), and *Eat Drink Man Woman* (1994), Lee made his English-language debut in 1995 with an intelligent adaptation of Jane Austen's *Sense and Sensibility.* Perhaps not wanting to be identified exclusively with lavish period comedies, Lee followed this up with *The Ice Storm* (1997), a tale of suburban adultery set in Connecticut in 1973. When he returned to the Mandarin language with *Crouching Tiger, Hidden Dragon* in 2000, Lee was one of the most sought-after directors in Hollywood. He extended his range even further by depicting a mythic comic-book character in *The Hulk* in 2003. More recently, in 2005, he won the Academy Award for his groundbreaking film *Brokeback Mountain.*

In the midst of these very public successes, Lee directed a much-overlooked film called *Ride with the Devil.* After a limited theatrical release around Thanksgiving 1999, this movie was rushed into video production early the following year. Critics who had lavished praise on everything else Lee had ever done found this film to be turgid and reactionary. By the same token, audiences that would never dream of seeing a movie with subtitles made *Ride with the Devil* a cult favorite. Both the negative and the positive reactions to this film seem to have been influenced by viewers' perceptions of the War Between the States.

Although we are accustomed to thinking of that war as taking place in the southeastern United States, many of the pressures that led to secession came from the West. Throughout the 1850s, the extension of slavery into the Western territories was hotly debated by sectional adversaries. If the Kansas-Nebraska Act of 1854 was supposed to effect an amicable compromise, it accomplished just the opposite. According to H. Arthur Scott Trask, the grand theory was that "Kansas, being contiguous to Missouri, would be settled by Southerners and that Nebraska, being contiguous to Iowa, would be settled by Northerners."[1] Unfortunately, the influx of abolitionists from New England to the Midwest deprived Kansas of a Southern majority.

The most infamous of these new settlers was Captain John Brown, whose self-styled Army of the Lord launched a bloody wave of terrorism along Pottawatomie Creek on May 24, 1856. After Kansas was admitted to the Union as a free state in 1860, bands of Kansas Jayhawkers began crossing the border into Missouri, ostensibly to continue Captain Brown's sacred mission. But the actual situation is more accurately described by the narrator of Daniel Woodrell's novel *Woe to Live On* (1987), which was the source for Lee's movie: "Jayhawkers said they raided to free slaves, but mostly they freed horseflesh from riders, furniture from houses, cattle from pastures, precious jewelry from family troves and wives from husbands. Sometimes they had so much plunder niggers were needed to haul it, so they took a few along. This, they said, made them abolitionists."[2]

Missourians, who overwhelmingly sympathized with the Confederacy, launched their own counteroffensive. Although the state did not secede from the Union, Governor Claibourne Fox Jackson refused Lincoln's call for volunteers to invade the South in 1861. As a result, the governor and state legislature were deposed by federalized militia and forced to flee the state capitol to avoid arrest. Several subsequent battles ensued between the Missouri State Guard and federal forces. Only a massive build-up of Union troops and a lack of support from the Confederate government in Richmond kept Missouri in the Union. In an effort to preserve their lives, property, and sacred honor, many rural Missourians either joined the Confederate army or fought their own guerrilla war against the invading forces. *Ride with the Devil* deals with a group of young men who chose the latter alternative.

Although the principal characters in this film are all sympathetic to the Southern cause, they also display a powerful streak of Western independence. The action begins at a wedding, where the story's protagonist, Jacob Roedel (played by Tobey Maguire), makes snide comments about domestic bondage worthy of Washington Irving. Although he is the son of an immigrant, Roedel refuses to flee to St. Louis "to live with the Lincoln-loving Germans." He then witnesses the murder of his best friend's father and the torching of the man's home by marauding Jayhawkers. One year later (in 1862), Roedel, his hair now grown to his shoulders, is riding with a band of Missouri bushwhackers, who give the Yankees and their sympathizers a taste of their own brutality.[3]

From a purely technical standpoint, Lee has achieved a remarkable degree of historical authenticity. The film was shot on location in western Missouri, and the characters look and sound like people from another era. Apparently, Lee put his actors through a kind of grueling boot camp, until they were comfortable handling antique firearms and acclimated to living out of doors. In addition to following the story line of Woodrell's *Woe to Live On*, Lee faithfully captures the language of that book in both vocabulary and cadence. (Reading Woodrell, one is reminded of what Ernest Hemingway meant when he said that all American literature comes from *Huckleberry Finn*.) That Lee should possess an eye for visual poetry is commendable but not surprising. That he should also assiduously maintain an archaic form of vernacular American English makes the film truly distinctive.

A typical example is a speech taken directly from the novel. Here, Jake is explaining to his friend Jack Bull Chiles the advantage to his having had his pinky finger shot off in an earlier skirmish. Anticipating the time when he will be shot by federal troops and hung in a tree to decompose, Jake says: "I would be a glob of rot hanging in a way tall tree, and people would ask, 'Who was that?' Surely, sometime somebody would look up there at my bones and see the tell-tale stump and reply, 'It is nubbin-fingered Jake Roedel.' Then you could go and tell my mother I was clearly murdered and she wouldn't be tortured by uncertain wonders."[4]

Although the violence on both sides of the conflict is unremitting, Lee's sympathies are clearly with the bushwhackers. Roedel and Chiles are initially radicalized by the murder of Chiles's father and become increasingly coarsened by their subsequent experiences. At one point, Jake frees one of their Unionist captives to take a message back to the federal command suggesting an exchange of prisoners. Not only does the man whom Jake has spared fail to deliver his message, he also promptly murders Jake's father, himself a staunch supporter of the Union. It is at this point that Jake realizes the reputation he has acquired as a secessionist and his inability to turn back. From then on, he and his companions become increasingly desperate men.

There is a romantic interlude when the band of bushwhackers hole up on the property of a Southern sympathizer named Evans. Jack Bull (played by Skeet Ulrich) is immediately smitten by the widow of Evans's son, who has joined the Confederate army and been slain. Although their time together is short, Chiles manages to impregnate the young widow (played by the folksinger Jewel) before meeting his own end. During a brief peaceful evening at his home, Evans tells his guests why their noble cause is doomed. Reflecting on what he had seen when his business took him to Lawrence, Kansas, Evans observes:

> As I saw those Northerners build that town, I witnessed the seeds of our destruction being sown. . . . I'm not speakin' of numbers nor even abolitionist trouble-makin'. It was the schoolhouse. Before they built their church even, they built that schoolhouse. And they let in every tailor's son and every farmer's daughter in that country. . . . [T]hey rounded up every pup into that schoolhouse because they fancied that everyone should think and talk the same free-thinkin' way they do with no regard to station, custom, propriety. And that's why they will win. Because they believe that everyone should live and think just like them. And we shall lose because we don't care one way or another how they live. We just worry about ourselves.

When Jack Bull asks him, "Are you sayin', sir, that we fight for nothing?" Evans replies, "Far from it, Mr. Chiles. You fight for everything that we ever had. As did my son. It's just that we don't have it anymore."[5]

Shortly thereafter, Evans is killed by the enemy and his family sent fleeing. With Chiles also dead, Roedel deposits his friend's beloved, Sue Lee, and unborn child with another sympathetic family and joins forces with William Clarke Quantrill's notorious raiders. If the killing of Jack Bull's father has prompted Roedel to join the bushwhackers and the even more treacherous murder of his own father has hardened his resolve, Jake's experience with Quantrill becomes another important turning point in the plot. A sort of Confederate counterpart to John Brown, Quantrill led an expedition that virtually leveled the town of Lawrence on August 21, 1863. Although women were generally spared, one hundred houses were burned and two hundred (mostly unarmed) boys and men were killed.

Quantrill has been so demonized in historical writing and popular culture (including at least ten previous films dating back to 1914) that he is clearly the devil referred to in the film's title. Lee manages to steer a middle course by initially showing how appealing Quantrill could be to young men with the background of Jake Roedel. In a review suggestively titled "A Southern Braveheart," Scott Trask reminds us that Lee has consistently shown the perfidy of the Union terrorists headquartered in Lawrence. He also films the rousing speech that Quantrill delivered prior to the invasion of the town:

> In that speech, Quantrill cited as justification for the raid the death at the hands of federal military authorities of some of the wives and sisters of the Missourians. By imprisoning and killing women, the federals had crossed the line into savagery and were no longer entitled to the protection of the laws of war. Justice requires retribution. In the words of one of the men, "We could stand no more. . . ." Any true Southerner should thrill at the beautifully filmed scenes of Quantrill's men, dressed in navy blue jackets for disguise, riding into Kansas, assembling on Mt. Oread above the town, shedding their jackets, forming into battlelines, and then swooping down with rebel yells on the radical Republican stronghold."[6]

Lee's point is not to justify Quantrill (who was an inexcusable butcher) but to demonstrate the extent of Jake Roedel's commitment and rage. As a result, we have a moral context in which to view Jake's decision to spare some of the truly innocent citizens of Lawrence. In doing so, he alienates several members of his own band, including John Ambrose (played by James Caviezel) and Pitt Mackeson (played by Jonathan Rhys Meyers). By the end of the film, Jake has made a kind of separate peace, in which he is hunted not only by the Unionists but also by some of his own former comrades.

Jake is domesticated and civilized when the farmer who is caring for Sue Lee and child orchestrates a marriage between the two young people. Roedel allows his "bushwhacker curls" to be cut and heads west with his new wife and his adopted child. Before the action ends, however, there is a final encounter with Pitt Mackeson, who declares his intention to return to his hometown of Newport for a drink. Because the town is overrun with Unionists and Mackeson himself is a notorious desperado, this declaration is tantamount to a death wish on the part of a psychotic young man who has nothing left to lose. Andrew O'Hehir is eerily correct in describing Mackeson as "an almost spectral figure of swishy, early-Jagger bigotry and hatred."[7]

From the time they are holed up on the Evanses' property until the final scene of the movie, Jake is increasingly paired with a black bushwhacker named Holt (played by Jeffrey Wright). Although initially little more than the anomalous figure of a black Confederate, Holt takes on a kind of dimension and dignity as the film progresses. Out of personal loyalty to his white friend and former owner George Clyde, Holt has ridden and fought with the pro-Southern forces. When Clyde is killed, however, Holt feels free for the first time and resolves to track down his mother, who is rumored to have been sold into Texas. Before he does so, he sees Jake, Sue Lee, and infant past some dangerous Indian territory. For his own part, Jake's friendship with Holt is another instance of the interethnic male bonding so prevalent in American culture. To his credit, Lee resists any temptation to corrupt this relationship with abolitionist sentimentality.

Although Ang Lee is finally more of an artist than a propagandist, *Ride with the Devil* expresses a definite point of view that is at odds with the pieties of nationalism and assimilation, and even more so with any belief in a global melting pot. One suspects that, as a Taiwanese, Lee might feel an affinity for the Confederate South as a province swallowed up by a larger superpower. In an interview that appears on the official website for *Ride with the Devil*, he says the following:

> I grew up in Taiwan, where older people always complained that kids are becoming Americanized; they don't follow tradition, and so we are losing our culture. As I got the chance to go around a large part of the world with my films, I would hear the same complaints. It seems so much of the world is becoming Americanized. When I read Daniel Woodrell's book *Woe to Live On*, which we based *Ride with the Devil* on, I realized that the American Civil War was, in a way, where it all started. It was where the Yankees won not only territory but, in a sense, a victory for a whole way of life and thinking.[8]

## I

The story told by Martin Scorsese's *Gangs of New York* (2002) takes place in the mid-nineteenth-century tenements of Manhattan, far from the South and without any explicit reference to the cause of the Confederacy. Like *Ride with the Devil*, however, it is a historically and philosophically subversive film that challenges some of our most deeply held political shibboleths. It is finally the sort of artifact that compels either assent or revulsion. The action begins in what appears to be a catacomb, as a man deliberately cuts his face with a razor while his son looks on. He admonishes his son not to wipe the blood from the blade and then affixes a clerical collar to his throat and hangs a medal of St. Michael around his son's neck. In a kind of catechism, the priest asks his son what St. Michael did and says "Good boy!" when the lad answers "He cast Satan out of Heaven." Clutching his son's hand with one hand and raising an iron Celtic cross with the other, the priest proceeds through the cave, eating the sacrament of Holy Communion. As the camera range widens, we see that an entire underground community is preparing for war. The atmosphere grows ever more intense as the camera follows the march to the entrance of the darkened chamber. Then the door is kicked open to a blinding wave of light reflected from the snow outside.[9]

This visually stunning sequence leads to a pitched battle between the band of Irish immigrants led by Priest Vallon (played by Liam Neeson) and a gang of Anglo-Dutch nativists who follow Vallon's archrival Bill the Butcher (played by Daniel Day-Lewis). Cinematically, the battle is like a jigsaw puzzle consisting of a large number of cuts intricately pieced together. The scene is highly impressionistic without losing any of its grounding in reality. At the end of the carnage, Bill kills Vallon as the priest's son looks on. Indicating his fallen foe, Bill announces to his own followers: "Ears and noses are the trophies of the day. But no hand shall touch him. He'll cross over whole. In honor."[10] The year is 1846, and the scene of the battle is the Five Points slum of New York City. It is not until sixteen years later, however, that the primary story of the film begins. Priest Vallon's son Amsterdam (now an adolescent played by Leonardo DiCaprio) is released from the reform facility where he has been raised and educated and heads toward the city to avenge his father's murder.

As the story progresses, we see that civil society, as we have come to know or at least imagine it, scarcely seems to exist in the New York of Five Points. Rival gangs, especially those representing the nativists and the Irish immigrants, inspire fierce tribal loyalty. The one ostensible political organization is the infamous Tammany Hall led by the implacably corrupt Boss Tweed (played by Jim Broadbent). One is apt to come away from this film believing that all of the historical pieties about our being a single nation united by what Augustine called "loved things held in common" is a whitewash of a more sinister national history. Not only was the American nation split into two warring regions, our urban neighborhoods were divided along ethnic lines. In this context, the federal government functions as a kind of vague entity that tries to control men's lives without commanding their respect, much less their affection. At least in offering the new immigrants greetings to their new country and a warm bowl of soup, Tweed's minions are giving the people something they want and need.

In an intriguing essay published in the Fall 2003 issue of *Perspectives on Political Science,* Sean Mattie argues convincingly that *Gangs of New York* is concerned with the difficulty of forging a civil community in the fractious America of the 1860s. The conflict between the nativists and the Irish immigrants is simply a microcosm of the tribal animosities afflicting the nation at large. Mattie errs, however, in seeing the Unionist philosophy of Abraham Lincoln as the solution to these animosities. If anything, the viewer of Scorsese's film finds himself admiring the anachronistic heroism of the rival gangs and seeing in their primitive sense of honor a quality conspicuously lacking in the overly civilized mass society that America has become in the ensuing 140 years.

This is not to say that Scorsese idealizes the savage violence and ethnic prejudices of the nativists and immigrants. To return to the state of affairs that existed in Five Points at that time would be almost as problematic as returning to the world of the *Iliad* or *Beowulf*. But at least these people knew who they were and what they believed in, and they were willing to fight and die to preserve a valued way of life. (Their preferred weapons are "bricks, bats, axes, knives, and fists. No pistols.") Bill the Butcher believes that citizenship is conferred not by a piece of paper but by a shared experience that is purchased with blood. When Tweed brags about the number of immigrants he can bring to the polls, Bill replies: "My father gave his life makin' this country what it is. Murdered with all his men, on the twenty-fifth of July, Anno Domini 1814. Now you want me to befoul his legacy by givin' this country over to them what's had no hand in fighting for it?"[11]

Although he has killed Priest Vallon, Bill admires him because he, too, fought for an inherited way of life. In a moment of reflection, Bill tells Amsterdam:

> The priest and me lived by the same principles. It was only faith that divided us. He gave me this, you know: [The scar on his face] It was the finest beating I ever took. My face was pulp. My guts was pierced. My ribs was swimmin'. But when he came to kill me, I couldn't look him in the eye. He spared me, because he wanted me to live in shame. This was a great man. So I cut out the eye that looked away, and sent it to him, wrapped in blue paper. I would have cut them both out if I could have fought him blind. Then I rose back up with full heart and buried him in his own blood.[12]

In contrast, Lincoln can offer only an army of conscripts, which any man of even moderate means can buy his way out of.

Mattie argues, quite unconvincingly, that "the film seems to hold that the [Civil] war is meaningful by giving the following speech to the priest who in 1862 sends Amsterdam from his orphanage into society: 'You go forth to a country torn apart by strife. . . . Lend your hand to the work that yet remains, that this war may end, and the plague of slavery that brought this conflagration down upon us, vanish forever from the earth.'" In a footnote, Mattie even contends that "in its themes and tone, this exhortation resembles, remarkably, Lincoln's second inaugural address." If Scorsese intended a parallel between this cleric and Lincoln, however, it was surely to denigrate Lincoln rather than to ennoble the cleric. This clergyman is a pompous Calvinist; he resembles the Puritans who blessed the slave market and then called for abolition in Griffith's *The Birth of a Nation*. After having been raised by this man, Amsterdam can hardly wait to toss the Bible he gives him into the river. In a voice-over, Amsterdam says, "The Five Points hadn't changed much since I was eight years old. . . . Every year the reformers came. And every year the Points got worse." In the next scene, one such reformer, the Reverend Raleigh, exhibits a beggar girl in an apparent plea for financial support. Even as Raleigh ignores her upturned hand, a policeman displaces a squatter, saying, "Move! The Reverend wants you out of here."[13]

In a stage production of *Uncle Tom's Cabin* in a theatre in the Bowery, an actor portrays Abraham Lincoln, suspended like an angel over the action with his arms outstretched, "as if crucified." While the figure of Lincoln exhorts the actors below ("Mr. Legree, lay down your whip! Miss Eliza, join hands with Mr. Shelby! And Topsy, dear little Topsy, cradle Uncle Tom's head"), Bill and Amsterdam both hurl catcalls and rotten fruit at the stage. As Uncle Tom stirs to life, one native screams, "Leave the nigger dead!" while Bill shouts, "Down with the Union!" Anyone laboring under the assumption that the North was united in a holy crusade to free the slaves, while worshipping Lincoln next to God himself, would find that delusion sorely tried by *Gangs of New York*.[14]

The climax of the film shows federal soldiers invading an American city and randomly shooting civilians. The setting, however, is not Atlanta but New York City. The definitive confrontation between the natives and the immigrants is interrupted by the infamous draft riots of July 1863. Contrary to the allegations of some reviewers, Scorsese does not romanticize the rioters or disguise the racist brutality they inflicted on defenseless blacks. It was an ugly chapter in American history but an instructive one as well. The War Between the States was a conflict over class as well as race. If the poor foot soldiers from the South often saw the dispute as a rich man's war and a poor man's fight, working-class Northern whites (native and immigrant) were largely indifferent to the plight of Southern blacks and resentful that they were being used as cannon fodder in Lincoln's jihad to preserve the Union.

In an extended discussion of the film in the May–June 2003 issue of *Social Education*, Benjamin Justice condemns Scorsese for emphasizing the class aspects of the draft riots at the expense of their racial dimension.[15] The problem, it seems to me, is that the black victims of the riots became pawns in what was essentially a class conflict. It may be that, from a strictly historical standpoint, the oppressed Irish immigrants are treated too favorably in the film. Leonardo DiCaprio, as Amsterdam Vallon, certainly lacks the menace that Daniel Day-Lewis brings to his portrayal of Bill the Butcher. But Day-Lewis's screen presence is such that Bill is a character to be respected, if not admired. There are certainly enough boobs and scoundrels among the rest of the Irish to disabuse anyone of the notion that oppression produces virtue. By the same token, one could admit that the poor Southern whites who join the Ku Klux Klan have legitimate grievances against the ruling elite without justifying their making blacks the targets of their frustration.

Scorsese's presentation of the riots seems designed to appeal to a kind of populist sentiment. The most clearly delineated victims of the mob are the aristocratic Schermerhorns, who are entertaining Boss Tweed, the mayor, and Horace Greeley. Right before the rioters rush his mansion, Schermerhorn quotes Tweed approvingly: "You can always hire one half of the poor to kill the other half." When Greeley says, "I have heard they are going from door to door in the Five Points asking those who wish to see further rioting to put lighted candles in the window. Irish, Pole, Germans," Schermerhorn smugly replies: "Ah, Mr. Greeley. The city is not mad. And I will prophesy a very dark night."[16] Only the sort of person who joins Edmund Burke in weeping for Marie Antoinette regrets the rock that immediately comes crashing through this prig's window. But we must remember that the same hand that threw the rock might have just gotten through lynching a freedman. What is a right-thinking liberal to do but excoriate Martin Scorsese for "whitewashing history"?

Those who pronounce a blanket condemnation on the "draft riots" are committing the opposite error of those who sentimentalize the disturbances. The events of July 13–17, 1863, included acts of looting, plunder, and murder deplored by all decent people. But so did the race riots that took place in America's cities a century later. By their very nature, popular uprisings are not tightly controlled, disciplined campaigns. It would nevertheless be a mistake to deny the legitimacy of the grievances that prompted opposition to the draft of the 1860s, just as it would be to accuse the ghetto dwellers of the 1960s of doing nothing but fouling their own nest. Many of the draft protests were peaceful, especially those led by cartman Thomas Fitzsimmons, who intended no more than a one-day "strike" against conscription.[17] In some cases, demonstrators helped protect the safety and property of persons targeted by those thugs who took advantage of the general disorder. And the troops that put down the riots rarely made distinctions between criminals and those who were merely exercising their First Amendment rights—assuming that the First Amendment even existed in Lincoln's America.

What is less well known is the fact that a class of respectable politicians and businessmen were themselves unenthusiastic about the policies of the national administration. Prior to the firing on Fort Sumter, at least, the merchants of New York shared the free-trade position championed by the South. They did not want to see the Port of New York isolated in a high-tariff North while Southern ports such as the one in Charleston became centers of international commerce. In 1860, New York mayor Fernando Wood even advocated that the city secede from the Union as a free-trade republic. President James Buchanan took the threat seriously enough to try to convince James Gordon Bennett, editor of the *New York Herald*, of the advisability of New York's remaining in the Union.

In a letter he wrote in 1860 to a Southern businessman, the prominent New York merchant August Belmont observed:

> If we did only look to our own material interests and those of our city, we should not deplore the dissolution of the Union. New-York, in such a catastrophe, would

> cut loose from the Puritanical East and her protective Tariff, and without linking her fortunes with our kind but somewhat exacting Southern friends, she would open her magnificent port to the commerce of the world. What Venice was once on the sluggish lagoons of the small Adriatic, New-York would ere long become to the two hemispheres, proudly resting on the bosom of the broad Atlantic, and I am afraid sadly interfering with the brilliant but fallacious hopes of the Palmetto and Crescent cities.

It was only when it became apparent that secession could not be accomplished short of war that such sentiment began to subside in New York.[18]

If *Gangs of New York* takes liberties with the historical record, it tells a mythic or metahistorical truth. To be sure, society cannot flourish in an atmosphere of perpetual strife among parochial interests. A spirit of compromise and respect for the common good are supremely civilized virtues. But civil society is also impossible when genuine group interests and tribal loyalties are ignored in the interest of ideology. One can surely admit this truth without endorsing a state of unending conflict between the forces of Bill the Butcher and Priest Vallon. If audiences instinctively side with the rioters against the federal troops, it is because they find totalitarianism more loathsome than anarchy. The solution is not to choose either alternative but to resent the sort of fanaticism that makes them the only options.

# FOURTEEN

# THE CAUSE OF US ALL

## RONALD F. MAXWELL'S *GETTYSBURG* (1993) AND *GODS AND GENERALS* (2003)

Ronald F. Maxwell has never been the darling of film critics. Unlike the pictures of Martin Scorsese and Ang Lee, Maxwell's work has often been greeted with lukewarm to hostile reviews. This is largely because his two most important films are "Civil War epics." Although there was a time when such movies were warmly received, they are now as aesthetically unfashionable in Hollywood as historical novels in highbrow literary circles. Part of the problem has to do with length. Each of Maxwell's two epics—*Gettysburg* (1993) and *Gods and Generals* (2003)—runs about four hours, even after being cut for theatrical release. "At four hours and fifteen minutes, *Gettysburg* is believed to be the second-longest American film ever made after Erich von Stroheim's *Greed*, a silent from 1924."[1]

The sort of scope that was seen as breathtaking when *The Birth of a Nation* was filmed in 1915 and still impressive when *Gone With the Wind* was produced in 1939 had become unacceptable by the 1990s. Widescreen spectaculars were no longer considered the novelty they were as recently as the 1950s and could generally be tolerated only if made by British directors about foreigners as exotic as Lawrence of Arabia or Mahatma Gandhi. The Civil War, unfortunately, had already been done. Anyone seeking to do yet another pop version of the American *Iliad* should think in terms of a TV miniseries. A small-screen version of Alex Haley's *Roots* had captivated the nation in 1977, and an even more protracted version of John Jakes's *North and South* had done well in 1985. Even Ken Burns's eleven-hour documentary, *The Civil War*, had generated surprisingly large audiences and considerable critical acclaim for PBS in 1989.

Fifteen years after he began the screenplay for *Gettysburg*—and after mortgaging his house to hold on to the screen rights to the movie's source, Michael Shaara's Pulitzer Prize–winning novel, *The Killer Angels* (1974)—Maxwell appeared to be destined for the miniseries ghetto when Ted Turner decided that the film should get some theatrical exposure before becoming a staple on TNT. Turner should be congratulated for this decision; the intensity of those three days that changed the world in July 1863 demands something akin to Aristotle's unity of time. In our own era, sitting through a four-hour movie seems like the least that a serious director might expect of his audience.

One of the reasons that *Gettysburg* is so long is that Maxwell is not content simply to show us what went on during that pivotal battle; he also delves into the characters of several of the men who made the fight, so that we will know what motivated them and what their sacrifice might mean for those of us who live in the world they made. For that reason, *Gettysburg* reminds us less of a potboiler such as *North and South* than it does of Edward Zwick's *Glory* (1989), one of the few Civil War epics (202 minutes) that actually did succeed in contemporary Hollywood. Because *Glory* depicts the fate of an all-black unit in the Union army, it is as much a racial film as it is a historical fiction. But, like all good historical fictions, it gives us a usable past rather than mere pageantry. In scenes that some reviewers found "overlong and lethargic," *Gettysburg* does much the same thing.[2]

In addition to its obvious cinematic excellence, *Glory* had the advantage of presenting a politically fashionable point of view. *Gettysburg*, like Shaara's novel before it, is much more evenhanded. To be sure, those who insist on seeing the Union effort as a crusade to free the slaves will find that point of view compellingly represented by Joshua Lawrence Chamberlain of Maine. In an effort to persuade some deserters to rejoin the fight, Chamberlain (as played brilliantly by Jeff Daniels) articulates some eloquent and noble sentiments. In a speech taken almost word for word from *The Killer Angels*, he says:

> This regiment was formed last fall back in Maine. There was a thousand of us then. There's not three hundred of us now. . . . Some of us volunteered to fight for the Union. Some came in mainly because we were bored at home and this looked like it might be fun. Some came because we were afraid not to. Many of us came . . . [in original] because it was the right thing to do. All of us have seen men die. Most of us never saw a black man back home. We think on that too. But freedom . . . [in original] is not just a word. . . . This is a different kind of army. If you look at history you'll see men fight for pay, or women, or some other kind of loot. They fight for land, or because a king makes them, or just because they like killing. But we're here for something new. . . . This hasn't happened much in the history of the world. We're an army out to set other men free.[3]

Had Maxwell been content to make a movie exclusively about Chamberlain, the film could have been filled with such righteous sentiments; its climax would probably have been Chamberlain's valorous stand in a pivotal skirmish on the second day of the battle; and it certainly would have been shorter. As it is, the presentation of Chamberlain as the best that the Union has to offer is actually made more credible by equally sympathetic portrayals of Confederate officers, who were fighting with just as much commitment and just as much heroism for other values. Even in the good old days when Hollywood depicted white Southerners in a generally benign light, the emphasis was almost always on such superficial matters as their flamboyant personalities. Maxwell's *Gettysburg* may be the first major picture since *The Birth of a Nation* to pay serious attention to Southern ideology. And, as a film of ideas, *Gettysburg* is far more likely to be taken seriously by modern audiences, who are understandably put off by the racist histrionics of D. W. Griffith.

Not long after Colonel Chamberlain delivers his moving oration to the deserters, his younger brother Tom (played by C. Thomas Howell) strikes up a conversation with some prisoners from Tennessee. (The scene begins with a couple of Yankee fiddlers playing "My Old Kentucky Home.") After Tom asks the prisoners where they are from, he admits that he has never been to Tennessee. "I reckon I never been to Maine, neither," one of the prisoners replies. "I don't mean no disrespect to you fighting men," Tom continues, "but sometimes I can't help but figure why are you fighting this war?" The prisoner turns the question around and asks Tom, "Why are you fighting it?" The response is automatic: "To free the slaves, of course. And to preserve the Union." To this, the prisoner replies: "I don't know about other folk, but I ain't fighting for no darkies one way or the other. I'm fighting for my rhats. That's what we're all fighting for." "For your what?" Tom asks. "For our rhats."[4]

The fact that Tom Chamberlain has such difficulty understanding the Tennessean's drawl is eloquently symbolic. The prisoner is correct: both sides are indeed fighting for their rights, but neither understands how that concept is defined by the other. The prisoner proceeds to state his case as follows: "Why is it you folks can't just live the way you want to live and let us live the way we do? 'Live and let live,' I hear some folks say. Be a might less fuss and bother if more folks took it to heart." After both young Chamberlain and the prisoner conclude that they have seen too much of the waste of war, the Tennessean salutes his captor and says, "See you in Hell, Billy Yank." To which Tom Chamberlain replies, "See you in Hell, Johnny Reb."

During the course of the film, the idealistic Colonel Chamberlain strikes up a warm friendship with an Irish enlisted man. One of the few fictional characters in the movie, Buster Kilrain (played by Kevin Conway) brings a realistic lower-class perspective to the issues at the heart of the conflict. Rather than claiming any special knowledge or wisdom, Buster frankly admits, "I can't understand anyone south of Mason-Dixon, Rebs or darkies." (Although the literal reference is to spoken accents, the larger implications are as clear here as they were in the earlier encounter between Tom Chamberlain and the Southern prisoners.) Although Buster and the colonel are both on the same side, they have fundamentally different views of human nature, as is reflected in the following exchange:

> "We used to have visitors from the South before the war. They were always very polite, academic, you understand. We stayed off the question of slavery out of courtesy. But toward the end there was no getting away from it. And yet, I could never understand,

> I don't now. I don't know why. And they fight so well. Tell me something, Buster. What do you think of Negroes?"
>
> "Well, if you mean the race, I don't really know. This is not a thing to be ashamed of. The thing is, you cannot judge a race. Any man who judges by the group is a pea-wit. You take men one at a time."
>
> "To me, there never was any difference."
>
> "None at all?"
>
> "None at all. Of course, I haven't known that many freedmen, but those I knew in Bangor, Portland—you look in the eye, there was a man. There was a 'divine spark,' as my mother used to call it. That is all there is to it. Races are men. 'What a piece of work is man. How infinite in faculties and form, and movement, how express and admirable. In action like an angel.'"

As much as he admires the colonel, Buster has seen too much of men at their worst to accept at face value the babbling of Shakespeare's mad prince:

> "Well, if he's an angel, all right then, but he damn well must be a killer angel. Colonel, darling, you're a lovely man. I see a vast difference between us, yet I admire you, lad. You're an idealist, praise be. The truth is, Colonel, there is no 'divine spark.' There's many a man alive no more of value than a dead dog. Believe me. When you've seen them hang each other the way I have back in the Old Country. Equality? What I'm fighting for is the right to prove I'm a better man than many of them. Where have you seen this 'divine spark' in operation, Colonel? Where have you noted this magnificent equality? No two things on earth are equal or have an equal chance. Not a leaf, not a tree. There's many a man worse than me and some better, but I don't think that race and country matters a damn. What matters, Colonel, is justice. Which is why I'm here. I'll be treated as I deserve, not as my father deserved. I'm Kilrain, and damn all gentlemen. There is only one aristocracy, and that is right here. [Points to his head] And that is why we've got to win this war."

Buster is arguing a familiar position—that the War Between the States was, at one level, a class conflict between the aristocratic South and the democratic North. If Chamberlain's vision amounts to a kind of *noblesse oblige*, the proletarian Buster believes in a society where rank and privilege are justified by individual merit.

Both Maxwell's film and the novel on which it is based give considerable credence to the notion that the Confederate cause, to the extent that it was defined by Virginians, was more European than American. An important observer in both *Gettysburg* and *The Killer Angels* is Lieutenant Colonel Arthur Lyon Fremantle, a former officer in Queen Victoria's Coldstream Guards. He is with the Confederates throughout the three days of battle and seems to share their interests, their sensibilities, and their beliefs. There is even a suggestion that an independent South might actually have found a way to rejoin the British commonwealth. Fremantle and, to a lesser extent, Buster Kilrain serve as useful devices for allowing the combatants to articulate their points of view for our benefit.

Perhaps because the Yankee position has been privileged in our history books, Maxwell gives the Confederates more than ample opportunity to make their case. In a campfire conversation on the evening of July 1, George Pickett (played by Stephen Lang) offers Fremantle a very simple analogy: "Colonel, think on it now. Suppose that we all joined a club. After a time, several of the members began to intrude themselves into our private lives, our home lives. Began telling us what we could and couldn't do. Well, then, wouldn't any one of us have the right to resign? I mean just resign. That's what we did. That's what I did, and now these people are telling us that we don't have that right." At no point does any Southerner in the film even suggest that the war is being fought over slavery. In fact, Longstreet regrets that the South was not sagacious enough to free the slaves before firing on Fort Sumter. This would have denied the Yankees any pretense to the moral high ground and might have persuaded the British to recognize the Confederacy.

In addition to different views of government, the two sides have different conceptions of the nature of man. If Chamberlain believes in human equality because we all possess the "divine spark," the Confederates believe in inequality because that conforms to their empirical observation. On the night between the second and third days of battle, several of the Confederate officers are discussing the writings of Charles Darwin. The only one who does not put at least some stock in the theory of evolution is Pickett. "I intend to lay this matter to rest for once and for all time," he declares. "Perhaps there are those among you who think that you are descended from an ape. I suppose it's possible there are those of you who believe that I am descended from an ape, but I challenge the man to step forward who believes that General Lee is descended from an ape."

In Shaara's novel, Longstreet recalls this conversation, but the principals are unidentified. Maxwell, it seems to me, is making several points by dramatizing the discussion and giving Pickett the punch line. Pickett wins the argument because Lee's natural superiority is widely recognized by his men. None of them thinks himself equal to Lee, and many continue to fight against formidable odds because they consider him to be almost a god (or at least a killer angel). This is a function of natural grace and breeding that is as far removed from Kilrain's immigrant dream of achieved merit as it is from Chamberlain's more metaphysical vision. Ironically, Pickett himself proves to be a touchstone against which to measure Darwin's reliability. His gallant and doomed charge on the third day of battle has little to do with the natural instinct for self-preservation. In the closing minutes of the film, Lee tells a dazed Pickett: "General, you must look to your Division." To which Pickett replies: "General Lee, I have no Division." Bereft of his men, George Pickett has lost his identity as a commander. He is like a dinosaur fallen in the struggle for survival.

The length of this film allows Maxwell to give us portraits of several individuals and their reasons for fighting. It also allows for a clear exposition of military strategy. Finally, the participation of well over five thousand historical reenactors, along with cinematographer Kees van Oostrum's use of a wide-lens camera, makes the battle scenes among the most authentic ever captured on film. One weakness of the movie, however, is its interpretation of the battle itself.

In his commentary on the DVD version of *Gettysburg*, Maxwell concedes that he may have relied too heavily on Michael Shaara's novel, which itself relied heavily on the postwar writings of Joshua Lawrence Chamberlain and James Longstreet. By seeing the Union victory from the perspective of a single participant, who was a particularly gifted writer, we are apt to get an unbalanced view of what happened. We do not need to accuse Chamberlain of deliberately inflating his own role in the battle to realize that any man's recollections will be colored by his own experience, especially when those recollections are recorded years later. The case of Longstreet raises more serious difficulties.

In praising Martin Sheen's superb portrayal of Robert E. Lee, Richard Schickel writes, "In our folklore (and in the hearts of his troops) the Confederate leader has been granted near saintly status. Sheen gives us the dark side of the holy warrior, a man of courtly manners who is possessed by a vision of a vainglorious, straight-ahead assault on the enemy's center—the vision that produced Pickett's disastrous charge. It was a course of action that defied reason (personified here by General James Longstreet)." This, of course, is Longstreet's self-serving interpretation of the battle, which seems confirmed by the fact that, at the end of both the book and the film, Lee graciously assumes blame for the Confederate defeat.[5]

It is more plausible, however, that the Confederacy erred in not being more aggressive on the first two days of the conflict. Because Jeb Stuart had not come back soon enough from a scouting expedition, Lee did not know the full strength of the enemy. Had his more cautious underlings showed their commander's resolve, the Virginians might have gained the high ground on either of the first two days. Having failed in his assault on both flanks, Lee logically concluded that the enemy was weakest in the middle. (This was standard Napoleonic reasoning.) The problem was that the only possible attack on the middle was over more than a mile of open farmland. Even that might have succeeded had the Southern artillery coverage been more adequate. (Such coverage was essential because the invention of the minie ball a few years earlier had made it possible for a defensive force to fire upon its attackers from a much greater distance than ever before.) Because everything that could go wrong did, the more timid Longstreet felt himself vindicated. And he wrote his memoirs, while Lee did not.

Although Ronald Maxwell's picture tells us much about the specific events that transpired on July 1–3, 1863, no film (not even one lasting more than four hours) can adequately place those events in the context of the larger war, much less of American history itself. If more recent occurrences have caused the significance of this epic battle to fade from the American consciousness, a movie such as *Gettysburg* is a good first step toward restoring our collective memory. Sensing that this was indeed only the beginning of a larger effort, Maxwell soon announced plans for two subsequent films—one leading to the conflict in Pennsylvania, the other covering the end of the war. When the first of these opened in February 2003, it became yet another battleground in a culture war that continues to rage nearly 140 years into Reconstruction.

## I

The reaction of elite critics to Maxwell's *Gods and Generals* is typified by Christopher Sharrett's extended review in the Summer 2003 issue of *Cineaste*. According to Sharrett: "The negative critical and public receptions of media mogul Ted Turner's new Civil War production *Gods and Generals* have been of such unanimity—denouncing the film as clumsy, ponderous, incompetent—that it might seem not very sensible to spend time giving this film serious evaluation, especially since it faded after a few weeks at the muliplexes." But a critic's gotta do what a critic's gotta do. So Sharrett informs us that "*Gods and Generals* says much about the reactionary, racist slant on the American past that saturates large sectors of 'liberal' mass media, in an era of neoconservative retrenchment."[6] The smug hostility of these opening sentences (and indeed of the essay that follows) actually says less about the merits and limitations of Maxwell's film than it does about the received view of history that the film challenges.

To begin with, when Sharrett asserts as fact that just about everybody found *Gods and Generals* to be clumsy, ponderous, and incompetent, he simply reveals his own ignorance. When the film critic Stephen Holden made a similar comment in the *New York Times*, Maxwell immediately cited twenty-three reputable critics who gave the film rave reviews. (Without even researching the question, I can think of half a dozen others to add to the list.) Leonard Maltin, who is not usually thought of as a shill for the Old Confederacy or the New Right, said: "Writer-director Ron Maxwell paints an incredibly vivid portrait of such legendary men as Stonewall Jackson and Robert E. Lee. More than that we get a real sense of life in those troubled times, the strategy and mechanics of battle, as well as the tragedy of pitting brother against brother. . . . I'm awfully glad I saw it, and if you have a taste for history, you should too."[7] The complaint that *Gods and Generals* was boring because it dealt with the concerns of a bunch of old dead white guys who lived before our time sounds like nothing so much as the course evaluations filled out by students going through Ritalin withdrawal. Maxwell's movie may not have had mass box-office appeal, but it boasted enough of a niche audience for the DVD to become the number-one seller in North America as soon as it was released. Maxwell's real sin was not that he made a long movie that asked its audience to think but rather the likelihood that they would think the wrong thoughts.

The ideological inclusiveness of *Gettysburg* was bad enough in a culture that has been told that the Confederates were a bunch of madmen trying to overthrow the American government in order to keep their slaves. This new film went several steps farther to humanize the madmen and to deemphasize slavery. It all begins with an in-your-face Confederate flag across the screen during the opening credits, while the haunting voice of Mary Fahl sings the lovely theme song, "Going Home." Then we read the film's defiant epigraph, from George Eliot's *Daniel Deronda* (1876):

> A human life, I think, should be well rooted in some spot of native land, where it may get the love of tender kinship for the face of the earth, for the labours men go forth to, for the sounds and accents that haunt it, for whatever will give that early home a familiar unmistakable difference amidst the future widening of knowledge. The best introduction to astronomy is to think of the nightly heavens as a little lot of stars belonging to one's own homestead.[8]

What sounds like a universal human truth (articulated by one of the world's great novelists) takes on specific dramatic significance in the next scene, when Colonel Robert E. Lee (played to perfection by Robert Duvall) refuses a promotion to general and the opportunity to lead the Union troops. As a career military man, he is passing up the chance of a lifetime. But in Lee's eyes, Lincoln is making war on his own countrymen. Even as the offer is being made, the legislature of

Virginia is voting on a resolution of secession. The prospect that he might be called upon to lead federal troops against his fellow Virginians is unthinkable to Lee. Philosophically, he is opposed to both slavery and secession, but his greatest *patriotic* loyalty is to his home. One is shocked, though not surprised, that Christopher Sharrett finds a scene of such moral and historical significance to be "stilted" and lacking in "dramatic tension."

Later on in the film, Lee explains to a subordinate (Major Walter Taylor) the source of his attachment to Virginia. When Taylor observes that they are close to where George Washington is rumored to have thrown a silver dollar across the Rappahannock River and to have "cut down that cherry tree," Lee replies:

> That may be so, Mister Taylor. But it has an even greater significance for me. It's where I met my wife. . . . It's something these Yankees do not understand, will never understand. Rivers, hills, valleys, fields, even towns: to those people they're just markings on a map from the war office in Washington. To us they're birthplaces and burial grounds, they're battlefields where our ancestors fought. They're places where we learned to walk, to talk, to pray. They're places where we made friendships and fell in love. . . . They're the incarnation of all our memories and all that we are.[9]

After Virginia responds to Lincoln's aggression with a vote to secede from the Union, the focus shifts to a classroom at the Virginia Military Institute, where a beleaguered professor tries unsuccessfully to teach his students some basic principles of warfare. That teacher is Thomas Jonathan Jackson, a colonel in the Virginia militia. From this point on, *Gods and Generals* largely becomes Jackson's story. If *Gettysburg* was more of an ensemble effort, its prequel is dominated by Stephen Lang's overpowering performance as one of the most revered and controversial figures in American history. Much of the negative reaction to Maxwell's film stems from the fact that its portrayal of Jackson is both favorable and historically accurate. It would have been easy to paint a heroic but one-dimensional portrait of Jackson. Given today's climate of opinion, it would have been easier still to present him as a mentally unbalanced religious fanatic. To give a sympathetic and accurate depiction of Jackson *as he actually was* is to run afoul of the thought police.

The two aspects of the film that trouble most of its ideological detractors are its treatments of race and religion. The charge is that Maxwell "whitewashes" the first and overemphasizes the second. In a truly extraordinary exercise in sophistry published in the February 25, 2003, issue of *National Review Online*, the military historian Mackubin Thomas Owens argues that the factual accuracy of a historical film is less important than its fidelity to a "deeper truth." As an example, he cites *Glory*, which is filled with inaccuracies both major and minor, but which leaves us with the stirring image of heroic black soldiers fighting for their freedom. ("By inaccurately depicting the 54th as a regiment of former slaves," Owens writes, "*Glory* reveals the deeper truth that blacks in general were not the natural slaves that Southerners believed them to be and that abolitionists feared they might be.")[10] Not surprisingly, Owens gives *Gods and Generals* high marks for getting the little things right while failing to convey the "deeper truth" that white Southerners were fighting not for states' rights but for the preservation of slavery. Consequently, he regards all this talk of defending one's homeland from invasion as just diversionary blather.

Owens, like so many of Maxwell's critics, is disturbed by what he considers the dishonesty of a scene depicting Stonewall Jackson praying with his black cook Jim Lewis (played by Frankie Faison). Both Jackson and Lewis are devout Christians and loyal sons of Virginia. To his credit, Owens does not express surprise that Lewis might respect Jackson as a man or that many Southern blacks might have at least mixed feelings about the imminent destruction of the only home they have ever known. What he utterly rejects is Jackson's suggestion to Lewis that blacks might be enlisted in the Confederate army as a condition for their freedom. It is true that the Confederate Congress did authorize precisely such a policy in March 1865, but it is anachronistic to suggest that this expedient was seriously considered as early as December 1862, which is the date of the scene in question. Here, Owens may have his facts right while missing a "deeper truth" that he finds philosophically unpalatable.

The future of slavery was debated in the South even before the war, and slaves did fight in the Confederate army. Would Jackson, who died in 1863, have agreed to make black soldiers free men? There is no solid evidence one way or the other. We do know that Jackson sponsored a black Sunday School in Lexington, Virginia, and helped teach slaves to read. Moreover, he seemed to lack the white supremacist ideology that Owens cites in the statements of other Southern leaders. What is perhaps more to the point is the fact that this scene pays full homage to the slave's desire for freedom. Listen in particular to the way in which Lewis uses his petition to God to speak indirectly to Jackson:

> Jackson (praying softly aloud): Lord, where you sit you can see the great distance that separates our Southern men from their wives and children. We pray that you watch over our families. Lord, I ask you to watch over Jim's family, over his friends, over his loved ones, wherever they may be.
>
> Jim Lewis (picking up with the prayer): L'od, I knows you sees into da heart of all men jes like you sees into da heart of ol' Jim Lewis. An Lo'd, I knows deres no lyin' or deceitfulness can hide from you. You find out de truth in de bottom of de deepest pit a darkness. Dy be no hidin from your truth an' your ever watchful eye.
>
> Jackson: Amen.
>
> Jim Lewis: How is it, Lo'd, can you 'splain sumpin' to dis ol' Virginy man? How is it a good Christian man like some folks I know can tolerate dey black brothers in bondage? How is it, Lo'd, dat dey don't jes break dem chains! How is it, Lo'd, my heart is open and achin' and I wants to know![11]

At least to modern ears, Jim Lewis and the antislavery position would seem to have the better of the implied argument. (It is only after this exchange that Jackson mentions the prospect of conditional emancipation.) But apparently for some deeper historians, that fact doesn't count unless the white Southerner is made into a cardboard villain in the process.

The other significant black character in the film is Martha, who is maid to the Beale family of Fredericksburg. When her owners flee ahead of marauding Yankee troops, Martha (played by Donzaleigh Abernathy, daughter of Ralph) insists on staying behind to protect the house. To the Federal looters approaching the door of the house,

Martha asks, "Can I be of service to you fine Northern gentlemen?" When they ask if it is her master's place, she tells them that it is hers, and they leave. But after the battle, when the Yankees requisition the house for a hospital, Martha welcomes them in and helps comfort the wounded by reading from the book of Esther. "Esther knew that it was not enough to save herself," Martha observes. "That she must save her people as well. . . . I love the folks you have chased out of this house. I have known them all my life. The Beales are good people. I was born a slave. My own children were born as slaves. Whatever you are doing here . . . whatever must be done for my children to grow up in freedom in a free country—may God bless you for it. Heaven help me, but may God bless you all."[12] Thus presented, Martha seems a far more credible character than if she were simply waiting for the first opportunity to slit her mistress's throat.

According to Owens, "the deeper truth of *Gods and Generals* seems to be that the war was the [S]outh's 'second war of independence' as Robert Duvall's Robert E. Lee describes the forthcoming conflict" when he says his farewell to the First Virginia Brigade. There is, of course, a less covert reason why Maxwell has Lee, Jackson, and other white Southerners assert this position. They actually believed it! Those members of the audience who persist in thinking that the war was fought over slavery will again find an eloquent spokesman for that belief in Joshua Lawrence Chamberlain (played again by Jeff Daniels). Shortly before the Battle of Chancellorsville, Chamberlain tells his brother Tom (played again by C. Thomas Howell) that "freeing the slaves wasn't a war aim when all this began. But war changes things. Sorts things out. Things get clarified." If this was Chamberlain's actual view at the time, it was one not widely shared in the Union army. Federal troops regularly returned fugitive slaves to their masters. As we know, John C. Fremont caught hell from Lincoln for practicing a little unauthorized emancipation in Missouri. So one might argue that Maxwell is using a tendentious portrayal of Chamberlain to whitewash Yankee indifference to slavery. And he is none too subtle in the effort.

A bit later in his homily to Tom, Brother Lawrence observes:

> Somewhere out there is the Confederate army. They claim they are fighting for their independence, for their freedom. I cannot question their integrity. I believe they

> are wrong, but I cannot question it. But I do question a system that defends its own freedom while it denies it to others—to an entire race of men. I will admit it, Tom, war is a scourge. But so is slavery. It is the systematic coercion of one group of men over another. It is as old as the Book of Genesis and has existed in every corner of the globe. But there is no excuse for us to tolerate it here, when we find it before our very eyes, in our own country. . . . As God is my witness, there is no one I hold in my heart dearer than you. But if your life, or mine, is part of the price to end this curse and free the Negro, then let God's will be done.[13]

To be sure, the white Southerners get more screen time in *Gods and Generals*, but can anyone think of *a single Confederate counterpart* to Chamberlain in *Roots*, *Mandingo* (1975), *Glory*, *Amistad* (1997), or any other of the myriad anti-Southern films churned out by Hollywood since World War II?

The use of the plural "Gods" in the title of the film is no rhetorical accident. Whereas the source novel by the late Michael Shaara's son Jeff simply meant to suggest that the generals were sometimes regarded as gods, Maxwell wanted the issue of religion (and religious differences) to be at the center of his film. To modern eyes, the sight of such blatant piety looks so strange as to be "unrealistic," especially if we concede that realism is a literary and dramatic convention that is often different from historical verisimilitude. If we were to get into a time machine and go back to the early 1860s, we would find characters who spoke and behaved very differently than we do now. In trying to be faithful to history, Maxwell shows Stonewall Jackson and his wife reading aloud from II Corinthians as he departs for battle. (When Chamberlain leaves for war, he and his wife read a more secular but equally high-minded text, Richard Lovelace's "To Lucasta, Going to the Wars.") "[T]he constant prayers became overbearing after a while," one smirking secularist writes. "I couldn't help wondering, as I watched scene after scene of bodies being blown to nearly bloodless smithereens . . . : what point did the filmmakers want to make by all this praying? That war is God's way of solving conflicts?"[14] If one believes in tribal gods, that is not an unreasonable inference. Although Christianity (like Judaism before it) makes claims to universality, God's actions in the Bible almost always benefited or punished a particular people.

As a Presbyterian, Stonewall Jackson was a fatalist. Believing that the hour of his death had already been decided, he claimed to be as serene in battle as in bed. As a reader of the Old Testament, he would have been familiar with God's orders to Joshua at the Battle of Jericho and to Saul when he went up against the Amalekites. In both cases, the Israelites were to take no prisoners and to slay civilians as if they were combatants. (Saul fell permanently afoul of the Lord when he spared the best of the Amalekites' livestock.) This style of warfare is known as the "black flag" and is generally unacceptable to modern sensibilities. While theologically a Christian, Jackson more nearly resembled the ancient Hebrew warriors or such recent ones as Menachem Begin and Ariel Sharon.

Although Maxwell does not show Jackson engaging in black-flag warfare, neither does he leave the general's ferocity in doubt. In fact, it is precisely at those moments when Jackson seems most tender and compassionate that he will say something to remind us of his complexity. When a dying colleague, General Maxcy Gregg, apologizes for the differences they have had in life, Jackson says: "The doctor tells me that you have not long to live. Let me ask you to dismiss this matter from your mind and turn your thoughts to God and the world to which you go." When Gregg says, "You know, General, that I am not a believer," Jackson replies: "Then I will have to believe for the both of us." Immediately after this moving display of Christian charity, Jackson leaves the hospital muttering about how horrible war is. "Horrible, yes," the attending physician, Dr. McGuire, admits. "But we have been invaded. What can we do?" With his jaw grimly set, Jackson declares: "Kill them, sir! Kill every last man of them!"[15]

Shortly thereafter, when he is staying at the Corbin home at Moss Neck Manor, where the Beale family has fled following the battle at Fredericksburg, Jackson develops a touching fondness for five-year-old Jane Corbin, even as his own daughter is born miles away. Hearing that young Jane has died of scarlet fever, Jackson is so stunned that he sits on a tree stump and sobs. When one of his aides says, "He's never cried before. Not for all the blood and death. Not for his young students from

VMI, not for his friends, not for anyone," Dr. McGuire replies: "Not so, Mister Pendleton. I think he's crying for them all." But during this same interlude, Jackson has ordered and presided over the execution of three deserters from his own Stonewall Brigade. As the critic Bill Kauffman observes, "Among Maxwell's great virtues as a filmmaker is his honesty. His respect for his subject never slips into hagiography."[16]

If Stonewall Jackson worships one kind of tribal deity, Joshua Lawrence Chamberlain pays homage to a very different but equally judgmental god. As we have seen, Chamberlain resembles Lincoln in imagining God to be exacting a terrible price in blood in order to eradicate the curse of slavery. And when Chamberlain invokes the name of God, he means something far more literal than the ceremonial deism of Lincoln. Theology is one of the subjects that he teaches at Bowdoin College. (The real Chamberlain was a friend of Calvin and Harriet Beecher Stowe.) Also, early in the film, we learn that Chamberlain almost abandoned his academic career in order to become a missionary. If the war had brother fighting brother, it also had god battling god.

For all his holy wrath against slavery, Chamberlain shared one perception with his Southern adversaries—he realized how momentous an act it was for the federal government to invade the provinces of its own country. When the Yankees are preparing to take the war to Southern civilians in Fredericksburg, Chamberlain compares it to Caesar's invasion of Rome. Film critics who believe that characters in historical dramas should all think and talk like the products of today's media-made culture would just as soon do without such esoteric allusions. But Maxwell has a point to make. And it is entirely in character for a classicist such as Chamberlain to appreciate the historical significance of what is about to happen. In a voice-over, he reads from the chronicle of Marcus Lucanus:

> Now swiftly Caesar had surmounted the icy alps and in his mind conceived immense upheavals, coming war. When he reached the water of the little Rubicon, clearly to the reader through the murky night appeared a mighty image of his country in distress, grief in her face, her white hair streaming from her tower-crowned head; with tresses torn and shoulders bare she stood before him and sighing said: "Where further do you march?

> Where do you take my standards warriors? If lawfully you come, if as citizens, this far only is allowed." Then trembling struck the leader's limbs, his hair grew stiff, and weakness checked his progress, holding his feet at the river's edge. At last he speaks: . . . "O Rome, the equal of the highest deity favors my plans. Not with impious weapons do I pursue you—here am I, Caesar, conqueror by land and sea, your own soldier everywhere, now too if I am permitted. The man who makes me your enemy, it is he will be the guilty one." Then he broke the barriers of war and through the swollen river quickly took his standards. When Caesar had crossed the flood and reached the opposite bank, on Hesperia's forbidden fields he took his stand and said: "Here I abandon peace and desecrated law; Fortune, it is you I follow. Farewell to treaties from now on; now war must be our judge!"[17]

What Chamberlain is doing in this speech is finding a usable past in a war that was fought in Rome two thousand years earlier. One suspects that he felt a more living connection with that past than many twenty-first-century Americans feel with the war that shaped their country's destiny a mere 140 years ago. That is unfortunate because, for all its authentic depiction of a bygone time, *Gods and Generals* recovers a usable past for our own time. What baffled and infuriated many critics was the fact that the lesson it offered was not the predictable one about race relations. Maxwell is concerned instead with the transformation of the United States from a federated republic into a nation-state. If the Confederate position on this issue seems quaint, even inexplicable, to contemporary audiences, that is a measure of how thorough the transformation has been. It is almost as if one cannot even raise the question without being accused of a retrograde nostalgia for dem ol' cotton fields back home.

When *Gods and Generals* was released in February 2003, the American nation-state was preparing to go to war with Iraq.[18] With the War Between the States, secession may have been dealt a death blow, and states' rights may have been put on life-support, but the desire to impose a preferred way of life at the point of a bayonet is still at the heart of American military policy. At least the victims now live in foreign lands rather than the United States itself. Even in an age of technological warfare, it took a full decade for as many Americans to lose their lives in Vietnam as fell in three days at Gettysburg.

In addition, regardless of what one thinks of Jackson's theory of black-flag warfare, he was certainly correct in assessing what was at stake in the conflict between the regions. In the interlude between the battles of Fredericksburg and Chancellorsville, Maxwell depicts him telling an aide, "If the Republicans lose their little war, they are voted out in the next election. They return to their homes in New York and Massachusetts and Illinois fat with their war profits. If we lose, we lose our country, we lose our independence. We lose it all."[19] The white South did indeed lose everything during war and Reconstruction. Even though the geographical region encompassed by the Confederacy eventually made an economic comeback as part of the Sunbelt, part of the price for that comeback has been a kind of cultural genocide. The NAACP may demand that Confederate symbols and memorials be removed from the public square and thrown down the memory hole of history, but it is white chambers of commerce that invariably close the deal.

But why should anyone other than diehard preservationists care? In other parts of the country, the culture of the Old South may have an academic and even an allegorical significance, but it lacks the symbolic resonance it possesses for those who are connected by blood memory to the cause that was lost at Appomattox. As time goes by, even that minority of persons grows ever smaller. It would seem that those who are not fanatical in their hatred of the traditional South might simply practice a policy of benign neglect in the hope that Southern heritage buffs will be content with dressing up and reenacting past battles before returning to the country clubs of the New South and the brokerage houses of the New World Order. If *Gods and Generals* were simply another dress-up ball, it would not have stirred such controversy. What is finally intolerable is not what it says about the Southern past but what it suggests about the American future.

Slavery was doomed even as Lincoln sent troops into the South, and no responsible public intellectual argues that it should be reinstated in the twenty-first century. When contemporary Americans (and people the world over) pay homage to the Confederacy, it is for reasons other than race. It is because they do not see globalization as an unmixed blessing and because they tire of the restrictions placed on their lives by the unholy alliance of the warfare and welfare states. When George Eliot wrote the words that Ron Maxwell uses as an epigraph to *Gods and Generals*, her native England was the world's dominant imperial power. The Gospel of Progress was fast replacing the Gospel of Christ. But Eliot's great novels are not a celebration of Empire or Progress. They are portraits of provincial life, and as such they speak a universal truth that has lasted long after the sun has set on the conquests of Queen Victoria. By the same token, the provincial life of the South has been preserved in a literature of memory that has outlasted the Confederacy and may well survive the American Empire itself.

The defeat of secession is an irrefutable historical truth. Whether that cause will rise again in some unforeseen future is hard to say. But those who are committed to exploring the "deeper truths" of history might note that the desire to secede from certain aspects of American life has never disappeared from the heart of the people. This is different from the utopian impulse to foment revolution so that other people might live under a more enlightened system of governance. Secession simply means withdrawing allegiance from a corporate entity to which one no longer wishes to belong. In an increasingly authoritarian society, the opportunities for doing so while simultaneously staying out of jail are few and far between. (Thoreau discovered as much when he refused to pay his poll tax.) Nevertheless, one can always strive to think freely and—within the parameters of the "Patriot Act"—to speak freely as well. Surely a separate peace is better than none at all.

Back in the 1950s, when Edmund Wilson was audited by the IRS in what he took to be an effort to pay for the Cold War, he began an intensive study of the "literature of the American Civil War." Quite to his surprise, the recovering Marxist found a kindred spirit in Alexander Stephens, vice president of the Confederacy. "There are moments," Wilson writes, "when one may wonder today—as one's living becomes more and more hampered by the exactions of centralized bureaucracies of both the state and the federal authorities—whether it may not be true, as Stephens said, that the cause of the South is the cause of us all."[20]

# BLOOD, SWEAT, AND GRACE

## MEL GIBSON'S *THE PASSION OF THE CHRIST* (2004)

Patrick J. Buchanan is certainly correct when he writes of Mel Gibson's *The Passion of the Christ*: "Not since D. W. Griffith portrayed the Klan as heroic defenders of white womanhood in *The Birth of a Nation* has a movie been so reviled." For a sample of the vituperation greeting this film, consider the following: "[A] wasted exercise in sadomasochism," writes Al Neuharth. "A repulsive masochistic fantasy, a sacred snuff film" that uses "classically anti-Semitic images," rants Leon Wieseltier in the *New Republic*. "A sickening death trip," says David Denby in the *New Yorker.* "It is sick," writes James Carroll in the *Boston Globe*. "A blood libel against the Jewish people," echoes Robert Scheer of the *Los Angeles Times*. "Jew-hating," says William Safire in the *New York Times*. "Fascistic," agrees Richard Cohen in the *Washington Post*. Daniel Goldhagen, author of *A Moral Reckoning: The Role of the Catholic Church in the Holocaust and Its Unfulfilled Duty of Repair*, calls *The Passion* "a sadomasochistic, orgiastic display that demonizes Jews as it degrades those who revel in viewing the horror." Gibson, Goldhagen writes, "restores a blood-drenched Christian culture of death."

These fulminations seem positively mild compared to the comments of Frank Rich, who wrote the following in the *New York Times* ten days after *The Passion* opened on Ash Wednesday 2004: "With its laborious buildup to its orgasmic spurtings of blood and other bodily fluids, Mr. Gibson's film is constructed like nothing so much as a porn movie, replete with slo-mo climaxes and pounding music for the money shots. Of all the *Passion* critics no one has nailed its artistic vision more precisely than Christopher Hitchens, who . . . called it a homoerotic 'exercise in lurid masochism' for those who 'like seeing handsome young men stripped and flayed alive over a long period of time.'"[1]

The object of this tirade of abuse is perhaps the most genuinely religious movie ever produced in Hollywood. For that reason, it drew an odd coalition on both sides of the debate. *The Passion* was embraced by conservative Christians, who had previously decried the graphic violence in motion pictures and would never even have thought of attending an R-rated film. At the same time, liberals, who ordinarily pride themselves on tolerating just about anything on First Amendment grounds, reviled this depiction of the final hours of Christ's life on earth. (One group in New Jersey—the Messiah Truth Project—demanded that the U.S. Justice Department investigate *The Passion* on the grounds that it violated "state and federal hate crime statutes for the purposeful encouragement of anti-Semitic violence.")[2] Although many in the media tried to portray the controversy as one pitting Jews against Christians, this is a gross oversimplification of the actual situation. Conservative Jews such as Rabbi Daniel Lapin, David Klinghoffer, Michael Medved, Don Feder, Matt Drudge, and Paul Gottfried defended Gibson's film, while many liberal Christians denounced it. The debate was finally more political and cultural than it was sectarian.

As we have already noted, the golden age of biblical epics has long been a thing of the past. In order to appeal to the broadest possible audiences, these films—even when dealing with the Christian Gospels—had tried to stress values that united a vast majority of Americans. Jesus was a great teacher who preached a message of love capable of changing people's lives. Reasonable Jews and even broad-minded secularists could agree with (or at least tolerate) this point of view.

It would have been more difficult, even in the old days, to produce a picture that unapologetically depicted Christ as God Incarnate who died for the sins of the world. This was precisely the message that the conservative Roman Catholic Mel Gibson wished to convey and was willing to invest thirty million dollars of his own money to produce. Such a project probably would not have been possible if Gibson had not had the money and clout that came with being the most popular star in Hollywood at the time.

One of the obvious problems with the attack on *The Passion of the Christ* was the fact that it began before Gibson had even finished filming the project. The *New York Times* got the ball rolling with an article based on an interview with Gibson's eighty-five-year-old father, who harbored some eccentric views about the role of Jews in world history. By June 2004, the Anti-Defamation League had gotten hold of a stolen version of an early script, which it proceeded to denounce to the press based on the analysis of five handpicked scholars, none of whom had seen any version of the movie. If this group had concerns about the way in which Jews were depicted in the film, voicing them to Gibson before going public might have been a more productive course of action.

At this point Michael Medved, who had good relations with both the ADL and the Gibson camp, offered his services as a behind-the-scenes mediator. He believed that gratuitous public attacks would only strengthen Gibson's resolve not to bow to pressure. This would assure that potentially objectionable aspects of the film went unchanged and would also demonstrate the fecklessness of the ADL. Medved even invited the organization's director, Abraham Foxman, to discuss his concerns either in private or on Medved's syndicated radio program. These overtures were declined. Unable to bring the ADL into any kind of dialogue, Medved did his best to represent Jewish interests to Gibson directly. On the basis of this experience, Medved concluded that it was absurd for Frank Rich and others to assert that Gibson had manufactured a controversy in order to build interest in his movie.

Because he had the confidence of Gibson and his partner Steve McEveety, Medved was allowed to see a preliminary screening of *The Passion* and spent three hours critiquing the film. The problem lay in the fact that for centuries European depictions of the Passion had portrayed first-century Jews as "Christ-killers." This attitude had fueled a history of prejudice and violence against subsequent generations of Jews. In the wake of the Holocaust, watchdog groups were particularly vigilant against anything that hinted at anti-Semitism. Although Medved did not believe that *The Passion*, even in its unedited form, was deliberately insensitive to Jews, he suggested alterations that were designed to head off controversy and make the film even more palatable to Jewish audiences.[3]

At Medved's suggestion, Gibson planned a "Jewish Initiative," which was to involve showing *The Passion* before synagogues and other community groups. This venture began with a private screening before thirty Jewish leaders and fifty prominent Christians, all of whom agreed not to discuss the film with the press prior to its release. This agreement did not prevent Rabbi Eugene Korn of the ADL from immediately telling *Jewish Week* magazine that *The Passion* "portrays Jews in the worst way as sinister enemies of God." When other press outlets picked up this story, Gibson's "Jewish Initiative" was abruptly canceled.[4]

At this point, Medved and other conservative Jews, who felt that the attacks on the film were unwarranted, did what they could to alleviate the concerns of fair-minded people who might be taken in by the allegations of anti-Semitism. In an article in the *Washington Post*, Tina Brown was prescient (or indiscreet) enough to suggest that anti-Semitism might actually be a red herring to conceal partisan political motivations. "The Gibson phenomenon makes Hollywood denizens nervous," she notes, "because it brings home the scary power of what they fear most: Bush country. It's not the supposed anti-Semitism of the movie they're worried about now. . . . No, it's Mad Mel's vaunted alliance with the alien armies of the right that are determined to return their mortal foe George W. Bush to the White House this November."[5] As we shall see, this analysis goes only part of the way toward telling a complex truth about cultural politics in twenty-first-century America.

## I

*The Passion of the Christ* begins in the Garden of Gethsemane with a shot of the back of Jesus' head. Our focus is on the natural setting, and only gradually do we discern the features of the savior's face. The Last Supper is over, and Jesus has gathered with his disciples to await his betrayal and arrest. According to the Gospels, this was a time of severe mental anguish. We hear the screech of a bird and then see a snake slithering toward Christ as he prays. This image reminds us of the form that Satan took in that earlier biblical garden when he tempted Eve. Rather than hear a dialogue between Jesus and Satan, who is tempting him to renounce his salvific destiny, the tension is depicted visually in the interaction of Christ and his immediate environment. The climax of this struggle occurs when Jesus crushes the serpent's head—a symbolic enactment of Christ's role as the second Adam who abolished the dominion of sin just as the first Adam had brought sin into the world.

This opening scene makes it clear that Gibson will be emphasizing the humanity of Jesus. Theologically, it has always been difficult to define the precise nature of the Incarnation. Dramatically, one must either emphasize the divinity or the humanity of Christ. The traditional biblical epics tended to fall short by splitting the difference in an unsatisfactory way—depicting Jesus as a distant magician who says wise things and even performs miracles but who seems the least real character in the film. (DeMille's original *King of Kings* [1927] may be an exception to this generalization.) Unlike Martin Scorsese, who depicts Christ as the most ordinary of mortals, Gibson gives us a suffering human being on a divine mission. This has led to the criticism that the resulting image of Jesus is too passive. But that is the aspect of Our Lord that Gibson has chosen to stress.

Early on in the film, the other character who dominates the action is Judas, the betrayer. Rather than being presented as the embodiment of unmitigated evil, he comes across as a tormented individual. At one point, the camera cuts away from the scene in Gethsemane to show Judas receiving the thirty pieces of silver that the leaders of the Temple pay him for turning over his master. Rather than delighting in the transaction, he seems conscience-stricken, as the bag of coins travels in slow motion from the priest's hands to his, with the contents spilling on the ground for him to gather. Later, in a scene that comes not from Scripture but from the mystical visions of the nineteenth-century nun Anne Catherine Emmerich, a buffeted and abused Jesus is knocked from a bridge where he dangles briefly from his chains. Judas, who has already betrayed his lord, is hiding under the bridge and flees in terror over what he has done.

But Judas cannot get away from his own conscience, which is symbolized by a group of demonic children who pursue him. If children traditionally represent innocence, these figures are a perversion of innocence, just as Satan is a perversion of the good. When they disappear from the screen, Judas is left alone either to live with his guilt or to seek forgiveness. It is at this point that he sees a donkey carcass infested with maggots. Apparently taking this to be an emblem of his own soul and perhaps a foretaste of Hell, he bursts into tears of despair and hangs himself.

Judas is not the only disciple to betray his master. Just as Jesus had foretold, before the cock crows Peter denies knowing him—three times. Although the consequences of this act are not as dire as those of Judas's treachery, Peter's conduct seems inexcusable for one who is to be the rock on which the church is built. Jesus, however, works in unpredictable ways. He did not choose perfect people to be his followers. The disciples were twelve ordinary and flawed human beings. Nevertheless, all were capable of picking themselves up when they fell and asking for forgiveness. Peter had the humility to do so. Judas did not.

Although this film is substantially based on Scripture, Gibson has used other sources to sharpen his message. In accordance with Roman Catholic tradition, he has emphasized the role of the Virgin Mary in her son's final hours. When Jesus goes to his first trial in *The Passion*, he sees a group of carpenters at work constructing his cross. There follows a flashback to when he was a young carpenter in Nazareth making a table. Here we get a glimpse of mother and son in a thoroughly conventional domestic life. They joke back and forth, and she even has to remind him to wash his hands before eating. This scene stands in sharp contrast to the present, when Mary witnesses the extreme suffering her son must endure.

## II

One of the most eccentric choices that Gibson made was to have his actors speak at various times in Aramaic, Hebrew, and Latin. This gave his film the sound of antiquity, while emphasizing its visual dimension. Moreover, as George McCartney has pointed out, "we do not have to make that extra effort of suspending our disbelief so necessary to tolerate the standard Hollywood Jesus speaking the King James Version by way of L.A." (Who among us can forget John Wayne as a Roman soldier in *The Greatest Story Ever Told* [1965] declaring, "Surely this must have been the Son of God"?) In what might strike some as a violation of probability, Jesus addresses Pilate in Latin. Even if it is more likely that he would have spoken Aramaic, Latin was used frequently enough in Galilee that Jesus might well have been familiar with the language. Why Gibson would have Jesus speak Latin (other than the fact that for nearly two millennia it was the universal language of the Roman Church) is dramatically intriguing. John Bartunek asserts that "Jesus wanted to make sure that Pilate fully understood Him. Pilate knows Aramaic, but it is not his mother tongue. If Jesus addresses him in Latin, there is no communication problem. The screenplay shows Jesus meeting Pilate on his terms, speaking his language."[6]

Another character who looms larger in *The Passion* than in Scripture is Pilate's wife, Claudia, who has a dream telling her that Jesus is a righteous man (see Matthew 27:19). This information simply exacerbates her husband's dilemma. To release this troublesome rabbi would anger Pilate's enemies among the Jewish hierarchy. To execute him would disturb Christ's followers. Add to that the fact that Pilate and his wife know in their heart of hearts that Jesus is an innocent man. A perfect archetype of indecision, Pilate offers the crowd the choice of Jesus or Barabbas. When the crowd makes the morally indefensible choice, Pilate washes his hands of Christ's blood and turns him over to the mob.

As soon as he does this, the film switches to a flashback of Jesus washing his hands at the Last Supper. This was, of course, a traditional Passover seder with a difference. On Passover, religious Jews remember the night on which the Angel of Death spared them the plague that killed the first-born in the houses of Egypt. The sacrificial lamb is the symbol of this covenant. Christ, the Lamb of God, becomes the sacrament of a New Covenant, one sealed with his blood. As Bartunek observes in his commentary on *The Passion*: "From then on His blood would become the tangible expression of the redeeming love that motivated His self-sacrifice, as well as the real instrument of that redemption—just as the lamb's blood had been a symbol of and instrument for Israel's salvation from Egypt."[7]

In addition to the warning in her dream, Claudia's unique visual perspective on the trial reinforces her belief in Our Lord's innocence. Gibson has her standing at a high window from which she can see her husband, the accused, and the crowd. She can also see the Blessed Virgin, John the Apostle, and Mary Magdalene. The screenplay emphasizes the effect on her: "It is [the Virgin Mary's] dignity that catches Claudia's attention. . . . Claudia studies Mary and her two companions with interest."[8] After the scene of Jesus' brutal flagellation, Claudia brings out cloth bandages with which she and Mary soak up the sacred blood.

The other woman who figures prominently in this story is Mary Magdalene, the reformed prostitute who became one of Christ's most devoted followers. It is believed that she may have been one of several sexually promiscuous women whom Jesus encountered and forgave in the course of his ministry. In the film, she is identified as the woman taken in adultery and sentenced to be stoned. Even as her Lord is being beaten in preparation for his own agonizing death, Mary Magdalene recalls the scene in which he saved her.

Jesus bent down in the dirt and began to write. He then said to the crowd: "He that is without sin among you, let him first cast a stone at her." As he continues to write, more and more of the woman's accusers disperse. Although we do not know what Christ wrote in the dirt, we can assume that they were the secret sins of the mob. He then tells the woman to go forth and sin no more. It is dramatically fitting to make this woman Mary Magdalene and to have this flashback here. "It's as if His blood reminds her of how He defended her against those who wanted to shed her blood," Bartunek writes. ". . . She goes back in her mind to a literal rescue, where her life was saved—not only her spiritual life, but even her physical life."[9]

## III

The attempted stoning of Mary Magdalene is only one of several flashbacks and crowd shots that periodically draw our attention away from the seemingly interminable beating of the Christ. At one point, there is what appears to be a staring match between the Virgin Mary (who Christians believe is responsible for Jesus' human nature) and a grotesque embodiment of the devil. This figure floats among the crowd, carrying a huge swaddling infant, a grotesque parody of the image of Madonna and Child. Here, when Satan would seem to have triumphed, the specter of Mary's maternal love for her son shines through. She remembers a time when he stumbled as a child and she wrapped her arms around him and said, "I am here." When she now makes the same gesture under much more dire circumstances, he reassures her by saying, "Behold, Mother, I make all things new."[10]

When the wounded savior looks at the devil in the crowd, the demon unfolds the swaddling clothes to reveal an adult face on top of a hunched body with hairy arms. In George McCartney's opinion, "Satan's baby is a ghastly visual variation of his earlier argument in the Garden [of Gethsemane]. This creature *is* human nature, he seems to say to Jesus. It is Your chosen nature. Look at it. It is ugly, animal, and quite beyond redemption. Only a fool would sacrifice himself for this thing. . . . [T]his sequence has an unnerving force that lingers well after the film ends."[11]

The image of the cross has become so much a part of Christian iconography that we are apt to forget that crucifixion was a horrific way for anyone to die. The pain of being nailed to a cross, which was certainly bad enough, was only the beginning. The condemned prisoner was defenseless against the elements. He could not protect himself from the sun, birds of prey, or insects, and even the act of breathing became progressively more difficult. The prisoner would either die of thirst from dehydration or suffocate because he could no longer raise his body enough to draw air into his lungs. Anticipating the manner of his death, Jesus tells his followers in the Gospel of Luke: "If any man would come after me, let him deny himself and take up his cross daily and follow me."

Although Christ's ministry is not the focus of this film, Gibson does not completely ignore the life the savior lived prior to his final hours. Even as he is dying on the hill called Calvary, a flashback takes us to the Sermon on the Mount. Whether this was a single sermon or a composite of several, it is a compendium of Jesus' teachings. The words are of a rabbi well schooled in the Law of Moses and other Old Testament texts. But he continually takes us beyond the Old Covenant to a radically new messianic vision. By including the Sermon on the Mount at this point in the story, *The Passion* emphasizes the authority behind the words. Jesus was not just a guru tossing out pretty thoughts for our consideration. Nor was he merely a man willing to pay the ultimate price for his beliefs. Christ was God Incarnate sacrificing himself for the Truth, so that all might live through him.

Jesus made several brief but profound comments while dying on the cross. These "last words" include the problematic cry of the heart: "My God, my God, Why have you forsaken me?" If we hear only those words, this sounds as if it is a statement of despair. Some have suggested that, at this moment, the burden of sinful humanity was so intense that God the Father could not look upon his son. This, however, would imply a separation of Christ's divine and human natures—which is a form of heresy. The savior's words here are actually the first line of Psalm 21 and would have been recognized as such by the religious Jews, both friends and enemies, gathered around the cross. Taken in its entirety, the psalm expresses faith in God's continuing presence, even when things *seem* to be hopeless. "By pronouncing the first verse of Psalm 21," Bartunek observes, "Jesus is engaging the entire psalm to express the prayer of His heart at that moment. As he hangs dying on the cross, rebuilding the bridge of trust between mankind and God that original sin had destroyed, the psalm shows that Christ's faith was not breaking as he cried aloud."[12]

In a departure from the literal record of the Scripture, in Gibson's film one of the final statements is spoken twice. "Father, forgive them, for they know not what they do." The rationale for this repetition is that two kinds of forgiveness are operative here. Jesus is forgiving both his physical torturers and those who are inflicting moral violence and humiliation upon him. The screenplay indicates that when Caiaphas hears this plea "he stops dead in his tracks. He slowly turns, looks at Jesus with amazement." At this point Dismas, the penitent thief, directly addresses Caiaphas: "Listen. . . . He prays for you."[13] Far from holding later generations of Jews responsible for his death, Christ was willing to absolve the one contemporaneous Jew who was most culpable for his crucifixion.

*The Passion* ends with the rock rolling back from the tomb on its own accord. A stream of light penetrates the darkened sepulcher and rests upon the shroud, even as Jesus is freed from it. Had the film gone on much longer, documenting the risen Lord's encounters with his followers during the forty days leading up to the Ascension, the dramatic intensity would have been dissipated. Although a biblical movie should be theologically sound, it is not itself a work of theology. Even if Scripture and cinema are telling the same story, they tell it in different ways.

Nevertheless, it would have been fatal to the story to end with the death of Jesus or to leave the physical reality of the Resurrection in doubt. Saint Paul makes it clear that the entire validity of the Christian faith rests not on the martyrdom of Christ but on his triumph over death. *The Passion* reminds us that we cannot have Easter without Good Friday. But Good Friday without Easter is martyrdom unrelieved.

## IV

Its graphic emphasis on the physical suffering of Jesus is the aspect of *The Passion* that has proven most controversial to the film's admirers and detractors alike. There are certainly other ways of telling the Christian story; however, Gibson's choice is both aesthetically and theologically justified. At one level, he may simply be doing what Flannery O'Connor thought necessary in an age of widespread unbelief. He is shouting for the hard of hearing and drawing big pictures for the half-blind. Sometimes even the faithful need to be reminded of the excruciating pain with which our salvation was purchased. Gibson's liberal critics have raked him over the coals for not making a movie that focused more on the sunnier aspects of Jesus' life and ministry. But the Christian drama is not solely a story of sweetness and light. To try to reduce it to that is to run the risk of making the Incarnate God into gentle Jesus meek and mild. That is the safe ecumenical path that Hollywood frequently took during its golden age. Mel Gibson chose to tell a harsher story.

The whole point of the Incarnation is that Jesus was fully human. Whether or not this means that he lusted after Mary Magdalene is a matter that Nikos Kazantzakis and Martin Scorsese have explored in prurient detail. If they have the right to do that, as they surely do, then Mel Gibson is equally justified in reminding audiences of Christ's suffering—an aspect of his humanity that bears more directly on his redemptive mission. Throughout the history of Christianity, believers have equated the extent of their Lord's suffering with the magnitude of his love. Even if this emphasis has sometimes been overdone, few would seriously argue that ours is an age bedeviled by an excess of penitence. Nevertheless, some of Gibson's harshest critics have dismissed *The Passion* as, at best, an antiquated expression of baroque Catholic piety and, at worst, an example of sadomasochism masquerading as religion.

Karen Jo Torjesen argues that the emphasis on Christ's physical suffering can be explained historically:

> Planted on native Irish soil just outside the reach of what remained of the Roman Empire, Irish Christians created a practice of penance so daunting, expressive, and formidable that it transformed and reformed Roman Christianity on the European continent. The suffering and naked body on the cross, the suffering flesh, and the open bleeding wounds became powerful religious symbols and took deep root in the religious imagination as a popular penitential piety. By the eleventh century, this piety had helped form a cultural context within which the doctrine of the atonement placed a passive, suffering Christ at the center of Christian theology.[14]

Explaining a phenomenon historically or anthropologically is not the same as dismissing it. In a sacramental world, all religion is grounded in time and place. That does not mean that the notion of blood atonement is nothing more than *Braveheart* with incense. Liberal Catholics and mainline Protestants may find this all rather embarrassing, but the vision of *The Passion* is shared by Catholic traditionalists such as Gibson and the hordes of evangelical Protestants who have made his film the highest grossing R-rated movie of all time. Thumb through a Baptist hymnal, and you will find songs such as "The Old Rugged Cross," "Are You Washed in the Blood?" "Nothing but the Blood," "Power in the Blood," and "There is a fountain filled with blood / Drawn from Immanuel's veins."[15] This is hardly an exhaustive list, but I think it makes my point.

The most damning accusation leveled against *The Passion of the Christ* is that the film is anti-Semitic. Essays that make this charge usually refer to the history of European anti-Semitism, which is assumed to have a religious base and to have been fueled by the performance of Passion plays, especially the one at Oberammergau in Germany. This is followed by a denunciation of the Holocaust and a celebration of the progress that has been made in Jewish-Christian relations since Vatican II. Now we have Mel Gibson, who has criticized some of the theological and liturgical changes made by Vatican II, producing a film about the

Passion. Exploiting these loose juxtapositions, Gibson's critics conclude that his film *must* be anti-Semitic. And once that assumption has been made, it is difficult to see what could have been done to allay it.[16]

Most of the characters in the film are Jewish. This includes Jesus, his mother, and his disciples. Even the minor character Simon of Cyrene, who carries Christ's cross for him when he is unable to do it himself, is identified as a Jew. To be sure, it is the Jewish hierarchy, particularly the high priest Caiaphas, who cry out for Jesus' blood. Because the gospels and independent historical texts confirm that this was the case, there is no way to dramatize the Passion without putting Caiaphas and his cronies in a bad light. No reasonable person would conclude that this means that subsequent generations of Jews bear responsibility for the behavior of these first-century villains. The only line of Scripture that could be misinterpreted to say that is Matthew 27:25, when the crowd cries out: "His blood be on us and on our children." Although Gibson thought that viewers would realize that the crowd was speaking for sinful humanity rather than Jews specifically, he removed that line entirely from the subtitles at Medved's urging.

Even more to the point, Medved has hit upon a crucial difference between Gibson's film and the European Passion plays. "The problem with traditional 'Passion plays,'" he writes, "was always the unmistakable association of contemporary Jews with the staged oppressive Judean religious authorities. The high priest often appeared with anachronistic European prayer shawls, skull caps, and side curls. [Gibson's film] avoids such imagery—costumes and ethnicity of the persecutors make them look far less recognizable as Jews than do the faces and practices of Jesus and his disciples. The words 'Jew' or 'Jewish' scarcely appear in the subtitles to this movie, spoken [mostly] in Aramaic and Latin."[17] If any ethnic group invites our rage and contempt, it is the sadistic Roman soldiers who beat and crucify the Christ.

As offensive as the traditional Passion plays may have been, it defies logic to draw a direct line between them and the horrors of Auschwitz. The Passion play at Oberammergau was first produced in 1633 when a group of Alpine villagers wished to express their thanks to God for sparing them from the Black Plague. This drama was performed thereafter at ten-year intervals. What can we conclude from this? Patrick Buchanan writes:

> Were that play a cause of the Holocaust, why was there no Holocaust in the centuries when Catholic kings ruled the Holy Roman Empire? Why did it happen only after Hitler came to power and Europe was convulsed in the worst war in its history, 300 years after the play was first performed? Blaming a six-hour play, put on once every ten years, by 2,000 amateur actors, in a tiny town of 5,000 buried in the Tyrolean Alps, for Hitler's pogrom against the Jews is so preposterous it calls up the old adage: "Anti-Catholicism is the anti-Semitism of the intellectuals."[18]

Gibson's preference for the Tridentine Latin Mass and other traditional practices of the Roman Church is frequently cited as an example of eccentricity if not downright deviancy. People who are quick to laud liberal critics of even the most fundamental doctrines of the church will not tolerate any criticism from the right. When John Paul II saw *The Passion* and purportedly said, "It is as it was," the spin doctors in the Vatican did their best to deny that such words were ever spoken. If they were, one must either condemn the pontiff as an anti-Semite or admit that the charges against Gibson's film were overblown.

It is also wrong to assert, as has been frequently done, that Vatican II represented a fundamental change in the church's view of the Jewish people. Father Thomas Williams, dean of the school of theology at Regina Apostolorum Pontifical University in Rome and an advisor to *The Passion of the Christ*, told the *National Catholic Register*: "[T]he fathers of the Second Vatican Council didn't see themselves as reversing any prior teachings on this question [of Jewish responsibility for Christ's death]. The council categorically *reaffirmed* perennial Catholic teaching that all of humanity's sins, and the sins of Christians in particular, are responsible for Christ's death, as stated, *inter alia*, in the catechism of the Council of Trent." This point is emphatically emphasized by the fact that it is Gibson's own hand that drives the first nail into the savior's palm.[19]

The charges of anti-Semitism seemed to abate when no attacks against Jews, either verbal or physical, could be traced to viewing Gibson's film. In fact, one began to suspect that the only people who found the movie hostile to Jews were those who had decided ahead of time that that was the case. Unfortunately, Mel Gibson severely damaged his own cause when he was apprehended speeding on the Pacific Coast Highway in late July 2006. An inebriated Gibson went on an anti-Semitic tirade before the arresting officer, who was Jewish. Gibson's enemies saw this incident as confirmation of what they had long believed, while his supporters considered it a betrayal of their trust.[20] The question before us is to what extent this encounter should color our evaluation of *The Passion of the Christ.*

Surely, there is a sense in which every work of art must stand or fall on its own, irrespective of the character of the artist. If Gibson's movie was anti-Semitic before his arrest, it did not become more so afterward. By the same token, if it was not anti-Semitic before July 2006, it did not become so because of the revelation of Gibson's personal demons. One of the most respected films ever made about Christ was Pier Pasolini's *The Gospel According to Matthew* (1964). The Vatican's initial response to this movie was negative, largely because Pasolini was a Marxist, which would seem to have disqualified him from telling the story of Jesus in a way that would satisfy orthodox believers. Over the years, however, the merits of this picture forced the church hierarchy to change its position. In 1996, the Vatican included *The Gospel According to Matthew* in its list of the fifteen greatest religious films of all time. It was the only picture about Christ so honored.[21] If Pasolini's film can be judged on its own merits, so can Gibson's.

The ideological enemies of *The Passion* (as opposed to those who criticize it on purely aesthetic grounds) fall into three broad categories. There are aggressive secularists, who are offended by any overt display of religious sentiment in our public culture. Then there are liberal Christians, who regard Gibson's theology as old-fashioned and ecumenically incorrect. Finally, there are neoconservatives, who understandably consider traditionalists such as Gibson as a threat to the hegemony of the American Right. Tina Brown was probably accurate in asserting that the Hollywood elite regarded the evangelical fans of *The Passion* as diehard Bush supporters. But Gibson himself is not of their number. His support for Pat Buchanan's presidential ambitions and his opposition to the war in Iraq would be enough to put him on any neoconservative enemies list. To call him an anti-Semite is simply an evasive way of saying that he is outside the mainstream of conservative opinion. The catch is that the neocons get to determine the limits of acceptable conservative thought.

If much of the debate over *The Passion of the Christ* has been political, the film makes no explicit comment on the mundane controversies of the twenty-first century. Its story is rooted in the specific reality of first-century Palestine. But none of the religious—indeed none of the *historical*—figures who lived before or since that time transformed civilization to the extent that Jesus did. "What did the crucifixion give mankind?" asks Patrick Buchanan. "Salvation, the opening of the gates of heaven, Western civilization, the greatest art, architecture, music, painting, sculpture, cathedrals, and churches in history, the idea that all men are children of God and that each has an innate worth and dignity, which puts limits on the power of any state—and an end to slavery."[22] That is why the Passion is both the greatest and the most controversial story ever told.

# PART FOUR

# ONE HUNDRED POLITICALLY INCORRECT FILMS

The eighteen films discussed in the preceding three sections of this book are broadly representative but by no means definitive. No doubt, similar points could have been made with a totally different selection of movies. Even when the entertainment industry has seemed most prone to a herd mentality, it has still been possible to find an independent vision on the screen—if one has looked hard enough. Ironically, this has often meant going back to older pictures made when official censorship was stronger but the pressure to be iconoclastic (seemingly at all costs) was weaker. But it should be clear by now that this volume is no exercise in nostalgia. Even if they are in a decided minority, films that challenge the conventional wisdom and values of Hollywood are made every year. Sometimes this is done deliberately. More often, I suspect, it is the happy result of an auteur remaining faithful to an independent vision.

Although the following list of one hundred politically incorrect films could be expanded or altered, it is long enough to suggest that the phenomenon we have been considering is neither a relic of the past nor an occasional quirk in the present. In each of the synopses below, I have tried to indicate both the content and the quality of the movie in question and to suggest why it is included in this book. Rather than arranging the list chronologically or thematically, I offer it in alphabetical order—a decision that I hope emphasizes the variety and eclecticism of the choices. The earliest movie on the list (*All Quiet on the Western Front*) was made in 1930, the most recent (*The Queen*) in 2006. There are a few British pictures, some foreign-language films, and even the first season of an animated television show. But most of the list consists of Hollywood productions that were originally shown in American theaters. All are available for home viewing on either DVD or VHS. Let the arguments begin.

## ABOUT SCHMIDT

2002 (125 minutes) • Comedy/Drama
Avery Pix/New Line • R

Cast: Jack Nicholson (Warren Schmidt), Kathy Bates (Roberta Hertzel), Hope Davis (Jeannie Schmidt), Dermot Mulroney (Randall Hertzel), June Squibb (Helen Schmidt), Howard Hesseman (Larry Hertzel), Len Cairou (Ray Nichols), Harry Groener (John Rusk), Connie Ray (Vicki Rusk), Mark Vehuizen (Duncan Hertzel)

Producers: Michael Besman, Harry Gittes; Director: Alexander Payne; Writers: Alexander Payne, Jim Taylor (based on the novel by Louis Begley and the screenplay *The Coward* by Alexander Payne); Photographer: James Glennon (color); Editor: Kevin Tent

Like all effective satires, this film is subtle enough to be misinterpreted by the terminally obtuse. Although it was blasted as an attack on American life by a reviewer for the neoconservative *Claremont Review of Books*, director Payne is attacking only the more tawdry aspects of our culture from what can only be described as an independent perspective. (In one scene, shrewd observers have even discerned a copy of the paleoconservative magazine *Chronicles* among Schmidt's reading matter.) Having just retired from the insurance industry, Warren Schmidt is forced to take stock of what is left of his life. He is spared the prospect of touring the country in a Winnebago with a wife he can't stand when he returns home one day to find said wife dead. He has already struck up a pen-pal relationship with a disadvantaged orphan, whom he has agreed to sponsor with a check for $22 a month. (This is a clever and hilarious expository device that allows Schmidt to vent many of his inner thoughts.) His primary mission in life, however, is to prevent his daughter from marrying an insipid waterbed salesman.

The heart of the film consists of a contrast between Schmidt and the family of his daughter's prospective husband—a household that includes Roberta Hertzel, matriarch of the clan, and her ex-husband Larry (a role for which Howard Hesseman is ideally cast). If Schmidt's conventional values seem a bit drab, the unconventional ones of the Hertzels are positively obnoxious. One suspects that Roberta and her former spouse (who has been banished from the marriage bed because of his inability to satisfy her voracious sexuality) are what geriatric hippies have become thirty years later. (No wonder their son is such a dweeb.) In what is perhaps the most memorable scene in the film—and the basis of parody on the Fox series *Family Guy*—Roberta disrobes and sinks into a hot tub next to the properly clad and appropriately embarrassed Warren. By now, the immensely talented Nicholson has won our empathy for the thoroughly middle-class Schmidt.

The temptation in such a film is to employ broad performances for easy laughs. Instead, the story possesses the fascination of a car wreck. As much as we might want to look away from these people, curiosity gets the best of us. However superior and condescending Schmidt may seem, we can't help wishing him well in his quest. The utter solemnity, bohemian self-righteousness, and ultimate cluelessness of the Hertzels make even the life of a retired insurance salesman seem filled with ambiguity and significance. Had Payne used a more dynamic foil, his point would have been more obviously made and, hence, lost. Nicholson's awkwardness plays off perfectly against Bates's total lack of self-awareness. (Both earned Academy Award nominations.) Although Alexander Payne had won favorable reviews for *Citizen Ruth* (1996) and *Election* (1999), *About Schmidt* was the film that established him as an important Hollywood director from whom much can be expected in the future.

## ADVISE AND CONSENT

1962 (140 minutes) • Drama
Columbia • Unrated

Cast: Henry Fonda (Robert Leffingwell), Charles Laughton (Senator Seab Cooley), Don Murray (Senator Brig Anderson), Walter Pidgeon (Senator Bob Munson), Peter Lawford (Senator Lafe Smith), George Grizzard (Senator Fred Van Ackerman), Gene Tierney (Dolly Harrison), Franchot Tone (the President), Burgess Meredith (Herbert Gelman), Eddie Hodges (Johnny Leffingwell), Paul Ford (Senator

Stanley Danta), Inga Swenson (Ellen Anderson), Paul McGrath (Hardiman Fletcher), Will Geer (Senate Minority Leader), Betty White (Senator Bessie Adams), Lew Ayres (Vice President Harley Hudson)

Producer: Otto Preminger; Director: Otto Preminger; Writer: Wendell Mayes (based on the novel by Allen Drury); Photographer: Sam Leavitt (black and white); Editor: Louis Loeffler

In an era when Congress seems to be held in universal contempt, it is useful to be reminded that this was not always the case. If there is a protagonist in *Advise and Consent*, it is not so much an individual character as the Senate itself. Because it was based on Allen Drury's novel, which had spent almost a year on the best-seller list, the story of *Advise and Consent* was at the time of the film's release well known. It is a political drama about the controversy a president creates when he nominates an ultraliberal egghead to be secretary of state. Majority leader Bob Munson tries to shepherd the nomination through a bitterly divided Senate, while contending with the nominee's overzealous champion, Senator Fred Van Ackerman, and his equally ardent opponent, Senator Seab Cooley.

As the drama intensifies, we find that Robert Leffingwell, the nominee, has concealed a youthful flirtation with communism, just as Brig Anderson, the chairman of the subcommittee considering his nomination, has concealed a homosexual affair. Cooley tries to scuttle the nomination by revealing Leffingwell's secret, while Van Ackerman tries to advance it by blackmailing Anderson with his. Without giving away the ending of this thriller, one can say that Leffingwell, Anderson, Cooley, and Van Ackerman all emerge diminished from this confrontation.

Otto Preminger manages to coax an ensemble performance from an all-star cast. (Such collegiality coincides with Drury's vision of the Senate.) Probably the most memorable portrayal is Charles Laughton's rendering of the Southern demagogue Seab Cooley. Although this role could have easily lent itself to caricature, Cooley comes across as a dedicated, if flawed, exponent of a legitimate point of view. The same could be said of most of the other senators—with the exception of those who seem to be nothing more than amiable members of the club. The most despicable and least collegial member of the body is the liberal peacenik Van Ackerman. That alone would be enough to qualify this film as "politically incorrect."

The political climate in 1962 was so different from what it is today that some senators actually thought this film to be an insult. Beverly Merrill Kelley tells us that, after a private screening for Congress, Senator Clinton P. Anderson (D-NM) sputtered: "The film creates a wholly incorrect impression of the Senate." Senator Stephen Young (D-OH) rose from the audience to announce he would introduce a bill preventing Columbia from distributing the picture outside the United States. U.S. Information Agency chief Edward R. Murrow raised strenuous objections, largely arguing that instead of giving our enemy ammunition, Hollywood should create a "favorable image" of Americans to show foreign nations. The American Legion protested in full force, decrying *Advise and Consent* as an "irresponsible defacement of the image of the U.S." and picketing theaters.

The problem was that Allen Drury was a veteran Washington reporter who had violated the press's tacit code by providing an inside view of Washington. This was before the era of investigative journalism (and long before the Internet), when far more salacious copy would be presented without the guise of fiction. Viewed from the perspective of the twenty-first century, one is apt to bemoan the proliferation of Van Ackermans and wax nostalgic for a few more Seab Cooleys.

## ALL QUIET ON THE WESTERN FRONT

1930 (133 minutes) • Drama
Universal • Unrated

Cast: Lew Ayres (Paul Baumer), Louis Wolheim (Kat Katczinsky), John Wray (Himmelstoss), Arnold Lucy (Professor Kantorek), Ben Alexander (Franz Kemmerich), Scott Kolk (Leer), Owen Davis Jr. (Peter), Walter Rogers (Behm), William Bakewell (Albert Kropp), Russell Gleason (Mueller), Richard Alexander (Westhus), Harold Goodwin (Detering), Slim Summerville (Tjaden), G. Pat Collins (Lieutenant Bertinick), Beryl Mercer (Mrs. Baumer), Edmund Breese (Herr Meyer)

Producer: Carl Laemmle Jr.; Director: Lewis Milestone; Writers: Erich Maria Remarque, Maxwell Anderson, George Abbott, Del Andrews, C. Gardner Sullivan, Walter Anthony, Lewis Milestone; Photographers: Arthur Edeson, Karl Freund (black and white); Editors: Edgar Adams, Edward L. Cahn, Milton Carruth

By the 1980s, antiwar films (*Platoon* [1986], *Full Metal Jacket* [1987], and the like) had become a staple commodity in Hollywood. The situation, however, was quite different in 1930 when Carl Laemmle Jr. produced a motion-picture version of Erich Maria Remarque's novel *All Quiet on the Western Front*. If elite opinion (of the sort characterized by Hemingway's "lost generation") had declared World War I a brutal farce even before the fighting was over, popular sentiment did not join in this judgment until the publication of Remarque's novel in 1929. In order to satisfy the international demand for this book, the German publisher had to keep six printing and ten bookbinding firms working full-time. The story lost none of its antiwar fervor when translated to the screen the following year.

The title card in the film's first frame sets the tone for what is to follow: "This story is neither an accusation nor a confession, and least of all an adventure to those who stand face to face with it. It will try simply to tell of a generation of men, who, even though they may have escaped its shells, were destroyed by the war." Early in the picture, a pompous professor lectures a class of schoolboys on the glories of war. (He uses the phrase "*Dulce et decorum est pro patria mori*," which had been employed so ironically by the British poet-soldier Wilfrid Owen.) What is even more extraordinary is the fact that these are German boys played by American actors with American accents. The Germans were our enemies in the great world war, but we are being asked to empathize with them and to see the world through their eyes. Like Henry Fleming in Stephen Crane's *The Red Badge of Courage*, the recruits soon learn that part of being in the army involves being deprived of the comforts of home. The former village postman turned drill sergeant becomes a one-man argument for fragging.

In one particularly memorable battle scene, we see the French infantry move on the Germans. This provokes machine-gun fire, which mows down a horde of French soldiers. Then our focus shifts from the general to the specific, when we see a pair of hands gripping a strand of barbed wire. The French soldier to whom the hands belong has been killed by a grenade. The battle itself is a wash, with neither side gaining ground. In yet another scene, the film's protagonist, Paul Baumer, finds himself trapped in a foxhole under heavy fire. When an enemy soldier jumps into the hole with him, Paul instinctively stabs him. Alone in the hole with the dying man, he must confront the reality of having killed another human being. The picture shows us amputees screaming in the hospital. Toward the end, Paul carries an old friend on his back, not realizing that the man, who was only slightly wounded when he picked him up, is now a corpse. Then, in a lyrical conclusion to the story, Paul sees a butterfly through his gunsight. Reaching out to the creature, he puts himself in the sight of a French soldier's gun. His hand clutches empty air, then goes limp.

Writing about this film on LewRockwell.com, Rick Gee observes: "Those of us who oppose the perpetual wars of the state should see it (or see it again) to reinforce our viewpoint. Those who support Leviathan's Total War should screw up the courage to see this significant film and ask themselves these questions: do I really support the state sending my loved ones to meet such a demise? Would I be willing to submit *myself* to such horrors? And if the answer to either question is 'no,' how can I continue to support the state in total war?"

## ALL THE KING'S MEN

2006 (140 minutes) • Drama
Columbia • PG-13

Cast: Sean Penn (Willie Stark), Jude Law (Jack Burden), Anthony Hopkins (Judge Irwin), Kate Winslet (Anne Stanton), Mark Ruffalo (Adam Stanton), Patricia Clarkson (Sadie Burke), James Gandolfini (Tiny Duffy), Jackie Earle Haley (Sugar Boy), Kathy Baker (Jack's mother)

Producers: Ken Lemberger, Michael Medavoy, Arnold Messer, and Steve Zaillian (Producers); Scott Budnick (Co-producer), James Carville, Andreas Grosch, Michael Hausman, Ryan Kavanaugh, Todd Phillips, Andreas Schmid, and David Thwaites (Executive Producers); Director: Steven Zaillian; Writer: Steven Zaillian (Based on the novel by Robert Penn Warren); Photographer: Pawel Edelman (color); Editor: Wayne Wahrman

This is one film where the remake is definitely superior to the original. The vastly overrated 1949 adaptation of Robert Penn Warren's Pulitzer Prize–winning novel was shot in California and might as well have been set there. Rather than building on that film, director Steven Zaillian has gone back to Warren's text and given us a remarkably faithful rendering of that great novel. His film, which was shot on location in Louisiana, depicts the rise and fall of a Southern populist named Willie Stark, who is loosely based on Huey P. Long. (Inexplicably, the time period of the story is switched from the 1930s to the 1950s.) Stark begins his career in politics by opposing a crooked bid for construction of a local school. After the bid is approved, three children die from the collapse of a fire escape. Stark immediately becomes a hero and is talked into running for governor by some slick political operatives intent on splitting the rural vote. When Willie learns that he is being used, his indignation fuels a winning race.

The narrator of the novel and film is a newspaper reporter named Jack Burden, who later goes to work for Stark. Coming from an aristocratic background, the cynical and introspective Burden provides us with perspective on the governor. Although his policies are benevolent toward the poor and dispossessed, Willie is ruthless in seizing and wielding power. Like Huey Long, he is a kind of democratic dictator who derives his strength from the support of the common people. Jack is torn between ties to his past and loyalty to the charismatic Stark. This contradiction brings havoc to his own life and helps to propel Willie to his doom.

Sean Penn's mesmerizing portrayal of Stark reminds us of why many critics consider him to be America's finest living actor. Jude Law turns in one of the best performances of his career as the less flamboyant Jack Burden. Kate Winslet, Mark Ruffalo, Patricia Clarkson, and Anthony Hopkins all do a fine job in supporting roles. James Gandolfini would have been more convincing as Tiny Duffy had he not resembled Tony Soprano affecting a Southern accent. Although this is a universal story, Zaillian was wise to stress the regional ambience that was so integral to Warren's novel.

Unlike so many other tales of politics in the South, *All the King's Men* is not about race. Although Huey Long was very much a man of his time on matters of civil rights, his economic reforms benefited blacks as well as whites. (Huey's brother Earl lived long enough to become a racial liberal.) Stark's magnetism is such that the audience is drawn to him. Nevertheless, the tragic consequences of his tactics show how corrupting power can be. As an honest public servant at the beginning of his career, Willie was ineffectual. It was only after he began to play dirty that he began getting results. What he faces is not just the politician's dilemma but the plight of any man who wishes to do good in a fallen world.

## BABETTE'S FEAST

1987 (102 minutes) • Drama
Panorama Films (Denmark) • G

Cast: Stéphane Audran (Babette Harsant), Birgitte Federspiel (Old Martina), Budil Kjer (Old Philippa), Jarl Kulle (Old Lorens Lowenhielm), Jean-Philippe Lafont (Achille Papin), Ghita Nørby (Narrator), Vibeke Hastrup (Young Martina), Pouel Kern (The Minister), Hanne Stensgaard (Young Philippa), Gudmar Wivesson (Young Lorens Lowenhielm)

Producers: Just Betzer, Bom Christensen, Benni Korzen, Pernille Siesbye; Director: Gabriel Axel; Writer: Gabriel Axel (based on a novel by Isak Dinesen); Photographer: Henning Kristiansen (Eastmancolor); Editor: Finn Henriksen

George Garrett has noted that even when Hollywood deals favorably with religious topics, it generally does so from a secular perspective. A film such as Gabriel Axel's *Babette's Feast*, however, is more in the tradition of Christian parables. "The meaning of a parabolic story," Garrett writes, "is inextricably part of the story, not separate from it. . . . Parables do not mean something else or even something more than themselves. . . . The story and its implications are one and the same." Based on a story by Isak Dinesen, *Babette's Feast* focuses on a pietistic Lutheran sect located in Norway toward the end of the nineteenth century.

More by his very presence than by any overt action, the patriarch of this sect has driven away any potential suitors for his daughters Martina and Philippa. In a flashback, we learn that a young army officer, Lorens Lowenhielm, has despaired of winning Martina's hand and has instead settled for a lady-in-waiting to the queen of Sweden. Later, a singing master from Paris, Achille Papin, is captivated—first by Philippa's voice, and subsequently by Philippa herself. He too departs when he realizes that the object of his affection belongs, body and soul, to a stern Protestant God indistinguishable from her father.

The two sisters grow old and take over the sect after their father's death. Years later, a young Parisian refugee named Babette arrives at their door. She has lost her family in a political uprising and has been sent to the sisters by Papin. Too poor to pay her wages, the sisters provide Babette with room and board in exchange for her service as a cook. Although she has been a gourmet chef in Paris, the sisters maintain a Spartan diet of cod and ale-bread soup. The years pass as a friend annually purchases a lottery ticket for Babette.

When Babette finally wins the lottery one year, she invests her money and her talents in preparing a special meal for the members of the sect. By this time, the coreligionists have grown old and embittered. They view the meal that is being prepared on their behalf with a certain trepidation. In a moment of startling irony, one of them says: "Like the wedding at Cana, the food is of no importance." To be sure, the transformation that this meal brings to the lives of the diners is more important than the mere food; however, the food is the sacramental vehicle through which the transformation takes place. Far from being a restrictive or exclusive affair, the feast is extended beyond the confines of the religious community with the unexpected arrival of the aged Mrs. Lowenhielm and her nephew Lars, now a general.

Several biblical comparisons suggest themselves. The most obvious ones are to the Eucharist or the heavenly banquet. When it is discovered that Babette has spent her entire winnings on the meal, we are reminded of the widow's mite or of Mary of Bethany spending a fortune on expensive ointment with which to bathe Christ's feet—both of which actions are commended in the Gospels. From a sectarian standpoint, we might see this story as a contrast between the rich sensuality of Catholicism and the ascetic renunciations of Protestantism. But the spirit of the film is one of reconciliation rather than the celebration of one tradition over another. At Christ's table, there is room for all.

## BANANAS

1971 (82 minutes) • Political Comedy
United Artists • PG-13

Cast: Woody Allen (Fielding Mellish), Louise Lasser (Nancy), Carlos Montalban (General Vargas), Howard Cosell (Himself), Roger Grimsby (Himself), Don Dunphy (Himself), Natividad Abascal (Yolanda), Jacobo Morales (Esposito), Miguel Ángel Suárez (Luis), David Ortiz (Sanchez), René Enriquez (Diaz), Jack Axelrod (Arroyo), Sylvester Stallone (Subway Thug #1), Danny DeVito (Man Sitting in Honeymoon Suite)

Producers: Axel Anderson, Antonio Encarnacion, Jack Grossberg, Manolon Villamil (Producers), Charles H. Joffe (Executive Producer), Ralph Rosenblum (Associate Producer); Director: Woody Allen; Writers: Woody Allen, Mickey Rose; Photographer: Andrew M. Costikyan (color); Editors: Ron Kalish, Ralph Rosenblum

Although Woody Allen is a man of the cultural Left, he is first and foremost a comedian. As such, he is capable of poking fun at liberal foibles—never more so than in his early film *Bananas*. The story opens with Howard Cosell covering the assassination of the dictator of San Marcos (which begins with the "traditional bombing of the American Embassy") for *The Wide World of Sports*. In equating a political uprising with a televised sporting attraction, the film lampoons an event that American radicals would have taken seriously. This becomes clear when an earnest young leftist named Nancy tries to get the Allen character, Fielding Mellish, to sign a petition for San Marcos. Because Mellish is interested only in getting Nancy in bed, he readily complies.

Like its immediate predecessor, *Take the Money and Run* (1969), *Bananas* is essentially a series of sight gags and one-liners loosely wrapped around the misadventures of the typical Allen nebbish. He has simply gone from being a failed criminal to an equally hapless revolutionary. For his part, the dictator Vargas is the standard-issue right-wing despot, who makes a reservation for one at the Miami Beach Hotel prior to the expected coup. ("Are we for or against the government?" a CIA agent asks on the plane into San Marcos. Not taking any chances, some of the agency will be for and some against.) When the rebel soldiers storm Vargas's palace, Allen alludes to Sergei Eisenstein's *The Battleship Potemkin* (1925) with a scene of a baby carriage rolling down the steps.

After the rebel leader Esposito briefly takes over, we see a stereotypical lust for power: "These people are peasants," he declares. "Too ignorant to vote." He immediately decrees that the official language of the country will be Swedish and that Vargas's men will be shot in the public square. (Mellish dutifully assigns them numbers like customers in a bakery.) When Esposito is predictably overthrown, Fielding takes over as leader of the country and makes a fundraising trip north of the border in a red Fidel Castro beard. He is soon arrested as a suspected Communist, which leads to a trial that is the occasion for a rapid-fire series of jokes. In one, a large black woman, who identifies herself as J. Edgar Hoover, takes the stand. (This was before the FBI director's cross-dressing had become common knowledge.) Later, in an allusion to the Chicago Seven trial, the judge orders Fielding bound and gagged. Muttering, he examines a witness who understands him perfectly.

Howard Cosell is brought back for the closing scene: the consummation of the Fielding Mellish marriage, which is itself another *Wide World of Sports* spectacular. Like the boxer to whom he is being equated, Fielding looks forward to a rematch next spring. While guffawing at this parody (which admittedly seemed funnier at the time than it does nearly four decades later), the audience cannot help recalling the opening assassination scene. Sex, sports, and politics are finally reduced to the level of mass entertainment.

## THE BARBARIAN INVASIONS

2003 (99 minutes) • Comedy/Drama
Astral Films • R

Cast: Rémy Girard (Rémy), Stéphane Rousseau (Sébastien), Marie-Josée Croze (Nathalie), Dorothée Berryman (Louise), Louise Portal (Diane), Dominique Michel (Dominique), Yves Jacques (Claude), Pierre Curzi (Pierre), Marina Hands (Gaëlle)

Producers: Daniel Louis, Denise Robert (Producers), Fabienne Vonier (Coproducer); Director: Denys Arcand; Writer: Denys Arcand; Photographer: Guy Dufaux (color); Editor: Isabelle Dedieu

At one level, this is a film about generational conflict and reconciliation. It is also such a trenchant critique of all concerned that one would be hard pressed to identify the barbarians referred to in the title. The story involves Rémy, a former history professor at the University of Montreal. Although we are not certain of his academic accomplishments, Rémy has lived a full hedonistic life and is now dying of cancer. The time has come for people he has neglected to determine what final obligation they might owe to this difficult man. This includes his wife, who divorced him years ago; his businessman son, who despises him; and an assortment of former female lovers and male friends.

The work of French-Canadian director Denys Arcand, *The Barbarian Invasions* can be seen as a sequel to *The Decline of the American Empire* (1986), which featured several of the same characters. Although Rémy is a socialist who rejects his son's suggestion that he go to America for treatment, he is perfectly willing to evade the law and the bureaucracy in order to bring comfort to his last days. Ironically, it is his capitalist son Sébastien who is able to make things happen. He bribes a union official into preparing a private room for Rémy on a floor that the hospital no longer uses. When it becomes clear that morphine is no longer strong enough to dull the old man's pain, Sébastien arranges for some heroin buys—at the suggestion of a nun, no less. (The cool efficiency of the young executive stands in stark contrast to the fecklessness of the welfare state.) The young man even pays three of Rémy's former students to visit him in the hospital, although one of them goes while refusing to take the money. Despite Rémy's contempt for the life his son has chosen, Sébastien becomes his father's chief caregiver.

There is an obvious irony in the fact that the father is a nonconformist and the son an establishmentarian. The personal dimensions of the story, however, transcend its social implications. As Rémy is dying, persons who shared his life years earlier begin to feel that they have lived vicariously through him. Regardless of the grudges they might hold toward him, there is a sense that a considerable energy and lust for life is about to be extinguished. One might argue that the film sentimentalizes the choices that Rémy has made in life in order to give him as pleasant a death as possible. Miraculously, the heroin not only eases his pain but makes it possible for him to enjoy food and wine. One almost expects him to engage in one final sexual fling rather than simply remembering past conquests. In a sense, Rémy is a static character who dies much as he lived. It is those around him who are changed. "The young embrace the fantasy that they will live forever," Roger Ebert writes. "The old cling to the equally seductive fantasy that they will die a happy death. This is a fantasy for adults."

## BARBERSHOP

2002 (102 minutes) • Comedy
State Street Pictures Cube Vision (MGM) • PG-13

Cast: Ice Cube (Calvin Palmer), Anthony Anderson (JD), Cedric the Entertainer (Eddie), Sean Patrick Thomas (Jimmy James), Eve (Terri Jones), Troy Garity (Isaac Rosenberg), Michael Ealy (Ricky Nash), Keith David (Lester), Parvesh Cheena (Samir), Lahmard Tate (Billy)

Producers: Mark Brown, Robert Teitel, George Tillman Jr.; Director: Tim Story; Writers: Mark Brown, Don D. Scott, Marshall Todd (from a story by Mark Brown); Photographer: Tom Priestly Jr. (color); Editor: John Carter.

This film offers a privileged view into the black community of South Chicago, where Calvin's barbershop is the one enduring symbol of social continuity. Established in 1968, the shop has been passed down through three generations of Calvin's family. Unfortunately, the business is heavily mortgaged, and Calvin has grand ambitions to set up a recording studio in his basement. Consequently, he sells the shop to Lester, a shady black investor who wants to turn it into a "gentlemen's club" with a barbershop motif.

It would appear that Calvin is too late in realizing that he has not only sacrificed a family legacy but also jeopardized the people who work for him. At the same time, an incredibly inept pair of thieves, JD and Billy, have stolen a brand-new ATM machine from a local (Indian-owned) grocery store. Their hilarious efforts to find a safe haven for this monstrosity serve as a counterpoint to the main story line. (The joke on them is that the machine is so new it has yet to be loaded with money.) In the meantime, Ricky Nash, a barber who already sports two felony convictions, is scrutinized by the police. The story ends happily when Lester is apprehended running a chop shop. A chastened Calvin gets his money back, and the barbershop remains open.

Director Tim Story blends an ensemble cast into a story with both specifically racial significance and universal meaning. The importance of the barbershop is heightened by the obvious difficulties of maintaining a sense of community and social order in the ghetto. Calvin's dream of obtaining a kind of vicarious stardom through a recording studio is typical of the dangerously unrealistic fantasies that often prevent the poor from gaining a sure foothold in the middle class. Isaac Rosenberg's portrayal of a white boy who convincingly takes on the trappings of black culture is only the most recent example of a phenomenon noted by Norman Mailer and Jack Kerouac back in the '50s. Probably the most memorable performance, however, is rendered by Cedric the Entertainer as Eddie, the oldest barber in the shop. This also turned out to be the most controversial aspect of the film.

While baiting his younger colleagues, Eddie makes some irreverent comments about Rosa Parks, Martin Luther King Jr., and Rodney King. This predictably brought down the wrath of the Reverend Al Sharpton and other civil-rights leaders. It was unfortunate that such an essentially positive portrayal of the African American community (made almost entirely by black artists) should be condemned for a few isolated lines. If these lines are heard in context, it is not clear that they are even meant seriously. Eddie's primary intention seems to be to get the goat of some kids too young to have lived through the civil-rights movement. Even if he is meant to be taken seriously, Eddie is only one character and not necessarily the spokesman for the movie. But the point of political correctness is that certain individuals cannot be denigrated—even in jest. Eddie's targets are among the very few figures in our culture who are afforded such deference. One wonders if "The Reverend Al" howled in protest over the presentation of Jesus in *The Last Temptation of Christ*.

## BARCELONA

1994 (101 minutes) • Romantic Comedy
Castle Rock • PG-13

Cast: Taylor Nichols (Ted Boynton), Chris Eigeman (Fred Boynton), Mira Sorvino (Marta), Tushka Bergen (Montserrat), Pepe Munné (Ramone) , Heléna Schmied (Greta), Núria Badia (Aurora), Thomas Gibson (Dickie Taylor), Jack Gilpin (The Consul), Pere Ponce (Young Doctor), Laura López (Ted's Assistant), Francis Creighton (Frank Robinson), Edmon Roch (Javier)

Producers: Whit Stillman, Antonio Lòrens, Jordi Tusell (Producers), Cecilia Kate Rocque (Associate Producer), Victoria Borrías, Rosa Romero (Line Producers); Director: Whit Stillman; Writer: Whit Stillman; Photographer: John Thomas (Technicolor); Editor: Christopher Tellefsen

In the late nineteenth and early twentieth centuries, Henry James created a genre of fiction focusing on American expatriates in Europe. Director Whit Stillman has given us a cinematic version of the same in *Barcelona.* In James's novels, the naïve and vulgar American usually experiences a moral epiphany when confronted with the culture of the Old World. (The one notable exception is his early novella *Daisy Miller* [1878].) The Americans in *Barcelona* are cousins—Ted and Fred Boynton. Ted works in sales for an Indianapolis car company, while Fred is an officer in the U.S. Navy during the last decade of the Cold War. After a brief period of euphoria and gratitude following World War II, sophisticated Europeans have resumed their disdain for America. Rather than endorsing that disdain, Stillman gradually reveals the moral superiority of his American characters.

The two cousins represent capitalism and the military, respectively. Although Ted seems to have reconciled himself to Spanish attitudes toward his vocation, Fred (who defiantly wears his naval uniform in Barcelona, at least in part because he has no suitable civilian clothes) expresses shock that he would be called a "fascist" when "young men wearing this uniform died to protect Europe from fascism." At the same time, he is not above spreading rumors that Ted follows the Marquis de Sade by wearing leather underwear. Ironically, this makes Ted more appealing to the Spanish trade-show girls, who are trying to peddle their native goods to American consumers.

In his own way, Ted is as committed to sales as Fred is to the military. He is a devoted reader of the commercial gurus Dale Carnegie and Frank Bettger, and his major worry in life is that he may not actually be "cut out for sales." Fred makes up the story about his cousin's devotion to the Marquis de Sade when he comes upon Ted reading the Bible (which had been hidden in a copy of the *Economist*) while dancing to a Glenn Miller tune. Although Fred's lie renders Ted more attractive to the Spanish women, the truth of Fred's patriotism makes him the target of a left-wing hit man.

After the shooting, Fred lies in a coma. Ted keeps a bedside vigil—reading him *The Scarlet Pimpernel*, while various local acquaintances read from *War and Peace*. In a fit of Protestant remorse, Ted, who has scored a perfect 1600 on his SATs, apologizes for not having believed that his cousin got a lower score because he was distracted by a girl adjusting her brassiere. At this point, Fred rises from the coma and says, "Give me a break." When he fully regains consciousness, he has lost an eye and suffers from partial amnesia. Ted, however, has received an important promotion from his dying employer, and both cousins end up back in America with Spanish trade-girl wives.(The final scene of the film takes place on the lake where Fred had stolen Ted's kayak back in their adolescence.) The happy couples are eating hamburgers—an American culinary triumph that Europe has never mastered.

## BECKET

1964 (148 minutes) • Historical Drama
Paramount • Unrated

Cast: Richard Burton (Thomas Becket), Peter O'Toole (Henry II), John Gielgud ( Louis VII of France), Donald Wolfit (Gilbert Folliot, Bishop of London), Martita Hunt (Empress Matilda), Pamela Brown (Eleanor of Aquitaine), Siân Phillips (Gwendolyn), Felix Aylmer (Theobold of Bec), Gino Cervi (Cardinal Zambelli), Paolo Stoppa (Pope Alexander III), David Weston (Brother John)

Producers: Hal B. Wallis (Producer), Joseph H. Hazen (Executive Producer); Director: Peter Glenville; Writers: Jean Anouilh, Edward Anhalt; Photographer: Geoffrey Unsworth (color); Editor: Anne V. Coates

Jean Anouilh's play *Becket or The Honor of God* (1959) is the most recent of five dramatic retellings of the story of Thomas Becket since the time of Alfred Lord Tennyson. In terms of theatrical conventions, it is also the most realistic. This, however, does not make it the most historically accurate version of the tale. Anouilh was working with a source that assumed that Becket was a Saxon. Although that notion had since been discredited, Anouilh found Thomas's identity with the defeated race so integral to his story that he left it in. Another innovation was to suggest a homoerotic element in Henry II's feelings for Becket. (Although this is not inherently implausible, there is no clear warrant for it in history.) Anouilh's play, therefore, is less a historical narrative than it is a fiction based on history. As such, it bears comparison to Robert Bolt's contemporaneous play *A Man for All Seasons* (1960).

Peter Glenville's adaptation of *Becket* is beautifully filmed. It also employs the talents of two of the greatest actors of the modern era—Richard Burton and Peter O'Toole. The story is of two friends who drink, hunt, and chase women together. The fact that one of these friends is the king of England scarcely seems to matter until Henry begins to rely on Thomas as a professional crony. He first appoints Becket chancellor of England and then engineers his consecration as archbishop of Canterbury. What Henry does not bargain for is the prospect that Thomas will take this latter job more seriously than he does his loyalty to the king.

Becket's transformation from a loose-living rake to a committed churchman is explained in part by the guilt he feels for being a Saxon collaborator with a Norman king. There is also the sense that he might simply have been waiting for a cause worthy of his devotion. If anything, Anouilh's Henry is even more conflicted than Becket. Instead of solving the long-festering conflicts between church and state, his designation of Thomas as archbishop has cost him his dearest friendship. One can well understand, if not approve, his anguished cry: "Will no one rid me of this troublesome priest?" Henry is now remembered as one of England's weaker kings, while Becket became a martyr and saint—the object of Chaucer's famous pilgrimage in *The Canterbury Tales.*

The subtitle of Anouilh's play is of prime significance. For modern audiences, honor is regarded as a medieval concept that has been superseded in recent years by more important values. If human "honor" calls up images of jousting knights or duels at dawn, however, the honor of God is an entirely different matter. Although the film version of *Becket* was probably never intended to have any contemporary relevance, it came out at the tail end of Vatican

II. Like *A Man for All Seasons*, it had an obvious appeal for conservative Roman Catholics, who sought to glamorize a time when church doctrine was defended to the death rather than compromised to appease a secular culture. And even non-Catholics could find something to admire in Becket's grace under pressure.

## BEING THERE

1979 (130 minutes) • Comedy
Lorimar • PG

Cast: Peter Sellers (Chance), Shirley MacLaine (Eve Rand), Melvyn Douglas (Benjamin Rand), Jack Warden (President Bobby), Richard Dysart (Dr. Robert Allenby), Richard Basehart (Vladmir Skrapinov), Ruth Attaway (Louise), David Clennon (Thomas Franklin), Fran Brill (Sally Hayes), Denise DuBarry (Johanna Franklin)

Producer: Andrew Braunsberg; Director: Hal Ashby; Writer: Jerzy Kosinski (based on his novel); Photographer: Caleb Deschanel (Technicolor); Editor: Don Zimmerman

Although he lost the Academy Award for best actor to Dustin Hoffman (for *Kramer vs. Kramer)*, Peter Sellers's performance as Chance the Gardener in *Being There* was probably his greatest job of acting. Most of his previous roles were flamboyant characters who could be played broadly by a professional comedian. The role of Chance, however, required a subtlety and nuance beyond the capability of most comics. A consummate actor, Sellers makes an implausible character seem totally convincing. Unfortunately, his untimely death made this the penultimate role of his career.

Based on Jerzy Kosinski's novel, *Being There* is the story of an illiterate gardener who is evicted from the only home he has ever known when his employer dies. Wandering around the streets of Washington, D.C., he is accidentally hit by the limousine of a tycoon's wife. In an effort to avoid a lawsuit, the tycoon (played by Melvyn Douglas) takes Chance under his wing. As a houseguest of the rich but dying Ben Rand, Chance impresses some of the most important people in the country (including the president of the United States) with homely aphorisms that they take for deep wisdom. They even misconstrue his name as Chauncey Gardiner.

A native of Poland, Jerzy Kosinski was born in 1933 and moved to America in 1958. As a result, he saw both the Nazi and Communist regimes up close during the first twenty-five years of his life. Like Franz Kafka, Kosinski has chosen to depict the totalitarian sensibility from an absurdist perspective rather than with the documentary realism employed for this task by so many other writers.

Although *Being There* is set in the United States and seems to be a satire of America's ruling class, the real object of ridicule is arbitrary power of any derivation. Because the rulers of the world have lost any sense of the meaning of the words they use, they attribute an unwarranted profundity to Chance's observations. (Or perhaps, in contrast to their empty bombast, his statements really do convey greater meaning. Kosinski allows us either interpretation.) John W. Aldridge argues that the condition satirized in *Being There* "is the kind that arises when the higher sensibilities of a people have become not so much brutalized as benumbed, when they have lost both skepticism and all hold on the real, and so fall victim to those agencies of propaganda which manipulate their thinking to accept whatever the state finds it expedient for them to accept."

Rather than being a con man who is trying to scam high society, Chance is a genuine naïf. No doubt, his elegant dress and courtly manners help to conceal his lack of education and worldly wisdom. Because he is used to having his life laid out for him by others, he is perfectly adaptable to radically changing circumstances. Although he becomes part of the Rand household and seems to develop a genuine affection for Ben, he does not adopt capitalist values. Nor does he particularly shun them. He seems to look beyond ideology to embrace individual personalities. This may account for the magnetism that draws people to him. But if Chance is a basically good person, he is also too shallow to be a moral norm. Everything that he knows in life comes from watching vapid television shows. That this elevates him to the level of a political guru tells us all we need to know about our media-made culture.

## THE BEST YEARS OF OUR LIVES

1946 (172 minutes) • Drama
RKO • Unrated

Cast: Frederic March (Al Stephenson), Myrna Loy (Milly Stephenson), Dana Andrews (Fred Derry), Teresa Wright (Peggy Stephenson), Virginia Mayo (Marie Derry), Cathy O'Donnell (Wilma Cameron), Hoagy Carmichael (Butch Engle), Harold Russell (Homer Parrish), Gladys George (Hortense Derry), Roman Bohnen (Pat Derry), Ray Collins (Mr. Milton), Steve Cochran (Cliff)

Producer: Samuel Goldwyn; Director: William Wyler; Writer: Robert E. Sherwood (based on the novel *Glory for Me* by MacKinlay Kantor); Photographer: Gregg Toland (black and white); Editor: Daniel Mandell

At the time of its release in 1946, *The Best Years of Our Lives* was well received by both audiences and critics. This depiction of returning veterans trying to readjust to civilian life won seven Academy Awards—including ones for best picture, best director, best screenplay (by former FDR speechwriter Robert Sherwood), best actor (March), and best supporting actor (Russell). The story follows three servicemen returning to the same Midwestern town. Al Stephenson, who has been a sergeant in the army, is now vice president of the local bank, where he must evaluate applications for small loans. As a captain in the air corps, Fred Derry is the highest ranking of the three veterans but also the one who experiences the most difficulty finding a job back home. He is finally able to regain his prewar position as a soda jerk and salesman at the local drug store, which has been absorbed by a national chain. The pay is low, and he must endure the humiliation of working for his own former assistant, who has risen in the store hierarchy while Fred and others were away at war. His personal life is complicated by the fact that his fun-loving wife is not content to live within her husband's limited means, even as he finds himself falling in love with Al's daughter Peggy. The third featured veteran is a sailor named Homer Parrish. A former high school athlete, he must return to his family and fiancée Wilma with hooks where his hands used to be.

While dealing with the personal lives of the major characters, the film also tackles larger social issues. In his position at the bank, Al approves a loan for a veteran whose only collateral is his character. Although this decision goes against traditional banking practice, there is every indication that he will continue to approve such loans in the future. In one crucial scene, Homer gets into a heated argument at the soda fountain with a man who believes that the war had been a mistake and that the United States should have joined with the Axis powers to fight the Soviets. When Fred joins the brawl, he quickly loses both his paycheck and his wife. Things look up, however, when he lands a job in the construction industry (building houses from the remains of bombers like the ones he used to fly) and his divorce leaves him free to pursue his romance with Peggy Stephenson. The film ends with the wedding of Homer and Wilma and the apparent engagement of Fred and Peggy.

If *The Best Years of Our Lives* was initially praised, it has subsequently elicited the disdain of elitist critics. Probably the most derisive analysis has been that of New York intellectual Robert Warshow, who thinks that the film is too evasive in its portrayal of both politics and sex. Warshow argues that if the movie wanted to depict the problems of veterans, it should have included some reference to veterans' organizations. He sneers at the significance of Al's giving a small loan to a veteran without collateral simply because it was not a large loan. (Given the constraints under which Al operates, it is clear that even a small loan is a big risk.) The confrontation in the drug store is also minimized by Warshow because Homer's antagonist is clearly a repulsive character. What makes him repulsive, however, are his views—or at least the truculent way in which he expresses them. One wonders if Warshow (who brands these views as "fascist') would have been more pleased had the antagonist been more likeable. The critic also surmises that Homer's lack of hands allows him to indulge himself guiltlessly in the male fantasy of remaining passive during sex. Whether that means that his handicap—the actor, Harold Russell, really did lose his hands in the war—is actually a stroke of luck, Warshow does not say. As a member of the adversary culture, he proably doesn't much care.

## BLAST FROM THE PAST

1999 (106 minutes) • Social Satire
New Line Cinema • PG-13

Cast: Brendan Fraser (Adam Webber), Alicia Silverstone (Eve Rustikoff), Christopher Walken (Calvin Webber), Sissy Spacek (Helen Webber), Dave Foley (Troy), Joey Slotnick (Archbishop Melker), Dale Raoul (Mom), Hayden Tank (Adam, Age 3 ½), Douglas Smith (Adam, Age 11), Ryan Sparks (Adam, Age 8), Don Yesso (Jerry), Scott Thomson (Young Pyscho), Rex Linn (Dave), Cynthia Mace (Betty), Jenifer Lewis (Dr. Nina Aron), Bill Gratton (Eve's Boss)

Producers: Renny Harlin, Hugh Wilson (Producers), Sunil Perkash, Claire Rudnick Polstein, Amanda Stern (Executive Producers), Mary Kane (Coproducer); Director: Hugh Wilson; Photographer: José Luis Alcaine (Deluxe color); Editor: Don Brochu

In 1888, Edward Bellamy wrote a futuristic novel called *Looking Backward.* Although largely forgotten today, this book ranked just behind *Uncle Tom's Cabin* and *Ben-Hur* among American best-sellers of the nineteenth century. It tells the story of an American plutocrat of the late 1880s who sleeps for 113 years, only to awaken to a socialist utopia in the year 2000. In *Blast from the Past*, a suburban American couple repairs to their fallout shelter in 1962. (It is the time of the Cuban Missile Crisis, and they assume that a nuclear attack has occurred when a plane crashes into their house.) The wife gives birth, and the entire family remains in the shelter for thirty-five years, waiting for the radioactivity to dissipate to safe levels. At this point the son, appropriately named Adam, ventures into what southern California has become in the late '90s. His innocent perspective on that world is the one the film asks us to adopt. Unlike Bellamy's protagonist, Adam has ventured into a dystopia.

Roger Ebert is no doubt correct in seeing this story as the antithesis of *Pleasantville*, made the previous year. In that film, kids from the present time travel back to an idealized '50s and gradually liberate the benighted souls of that era from the various repressions from which they suffer. In *Blast from the Past*, the people of the '90s have much to learn from the wisdom of an earlier time. Adam finds true love with a woman named (what else?) Eve, who finds his basic decency and näiveté too much to believe. When he tells her the true story of his life, she takes the logical course of action and tries to have him committed. Fortunately, Adam escapes from the shrink, leading to what has to be one of the funniest lines in the history of cinema: "I think I'm being chased by a psychiatrist." He later convinces Eve that he is on the level and takes her home to meet the folks at their shelter, a luxurious (if underground) simulation of their house. (Because it has been assumed that the family perished when the plane crashed into their abode, a succession of seedy commercial establishments have been erected on the ruins.) With a box of vintage baseball cards and some stock certificates that have appreciated greatly in value, Adam is able to lavish phenomenal wealth on his parents and his newfound helpmeet. The old man, however, has a hard time believing that the Soviet Empire disappeared—without a shot being fired.

Given the relentless disparagement of the '50s by the chattering class, it is both unusual and refreshing to see a movie in which the moral norm is a family that could have lived down the street from the Cleavers in *Leave It to Beaver.* I suspect that many aging baby boomers have grown nostalgic for the simpler values of their childhood, while younger generations are curious about an era they know only from reruns on TV Land. Director Hugh Wilson does not need to make either the traditional family or the time in which they lived seem better than they were for them to appear superior to the rootless and vulgar culture of the new millennium. Simply by letting us hear the voice of Perry Como and see the face of Jackie Gleason, he reminds us of the way we were.

## BLAZING SADDLES

1974 (93 minutes) • Comedy
Warner Brothers • R

Cast: Cleavon Little (Bart), Madeline Kahn (Lili Von Shtupp), Gene Wilder (Jim), Slim Pickens (Taggart), Harvey Korman (Hedley Lamarr), Alex Karras (Mongo), Mel Brooks (Governor LePetomaine / Indian Chief), David Huddleston (Olson Johnson), Liam Dunn (The Reverend Johnson), John Hillerman (Howard Johnson), George Furth (Van Johnson)

Producer: Michael Hertzberg; Director: Mel Brooks; Writers: Mel Brooks, Norman Steinberg, Andrew Bergman,

Richard Pryor, Alan Uger (based on a story by Andrew Bergman); Photographer: Joseph Biroc (Technicolor); Editors: John C. Howard, Danford B. Greene

Voted the sixth-funniest movie comedy of all time by the American Film Institute, Mel Brooks's *Blazing Saddles* was regarded as a taboo-shattering picture when it was released in 1974. Its scatological humor is epitomized by a legendary scene of campfire flatulence. Persons acquainted with Yiddish will recognize some vulgar expressions unfamiliar to the majority of the audience. But the real scandal consisted of the racial epithets and attitudes expressed by the stock Western characters in the film. Some earnest social critics have argued that Brooks was attempting to satirize the racism behind the winning of the American West. Others suspect that he was just trying to capitalize on a contemporaneous trend in popular culture. At the time that *Blazing Saddles* was released, the highest-rated show on American television, *All in the Family*, featured a racist character who thought and said things that were not supposed to be expressed in polite company. The experience proved cathartic both for closet bigots and for those who liked nothing better than to see pious liberals squirm.

Brooks's story concerns a greedy speculator (Hedley Lamarr) who seeks to depopulate the Western town of Rock Ridge because the railroad craves the land on which it stands. After considering several sure-fire scare tactics, Lamarr persuades the governor to appoint a black sheriff for the town. Although this predictably raises the ire of the townspeople, almost all of whom are surnamed Johnson (in a likely allusion to black slang for the male genitalia), the sheriff manages to survive with the aid of a drunken prisoner who used to be the fastest gun in the West. Played respectively by Cleavon Little and Gene Wilder, the sheriff (Bart) and the drunk (Jim) form the sort of interethnic male bond that Leslie Fiedler claims was integral to the myth of the American West.

The problem with reading this movie as an indictment of the white conquest of the frontier is that the victims of that conquest were red rather than black. The only red presence in the film comes when a Yiddish Indian played by Brooks attacks a wagon train with which Bart's family has been riding. (In an obvious spoof of segregation, the white pioneers will not let the blacks join their protective circle, thus forcing Bart's family to drive their wagon around in a single feckless circle.) Noting that "they're darker than we are," the chief lets the blacks go.

Far from being a coherent anti-Western, *Blazing Saddles* may be viewed as yet another episode in the annals of the vexed relations between American blacks and Jews. From the vitriol of the Black Muslims to Jesse Jackson's reference to New York as "Hymietown" and the more recent scapegoating of Jews by black politicians such as Cynthia McKinney (D-GA), anti-Semitism in the black community has become increasingly evident in recent decades. By the same token, Jewish comedians such as Lenny Bruce and Kinky Friedman have freely used the toxic "N" word for allegedly satiric purposes. Brooks, however, must have set some kind of record in *Blazing Saddles* (including having his Indian chief refer to Bart's family as "shvartzers," the Yiddish equivalent for "niggers"). In November 2006, the racist rant of the Jewish comedian Michael Richards threatened to take the word permanently out of circulation. It is no small irony that, more than thirty years after the filming of his most outrageous movie, one of the linguistic taboos that Brooks sought to shatter has returned with a vengeance—thus making *Blazing Saddles* more politically incorrect than ever.

## BORAT: CULTURAL LEARNINGS OF AMERICA FOR MAKE BENEFIT GLORIOUS NATION OF KAZAKHSTAN

2006 (84 minutes) • Comedy
Twentieth Century-Fox • R

Cast: Sacha Baron Cohen (Borat Sagdiyev), Ken Davitian (Azamat Bagatov), Luenell (Luenell), Bob Barr (Himself), Pamela Anderson (Herself)

Producers: Sacha Baron Cohen, Jay Roach (Producers), Monica Levinson, Dan Mazer (Executive Producers), Jonathan Sacher (Coproducer); Director: Larry Charles; Writers: Sacha Baron Cohen, Anthony Hines, Peter Baynham, Dan Mazer, Todd Phillips; Photographers: Luke Geissbuhler, Anthony Hardwick (color); Editors: Craig Alpert, Peter Teschner, James Thomas

It is difficult to place Sacha Baron Cohen and his cinematic persona Borat on any conventional political spectrum. Everyone from the poverty-stricken masses of the Third World to the upper reaches of American society is fair game for Cohen's satire. This remarkable film is a kind of guerilla documentary in which real people are allowed (even encouraged) to make fools of themselves without benefit of a script. Apparently, several of Cohen's victims gulled themselves into thinking that they were involved in a serious venture in cultural exchange. After seeing the results, they have—unsurprisingly—besieged him with lawsuits.

The premise of the film is that Borat Sagdiyev, a TV reporter from the former Soviet satellite of Kazakhstan, is touring America to learn how to elevate the cultural standing of his own country. The movie begins in what purports to be the documentarian's hometown. Borat introduces his sister as the "number-four prostitute" in the country and his aged mother as the oldest woman in the town at the age of forty-three. We then see one of the country's favorite sports—"the running of the Jew," in which Kazakhs attack larger than life anti-Semitic caricatures of both the Jew and his wife. (The purpose of the game is to destroy "Mrs. Jew" before she "hatches her young.") Rarely has a Hollywood film so mercilessly parodied the backwardness and prejudice of the Third World. And this is just the opening sequence!

Borat's American odyssey takes him from the East to the West coast. In the process, he sings a fictitious version of the Kazakhstan national anthem to the tune of the "Star-Spangled Banner" at a rodeo in Virginia, brings a black prostitute to an elegant dinner party at a plantation in Mississippi, converts to Christianity at a Pentecostal church service, and literally bags Pamela Anderson at a book signing. On the way, he encounters everyone from black street people to white frat boys and asks a gun store owner to recommend the best weapon for defending himself against a Jew. The deliberately offensive content of this film, including a particularly gross nude male wrestling scene, fully justifies its R rating and makes it inappropriate viewing for the young and the squeamish. Others are apt to share the reaction of *Simpsons* writer George Meyer, who said upon seeing the film: "I feel like someone just played me *Sgt. Pepper's* for the first time."

Writing in *Entertainment Weekly*, Josh Rottenberg compared *Borat* to the classic TV series *Candid Camera*, a program in which the victims of various practical jokes were caught on a hidden camera. The practical jokes in this film, however, are photographed on a visible camera and perpetrated by an even more visible provocateur. Moreover, the finished picture consists of more than mere adolescent pranks. Through the persona of Borat, Sacha Baron Cohen does what all true art should do. He holds a mirror up to human nature. It was perhaps for that very reason that this enormously successful film was initially pulled from theaters all over the country.

## BRAVEHEART

1995 (177 minutes) • Historical Drama
Icon Pictures/The Ladd Company/Marquis Film/
Paramount • R

Cast: Mel Gibson (William Wallace), Sophie Marceau (Princess Isabelle), Patrick McGoohan (King Edward I—Longshanks), Catherine McCormack (Murron), Brendan Gleeson (Hamish), James Cosmo (Campbell), David O'Hara (Stephen), Angus Macfadyen (Robert the Bruce), Ian Bannen (The Leper), Peter Hanly (Prince Edward)

Producers: Mel Gibson, Alan Ladd Jr., Bruce Davey; Director: Mel Gibson; Writer: Randall Wallace; Photographer: John Toll (color); Editor: Steven Rosenblum

Although the critical reaction to this film was mixed, it was nominated for nine Academy Awards and won four (including best picture and best director). The narrative follows the Scottish national hero William Wallace from childhood to martyrdom at the hands of the perfidious British. While only a boy, Wallace sees the forces of Edward I massacre a group of unarmed Scottish landowners. The orphaned hero is adopted by his uncle and educated abroad. As an adult, he returns to his native hamlet to find the British still treacherous and the Scots still gullible. A brief romantic interlude, in which he courts and weds a local girl, is interrupted when his wife is raped and murdered by the Brits.

At that point, Wallace becomes an effective guerilla warrior, leading his people in a surprising victory against a much larger English contingent at the Battle of Stirling. In a daring move he invades England and captures the town of York. Unfortunately, the superior British forces combined with the treachery of Robert Bruce, leader of the nobles and aspirant to the Scottish throne, prove Wallace's undoing. In a death agony that may anticipate *The Passion of the Christ,* he is brutally tortured on the rack before being beheaded. Through it all, he is sustained by the single word "freedom."

At a time when he was already the most bankable star in Hollywood, Gibson achieved his first directorial triumph with a film that seemed to transfer the action of his highly successful *Lethal Weapon* movies to the low-tech thirteenth century. Although some reviewers faulted the movie's sluggish pace and Gibson's trite use of slow motion during some action sequences, the battle scenes are magnificently orchestrated. More problematic are the liberties Gibson takes with the historical record, particularly in manufacturing a romance between Wallace and Queen Isabelle. Nevertheless, the imaginative vision of the film is true to the spirit of ethnic nationalism. That might have been good enough for the liberal establishment—had the ethnics not been the politically incorrect Scots.

William Wallace is no Gandhi or Mandela. Like Gibson, he is an unapologetic white Anglo-Celtic Roman Catholic. (In an essay on the film, the Celtic historian Michael Hill writes: "Several scenes might serve as editorials for the *Latin Mass* magazine, and Wallace's Latinity is harped upon almost as much as his ferocity.") Wallace and his followers have no grand social vision beyond a desire to be left alone to live according to their own lights. Gibson leaves little doubt in our minds that such a life would be conservative, if not reactionary, when judged by contemporary standards. The values of the Scots, as enumerated by Hill, include "the things that New York despises, namely Christian devotion, populism, patriotism, home rule, self-defense, well-defined sex roles, traditional morality, and self-sacrifice for a noble cause." Perhaps the harshest political criticism to be leveled at the film came from the gay community, which objected to Gibson's depiction of the homosexual prince Edward II. In contrast, the audience actually feels some sympathy for the prince's utterly despicable but unmistakably heterosexual father, Edward I.

## BRAZIL

1985 (143 minutes) • Futuristic Satire
Universal • R

Cast: Jonathan Pryce (Sam Lowry), Robert De Niro (Tuttle), Katherine Helmond (Ida Lowry), Ian Holm (Kurtzmann), Bob Hoskins (Spoor), Michael Palin (Jack Lint)

Producer: Arnon Milchan; Director: Terry Gilliam; Writers: Terry Gilliam, Tom Stoppard, Charles McKeown; Photographer: Roger Pratt (color); Editor: Julian Doyle

Visions of the future are often problematic, especially if the future in question is close at hand. (Although George Orwell died in 1950, most of his readers were around to measure the actual year 1984 against the prophecies of his novel.) I vividly recall a mock ad in *National Lampoon* showing a family from the 1950s heading toward a space station in the rocket-powered equivalent of a station wagon. One family member says to another: "I sure hope the desk clerk knows Esperanto." The future, as Paul Valéry once noted, isn't what it used to be. That would seem to be one of many points in Terry Gilliam's *Brazil*, a film that at times appears either pointless or confused about its message. But then, the confusion itself may be part of the design. Robert Ross characterizes this picture as "Walter Mitty meets Franz Kafka." One could just as easily pitch it as "Monty Python meets Fritz Lang" or "George Orwell meets the Marx Brothers."

Set "sometime in the twentieth century" (which is enough to date it already), *Brazil* resembles the grim and mechanized landscape of Lang's *Metropolis* (1926). It is a technological society in which none of the technology seems to work. The computer screens are like clouded mirrors and the keyboards resemble very old manual typewriters. In one of the opening scenes, a clerk climbs on his desk to squash a bug on the ceiling. The dead bug falls onto the keyboard, transforming the name "Tuttle" to "Buttle." The resulting confusion sends an innocent man to his death and unleashes a series of misadventures, in which a bumbling bureaucrat named Sam Lowry tries to find both love and freedom in a world bent on denying him both.

Because most of the characters speak with a British accent, we assume that the story is set in England. We might also assume that the bureaucratic mindlessness depicted on the screen is, at least in part, a satire on the inefficiencies of a socialist society. When Lowry's air-conditioning unit breaks down, a renegade private repairman arrives and fixes it before the official government workers even show up to discover that Lowry does not have the proper form for the job. Always in the background are terrorist explosions and the sight of rogue police arresting innocent citizens. (Talk about prescience!) The only release from this oppressive environment lies in the imagination. Many of the characters live a vicarious life in old films. (References to classic pictures and old movie posters abound.) In addition, Sam dreams of flying—like Icarus or an angel, take your pick—with his feminine ideal. When he finally meets this woman, she turns out to be a take-charge truck driver with short hair and a no-nonsense attitude. Rather than dampening his ardor, this turns out to be just the sort of woman Lowry needs.

I would not reveal the ending of this movie, even if I understood it. Suffice it to say that it is not a testament to the triumph of the human spirit. In fact, the romantic 1930s song "Brazil" mocks the lack of romance and idealism in the world of this film. What we see is not so much a possible dystopia as a bad dream or life in the funhouse mirror. If anything, Gilliam has learned too well that film is a visual medium. The movie may not have been conceived in a psychedelic haze, but one suspects that that is the best way to view it.

## CHARIOTS OF FIRE

1981 (123 minutes) •Historical Drama
Enigma (UK) • PG

Cast: Ben Cross (Harold Abrahams), Ian Charleson (Eric Liddell), Nigel Havers (Lord Andrew Lindsay), Nicholas Farrell (Aubrey Montague), Ian Holm (Sam Mussabini), John Gielgud (Master of Trinity), Lindsay Anderson (Master of Caius), Nigel Davenport (Lord Birkenhead), Cheryl Campbell (Jennie Liddell), Alice Krige (Sybil Gordon)

Producer: David Putnam; Director: Hugh Hudson; Writer: Colin Welland; Photographer: David Watkin (color); Editor: Terry Rawlings

Audiences and critics responded so well to *Chariots of Fire* that it won Academy Awards for best picture, best original screenplay, best original score, and best costume design, while being nominated for three other Oscars. The movie came out the year after the United States had boycotted the Moscow Olympics because of the Soviet invasion of Afghanistan. It was therefore a propitious time for a film that analyzed the relative importance of sports within the broader range of human values. The story focuses on two very different British runners—the Jew Harold Abrahams and the Scottish Christian Eric Liddell. Despite their dissimilarities, the film does not condescend to either individual. In a sense, both are outsiders within the elitist caste system of the British upper class and are tolerated only because of the international glory their athletic gifts can bring to the empire at the 1924 Olympics in Paris. Although England had been on the winning side in World War I, we are made keenly aware of the toll that that conflict had taken on an entire generation of young Britons.

If Abrahams is running with a chip on his shoulder, it is because of the anti-Semitic treatment he receives at Cambridge and elsewhere. His mission is not only to win Olympic gold but to prove himself a more loyal subject of the king than all of the upper-class WASP dilettantes who are running just for fun (an attitude that is mistaken for the amateur ideal). As part of his quest for glory, Abrahams hires a private trainer, who is part Italian and part Arab. At the same time, he is trying to win the love of a beautiful opera singer. Abrahams comes across as a sympathetic character because of his determination and the degree to which he anticipates a more contemporary attitude toward sports. It is ironically fitting that in real life he was the elder statesman of British athletics until his death in 1978—three years before the release of the movie.

If Abrahams is a modern athlete before his time, Liddell is a throwback to an age when religious faith meant more than worldly glory. A deeply devout member of the Church of Scotland, Eric convinces himself that his ability to run is a gift from God. Despite objections from his family (particularly his fiancée), he persists in his athletic career until he has established himself as the fastest man alive and his country's best hope for Olympic success. Then he learns that a qualifying heat in which he is supposed to run is scheduled for Sunday. Not even the prince of Wales (the future Edward VIII) can persuade him to violate the Sabbath. A solution emerges when one of the less committed runners, who has already won a medal, offers to drop out of the competition so that Liddell can run in a non-Sunday heat. Abrahams will then be able to take Liddell's place on Sunday. (This would appear to be an example of the amateur ideal at its best.) In an industry that often maligns what it takes to be religious fanaticism, the story of Eric Liddell is treated with admirable sensitivity.

## THE CHRONICLES OF NARNIA: THE LION, THE WITCH, AND THE WARDROBE

2005 (143 minutes) • Animated Fantasy
Walden/Disney • PG

Cast: Georgie Henley (Lucy), Skander Keynes (Edmund), William Moseley (Peter), Anna Popplewell (Susan), Tilda Swinton (White Witch), James McAvoy (Mr. Tumnus), Jim Broadbent (Professor Kirke), Kiran Shah (Ginarrbrik), James Cosmo (Father Christmas), Elizabeth Hawthorne (Mrs. MacReady), Liam Neeson (Voice of Aslan), Ray Winstone (Voice of Mr. Beaver), Dawn French (Voice of Mrs. Beaver), Rupert Everett (Voice of Fox), Douglas Gresham (Voice of the Radio Announcer)

Producers: Mark Johnson, Philip Steuer (Producers), Andrew Adamson, Perry Moore (Executive Producers), K. C. Hodenfield (Associate Producer), Douglas Gresham (Coproducer); Director: Andrew Adamson; Writers: Ann Peacock, Andrew Adamson, Christopher Markus, Stephen McFeely (based on the book by C. S. Lewis); Photographer: Donald McAlpine (color); Editors: Sim Evan-Jones, Jim May

Despite his many scholarly accomplishments and his books of lay theology, C. S. Lewis is best remembered as the creator of the magical kingdom of Narnia in a series of children's books beginning with *The Lion, the Witch, and the Wardrobe* (1950). Unlike America, where children's literature is too often relegated to low-rent or mass culture, such works (from the time of Mother Goose to the current era of J. K. Rowling) have always been treated respectfully in England. One thinks particularly of *The Lord of the Rings* (1954–55), by Lewis's friend and colleague J. R. R. Tolkien. *The Narnia Chronicles*, however, more closely resemble *Peter Pan* (1904), *Through the Looking Glass* (1872), and *The Wizard of Oz* (1900) in transporting ordinary children from their mundane world into a land of fantasy. In *The Lion, the Witch, and the Wardrobe*, two brothers and two sisters are removed from war-torn London to the country house of an eccentric relative (a professor, of course), where they play hide-and-seek in an attempt to evade the relative's tyrannical housekeeper. In the midst of the game, the youngest child, Lucy, climbs into an old wardrobe, which leads to a snowy landscape and her encounter with a faun named Mr. Tumnus.

Although her siblings initially disbelieve Lucy's tale, all of them eventually find themselves on the other side of the wardrobe. Narnia is a wintry kingdom temporarily ruled by a wicked witch who can turn her enemies to stone with the wave of her wand. The plot thickens when the witch captures one of the children, the obnoxious Edmund, and holds him hostage in her conflict with the kingdom's rightful ruler, the lion Aslan. In the meantime, the other three children are taken in by a family of friendly beavers. All seems lost when the witch, who has been granted safe passage by the lion, maliciously slays the noble Aslan in exchange for the return of Edmund. Aslan, however, is resurrected because a truth deeper and older than the witch's magic held that "when a willing victim who had committed no treachery was killed in a traitor's stead, . . . Death itself would start working backward." What follows is a final Armageddon-like battle, in which the forces of Aslan defeat those of the witch. The children are then installed as rulers of Narnia.

In most respects the film remains faithful to Lewis's text. (In the one major divergence, the book brings the children back through the wardrobe to their quotidian lives, whereas the movie leaves them on their Narnian thrones.) The computer-generated animation allows human beings, animals, and mythical creatures to interact with each other as naturally as they should in this supernatural world. Beyond the pyrotechnics, however, is a vision as ancient as Scripture. Edmund and Peter are referred to as "Sons of Adam" and Lucy and Susan as "Daughters of Eve." Thus, humanity is defined in terms of the primordial fall in Eden. The witch would seem to be a female embodiment of Satan. And Aslan, who is resurrected after dying for Edmund's sins, is the Lamb of God masquerading as the King of the Jungle. In *The Chronicles of Narnia* (as well as in Tolkien's tales of Middle-earth), Christianity has returned to the screen in the form of allegory.

## CITIZEN RUTH

1996 (109 minutes) • Social Satire
Miramax • R

Cast: Laura Dern (Ruth Stoops), Swoosie Kurtz (Diane), Kurtwood Smith (Norm Stoney), Mary Kay Place (Gail Stoney), Tippi Hedren (Jessica Weiss), Burt Reynolds (Blaine Gibbons)

Producers: Cathy Konrad, Cary Woods, Andrew Stone (Coproducers), Michael Zimbrich (Assistant Producer); Director: Alexander Payne; Writers: Alexander Payne, Jim Taylor; Photographer: James Glennon (color); Editor: Kevin Tent

John Simon begins his review of this film with the following observation: "True satire, it should be recalled, is equitable. It sees not black to the left and white to the right, but ridiculous and appalling mud-grey all over. That is how Swift, Voltaire, and Brecht did it, and that, in its sometimes a bit heavy-handed, not always quite funny enough way, is what *Citizen Ruth* does. It is quite simply the boldest satire out of Hollywood since, roughly, the year one." The story concerns Ruth Stoops, a virtual poster girl for forced sterilization. We first meet her in bed with the latest in a string of losers, who takes his pleasure and then tosses her out on the street. She then visits the male relative who is taking care of two of her four children (the others having been given up for adoption)—not to inquire about their welfare but to bum fifteen dollars, which she uses for recreational purposes. As Roger Ebert sagely observes, "One of the danger signals of substance abuse, I'm pretty sure, is finding yourself sniffing patio sealant."

When the cops, who know her by name, bust Ruth for the sixteenth time that year, the judge deems her an unfit mother and offers her a reduced sentence if she will terminate her pregnancy. While in jail, however, she meets some abortion protesters, who agree to give her nine months' room and board if she will keep the child. At this point, advocates of legal abortion must think that director Alexander Payne is on their side. The baby-savers are presented as hopelessly bourgeois hypocrites, every bit as tawdry as their enemies have imagined them to be. Ruth manages to play the scam reasonably well until she sneaks out for a party with the host family's teenage daughter. The laughs are so predictable that we are apt to lose sight of the fact that these people are indeed opening their home to a woman who would otherwise be in the gutter inhaling a bag of airplane glue. One wonders if their daughter is a praiseworthy rebel or yet another example of the unwitting sacrifices made by zealots out to save the world? Alas, Payne's satire is not sufficiently nuanced even to raise this question.

But don't turn the DVD player off just yet. The tables are turned when one of the pro-life stalwarts, who turns out to be a double agent for the other side, kidnaps Ruth. The "pro-choice" side proceeds to hold her prisoner in the rural hideaway shared by the double agent and her lesbian lover. Although Payne is relentless in his lampooning of the Christian Right, he is equally savage in depicting the boutique Left. Eventually, the future of Ruth's pregnancy becomes the object of a bidding war between both sides, as Ruth herself walks off undetected and apparently irrelevant. If the pro-life forces come off as less than admirable because they finally care more for the fetus than the mother, they at least do not hold her prisoner in order to vindicate her "right to choose." This is a movie designed to infuriate both sides in the abortion controversy, even if it fails to stake out a morally coherent position of its own. Fortunately, the ambivalence of the film is not fatal for social satire, as disappointing as it may be for those who already have their minds made up.

## COLONEL EFFINGHAM'S RAID

1945 (72 minutes) • Comedy
Twentieth Century-Fox • Unrated

Cast: Charles Coburn (Col. W. Seaborn Effingham), Joan Bennett (Ella Sue Dozier), William Eythe (Albert Marbury), Allyn Joslyn (Earl Hoats), Elizabeth Patterson (Cousin Emma), Donald Meek (Doc Burden), Frank Craven (Dewey), Thurston Hall (Ed, the Mayor), Cora Witherspoon (Clara Meigs), Emory Parnell (Joe Alsobrook), Henry Armetta (Jimmy Economy), Stephen Dunne (Professor Edward Bland), Roy Roberts (Army Captain Rampsey)

Producer: Lamar Trotti; Director: Irving Pichel; Writers: Berry Fleming, Kathryn Scola; Photographer: Edward Cronjager (black and white); Editor: Harmon Jones

This gem of a movie takes us back to an earlier time in both Hollywood and America. It is 1940, and a kind of patriotic fever (along with the desire to impress a girl) inspires young Al Marbury to join the army. At the same time, Al's Cousin Willie—a career military officer—retires to the small Southern town where the family has always lived. When Willie signs on as a columnist for the local newspaper, the editor assumes that all he will get are human interest stories about the colonel's experiences in the larger world. Much to his surprise, the writer who signs his name W. Seaborn Effingham is as concerned with local politics as he had been with building the Panama Canal decades earlier. (One wonders what the town officials were doing while Willie was in the army.) In the meantime, there is a romantic subplot involving Marbury and Ella Sue Dozier.

This well-paced comedy features a typically excellent performance by Coburn, along with a strong supporting cast. (One local eccentric keeps appearing at public meetings to distribute cards announcing the end of the world.) The major conflict in the story concerns the effort of local officials to rename Confederate Monument Square in honor of a shady politician. The courageous and morally upright Colonel Effingham uses his newspaper column to arouse the indignation of a previously apathetic populace. Even though he is retired from military service, he maintains a sense of civic duty and predictably carries the day. When someone asks why he is in such a hurry, the Colonel replies: "At sixty-five, you have to be in a hurry."

Were this movie made today, it would almost certainly be set somewhere other than the small-town South. Nineteen forty-five, however, was a time when it was still possible for one to be both a patriotic American and a loyal Southerner (even in a movie made by the Communist director Irving Pichel). This was the unspoken cultural truce that existed from the time that the South rejoined the Union until the dawn of the civil-rights era. According to the Southern historian Clyde Wilson: "The terms of the truce went something like this. Northerners agreed to stop demonizing Southerners and to recognize that we had been brave and sincere and honorable in the War, although misguided in trying to break up the Union. Northerners agreed also that Reconstruction was a great wrong that would not have happened if Lincoln had lived. And they willingly accepted Confederate heroes like Lee and Jefferson as *American* heroes." When Colonel Effingham speaks against the destruction of the old courthouse, he cites its heritage from Revolutionary times to the present. Included in that history is the legacy of the Confederacy. He equates modernism with corruption, and it is to the people's credit that they stand with tradition.

## CRASH

2004 (122 minutes) • Drama
Lion's Gate • R

Cast: Sandra Bullock (Jean Cabot), Don Cheadle (Det. Graham Waters), Art Chudabala (Ken Ho), Tony Danza (Fred), Keith David (Lieutenant Dixon), Loretta Devine (Shaniqua Johnson), Matt Dillon (Officer John Ryan), Michael Peña (Daniel), Jennifer Esposito (Ria), William Fichtner (Flanagan), Nona Gaye (Karen), Brendan Fraser (Rick Cabot), Terrence Howard (Cameron Thayer), Bruce Kirby (Pop Ryan), Ludicras (Anthony), Thandie Newton (Christine Thayer), Ryan Phillippe (Officer Tom Hansen), Peter (Larenz Tate), Farhad (Shaun Toub), Beverly Todd (Graham's mother)

Producers: Don Cheadle, Paul Haggis, Mark R. Harris, Bobby Moresco, Cathy Schulman, Bob Yari (Producers), Betsy Danbury, Sarah Finn, Randi Hiller (Coproducers), Marina Grassic, Jan Körbelin, Tom Nunan, Andre Reimer (Executive Producers), Dana Maksimovich (Associate Producer); Director: Paul Haggis; Writers: Paul Haggis and Bobby Moresco; Photographer: J. Michael Muro (color); Editor: Hughes Winborne

When *Crash* became the surprise winner of the 2006 Academy Award for best picture, it was clearly a triumph for the individual vision of director Paul Haggis. Although Haggis had won an Oscar the previous year for his screenplay *Million Dollar Baby*, he and his partner Bobby Moresco wrote the script for *Crash* on speculation and then sought financial backing. As risky as this procedure might have been, it assured them a high degree of artistic freedom. The story they tell involves a dozen people, of various ethnic backgrounds, whose lives cross simply because they live in Los Angeles.

The film opens when a Chinese woman rams her car into the back of a vehicle driven by a Hispanic female, who happens to be a police officer having an affair with a black colleague. The latter officer is the older brother of a street criminal who plays an important role in the tale. In fact, little brother and his partner in crime steal the district attorney's Lincoln Navigator at gunpoint. (The D.A. seems primarily concerned with whether the theft will harm his efforts to win the black vote in the upcoming election.) In the meantime, the D.A.'s wife insists that the locks be changed on her house, even as a racist cop and his partner pull over a Lincoln Navigator that is obviously not the stolen vehicle but is being driven by an upscale black couple, the female member of which is light enough to be mistaken for white.

One could go on, but the general direction of the film should be apparent from the summary of these few opening scenes. Like several earlier movies set in Los Angeles (*Grand Canyon* [1991], *Short Cuts* [1993], and *Magnolia* [1999]), *Crash* is organized around a series of vignettes rather than a single main plot. Despite this episodic structure, the emphasis on race gives the picture its coherence. In Los Angeles, the much-ballyhooed experiment in multiculturalism seems not to be working.

It is to his credit that Haggis refuses to lay the blame on a particular ethnic group—not even white middle-class males. One of the most complex characters in the film is the racist cop who stops the wrong Lincoln Navigator and then proceeds to subject the female passenger to a humiliating groping under the guise of searching for hidden weapons. Just when our disgust with this cretin is at its highest, we see him battling his father's HMO in a vain attempt to secure treatment for the old man's prostrate cancer, which the HMO has repeatedly diagnosed as a bladder infection. To complicate matters, the official who denies the claim is a black woman whom the cop suspects got her position through affirmative action. The cop's father, who has always treated black people fairly, lost his business, his livelihood, and his wife when the city began contracting exclusively with minority-owned suppliers. In one of the movie's many coincidences, the cop later pulls the woman he has groped out of a burning car and saves her life.

The evenhandedness of this film is remarkable, especially since it negotiates a minefield of issues noted for their political sensitivity. (Surprisingly, one explosive issue that it does not tackle is illegal immigration.) Noting the Christmas setting and the pervasiveness of Christian imagery, the critic George McCartney suggests that *Crash* may actually be a religious movie.

It "lifts our spirits because it never flinches from exhibiting the ugliness of which we are capable," he writes, "yet it never fails to remind us of the redemption that awaits those who rise to the challenge of rescuing one another."

## DAWN OF THE DEAD

1979 (125 minutes) • Horror
Dawn Associates/Laurel Group • R

Cast: David Emge (Stephen), Ken Foree (Peter), Scott Reiniger (Roger), Gaylen Ross (Francine), David Crawford (Dr. Foster), David Early (Mr. Berman), Richard France (Scientist), Howard K. Smith (Television Commentator), James A. Baffico (Wooley), George A. Romero (Television Director)

Producers: Richard P. Rubinstein, Herbert Steinman, Billy Baxter, Alfredo Cuomo; Director: George A. Romero; Writer: George A. Romero; Photographer: Michael Gornick (Technicolor); Editors: George A. Romero, Kevin Davidow

The imminent demise of civilization was an obsession of American culture during the 1960s and '70s. In *Dawn of the Dead*, George A. Romero deals with this theme metaphorically and, in the process, returns the genre of the horror story to its roots in social commentary. At the end of Romero's first feature film, *Night of the Living Dead* (1968), the state of Pennsylvania was inundated by zombies who devoured human beings. Although the main characters in that picture have all been destroyed, in *Dawn of the Dead* Romero picks up where he left off with the general catastrophe. The new film begins in a television studio whose news division purveys inaccurate information to boost ratings, even as the police pursue zombies and racial minorities with equal vigor. Unlike more sentimental horror movies, however, this film does not elicit sympathy for the monsters, who are blood-curdling cretins. In a sense, though, they are also exaggerations of our own human impulses.

Three men (Roger, Peter, and Stephen) and one woman (Fran) escape to the precarious safety of a shopping mall. Fran and Stephen are lovers and the parents of an unborn child. Roger and Peter are a couple of SWAT team cops who are white and black, respectively. Unfortunately, the mall is no certain defense against the zombies, who easily outnumber their potential victims. Eventually the living are forced to barricade themselves inside the mall's stores. Roger and Peter, in particular, take advantage of the situation to go on a plunder spree. With the breakdown of social order, the concept of private property is now meaningless. (The irony is compounded by the fact that Peter and Roger are ostensibly law officers who have lost sight of their vocation.) Their wanton greed contrasts markedly with the idyllic night that Charlie Chaplin spent in a department store in *Modern Times* (1936). The zombies differ from this pair in little more than the awkwardness of their looting. The distinction between the living and the undead is further collapsed when Stephen and Roger are both attacked and transformed into zombies. Peter is thus required to kill them both.

In addition to zombies (who include such recognizable types as nuns and Hare Krishnas), the mall is invaded by anarchic bikers. Unlike the principal characters of the film, these individuals seem less interested in acquiring physical booty than in wreaking havoc and destruction for their own sake—often with a slapstick touch, as when they pelt the zombies with cream pies and seltzer water. Unlike the zombies, they are under no biological compulsion to behave as they do. They simply take advantage of the existing chaos to throw off any inhibitions the vanishing social order might have placed upon them. The tale concludes when Fran (who had earlier insisted that Stephen teach her how to fly the traffic helicopter he pilots) and Peter fly from the roof of the mall with a limited supply of gasoline and an uncertain future. Before joining her, Peter had contemplated suicide, holding a gun to his head. Whether intended by Romero or not, this gesture reminds one of a scene in *The Birth of a Nation*, when a beleaguered white man holds a gun against the head of a white woman to prevent her from being raped by a gang of blacks.

Romero is often regarded as a left-wing ideologue and may even think of himself as such. Nevertheless, *Dawn of the Dead* contains elements that a conservative can admire. No one but a crass materialist would celebrate the commercialism of a shopping mall, which Romero shrewdly portrays as a temple to unbridled greed. Also, he shows that the collapse of civil order results not in liberation but in a threat to all humane values. If the zombies are a symbolic representation of the demonic within us, the bikers are literal presences within our society. And even the ostensibly decent characters remind us of the misdeeds that ordinary people are capable of under extraordinary circumstances.

## THE DECALOGUE

In 1988, a year before the fall of the Soviet Empire, the director Krzysztof Kieslowski produced an extraordinary series of ten one-hour dramas for Polish television. Called *The Decalogue*, these films were loosely based on the Ten Commandments. Critics trying to find a direct correspondence between the decalogues of Moses and Kieslowski, however, have been frustrated. Whether one employs the Catholic or Protestant enumeration, not all of the films bear an obvious and direct connection to a specific commandment. In a general sense, however, one can say that Kieslowski perceives the moral dimension of life and believes that human behavior has transcendent implications.

Speaking of himself and his collaborator, Krzysztof Piesiewicz, Kieslowski writes: "We were aware that no philosophy or ideology had ever challenged the fundamental tenets of the Commandments during their several thousand years of existence, yet they are transgressed on a routine basis." Although there was a time when such assumptions would have been taken for granted, the final decade of the twentieth century was not such a time. In comparison to most American cinema (much less the drivel that appears on American television), *The Decalogue* is both thought-provoking and emotionally riveting.

## DECALOGUE ONE

53 minutes

Cast: Henryk Baranowski (Krzysztof), Maja Komorowska (Irena), Wojciech Klata (Pawel), Artur Barcis (Man in the Sheepskin), Maria Gladkowska (Girl), Ewa Kania (Ewa Jezierska), Aleksandra Majsiuk (Ola), Magda Sroga-Mikolajczyk (Journalist)

Producer: Ryszard Chutkowski; Director: Krzysztof Kieslowski; Writers: Krzysztof Kieslowski, Krzysztof Piesiewicz; Photographer: Wieslaw Zdort (color); Editor: Ewa Smal

The first film in the series is a fairly straightforward depiction of the first commandment: "I am the Lord thy God. . . . Thou shalt not have other gods before me." In modern civilization, the worship of golden calves and similar "false gods" of the Old Testament is virtually obsolete. For the most part, it has been replaced by scientism—a naïve confidence in the ability of science and technology to solve all human problems. The protagonist of *Decalogue One* is a thoroughly likable young professor named Krzysztof. (It is notable that he shares the name of both the director of the film and the Son of God.) A single father, Krzysztof is devoted to his young son Pawel, who shares his father's love of computers and penchant for solving complex mathematical problems. Although raised in a Catholic family, Krzysztof is now a virtual skeptic. He nevertheless allows his devout sister, Irena, to enroll Pawel in religious classes.

Krzysztof is so convinced of the potential of computers that he tells his class at the university that these machines will someday be capable of expressing aesthetic preferences. (The near-human qualities Krzysztof ascribes to computers causes critic Joseph G. Kickasola to see ominous parallels to Stanley Kubrick's *2001: A Space Odyssey* [1968].) Pawel is a budding chess prodigy who devises a move that enables his father to defeat a female master at the game. The lad is also filled with philosophical questions concerning such matters as the nature of death and the reality of the soul. He is still young enough to be torn between the very different answers given by his father and his aunt. When he asks his father's permission to try out the skates he is to get for Christmas,

Krzysztof dutifully calculates the thickness of the ice and gives his blessing. Unfortunately, an unexpected thaw results in Pawel's drowning.

For reasons known only to himself, Krzysztof enters a church and turns over an entire bank of votive candles. We see a picture of the Madonna apparently weeping. And then, in a final touch of irony, Krzysztof reaches into the baptismal fount only to find the holy water frozen. It would probably be an exaggeration to say that Pawel's death is God's judgment on his father's infidelity. Kieslowski does not conceive of the world in terms of such simplistic moralism. True believers also lose their children to freak accidents. But the limits of scientism are evident in this film. Logical inquiry falls short of religion not so much in giving us an inaccurate perception of the world as in its failure to provide consolation when the world doesn't behave as we might like. In purely instrumental terms, science may supplant the proverbial god of the gaps by explaining phenomena that were previously inexplicable. But by its very nature, science will not speak to the ends and purposes of life. When we expect it to do so, we create false gods, however benign those gods may appear to be.

## DECALOGUE TWO

57 minutes

Cast: Krystyna Janda (Dorota), Aleksander Bardini (Doctor), Olgierd Lukaszewicz (Andrzej), Artur Barcis (Young Man)

Producer: Ryszard Chutkowski; Director: Krzysztof Kieslowski; Writers: Krzysztof Kieslowski, Krzysztof Piesiewicz; Photographer: Edward Klosinski (color); Editor: Ewa Smal

The second film of the series is fraught with a moral ambiguity that initially seems far removed from the dogmatic legalism of the Ten Commandments. It certainly does not appear to illustrate a specific stricture of the Decalogue. Buried within the story, however, is a false oath taken in the name of God. Although this would appear to violate the Second Commandment ("Thou shalt not take the name of the Lord thy God in vain"), the consequences of this transgression are all positive. One suspects that this is an example of the fortunate fall or, at the very least, situation ethics. The two principal characters in this episode are a crusty old doctor and a glamorous young woman named Dorota. The doctor is treating Dorota's husband, Andrzej, who is probably dying of cancer. When she shows up at the doctor's flat (just about all of the characters in these films live in the same housing complex), he will give her no information concerning her husband's condition. Families are supposed to limit their inquiries to certain hours on Wednesday, and it is now only Monday. As disagreeable as the doctor may seem, he too has suffered greatly. Through overhearing conversations with his housekeeper, we learn that his own family was wiped out in a bombing raid during the Second World War. Although one would like to believe that the Nazis were responsible, it is even more likely that the Allies were the unwitting culprits here. Yet another example of the unintended consequences of good intentions.

The plot involves much more than a wife's grief for a dying husband. When she again forces the doctor to listen to her, Dorota reveals that she is pregnant with another man's child. Although this will probably be her last chance to have children, she will have an abortion if her husband lives. The ethical dilemma here is far more complex than the political debates we are accustomed to in the United States. Although it is not immediately clear whether Dorota could have conned her husband into believing that the child was his, she would certainly have considered it a betrayal to do so. The doctor's verdict, therefore, will determine whether her child lives or dies.

If the protagonist of *Decalogue One* shows too much confidence in scientific evidence, the doctor in this film appreciates the limits of human knowledge. (Although he is not conventionally religious, he professes to believe in a private god.) But, when pressed to render an opinion, he tells Dorota that her husband will die and swears to God that it is the truth. The information we have concerning Andrzej's condition is ambiguous enough that we are not certain whether the doctor is offering his best judgment. Probably he should have remained dogmatically uncertain. Instead, he pronounces the oath that will save Dorota's child. In any event, Andrzej miraculously recovers and rejoices in the fact that he and his wife are to be parents. (Has his wife, in a failure of nerve or an excess of compassion, lied to him after all?) We are left to wonder whether the doctor has taken the Lord's name in vain or has served as an inadvertent vehicle of grace.

## DECALOGUE THREE

56 minutes

Cast: Daniel Olbrychski (Janusz), Maria Pakulnis (Ewa), Joanna Szczepkowska (Janusz's Wife), Artur Barcis (Tram Driver), Krystyna Drochocka (Aunt)

Producer: Ryszard Chutkowski; Director Krzysztof Kieslowski; Writers: Krzysztof Kieslowski, Krzysztof Piesiewicz; Photographer: Piotr Sobocinski (color); Editor: Ewa Smal

*Decalogue Three* seems to be based loosely on the Third Commandment: "Remember the Sabbath Day to Keep It Holy." In this case, however, the Sabbath is not a Sunday at all but rather the Feast of the Nativity. The principal female character in this film is a woman named Ewa, who apparently suffers from severe holiday depression. Most directors would find that to be a sufficient premise on which to base the story, but Kieslowski's concern with moral and theological issues takes us far beyond mundane psychological considerations. Paul Tillich has suggested that the atheist may actually take religion more seriously than the casual believer. By the same token, the person who comes close to suicide on Christmas Eve may actually be closer to the true meaning of the season than the purely secular observer.

The film begins with the principal male character, Janusz, dressed as Santa Claus distributing presents to his children. Afterward, he, his wife, and his daughter dutifully attend Midnight Mass. It is here that he sees Ewa, who is a former lover, and the complications begin.

In contrast to Janusz, Ewa has no family life to speak of. Although she visits her aging aunt in a retirement home, the old lady is too feeble-minded to understand much of anything. Shortly thereafter, the festivities at Janusz's flat are interrupted by a telephone call. He informs his wife that the taxicab he drives for a living has been stolen. The call, however, is actually from a lonely and desperate Ewa. (Janusz's wife later sees them outside her window and assumes that the old affair has been rekindled.) Ewa tells Janusz that her husband Edward has been missing since noon and that she is desperate to find him. Although Janusz suspects that the story is a fabrication, he joins Ewa's "search" until the early hours of the dawn. At one point, this leads them to a hospital, where Ewa recoils in horror from the sight of a legless corpse who is not her husband. An embittered Ewa then tells Janusz: "I wanted it to be him. Or you. I wanted it to be your face and your teeth. . . . I dreamt once that you had broken your neck—your tongue was hanging out—it was a wonderful dream." In another nighttime sequence, a sadistic jailer sprays a couple of naked drunks with cold water. Neither of them is Edward.

By the end of the evening, Ewa shows Janusz a picture of Edward and his family, who live in another city. She has never been married to him, and their relationship has been over for several years. (When Edward had walked in on Ewa and Janusz making love, she chose Edward—mistakenly suspecting that Janusz had alerted Edward to their tryst in an attempt to break off his own affair with her.) The overdose of sedatives that Ewa carries with her confirms the fact that, without Janusz's comforting presence, she might well have taken her life that night. But as much as we might want to credit him with Christian charity on this holiest of nights, Janusz's own family situation seems compromised. When he returns in the morning, his wife asks him: "Does this mean that you'll be wandering off at all hours of the night again?" Although he says it does not, it isn't clear whether she—or we—can believe him.

## DECALOGUE FOUR

56 minutes

Cast: Adrianna Biedrzynska (Anka), Janusz Gajos (Michal), Artur Barcis (Young Man), Adam Hanuszkiewicz (Professor), Jan Tesarz (Taxi Driver), Andrzej Blumenfeld (Michal's Friend), Tomasz Kozlowicz (Jarek), Elzbieta Kilarska (Jarek's Mother), Helena Norowicz (Doctor)

Producer: Ryszard Chutkowski; Director: Krzysztof Kieslowski; Writers: Krzysztof Kieslowski; Krzysztof Piesiewicz; Photographer: Krzysztof Pakulski (color); Editor: Ewa Smal

In comparison to the rest of the Decalogue, the Fourth Commandment seems narrowly traditional, if not downright old-fashioned—"Honor Thy Father and Thy Mother." As one might expect, however, Kieslowski does not give us a simplistic tale about childhood obedience. The greatest artists, from the time of Sophocles on, have realized that the ties that bind parents and children have as much to do with libidinal mystery as legal obligation. As much as middle-class moralists might object, the nuclear family has been the historical exception rather than the rule. Polygamy was as common among the ancient Israelites as serial monogamy is in the modern world. To honor one's parents, it is first necessary to know who they are. This turns out to be the central dilemma of *Decalogue Four.*

Michal and Anka have lived as father and daughter ever since Anka's mother died when the child was five days old. Although there is no particular reason to believe that Michal is not her father, a weird sexual tension has always pervaded their relationship.

Toward the beginning of the film, Anka discovers a letter that her mother wrote to her just prior to her death. Suspecting that the contents might alter her life, she is reluctant to open the envelope, even as she speculates about its contents. Ever since the onset of puberty, she has felt that every romantic experience has been a betrayal of Michal. (The previous year, she secretly had an abortion because she did not want the child and wished to avoid Michal's reaction to the situation—whatever it might be.) An acting student, she is capable of striking poses in real life. Still not wanting to know for sure what her mother's letter says, she forges a copy telling her that Michal is not her biological father. She then tells him this "secret" to gauge his reaction. Having suspected all along that he is not the girl's father and having desired her sexually, Michal is devastated to discover what purports to be the truth. He does not, however, alter his conduct toward the girl. Having lived all his life as her father, he is not about to stop now, even if that is what they both want. Although he does not articulate his reasons, he may well think that Anka needs a father more than a lover and that the girl will never be whole as long as she thinks of him in other than paternal terms.

After Michal refuses the opportunity to seduce Anka, we next see her awakening in her childlike bedclothes, searching for him in their empty apartment. He has not abandoned her but has simply left to buy milk. Seeing him out the window, she runs to Michal confessing her ruse. What we still do not know, however, are the actual contents of the mother's letter. Having decided that the fact of the matter is less important than the truth they have decided to live, they burn the letter. As Joseph G. Kickasola concludes: "Anka needs to know, beyond all doubt, that Michal will be her father whatever the biological circumstance; in essence, it is the relationship that is fundamental and must never be undermined."

## DECALOGUE FIVE

57 minutes

Cast: Miroslaw Baka (Jacek), Krzysztof Globisz (Piotr), Jan Tesarz (Taxi Driver), Zbigniew Zapasiewicz (Police Inspector), Barbara Dziekan-Wajda (Cashier)

Producer: Ryszard Chutkowski; Director: Krzysztof Kieslowski; Writers: Krzysztof Kieslowski, Krzysztof Piesiewicz; Photographer: Slawomir Idziak (color); Editor: Ewa Smal

"Thou Shalt Not Kill" may be the best known and most problematic of the commandments. At the time it was given, the Mosaic law mandated death for a host of infractions, most of which would be considered petty by today's standards. *Decalogue Five* concerns a cold-blooded murderer who is subjected to capital punishment. Because this film was set prior to the fall of communism, it would have been simple for Kieslowski to make the prisoner a political criminal who was victimized by the state. In choosing to make him an unrepentant killer, the film raises the issue of capital punishment in a manner that is relevant to the Western democracies as well. *Decalogue Five* focuses on three principal characters—Jacek, the murderer; his victim, Waldemar; and his attorney, Piotr. Jacek and Waldemar are both contemptible individuals, while Piotr is a high-minded idealist. At first, we see them going their separate ways until circumstance brings them together.

At one level, Jacek is a sociopath, a prime example of what Coleridge called motiveless malignity. As he wanders through town, he pushes a piece of pavement off a highway overpass, causing what sounds like a serious wreck. In other scenes, he scares an old woman's pigeons away from the town square and pushes a man into a latrine. Even his eating habits are filthy. The only scene in which he appears even mildly sympathetic is one in which he takes a picture of a young girl into a photo shop to be enlarged. It is only after he has been condemned that we learn that the photograph is of his dead sister's First Communion. The young girl, who may have been the only human being he truly loved, had been killed by a tractor driven by one of Jacek's drunken friends.

Although the cab driver Waldemar surely does not deserve to be murdered, he is initially presented as a jerk who sexually harasses women and delights in playing practical jokes on potential customers. For reasons that are not made clear, Jacek decides to garrote him with a length of rope. When that fails to do the trick, he beats his victim to death and then casually finishes a sandwich the driver has been eating in the cab. In a feature film that Kieslowski developed from this episode, Jacek drives the cab into town to impress a girl. In *Decalogue Five*, however, the murder is presented without rational motivation.

When we first see Piotr, he is being interviewed for a position as a lawyer. Although he has not yet come in contact with Jacek, he expresses his strong skepticism about both the efficacy and justice of deterrent punishment. Later, he sees Jacek in a café with the rope that he will use for his crime. (After the fact, Piotr is tormented by the irrational belief that he might have done something at that point to prevent the crime.) In the closing scenes, we learn of Jacek's love for his sister and of his selfish desire that his mother give him her place in the family burial plot. Finally, we witness the harrowing mechanics of execution. The film ends with Piotr sitting in his car, screaming, "I abhor it!" Although his obvious reference is to the death of his client, he might also be thinking of his own failure as both an attorney and a human being to reduce the level of murder in the world around him.

## DECALOGUE SIX

58 minutes

Cast: Grazyna Szapolowska (Magda), Olaf Lubaszenko (Tomek), Stefania Iwinska (Godmother), Artur Barcis (Young Man), Stanislaw Gawlik (Postman), Piotr Machalica (Roman), Rafal Imbro (Bearded Man), Jan Piechocinski (Blond Man)

Producer: Ryszard Chutkowski; Director: Krzysztof Kieslowski; Writers: Krzysztof Kieslowki, Krzysztof Piesiewicz; Photographer: Witold Adamek (color); Editor: Ewa Smal

The Sixth Commandment—"Thou Shalt Not Commit Adultery"—is so widely violated in the modern world that it would seem difficult to find an original way of illustrating its moral ramifications. What Kieslowski has done is to focus on Christ's more severe interpretation of the commandment—that one who lusts in his heart has committed adultery already. In this case, the lust is that of a voyeur named Tomek, who is obsessed with Magda, a sexually active woman whose conduct he observes through a telescope. If just about everyone (including born-again American presidents) has experienced lust, few people actually become peeping Toms. Those who do are considered perverts and may be forced to register as criminal sex offenders. It is a tall order to create sympathy for such a person, much less in the mind of his victim. But that is exactly what Kieslowski does.

To begin with, Tomek's interest in Magda appears to be more aesthetic than erotic. When he spies on her, takes a route as a milkman to be close to her, puts fake money orders in her mailbox to arouse her interest, and calls in phony reports of gas leaks in her apartment to foil a tryst with one of her many boyfriends, Tomek is almost indifferent to concealing his own identity. When one of Magda's boyfriends calls him out, he appears obediently to take a punch in the face. He even reveals himself and his antics to Magda rather than allow her to continue worrying about the source of the money orders. Although her initial reaction to him is, predictably, revulsion, she is eventually drawn to him, perhaps finding his strange devotion touching in contrast to the temporary and tawdry affairs she is used to. Tomek does not want to go away with her, make love to her, or even kiss her. He doesn't even masturbate anymore when looking at her through his telescope.

One evening, Magda invites Tomek to her apartment and tries to seduce him by putting his hand under her dress so that he can feel her arousal. When this produces a premature ejaculation in Tomek, who is still fully clothed, Magda tells him: "That's all it comes down to, Love. Now go to the bathroom and clean yourself up." After he leaves, Magda feels remorse and puts a big sign in her window that says "COME OVER" and "FORGIVE ME." Whether or not Tomek sees the sign, he goes home, slits his wrists, and ends up in the hospital.

At this point, Magda goes from being pursued to being the pursuer. Not knowing what Tomek has done until she is finally informed by one of his fellow postal workers, she searches for him—even looking for him through her window with opera glasses. When she stops by his apartment to return a coat he had left at her place, Magda meets the mother of one of Tomek's friends, who is now his landlady and surrogate mother. (The old lady's own son lives in another country.) After he is released from the hospital, Tomek no longer wishes to spy on Magda. If this can be seen as a moral triumph on his part, she experiences it as an emotional loss. One can only assume that she will return to her earlier life of casual fornication, which is surely the modern equivalent of adultery.

## DECALOGUE SEVEN

55 minutes

Cast: Anna Polony (Ewa), Maja Barelkowska (Majka), Wladyslaw Kowalski (Stefan), Boguslaw Linda (Wojtek), Bozena Dykiel (Ticket Woman), Katarzyna Piwowarczyk (Ania)

Producer: Ryszard Chutkowski; Drector Krzysztof Kieslowski; Writers: Krzysztof Kieslowki, Krzysztof Piesiewicz; Photographer: Andrzej Jaroszewicz (color); Editor: Ewa Smal

The Seventh Commandment—"Thou Shalt Not Steal"—affirms the sanctity of private property. This is a principle officially rejected in collectivist economies and one that is often minimized by democratic liberals, who make a false distinction between *human* rights and *property* rights. But even if one can make the metaphysical argument that the right to property is one of the most fundamental human rights, that still leaves the task of rendering this truth in a dramatically compelling manner. In *Decalogue Seven,* Kieslowski has met that challenge by equating property with the more emotionally charged concept of custody. Majka, a young woman in her twenties, had given birth to a child when she was only sixteen. The baby's father, Wojtek, was a teacher at the school she attended. The entire incident was covered up by Majka's mother, the headmistress of the school, who has adopted the baby as her own. Now that Majka has been expelled from college, for reasons that are never made entirely clear, she decides that it is time to take control of her life by seizing her child and fleeing to Canada.

Majka and her mother, Ewa, are both strong-willed women who have never gotten along with each other. Although Majka enjoys a better relationship with her father, Stefan, the man is too weak to be much of a force in the family conflict. If anything, Wojtek is even worse. Feeling blackmailed by Ewa, he has retired from teaching to write poetry and make teddy bears. When Majka steals her six-year-old child, Ania, and takes her to Wojtek's house, the biological father tries to persuade her to return the girl to Ewa and Stefan. Bargaining from a position of strength, Majka calls her mother on the phone and demands that she be given legal custody of the child. At first, Ewa tries to negotiate a middle position but soon capitulates for fear of never seeing Ania again. (In her relationship with the child, she has tried to forge the mother-daughter bond she has never had with Majka.) Unfortunately, a nervous Majka hangs up the phone before hearing her mother's surrender. The film concludes with Ewa tracking down her estranged and adopted daughters at the train station. She recovers Ania, even as a bewildered Majka jumps aboard the train in what will apparently be the first leg of her journey to Canada.

Throughout the film, Ewa and Majka have treated Ania as if she were property. Legally, we speak of whom a child *belongs* to. The law, however, is at best a vestigial presence in this tale. More important are the moral claims of these two women. If we are concerned with the welfare of the child, it is difficult to see how her interests will be served by being removed from the only home she has ever known to make a new life, with no visible means of support, in the custody of a woman she has always regarded as her sister. Majka's final act of escape may also be an act of resignation and love—although it seems totally spontaneous in the context of the story. Ewa has won the contest of wills by repossessing what is *legally* hers. But it hardly takes the wisdom of Solomon to discern the behavior of the true mother.

## DECALOGUE EIGHT

55 minutes

Cast: Maria Koscialkowska (Zofia), Teresa Marczewska (Elzbieta), Artur Barcis (Young Man), Tadeusz Lomnicki (Tailor)

Producer: Ryszard Chutkowski; Director Krzysztof Kieslowski; Writers: Krzysztof Kieslowski, Krzysztof Piesiewicz; Photographer: Andrzej Jaroszewicz (color); Editor: Ewa Smal

Like several of the other episodes in *The Decalogue*, Kieslowski's depiction of the Eighth Commandment ("Thou Shalt Not Bear False Witness Against Thy Neighbor") occurs in a complex moral environment. In this case, it is that of the anti-Nazi underground. If fidelity to the truth is an absolute ideal, then one must adhere to it regardless of the consequences. That means, however, that one must also assume moral responsibility for those consequences. The dilemma in question involved a young Jewish girl who was to be taken into hiding in Poland during World War II. The plan was for her to be received by a Catholic family with a certificate of christening. At the last minute, the couple that was to provide the certificate reneged on the agreement, ostensibly because it would require them to swear to something that was false—namely, that the girl was a Christian. The child was then sent out to what would have been a likely death at the hands of the Nazis.

This story is told in an ethics class in Poland more than forty years later by an American woman, Elzbieta, who has translated the works of Zofia, the woman who teaches the class. Just before this exposition, a student in the class has told the story we witnessed in *Decalogue Two*. Zofia unquestioningly asserts that the doctor had done the right thing in telling Dorota that her husband would die, because nothing is more important than the life of a child. If the doctor has done right in making what was at best a questionable oath before Almighty God, what can one say about the couple in the second story, who were apparently willing to sacrifice the life of a child rather than swear to a bogus baptism? The situation is further complicated when we learn that Elzbieta was the child in question and that Zofia and her husband were the couple.

Elzbieta seems more curious than embittered, while Zofia clearly feels guilt about her conduct. The situation, however, was not as simple as Elzbieta had assumed. The family that had been designated as Elzbieta's new guardians were suspected of being Nazi collaborators. Zofia had every reason to believe that turning the child over to them would jeopardize the entire underground. Thus, in addition to bearing false witness, Zofia and her husband believed that going through with their plan would mean risking the lives of many innocent people against that of a single individual. But they also realized that they were subjecting a child to almost certain death on the basis of information that might not be reliable. As things turned out, the supposed collaborators were innocent, although one man remained imprisoned until 1955. When Elzbieta goes to see the man, who is now a tailor, he is too traumatized even to speak about the war or its aftermath.

This film raises, but does not answer, the thorny question of what constitutes right action. If Zofia is correct in her current position that nothing is more important than the life of a child, then her wartime actions were wrong. Certainly they had horrific consequences for the suspected collaborators. It is not clear, however, that Zofia would have been unambiguously right to risk collapse of the entire underground movement. As things stand, Elzbieta appears more ready to forgive Zofia than she is to forgive herself.

## DECALOGUE NINE

58 minutes

Cast: Ewa Blaszczyk (Hanka), Piotr Machalica (Roman), Artur Barcis (Young Man), Jan Jankowski (Mariusz), Jolanta Pietek-Górecka (Ola), Katarzyna Piwowarczyk (Ania), Jerzy Trela (Mikolaj)

Producer: Ryszard Chutkowski; Director: Krzysztof Kieslowski; Writers: Krzysztof Kieslowski, Krzysztof Piesiewicz; Photographer Piotr Sobocinski (color); Editor: Ewa Smal

At first glance, *Decalogue Nine* seems to be more closely related to the prohibition against adultery than it does to the Ninth Commandment—"Thou Shalt Not Covet Thy Neighbor's Wife." This is particularly true when one considers that the only character who covets another's wife is the relatively minor figure of Mariusz. The story focuses on Roman and Hanka, a loving couple caught in a troubled marriage. Perhaps as a result of his philandering past, Roman suffers from what we now call erectile dysfunction. His physician tells him that this condition is permanent and that he should probably seek a divorce. When he tells his wife that, under the circumstances, she should at least seek a lover, she pledges her love and fidelity to him.

Despite her genuine feeling for Roman, we soon learn that Hanka is already involved in a casual affair with a young physics student. When Roman discovers the young man's notebook in the glove compartment of his car, he becomes jealous and begins to spy on his wife and her paramour. Although Roman is an object of genuine pity, his jealousy runs counter to his explicit instructions to his wife. Moreover, we cannot be certain that he has not been unfaithful to her at some point in their marriage.

In his role as a surgeon, Roman encounters a young woman named Ola with a gift for singing. Unfortunately, her heart condition effectively precludes a professional career. The ethical dilemma she faces is whether to undergo a risky operation or remain content with her lot in life. Although she would prefer the latter, her mother pushes her to have the operation and the career it would make possible. In the script for *Decalogue Nine*, Roman performs the surgery only to have Ola die on the operating table. In the actual film, however, the issue is left unresolved. In either case, Ola serves as a foil for Roman. Although both suffer from a disability, Ola has reconciled herself to this fact. Roman behaves in a self-destructive manner, which ultimately leads to a suicide attempt.

Upon confronting his wife with evidence of her affair, she vows to break it off. (In fact, she has already told her boy toy to get lost.) The young physics student, however, follows Hanka on a skiing vacation. When he presents himself to her, she flees back to her husband. Unfortunately Roman has already discovered that the two former lovers are at the same resort and drives his bicycle over an embankment. Although he is beat up, he lives and seems to effect a permanent reconciliation with his wife over the telephone.

Although the impulse to covet is rooted in envy, Kieslowski realizes that that emotion is closely connected with jealousy. To want what one cannot have is surely a form of coveting. It is probably pointless to speculate whether, in the film, God (or nature) is punishing Roman for his checkered past. What is important is his conduct in the present. As psychologically credible as it may be, it clearly falls short of the ideal embodied in the Commandments. One can only hope that his brush with death has brought him to a new appreciation of life, despite the limitations with which he will have to cope.

## DECALOGUE TEN

57 minutes

Cast: Jerzy Stuhr (Jerzy), Zbigniew Zamachowski (Artur), Henryk Bista (Shopkeeper), Olaf Lubaszenko (Tomek), Maciej Stuhr (Piotrek)

Producer: Ryszard Chutkowski; Director: Krzysztof Kieslowski; Writers: Krzysztof Kieslowski, Krzysztof Piesiewicz; Photographer: Jacek Blawut (color); Editor: Ewa Smal

If the coveting of another's wife involves lust, the coveting of his goods consists of greed. In *Decalogue Ten*, two brothers (Jerzy and Artur) actually covet something that is legally theirs—a stamp collection they have inherited from their late father. The funeral oration by the president of the philatelic association makes clear that the dead man's devotion to stamp collecting was so intense that it transcended everything else in his life. Understandably embittered by their father's neglect, the two brothers eagerly look forward to dividing the proceeds of their inheritance. At this point mishaps ensue. To begin with, Jerzy makes the mistake of giving a few stamps to his son as a memento of the boy's grandfather. Unaware of the value of the stamps, the lad immediately trades them away for a fraction of their value. Following the transaction, Jerzy encounters a well-connected stamp dealer with questionable ethics. The dealer offers the brothers the rare stamp that will complete their collection and ensure them previously undreamed-of wealth if Jerzy, who has the proper blood type, will donate a kidney to his seriously ill daughter. Artur, who sings lead for a rock band that proclaims a completely self-serving philosophy of life, disingenuously stresses the altruistic qualities of the transaction.

The ethics of selling an organ are thorny enough for poverty-stricken donors. Jerzy, however, simply wants to enhance the comfort of his bourgeois life. In his obsession with the stamp collection, he is becoming more like his father than he might wish or even realize. (In the script to the film, this obsession finally prompts his wife to file for divorce.) If anything, his brother—who sacrifices nothing—is even worse. At the same time, we become so involved in the story that it is difficult to judge the brothers. They are simply trying to lay claim to what belongs to them against the machinations of unscrupulous speculators and the caprice of fate.

While Jerzy is donating his kidney and Artur is at the hospital to lend him moral support (while seducing a nurse in his spare time), someone robs the apartment that houses the stamp collection. It is revealing that each of the brothers suspects the other of being in on some kind of scam. They had been estranged from each other before the death of their father and seem to be divided even further by his patrimony. The film has a comic ending, however, when the brothers confess their suspicions to each other and realize that each has purchased the same stamps in an attempt to complete a collection that is now gone. If we can believe that these two men would laugh in the face of such massive misfortune, we can conclude that this experience has brought them together in a way that the inheritance itself might not have. The greed that causes one to covet is essentially a perversion of values. Kieslowski suggests that Jerzy and Artur had to lose their prospective fortune in order to discover what is of true value.

## THE DECLINE OF THE AMERICAN EMPIRE

1986 (101 minutes) • Satire
Cineplex Odeon • R

Cast: Dominique Michel (Dominique), Dorothee Berryman (Louise), Louise Portal (Diane), Geneviève Rioux (Danielle), Pierre Curzi (Pierre), Rémy Girard (Rémy), Yves Jacques (Claude), Daniel Brière (Alain), Gabriel Arcand (Mario)

Producers: Renè Malo, Roger Frappier; Director: Denys

Arcand; Writer: Denys Arcand; Photographer: Guy Dufaux (color); Editor: Monique Fortier

In one of the opening scenes of this film, the woman who chairs the history department at the University of Montreal gives a radio interview about her new book. Her thesis is that a civilization becomes obsessed with the personal happiness of its members only when it is at the point of decline. This theory would suggest that the days are numbered for the hedonistic American Empire. In retrospect, such a prophecy would seem to have missed the mark. *The Decline of the American Empire* was made in 1986, three years before the spectacular fall of the *Soviet* Empire. Despite the war in Iraq and other setbacks, American power and influence have rarely been higher. The knee-jerk neoconservative response would be that French-Canadian filmmaker Denys Arcand is simply airing a fashionable disdain for the United States.

I suspect that a far different interpretation is even more plausible. The learned chairwoman (who is asked to extend her interview because Milan Kundera failed to show up) is one of several characters in an ensemble cast. (As Roger Ebert points out, all of these characters "either work in the history department at a Canadian university, or sleep with people who do.") These individuals gather for a dinner that features food, wine, and endless conversation about sex. As one of the participants, chairwoman Dominique reflects the decadence that she writes about. Like the college in Edward Albee's *Who's Afraid of Virginia Woolf?* (1962), the preferred faculty sport on this campus is musical beds.

In addition to Dominique, the diners include Rémy, the undisputed departmental satyr; his mostly clueless wife Louise; a colleague named Pierre and his student mistress, whom he met at a massage parlor; a promiscuous homosexual named Claude, who teaches art history; and a young student named Alain. Also appearing are Diane, a neighbor, and her biker boyfriend. Prior to the dinner, Louise, Danielle, and Diane warm up at the local health club—talking about men, their own bodies, and, of course, sex. In fact, for a movie so concerned with sex, *Decline* features a lot of talk and not much action, which may well be one of the points of the satire.

Can a society thrive militarily and economically and still be rotten morally? Social conservatives (particularly religious fundamentalists) say that it can. One of the most telling denunciations of Western culture came in Aleksandr Solzhenitsyn's controversial 1978 commencement address at Harvard.

Many assumed that the Russian prophet would be so glad to be removed from Soviet tyranny that he would spontaneously embrace all aspects of non-Soviet life. Instead, he skewered the weakness and depravity of our own civilization. There is no evidence that Arcand fancies himself a Solzhenitsyn, much less a Gibbon. Nevertheless, the title and subject matter of his film allow—almost demand—a conservative reading. Some viewers may miss this simply because there is enough vulgarity (and occasional nudity) to warrant an "R" rating. Moreover, the characters possess enough charm and wit to be entertaining company. Only when we see Claude urinating blood and witness the effect of Rémy's previously unsuspected infidelities on his wife do we realize that pleasure has its price. Like ideas, behavior has consequences.

## DELIVERANCE

1972 (109 minutes) • Action Adventure
Warner Brothers • R

Cast: Jon Voight (Ed Gentry), Burt Reynolds (Lewis Medlock), Ned Beatty (Bobby Trippe), Ronny Cox (Drew Ballenger), Bill McKinney (Mountain Man), Herbert "Cowboy" Coward (Toothless Man), James Dickey (Sheriff Bullard), Ed Ramey (Old Man), Billy Redden (Lonnie)

Producer: John Boorman; Director: John Boorman; Writer: James Dickey (Based on his novel); Photographer: Vilmos Zsigmond (Panavision, Technicolor); Editor: Tom Priestly

*Deliverance* is the story of four suburbanites from Atlanta who decide to spend a weekend riding down a wild river that is due to be dynamited to form a man-made lake. The leader of the group is Lewis Medlock, a physical-fitness nut who fancies himself a superman. He is joined by the sensitive guitar-strumming Drew Ballenger, a soft country club man named Bobby Trippe, and the narrator, Ed Gentry. Ed runs his own commercial art studio, even as he dreams about more serious aesthetic endeavors. He sees the journey down-river as an opportunity both to test himself physically and to get in touch with a natural world from which he has been cut off. Describing the theme of the book on which the movie was based, author James Dickey has said that it is about "this business of the element of danger which men think they want; but when they find they are into something far more dangerous than they could ever have imagined, they want deliverance from it."

While on the river, they are accosted by a couple of hideous mountain men who sodomize Bobby for daring to intrude upon their territory. When Lewis kills one of the attackers with a bow and arrow, he and his companions become marked men. Shortly after they continue their trip by canoe, Drew is ambushed, and Lewis breaks his leg. It is therefore up to Ed to climb a steep cliff so that he can surprise and kill the remaining mountaineer. Both the violence and the beauty of this story are rendered magnificently on screen in what amounts to the visual equivalent of Dickey's poetic prose. Not only did Dickey write the novel *Deliverance*, he also provided the screenplay and appeared in a cameo role as the sheriff who interrogates Lewis, Ed, and Bobby at the end of their adventure.

Although no film can capture a character's inner life as well as a book, the movie possesses virtues not found in the novel. In one unforgettable scene, Drew plays an impromptu duet with an albino mountain boy. Although this "dueling banjoes" encounter is described in the novel, the music has to heard to be appreciated. The four principal actors—Jon Voight, Burt Reynolds, Ned Beatty, and Ronny Cox—are all well cast and deliver fine performances. Bill McKinney and Herbert "Cowboy" Coward are appropriately grotesque as the mountain men, and even the neophyte Dickey is convincing in his role as sheriff.

Both the novel and the film versions of *Deliverance* have been criticized for glorifying violence. If we consider the situation in which the suburbanites find themselves, however, they have little choice but to defend themselves. What Ed experiences is a kind of midlife initiation into manhood. Had he lived in a more primitive society, this initiation probably would have been more ritualized and would have occurred closer to puberty. When Dickey was an undergraduate at Vanderbilt, he was greatly impressed with Stanley Edgar Hyman's review of Joseph Campbell's *Hero with a Thousand Faces* (1949) in the *Sewanee Review*. *Deliverance* is, in many ways, a contemporary American enactment of the universal myth that Campbell describes. If Dickey rejects the belief that modern man is necessarily civilized, he even more emphatically rejects the idea of the noble savage.

## DESTINATION MOON

1950 (91 minutes) • Space Adventure
George Pal Productions • Unrated

Cast: John Archer (Jim Barnes), Warner Anderson (Dr. Charles Cargraves), Tom Powers (General Thayer), Dick Wesson (Joe Sweeney), Erin O'Brien-Moore (Emily Cargraves), Ted Warde (Brown)

Producer: George Pal; Director: Irving Pichel; Writers: Robert A. Heinlein, Alford Van Ronkel, James O'Hanlon (based on the novel *Rocket Ship Galileo* by Robert A. Heinlein); Photographer: Lionel Lindon (Technicolor); Editor: Duke Goldstone

In England, highbrow writers such as H. G. Wells, Aldous Huxley, C. S. Lewis, and Anthony Burgess have been able to work in the lowbrow medium of science fiction without any loss of status. This has not been true in the United States, where science-fiction writers have generally been considered crass popularizers. The same was long true in film. Despite the fact that the cinema virtually began with Georges Méliès's *Voyage to the Moon* (1902), Hollywood's treatment of futuristic fantasy was at first largely confined to low-budget serials featuring such improbable characters as Flash Gordon, Buck Rogers, and Captain Video.

In 1950, all of this began to change with the production of Irving Pichel's *Destination Moon*. Although this film seems dated and wooden today, it was the first space movie to give serious consideration to issues of technical realism. Certainly, a good deal of the credit must go to Robert A. Heinlein, whose novel *Rocket Ship Galileo* (1947) served as the inspiration for *Destination Moon* and whose presence on the set helped to keep the moviemakers honest.

For years, Heinlein labored in the obscurity of the sci-fi desert until his novel *Stranger in a Strange Land* (1961) became a virtual sacred text for the youth culture of the 1960s. The irony of this "discovery" is that Heinlein's own politics put him far to the right of many of his newfound devotees. His narratives of space travel, in particular, are often seen as a tribute to the frontier spirit of America so despised by revisionist historians. (Next to Ayn Rand, Heinlein is probably the most admired novelist among American libertarians.) Add to this the fact that the race to beat the Soviets into outer space was a prime goal of the Cold War—a point made repeatedly in *Destination Moon*, despite the fact that Sputnik was still seven years in the future.

Nevertheless, the Maoist literary critic H. Bruce Franklin is wrong to view Heinlein's narrative as an unblinking tribute to the military-industrial complex. The moon mission depicted in the book and movie is privately funded by a maverick industrialist named Jim Barnes. Although the government is nominally behind his project, it is timid about giving the go-ahead. Barnes is a rebellious and far-seeing patriot who keeps the bureaucracy at bay long enough to launch the missile on his own authority. (He is, of course, a member of the crew as well.) The four men on this mission are all willing to risk the lethal possibility of equipment malfunction in order to claim the lunar surface for their country. (The voyage is called Project Luna, and the men refer to themselves as "lunatics.") There is even a scary moment toward the end when it seems as if one of the crew will have to stay on the moon for the return trip to be launched at all. Fortunately, the rocket gets back into flight, thanks to the ingenuity of the private sector. Although the real moon landing was not to occur for another nineteen years and Stanley Kubrick's *2001: A Space Odyssey* (1968) was nearly as far off, a new era had been launched in American filmmaking.

## DIRTY HARRY

1971 (102 minutes) • Crime Drama
Malpaso/Warner Brothers • R

Cast: Clint Eastwood (Harry Callahan), Reni Santoni (Chico), Harry Guardino (Bressler), Andy Robinson (Scorpio), John Mitchum (DiGiorgio), John Larch (Chief), John Vernon (Mayor), Mae Mercer (Mrs. Russell), Lyn Edgington (Norma), Ruth Kobart (Bus Driver)

Producer: Don Siegel; Director: Don Siegel; Writers: Harry Julian Fink, Rita M. Fink, John Milius (uncredited), Dean Riesner (based on an unpublished story by Rita M.

and Harry Julian Fink); Photographer: Bruce Surtees (Panavision, Technicolor); Editor: Carl Pingitore

During the late sixties and early seventies, violent street crime was one of the great polarizing issues of American culture. There was little question where director Don Siegel came down on this issue. His support for vigorous, no-holds-barred law enforcement struck a responsive chord among audiences, even as it raised the hackles of civil libertarians. Although Siegel had endorsed what seemed like vigilante justice in a series of films, including *Hell Is for Heroes* (1962) and *Madigan* (1968), *Dirty Harry* was his breakthrough movie, perhaps because Clint Eastwood (fresh from a string of spaghetti Westerns) was perfectly cast as police inspector Harry Callahan. The story involves a serial killer who always seems one step ahead of the San Francisco police department. When the killer buries a teenage girl alive and demands $200,000 in ransom, the feckless city officials knuckle under to his demands and assign Harry to deliver the money.

As the killer chases Harry all over the city in an attempt to collect ransom for a girl who is already dead, our sympathies are with the lawman. Despite apprehending the criminal (at considerable personal risk), Harry is informed that he violated several of the cretin's constitutional rights. With most of the incriminating evidence excluded, the authorities are forced to release the suspect to kill again. Harry is reprimanded for his conduct and ordered off the case. At this point, he pursues the killer on his own time. In the climactic scene of the film, the criminal kidnaps a bus full of children and demands an airplane to give him safe passage out of the city. Not surprisingly, Harry captures him single-handedly and dispatches him to the hereafter. In a finale reminiscent of *High Noon*, Harry tosses his police badge into the ocean.

The enthusiastic popular response to *Dirty Harry* was no doubt based on the widespread belief that civil order was breaking down in American society. The perception that criminals had more rights than their victims led many to look for a strong man to enforce justice, even if it meant cutting through constitutional red tape. Although some liberal critics saw this as the emergence of fascism in American society, Harry Callahan actually walks in a venerable tradition of American heroes. Not only does he possess a rigid sense of right and wrong, he is also a rebel who bucks the system. As a widower, Harry is the womanless hero to whom we have grown accustomed. He is even supplied with an ethnic sidekick in the form of an Hispanic partner. Unfortunately, the urban frontier has become so corrupted that not even this surrogate marriage works out. As soon as the partner overcomes Harry's racist suspicions, the manifest dangers of a cop's life drive him back to the safety of a college campus. This film spawned four sequels, influenced a host of subsequent cop dramas, and helped to make Eastwood a major Hollywood star.

## EDMOND

2005 (82 minutes) • Drama
Code Entertainment • R

Cast: William H. Macy (Edmond Burke), Julia Stiles (Glenna), Joe Mantegna (Man in Bar), Ling Bai (Peep-Show Girl), Jeffrey Combs (Desk Clerk), Denise Richards (Allegro-B Girl), Mena Suvari (Whore), Dylan Walsh (Interrogator), Russell Hornsby (Shill), Debi Mazar (Atlantic Leisure Club Matron), Rebecca Pidgeon (Edmond's Wife), Lionel Mark Smith (Pimp), Marcus Thomas (Window Man), Jack Wallace (Chaplain), George Wendt (Pawn Shop Guy), Dulé Hill (Sharper)

Producers: Stuart Gordon, Chris Hanley, Molly Hassell, Duffy Hecht, Roger Kass, Mary B. McCann, Kevin Ragsdale. Lionel Mark Smith (Producers), Art Spigel, Chad Troutwine (Coproducers), Al Corley, Sam Englebardt, Stephen Hays, Ryan R. Johnson, Eugene Musso, Bart Rosenblatt, Gary Rubin, Tricia Van Klaveren, Felix Werner, Katherin Werner (Executive Producers), Roger Mende (Co–Executive Producer), Amy Gunzenhauser, Jade Healy, Jasper Jan, Kim Olsen, Lorna Umphrey, Allison Wolf (Associate Producers), Michael O. Gallant (Line Producer); Director: Stuart Gordon; Writer: David Mamet; Photographer: Denis Maloney (color); Editor: Andy Horvitch

Although this film is not recommended for family viewing, neither is it the sort that is likely to give much comfort to elite opinion on the matters of race, sex, and class. Fairly early in his career, David Mamet discovered that white male rage was a sentiment with considerable dramatic potential. Although it took twenty-three years for his play *Edmond* (1982) to make it onto the motion-picture screen, his major themes are as relevant in the early twenty-first century as they were more than two decades earlier. In the opening scene, a fortune teller convinces the outwardly comfortable Edmond Burke that he is special and that his life can be different. Perhaps needing little persuasion, Edmond decides to leave his wife and embark on what turns out to be a Dantean tour of New York nightlife. After spending most of his loose cash at a peep show and leisure club/bordello, without obtaining even the sordid gratification offered by such establishments, he is beaten up by a card sharp and a shill who are running a crooked three-card monte game on the street. Getting no sympathy from the clerk in a flea-bag hotel, he wanders into a pawnshop and hocks a ring for a knife. This proves liberating when Edmond is accosted by a black pimp who tries to rob him of what little he has left. Although he doesn't use the knife, he gives the pimp a well-deserved beating, accompanied by a racist tongue-lashing.

Newly emboldened, Edmond goes into a coffeehouse, orders an Irish whiskey with a beer chaser, and picks up a waitress. Unfortunately, his newfound sense of self-worth is mainly a delusion. After a sexual encounter back in the waitress's apartment, he forces her into a pointless argument. This time he does use the knife and suddenly finds himself guilty of murder. Soon thereafter, he is apprehended trying to enter a street-front mission. (He is identified to the police by a woman he had verbally abused after a failed attempt to engage her in conversation earlier in the evening.) By this time, the evidence of the waitress's murder has caught up with Edmond, and he faces a long prison sentence. With his wife understandably unwilling to reconcile with him, Edmond's future consists of life with a black cellmate who immediately demands oral sex. In the final scene, Edmond and the black man engage in a sophomoric philosophical discussion reminiscent of Huck and Jim on the raft. The story ends with Edmond giving his cellmate a goodnight kiss and sitting back down in his own bed.

By any estimation, this is a bleak view of American civilization. Although the protagonist has the same name as the godfather of British conservatism, Mamet gives his first name a French spelling. Is it reading too much into the text to recall that the English Edmund Burke was horrified by the moral and social anarchy of the *French* Revolution? If anything, the forces that defeat

Mamet's Edmond represent an even greater threat to civilized values. Rather than realizing the situation for what it is, Edmond simply projects it into a bitter image of black people and the freer instinctual life he assumes they represent. Those who empathize with the phenomenon of white male rage are tempted to sympathize with Edmond until they realize the poetic justice of his ultimate fate. If Leslie Fiedler was correct in suggesting that an image of interracial male bonding is at the heart of one our most persistent American dreams, perhaps the fear of being sodomized by a black man is some kind of white American nightmare. Edmond's total defeat is symbolized by the fact that, by the end of the film, he willingly succumbs to that nightmare.

## THE EDGE OF THE WORLD

1937 (81 minutes) • Drama
Joe Rock • Unrated

Cast: John Laurie (Peter Manson), Belle Chrystall (Ruth Manson), Eric Berry (Robbie Manson), Kitty Kirwan (Jean Manson), Finlay Currie (James Gray), Niall MacGinnis (Andrew Gray), Grant Sutherland (John, the Catechist), Campbell Robson (Mr. Dunbar), George Summers (Trawler Skipper)

Producer: Joe Rock; Director: Michael Powell; Writer: Michael Powell; Photographers: Monty Berman, Skeets Kelly, Ernest Palmer (black and white); Editors: Derek Twist, Robert Walters

Early in *The Edge of the World*, a parishioner compliments a Scottish preacher on the sermon he has just delivered: "One hour and fifteen minutes. Let them beat that in Edinburgh if they can!" As it turns out, the entire film is scarcely longer than an hour and fifteen minutes. Although it is no sermon (not even of the sort that Father Mapple delivers at the beginning of *Moby-Dick*), the story it tells deals with themes of universal significance—Man against Nature, the individual and the community, love of home versus the lure of other lands. And it does so within the most constrained setting imaginable. Shot on location on the North Sea island of Foula, this movie tells the story of a Scottish village that must decide whether it will continue as an independent polity or evacuate its dwindling population to the mainland. With trawlers cutting into their traditional fishing rights, the townspeople are being strangled economically, and the aging inhabitants are not even coming close to replacing themselves. If there were an Endangered Species List for a way of life, the age-old customs of this island would be on it.

The initial conflict involves Andrew and Robbie, two young men who have opposite views of the future. Andrew argues that assimilation with the mainland offers the community its only chance for survival, while Robbie is just as adamant about staying put. Since the other villagers are also evenly split on the matter, the two youths decide to resolve the issue with a race to the top of a 1,300-foot sea cliff. In shooting this race, director Michael Powell visually demonstrates the immensity of nature in contrast to these two lone men against the sky. Failing to heed Andrew's advice to take a longer but safer route, Robbie falls to his death, thus diminishing the young male population of the town by 50 percent. When Robbie's embittered father refuses to sanction his daughter's marriage to Andrew, the lad follows his own advice and ships out to the mainland. Ruth, the girl he leaves behind, soon discovers that she is pregnant with Andrew's child. But the lack of a doctor on the island endangers even this infant's chance of survival. The film ends with the return of Andrew to lead a mournful evacuation of the island and the abandonment of a way of life.

Even as we admire the fierce independence of these people, we realize that they have taken the only path that will allow them to survive as a community. If the pioneer strikes out for new frontiers, we really don't have a name for what the people of Foula are forced to do. Their attachment to even the most barren land is rooted in memory, which is certainly a conservative value. But so too is the prudence they reluctantly demonstrate. If we wish to see the invasion of the trawlers as the fell hand of technology—or perhaps of modernity itself—we can do so. Unlike Faulkner's characters on their little postage stamp of soil, the people of this island do not prevail. But at least they survive.

## A FACE IN THE CROWD

1957 (125 minutes) • Drama
Warner Brothers • Unrated

Cast: Andy Griffith (Lonesome Rhodes), Patricia Neal (Marcia Jeffries), Anthony Franciosa (Joey DePalma), Walter Matthau (Mel Miller), Lee Remick (Betty Lou Fleckum), Rod Brasfield (Beanie), Marshall Neilan (Senator Worthington Fuller)

Producer: Elia Kazan; Director: Elia Kazan; Writer: Budd Schulberg (based on his story "The Arkansas Traveler"); Photographers: Gayne Rescher, Harry Stradling Sr. (black and white); Editor: Gene Milford

The new medium of television began to sweep the nation in the 1950s. By the time *A Face in the Crowd* was released in 1957, 78.6 percent of American homes had TV sets. Whether this helped to create a global village (as Marshall McLuhan argued) or a vast wasteland (as FCC commissioner Newton Minow contended), the nation would never be the same again. In the early '50s, the Kefauver hearings into organized crime brought the American government into American living rooms and made Senator Estes Kefauver a presidential candidate. (He would later campaign in a coonskin cap of the sort made popular by Walt Disney's telecast of the saga of Davy Crockett.) By the middle of the decade, the medium helped to account for the rise and fall of Senator Joe McCarthy, whose pursuit of subversives in the American government exposed remarkably few traitors (they were mostly routed out by others) but did reveal McCarthy's own demagoguery. In *A Face in the Crowd*, director Elia Kazan and writer Budd Schulberg, who were themselves repentant ex-Communists (see the note on *On the Waterfront* below), show how television might be manipulated for base ends by a charismatic personality.

Lonesome Rhodes (played brilliantly by Andy Griffith, who had yet to become a mainstay on American television himself) is discovered in the drunk tank of an Alabama jail by radio producer Marcia Jeffries. Rhodes soon becomes a radio personality in Memphis, appealing directly to the little people in his audience and gently chiding his sponsors (whose sales soar on the strength of his popularity). Proving too big for a regional radio market, Rhodes moves his show to New York and to television, where he soon becomes a national phenomenon.

To some degree, the character of Lonesome Rhodes seems to have been based on Arthur Godfrey, who so dominated television in the early '50s that his shows once accounted for a full 10 percent of CBS's total revenue. But, unlike Godfrey, Rhodes is not content simply to be an entertainer. He takes an otherwise dull politician (Senator Worthington Fuller) under his wing, gives him a folksy personality, and makes him into a presidential contender. Alarmed by the Frankenstein monster she has helped to create and incensed that she has been jilted for a baton-twirling high school girl, Marcia exposes Rhodes by leaving the microphones turned on while he is mocking his gullible audience after a show one night. Because Lonesome's appeal is tied to his presumed sincerity, this ploy ruins his popularity and leaves him a pathetic wreck of a man.

Although the majority of critics read *A Face in the Crowd* as a cautionary tale about possible right-wing exploitation of television (which admittedly is what Kazan and Schulberg intended), slick operators on the left could just as easily use the medium for their ends. Kefauver, after all, was a liberal, and a generation earlier, Huey Long had employed radio to promote his schemes for the redistribution of the nation's wealth. In contrast, Will Rogers, who was more popular than any politician, used stage, screen, and radio to poke fun at all politicians rather than to advance a nefarious ideological agenda. And for all his supposed power, the worst thing that Arthur Godfrey ever did on the air was to fire singer Julius La Rosa from his show.

## THE FANNY TRILOGY: MARIUS

1931 (130 minutes) • Romantic Comedy
Paramount • Unrated

Cast: Raimu (César), Pierre Fresnay (Marius), Orane Demazis (Fanny), Fernand Charpin (Honoré Panisse), Alida Rouffe (Honorine Cabanis), Paul Dullac (Felix Escartefigue), Alexandre Mihalesco (Piquoiseau), Robert Vattier (Albert Brun)

Producers: Robert Kane, Marcel Pagnol; Director: Alexander Korda; Writer: Marcel Pagnol; Photographer: Theodore J. Pahle (black and white); Editor: Roger Mercanton

*The Fanny Trilogy* began as stage productions prior to the advent of talking motion pictures. Although each film is self-contained, all three feature common characters and a continuing story line. The setting is the seaport town of Marseilles, more specifically a local bar run by César and his twenty-year-old son, Marius. Outside the bar, a young woman named Fanny operates a fish stall. If the main action of the story involves the romance of Marius and Fanny, much of the dialogue consists of humorous exchanges between César and his circle of middle-aged cronies. One of these, the sailmaker Panisse, seeks Fanny's hand in marriage. Ordinarily, such a match would be out of the question, but Panisse's wealth and Marius's desire to run away to sea make the marriage seem at least plausible.

In an effort to divert Marius's attentions away from the sea and toward her, Fanny pretends to be interested in Panisse. While this does arouse his jealousy, it does not extinguish his fascination with faraway places. When Fanny realizes that Marius will never be happy on land, she affects an indifference for him that effectively sends him out to sea. This plot development allows Marius to return in subsequent films while bringing the first one to a dramatic close. What we do not learn until the second film is that Fanny is pregnant with Marius's child and looks upon a match with Panisse as the one way to save her own reputation.

Although César and his cronies are not essential to the love plot, they continually threaten to steal the show with their games, quarrels, and one-liners. It is a good life and a substantial inheritance (as well as a beautiful girl) that Marius abandons to satisfy his wanderlust. (Although treated in semicomic terms here, the desire for exotic experience at sea is an important theme in much nineteenth-century literature—from *Moby-Dick* [1851] to the poetry of Baudelaire.) Whether he would have left had he known that Fanny was pregnant remains an unanswered question. It is to her moral credit, however, that she refuses to use this information to trap him. If Marius seems callous and self-absorbed, Fanny's mother is preoccupied with greed and an excessive concern for appearances. Not only does she covet Panisse's money, she is also concerned that her daughter not acquire the reputation of the family's black sheep, Aunt Zoe. She serves primarily as a foil to César, whose concern for the happiness of both young people is genuine.

The driving force behind this production was the French playwright and filmmaker Marcel Pagnol. Because *Marius* began as a play and because Pagnol thought of himself as the champion of *filmed theater*, some critics have thought his vision insufficiently cinematic. Nevertheless, Andre Bazin writes: "If Pagnol is not the greatest *auteur* of sound film, he is in any case something like its genius. He is perhaps the only one who, since 1930, has dared a verbal plenitude comparable to the visual plenitude of Griffith or von Stroheim."

## THE FANNY TRILOGY: FANNY

1932 (140 minutes) • Romantic Comedy
Les Films Marcel Pagnol • Unrated

Cast: Raimu (César), Pierre Fresnay (Marius), Orane Demazis (Fanny), Fernand Charpin (Panisse), Auguste Mouriès (Félix Escartifigue), Robert Vattier (Albert Brun)

Producers: Marcel Pagnol, Roger Richebée; Director: Marc Allégret; Writer: Marcel Pagnol; Photographers: Georges Benoit, Coutelier, André Dantan, Roger Hubert, Nikolai Toporkoff (black and white); Editors: Raymond Lamy, Jean Mamy

*Fanny* commences moments after Marius's departure, with César believing that his son and Fanny will marry. It is at this point that Fanny informs him that she has sent Marius away. For the next month, the father and the girl await word from Marius, who finally sends a short letter to César. His only mention of Fanny is his fond hope that she will be happy marrying Panisse. With what amounts to her lover's permission, Fanny is now faced with a moral dilemma. Her mother, Norine, thinks that she should marry Panisse as soon as possible and let him think that the child she is carrying is his. Fanny, however, prefers to be honest and tells Panisse the truth. Rather than being offended, the sailmaker is delighted to have both a young bride and a son he can claim as his own. (The possibility that the child will be female seems not to occur to him.) César is persuaded to go along with the plan when Fanny promises that he will be the godfather and that the child will be named after him.

The marriage of convenience proceeds better than anyone had expected. Panisse is both a faithful husband and a devoted father—qualities notably lacking in Marius. Although Marius does not yet know that the child is his, the fact that he is still alive leaves open the possibility of his return. One night he does appear for a brief visit at César's bar. With his life at sea finished, he is heading to Paris to sell automobiles. Not wanting to leave without seeing Fanny, he visits his former girlfriend. While Panisse sleeps, they become reacquainted, and Marius realizes that the child is his. Just as he is about ready to kiss Fanny, César arrives and will not leave the two alone. Sensing that she still loves him, Marius wants both Fanny and his child. She refuses to forsake Panisse, however, and sends Marius away for a second time. As much as César would like to see Marius and Fanny together, he too realizes that Panisse's selfless behavior has established him as the rightful husband and father. Realizing too late that he will never love anyone but Fanny, Marius departs.

The situation in *Fanny* is one that could easily evolve into a tale of cuckoldry. A young woman is separated from the young man she loves and wed to an unattractive older man for whom she feels no passion. When the young man returns and sees the error of his ways, nothing would be more "natural" than for the young people to get back together. The moral vision of this film, however, will not allow such a predictable outcome. For one thing, Panisse refuses to play the role of the stereotypical cuckold. Far from being a jealous dupe, he is grateful for the opportunity to become a husband and "father" so late in life and devotes himself altruistically to both roles. Rather than being ruled by hormones, Fanny allows Marius to leave when she senses that he will not be happy tied down on land and insists on maintaining the sanctity of her marriage when he experiences belated second thoughts. Even the buffoonish César rises to a level of moral seriousness in this situation. This film leaves us with the antiromantic message that physical passion is *not* the highest human value.

## THE FANNY TRILOGY: CÉSAR

1936 (168 minutes) • Romantic Comedy
Les Films Marcel Pagnol • Unrated

Cast: Raimu (César), Pierre Fresnay (Marius), Fernand Charpin (Panisse), Orane Demazis (Fanny), André Fouché

(Césariot), Robert Vattier (Albert Brun), Paul Dullac (Escartefigue), Alida Rouffe (Honorine)

Producer: Marcel Pagnol; Director: Marcel Pagnol; Writer: Marcel Pagnol; Photographer: Willy Faktorovitch (black and white); Editors: Suzanne de Troeye, Jeanette Ginestet

Although Pagnol was arguably the *auteur* of both *Marius* and *Fanny*, *César* is the only film of the trilogy that he actually directed. It takes place twenty years after *Fanny*. Césariot, Fanny's son, is now grown, Panisse has reached the biblical age of threescore years and ten, and no one has seen or heard from Marius in the past two decades. At the beginning of the story, Panisse suffers a heart attack that everyone realizes will be fatal. Not wanting to alarm him more than is necessary, his friends contrive to get the parish priest to drop by as if he were simply in the neighborhood. In a scene that is both sad and humorous, Panisse insists on making his final confession in the presence of his friends. (After all, in the early church confessions were made before the entire congregation.) None of his petty transgressions seem to disturb the priest until Panisse admits that he has concealed Césariot's true paternity from the boy. Despite the priest's admonition, Panisse goes to his grave without telling his foster son that he is not his biological father. Instead, Fanny assumes this difficult task herself.

Initially, Césariot appears traumatized to learn that he is not the son of the saintly man he has always thought was his father. He is angry with his mother for both the years of deception and the fact that she still harbors fond memories of Marius. Within a few days, however, curiosity gets the better of him, and he sets out to find his biological father, who is working as a mechanic across the bay. Without divulging his true identity, Césariot strikes up an acquaintance with Marius and even goes fishing with him. Although the two get along well enough together, Césariot is appalled to learn that his father has been arrested for some petty crimes. The situation is exacerbated when Marius's partner at the garage plays a practical joke on the boy by telling him that the two mechanics are engaged in drug smuggling.

If anything, Panisse's stature increases after his death. We learn that he has kept Marius afloat financially by advancing him money and guaranteeing other loans. In a bittersweet scene, César and a couple of Panisse's other friends realize the extent of their loss when they sit down for a game of cards and try to imagine how the sailmaker would have played his hand. Trying to imagine Panisse in the afterlife, César has already wondered what it would be like if his shriven friend encountered an exotic non-Christian god somewhere in the clouds.

The film ends when Marius makes a final return to Marseilles and tries yet again to pick up the pieces of his past life. From his perspective, his life has been a hard-luck story. Believing himself abandoned by his father and his fiancée, he had tried to return home and make amends only to be turned away again. Although he was arrested years earlier, he has spent the past fifteen years as an honest mechanic. With Panisse dead, it is now possible for Marius to be reunited with Fanny and finally to claim his son without any loss of honor. We believe that he has suffered enough and is a truly changed man. Thus, the happy ending of the trilogy is morally as well as dramatically justified.

## THE GREAT MCGINTY

1940 (82 minutes) • Political Comedy
Paramount • Unrated

Cast: Brian Donlevy (Dan McGinty), Muriel Angelus (Catherine McGinty), Akim Tamiroff (The Boss), William Demarest (The Politician), Allyn Joslyn (George), Louis Jean Heydt (Tommy Thompson), Harry Rosenthal (Louie), Arthur Hoyt (Mayor Tillinghast), Libby Taylor (Bessy), Thurston Hall (Mr. Maxwell)

Producer: Paul Jones; Director: Preston Sturges; Writer: Preston Sturges; Photographer: William C. Mellor (black and white); Editor: Hugh Bennett

Filmed in 1939 and released the following year, *The Great McGinty,* which won an Oscar for best screenplay, was the first directorial effort in the brilliant but short-lived career of Preston Sturges. (Already an accomplished writer for stage and screen, Sturges gave Paramount this script free of charge, on the condition that he be allowed to direct.) At a time when political films appealed to the populist sentimentality of the audience, Sturges maintained the cynicism that is essential to any effective satirist. Whether intended as such or not,

*The Great McGinty* was a rebuke to Frank Capra's *Mr. Smith Goes to Washington*, which had taken the nation by storm a year earlier and remains the better known and loved of the two films.

*The Great McGinty* opens in a South American bar, where two men from north of the border have fled for refuge. One is described as an honest man who did only one dishonest thing in his life and the other—the bartender—as a dishonest man who did only one honest thing in *his* life. Although we expect these to be intersecting or parallel stories, the basically honest man (who might have been a Capra hero gone bad) is only a device to introduce the far more interesting story of the film's protagonist. When the "honest" man, who had embezzled some money from the bank where he worked, prepares to shoot himself in shame over how far down he has come in the world, the bartender informs him that he had once been governor of his state. The rest of the story is told in flashback.

The expatriate bartender had started out as a street bum hired by a political boss to vote multiple times for the machine's candidate for mayor. Impressed by the fact that the bum, Dan McGinty, has voted thirty-five times in a single day, the unnamed and generic boss (played by Akim Tamiroff) puts him to work collecting old debts. McGinty is so effective at this job that the boss decides to run him for mayor. (The actual machine candidates are interchangeable pawns.) The boss's one mistake is to suggest that McGinty arrange a marriage of convenience to woo the women's vote. This ploy proves too successful when McGinty and his wife eventually fall in love with each other and she becomes a fatally civilizing influence on him.

Because of McGinty's popularity as mayor, the boss decides to run him for governor. By this time, however, Mrs. McGinty has convinced her husband that the power of office will allow him to do good for the common man by eliminating tenements and sweatshops. Unlike Willie Stark in *All the King's Men*, McGinty acquires rather than loses idealism by climbing the political ladder. But, like Willie, he is undone by past transgressions. When he betrays his mentor, the boss reveals some graft that McGinty had taken when building a bridge as mayor. He is briefly imprisoned but then spirited away by a former underling who is now a prison guard. (Both men and the boss end up working in the South American bar.) Before leaving the United States forever, McGinty calls his wife and ruefully admonishes her that "you can't make a silk purse from a pig's ear." This line may well serve as Sturges's comment on our entire political system.

## HARDCORE

1979 (105 minutes) • Drama
Columbia • R

Cast: George C. Scott (Jake VanDorn), Peter Boyle (Andy Mast), Season Hubley (Niki), Dick Sargent (Wes DeJong), Leonard Gaines (Ramada), David Nichols (Kurt), Gary Graham (Tod), Larry Block (Detective Burrows), Marc Alaimo (Ratan), Leslie Ackerman (Felice)

Producer: Buzz Feitshans; Director: Paul Schrader; Writer: Paul Schrader; Photographer: Michael Chapman (Metrocolor); Editor: Tom Rolf

Although there is probably not much competition for the honor, Paul Schrader's *Hardcore* may well be the greatest Calvinist movie ever made. Schrader grew up in Grand Rapids, Michigan, in a family devoutly committed to the Dutch Reformed Church. He was a pre-ministerial student at Calvin College before turning away from his upbringing. He later went on to write the scripts for such powerful Martin Scorsese films as *Taxi Driver* (1975), *Raging Bull* (1980), and *The Last Temptation of Christ* (1988). *Hardcore*, which was the second professional film he directed, begins in the Grand Rapids he remembers from childhood.

Jake VanDorn is a devout and hard-bitten furniture maker who lives alone with his teenage daughter Kristin. On the day after Christmas, the daughter leaves what Frederic and Mary Ann Brusatt aptly call this "winter wonderland" for a church trip to California. Soon thereafter, she turns up missing during an excursion to Knotts' Berry Farm. Frustrated with the failure of the police to find her, Jake hires a private investigator named Andy Mast to track her down. After a few weeks, Mast turns up an eight-millimeter peep-show film featuring Kristin. When the trail runs cold, Jake flies out to California to take up the search himself.

Jake's tour through the pornographic sewer of Los Angeles is a cross between Dante's descent into the Inferno and Leopold Bloom's journey through Nighttown. As such, it is a remarkable confirmation of the Calvinist worldview. The world of pornography, which degenerates to the level of snuff films, is clearly an example of total depravity, a doctrine that Jake believes in abstractly but has never had to confront quite so directly. What he is also forced to confront is his own sin of pride, which apparently caused his daughter to leave him for life in the gutter and had prompted his wife to leave them both years earlier.

If the plot seems a bit heavy-handed, that is only fitting for a Calvinist narrative. Because Jake and Kristin are presumably among the elect, the fact that they are reunited at the end of the film should come as no surprise. Her sojourn in hell has been a learning experience for them both. In strict Calvinist terms, they are not exactly redeemed by this experience. (Their state of grace was predetermined by God from the beginning of time.) What they have undergone is closer to a rite of purification, which is more than a little ironic considering where and how it occurs.

Jake's guide through the underworld is a streetwise girl named Niki who has been selling herself since age fifteen. By the end of the film, Jake would like to do something to help her, but Mast convinces him that it is too late. Of course, that is true only if Niki is not among the elect. Although only God knows, the film seems to suggest that that is the case. At one point, Jake (whose biblical namesake wrestled with an angel of the Lord) says to her: "I'm a mystery to you. You can never understand a man like me—a man who believes in God, who doesn't pursue women, who believes in social order, and believes that at the end of his life he will be redeemed. You can't imagine someone who doesn't know what's going on in New York or Los Angeles, or what's happening on TV and in the movies, or who's on Johnny Carson!" Fortunately, this lack of understanding does not prevent Niki from being an agent of irresistible grace, surely the most appealing of Calvinist doctrines.

## HOFFA

1992 (140 minutes) • Drama
Twentieth Century-Fox • R

Cast: Jack Nicholson (Jimmy Hoffa), Danny DeVito (Bobby Ciaro), Armand Assante (Carol D'Allesandro), J. T. Walsh (Frank Fitzsimmons), John C. Reilly (Pete Connelly), Kevin Anderson (Bobby Kennedy), Cliff Gorman (Solly Stein)

Producers: Caldecott Chubb, Danny DeVito, Edwin R. Pressman (Producers), Joseph Isgro (Executive Producer), William Barclay Malcolm, David Mamet (Associate Producers); Harold Schneider (Coproducer); Director: Danny DeVito; Writer: David Mamet; Photographer: Stephen H. Burum (color); Editors: Lynzee Klingman, Ronald Roose

For most Americans who came of age after the mid-1960s, Jimmy Hoffa (if he is remembered at all) is simply America's most famous missing person—the ultimate cold-case file, a man who disappeared in 1975 and hasn't been heard from since. To those of us who lived through Hoffa's moment in the national spotlight, however, he is remembered as a brutal and corrupt union boss who was brought down by the sainted Bobby Kennedy. Only among a select few, mostly members of his own Teamsters Union, is Hoffa lionized as the great organizer who brought economic justice to America's truck drivers. That is essentially the point of view of this film. Directed by Danny DeVito and written by David Mamet, *Hoffa* is uncompromisingly revisionist in its perspective. Older viewers will be particularly struck by the degree to which Jack Nicholson captures the look and sound of the man they remember from old newsreels and Senate hearings. Only the meanings have been changed.

The point of view of the movie is that of a generic truck driver named Bobby Ciaro. Bobby knew Hoffa when he was only an official in the Detroit local and remains loyal to him during his subsequent rise and fall. Although Hoffa is shown dealing with the mob, we have the sense that he used them as much as they used him. (As we now know, his arch-enemies the Kennedys did pretty much the same.) This is a cynical and pragmatic, though not necessarily inaccurate, portrayal of life in America. One almost expects the film to turn into a blue-collar version of *All the King's Men* or *Viva Zapata*, showing how power ultimately corrupts idealism. But as Roger Ebert points out, "we can never quite glimpse the idealism that should be there somewhere." The tough-guy tone of this picture precludes such moralizing. We must settle for populism without piety.

*Hoffa* is an episodic narrative that blends fact and fiction in a manner that sober historians decry. What we have here, however, is not documentary realism so much as myth. By that I do not mean that it is false but that it conveys a vision that may be truer than fact. Surely the demonic image of Hoffa is the product of a myth made by politicians and the press during his own lifetime. It is a measure of the man's integrity (or stubbornness) that he didn't seem to care—as long as the Teamsters continued to love him. Tribal loyalty alone is not a quality sufficient to make Hoffa a conservative, which is something he certainly never claimed to be, even if he did deal with Republicans as freely as he did with mobsters. But this cinematic version of his career does help show why the New Deal coalition had come apart at the seams by the late '60s. White working-class stiffs, such as those Hoffa represented, had become unfashionable in the eyes of the nation's moral elite. It may just be coincidence, but since Hoffa's disappearance from the scene, both liberalism and the labor movement have become diminished forces in American life.

## HOOSIERS

1987 (114 minutes) • Sports Drama
Orion • PG

Cast: Gene Hackman (Norman Dale), Dennis Hopper (Shooter), Barbara Hershey (Myra Fleener), Sheb Wooley (Cletus), Fern Parsons (Opal Fleener), Ross Rollin (George Chelice), Michael O'Guinne (Robert Swan Rooster)

Producers: Carter Dehaven, Angelo Pizzo; Director: David Anspaugh; Writer: Angelo Pizzo; Photographer: Fred Murphy (color); Editor: Timothy C. O'Meara

Sports have always held a special place in American life. Not only do the games themselves evoke passion, they also provide metaphors for other aspects of life. "Playing by the rules," "giving 100 percent" (or more) are but two of the many clichés that athletics have given to our workaday world. Unfortunately, as covert professionalism makes a mockery of the term "student athlete" and performance-enhancing drugs cause competition itself to seem suspect, our gladiators have been inevitably compromised by the world in which the rest of us must live. But in sports, as in so many other realms of experience, there is the myth of a golden age when things were as we like to imagine them to have been. David Anspaugh's film *Hoosiers* takes us back to such a time.

The year is 1951, and the setting is a small Indiana farming community where high school basketball is as much a religion as a pastime. When the incumbent coach dies suddenly, he is replaced by Norman Dale, a mysterious stranger who had been a college classmate of the school's principal. For reasons that are not immediately made clear, Dale's career as a successful college coach in Ithaca, New York, had ended abruptly a decade earlier. Fresh out of the military, he is starting life over as an apparently middle-aged loser.

*Hoosiers* gives us a realistic depiction of life in a small midwestern community. Hickory, Indiana, is neither the soul-numbing hell one finds in the fiction of Sherwood Anderson and Sinclair Lewis nor the sunny utopia of the Andy Hardy movies. It is an insular community where a newcomer must earn the right to belong. The school itself is so small that there are only six players on the basketball squad and the team manager has to be sent into a crucial game. Despite initial resistance to Dale and his way of doing things, the team eventually comes together and starts winning games. The star player from the previous year, who had dropped off the team, returns in time for the Hickory Huskers to be at their peak come tournament time.

Like that later Hoosier coach Bobby Knight (who also began his head coaching career in New York), Dale is a disciplinarian who picks up a ton of technical fouls and is thrown out of more than his share of games. Only then is it revealed that he lost his previous position when he punched out one of his own players. Believing in redemption, Dale hires the town drunk as an assistant coach on the condition that he clean up his act. Although this reclamation project is only partially successful, it shows that Dale has a good heart under his rough exterior. The drunk (known as Shooter) started his spiral downward after missing an important shot in a key game during his own high school career. Dennis Hopper as Shooter and Gene Hackman as Dale both turn in mesmerizing performances.

This film recaptures the gee-whiz innocence of a time when white farm boys spent long winter afternoons shooting at hoops on the sides of barns. At the same time, black kids were perfecting their games on inner-city playgrounds. (The best discussion of these two cultures is Jeff Greenfield's classic essay "The Black and White Truth about Basketball.") In the climax of *Hoosiers*, the farm boys play against a racially mixed city team for the state championship (just as did Hickory's real-life counterpart, Milan, in the 1954 Indiana state championship game). The point of the story, however, is not a racial one but rather the transracial truth that David sometimes can slay Goliath. That fact alone makes this picture a welcome departure from tendentious racial politics and a reaffirmation of values routinely scorned by the adversary culture.

## I LOVE YOU, ALICE B. TOKLAS!

1968 (92 minutes) • Comedy
Warner Brothers/Seven Arts • R

Cast: Peter Sellers (Harold Fine), Jo Van Fleet (Mrs. Fine), Leigh Taylor-Young (Nancy), Joyce Van Patten (Joyce Miller), David Arkin (Herbie Fine), Herb Edelman (Murray), Salem Ludwig (Mr. Fine), Louis Gottlieb (Guru), Grady Sutton (Funeral Director), Janet Clark (Mrs. Foley), Jorge Moreno (Mr. Rodriguez), Ed Peck (Man in Dress Shop), Jack Margolis (Big Bear), Eddra Gale (Love Lady), Carol O'Leary (Anita)

Producers: Charles A. Maguire (Producer), Paul Mazursky, Larry Tucker (Executive Producers); Director: Hy Averback; Writers: Paul Mazursky, Larry Tucker; Photographer: Philip Lathrop (color); Editor: Robert C. Jones

If it were not for the presence of Peter Sellers, *I Love You, Alice B. Toklas!* would be little more than a dated spoof of the psychedelic generation. Sellers delivers a flawless performance as a neurotic Jewish lawyer named Harold Fine. (Look also for Grady Sutton, who played W. C. Fields's prospective son-in-law in *The Bank Dick* [1940], in the role of the funeral director.) Harold has a high-figure salary, a Lincoln automobile, and a beautiful and devoted fiancée. In short, he seems to be the Walter Mitty image of countless Woody Allen characters. Unfortunately, Harold is also asthmatic, uptight, and unfulfilled. It seems as if things will only get worse when his fiancée, Joyce, pressures him to set a date for their wedding. His entire outlook on life changes, however, when his brother's hippie girlfriend, Nancy, bakes him a plate of very special brownies. For the benefit of the uninformed, these brownies come from the cookbook of Alice B. Toklas, lesbian consort of Gertrude Stein, the grand dame of literary modernism. Because the brownies are laced with hashish, Harold is freed of his middle-class hang-ups. In one of the most hilarious scenes in the film, Harold shares the brownies with his aging parents, who immediately become giddy and lascivious.

Suspecting that the hippie lifestyle may offer him the freedom he's been looking for, Harold leaves Joyce at the altar to drop out, tune in, and turn on. Although cameo appearances by Allen Ginsberg and Timothy Leary were cut, there is one extremely funny scene in which a newly liberated Harold seeks advice from a white-robed guru. "But how do you know what a flower is, Harold," the guru asks, "if you don't know who *you* are?" "I'm trying, guru," Harold replies, "I'm really trying." To this, the guru replies: "When you stop trying, then you'll know who you are." As one might predict, long hair and strange clothes are not enough to bring true liberation. When a group of hippie squatters invade his apartment, Harold soon returns to the straitlaced life and to the altar where he has left the long-suffering Joyce. In an act that stretches credulity, he abandons her a second time. Although we suspect that he is not going to go off the psychedelic deep end again, he will be looking for his own individual mode of freedom.

Sellers is such an accomplished actor that he need never play himself. In real life, however, he was a driven professional who sought release in recreational drugs and sex. On the screen, he was able to establish some ironic distance from such a persona. If the film fails as satire, it is because all the jokes are directed at the surface rather than the substance of hippie culture. Because the film does not have the nerve to return a chastened Harold to the life he has abandoned and cannot find a convincing rationale to return him to his failed bohemian existence, the most that can be done is to leave him searching for something better than anything he has known before. In 1968, it was easier to believe that he might find that elusive happiness. In retrospect, Harold seems as lost as Peter Sellers himself.

## JEZEBEL

1938 (104 minutes) • Drama
Warner Brothers • Unrated

Cast: Bette Davis (Julie Morrison), Henry Fonda (Preston Dillard), George Brent (Buck Cantrell), Margaret Lindsay

(Amy Bradford Dillard), Fay Bainter (Aunt Belle Massey), Richard Cromwell (Ted Dillard), Donald Crisp (Dr. Livingstone), Henry O'Neill (General Theopholus Bogardus), John Litel (Jean La Cour), Gordon Oliver (Dick Allen)

Producer: Henry Blanke; Director: William Wyler; Writers: Clements Ripley, Abem Finkel, John Huston, Robert Buckner (based on the play by Owen Davis Sr.); Photographer: Ernest Haller (black and white); Editor: Warren Low

This film appeared a year before the blockbuster *Gone With the Wind* and has languished in its shadow ever since. While *GWTW* was filmed in Technicolor, *Jezebel* was a typical black-and-white product of the '30s. Whereas *GWTW* was a 220-minute epic, *Jezebel* managed to tell its story in a mere 104 minutes. Moreover, the star of the movie (Bette Davis) had already been turned down for the role of Scarlett O'Hara. Despite these limitations, *Jezebel* has held up remarkably well over the years. For her performance as the spoiled and fiery belle Julie Morrison, Davis won the Academy Award for best actress. Like Scarlett O'Hara, Julie loses her chances for happiness by wanting too much. When her fiancé, Press Dillard, stays at a business meeting at his bank rather than go shopping with her, Julie spitefully purchases an inappropriate red dress to wear at an upcoming ball. (Unmarried women are expected to wear white.) The battle of wills between Julie and Press, which is played out on the dance floor, effectively ends their engagement.

The following year, when Julie hears that Press is to return to Louisiana from New York, she confidently assumes that she will win him back. In an unforgettable scene, she kneels before him, in a white dress, and apologizes profusely for her past indiscretions. Unfortunately, Press is now married to a woman from New York and has brought his new wife with him. Almost reflexively, Julie directs her charm to a more typically Southern beau, Buck Cantrell. While Press makes a business trip to New Orleans, which is infested with yellow fever, his brother Ted and Buck trade insults and eventually fight a duel that results in Buck's death. When they hear that Press has been stricken by yellow fever, both his wife, Amy, and Julie rush to his side. According to the quarantine laws, Press is sent to a special island to fend for himself along with other victims of the epidemic. Having destroyed herself with her own selfishness, Julie persuades Amy to let her accompany Press because she will be better able to take care of him. In the final scene of the film, a redeemed Julie rides in a cart to almost certain death with the man she loved and lost.

On the surface, Julie's turn in character might seem contrived. What makes it convincing, however, is the emotional intensity that Bette Davis brings to the role. Although we cannot help agreeing with Press in his practical criticisms of Southern culture, there is a grandeur about plantation life that captures the imagination of the audience. Unfortunately, this is mixed with enough Jim Crow humor to make the film seem anachronistic to contemporary viewers. (Nevertheless, the scene in which Julie leads the slave children in a Stephen Foster song after she learns of Buck's death is one of the dramatic high points of the movie.) If the South was a land of beautiful losers, Julie Morrison's final sacrifice makes her emblematic of an entire class of people.

## JUDGE PRIEST

1934 (80 minutes) • Comedy
Fox • Unrated

Cast: Will Rogers (Judge William "Billy" Priest), Henry B. Walthall (The Reverend Ashby Brand), Tom Brown (Jerome Priest), Anita Louise (Ellie May Gillespie), Rochelle Hudson (Virginia Maydew), David Landau (Bob Gillis), Brenda Fowler (Mrs. Caroline Priest), Hattie McDaniel (Aunt Dilsey), Stepin Fetchit (Jeff Poindexter), Berton Churchill (Senator Horace K. Maydew)

Producer: Sol Wurtzel; Director: John Ford; Writers: Dudley Nichols, Lamar Trotti (from stories by Irvin S. Cobb); Photographer: George Schneiderman (black and white); Editor: Paul Weatherwax

In a life cut short by an airplane crash in 1935, Will Rogers was one of America's most beloved entertainers. In addition to being a stand-up comedian, actor, and newspaper columnist, Rogers was our greatest satirist since Mark Twain. The most substantial remaining record of his work lies in his motion pictures. As one of the earliest sound pictures for both Rogers and John Ford,

*Judge Priest* would be important simply as a historical document. But it is also a charming and well-made film that calls forth memories of an earlier pastoral America which now exists only in memory. The fact that this America is set in a South that still reveres its Confederate heritage makes *Judge Priest* the sort of "culturally insensitive" film that would not be made today.

In the role of Judge William Priest, a small-town Southern jurist, Rogers is the very soul of tolerance and moderation. In the opening scene, a white racist windbag brings the black Jeff Poindexter to court on the grounds that he is "a confirmed chicken thief" who has "no place in this God-fearing community." The judge shows his contempt for this blather by reading the newspaper on the bench, while Poindexter sleeps on the witness stand. Instead of showing an official judicial verdict, the screen dissolves into a scene of Judge Priest and Jeff going fishing.

In his private life, the judge also displays an uncanny sense for what is right and a knack for bringing it about. At one point, he contrives to reunite his nephew and the lad's estranged girlfriend. (The judge's own wife and two children are all dead.) When the nephew's imperious mother objects to her son's match with a poor girl of unknown parentage, she observes: "The name of Priest means something in Kentucky!" To this, the judge replies: "I never heard it meant intolerance." If Judge Priest seems to be the conscience of this small Kentucky town, it can be argued that Will Rogers was close to being the conscience of America—a kind of priest as well as a judge.

The public and private plots merge when the town blacksmith, Bob Gillis, is brought to trial for stabbing the barber Tully. Not only does this turn out to be the first case for the Judge's nephew Rome, who has just recently graduated from law school, it is also the climax of the movie. Things seem to be going against Gillis when he offers no reason for having defended the honor of Rome's girlfriend, Ellie May. Then the Reverend Brand takes the stand and reveals that Gillis had once been released from a life sentence on a chain gang and had fought valiantly for the Confederacy. Moreover, for the past few years, he has secretly watched over and provided for Ellie May—his daughter. By this time, Jeff (at the Judge's instigation) is leading a band in "Dixie" just outside the courthouse window. Gillis is pronounced innocent by acclamation of the town.

The Southern nationalism that permeates this film perfectly fits its elegiac mood. Less than twenty years earlier, Henry B. Walthall, who plays the Reverend Brand, had portrayed the Little Colonel in D. W. Griffith's *The Birth of a Nation*. Although his account of Gillis's heroics (which resemble those of the Little Colonel in several particulars) are rendered in flashback, Ford never allows Gillis's face to vanish from the screen. If the racial stereotypes portrayed by Fetchit and McDaniel seem problematic today, they were less so in 1934. As Fetchit himself observed, "When people saw me and Will Rogers like brothers, that said something to them." Or as the critic Martin Rubin put it: "*Judge Priest* suggests that, by lying long enough in the dappled Southern sunlight, white and black will overlap . . . without the boundaries of miscegenation ever being crossed."

## KATE AND LEOPOLD

2001 (118 minutes) • Romantic Comedy
Konrad Pictures/Miramax Films • PG-13

Cast: Meg Ryan (Kate McKay), Hugh Jackman (Leopold), Liev Schreiber (Stuart Besser), Breckin Meyer (Charlie McKay), Natasha Lyonne (Darci), Bradley Whitford (J. J. Camden), Paxton Whitehead (Uncle Millard), Spalding Gray (Dr. Geisler), Josh Stamberg (Colleague Bob), Matthew Sussman (Ad Executive Phil), Charlotte Ayanna (Patrice), Philip Bosco (Otis), Andrew Jack (Roebling), Stan Tracy (Photographer), Kristen Schaal (Miss Tree)

Producers: Cathy Konrad (Producer), Kerry Orent, Meryl Poster, Bob Weinstein, Harvey Weinstein (Executive Producers), Christopher Goode (Coproducer); Director: James Mangold; Writers: Steven Rogers, James Mangold; Photographer: Stuart Dryburg (color); Editor: David Brenner

On the surface, this film would seem to be nothing more than a moderately amusing romantic comedy based on a flimsy science-fiction premise. Leopold, who is a proper if somewhat progressive Victorian gentleman, falls into a time warp that lands him in twenty-first-century Manhattan. The conflict of cultures, especially as he interacts with the very modern career woman Kate, provides predictable laughs. Surprisingly, however, not all of the laughs are at the expense of Victorian propriety. As certain as he is of his place in society, Leopold is no prig. He represents the dilemma of the man who wishes to bring progress to the world in which he lives until he sees the actual future. As viewers, we are forced to see our world through the eyes of a man who must regard it as a confused, if not exactly dystopian, fantasy. The charm of Jackman's performance makes this all seem real.

As the epitome of the liberated woman, Kate is the antithesis of the Victorian lady; however, her growing infatuation with Leopold prompts her to take a trip back in time to his world. Contrary to the lessons of feminism, she does not find this to be a hideously repressive environment. The contrast with *Pleasantville*, a film made only a few years earlier, is striking. In that movie, some contemporary kids manage to enter the black-and-white world of a television show set in the drab 1950s. As they bring enlightenment (mostly in the form of sexual awareness) to that environment, it begins to take on cautious shades of color. One finds no such condescension toward the past in *Kate and Leopold*. Instead, the contrast of cultures reveals some of the deficiencies of the contemporary world.

The fact that this film did not raise the ire of feminists, and indeed the entire liberal establishment, can only be attributed to deceptive packaging. Chick flicks are not meant to raise serious social issues—especially not at the expense of women, who were not even allowed to vote in the Victorian era. (Let us not forget, however, that the period was named for a woman, who remained on the throne longer than any other British monarch.) By the end of the film, Kate must decide whether to remain in the liberated modern world or follow Leopold back through the time warp and become a Victorian lady. Although I will not reveal her choice, the fact that both options are given a kind of moral equivalency is itself an example of political incorrectness rarely seen in contemporary cinema.

## KHARTOUM

1966 (134 minutes) • Historical Drama
United Artists • Unrated

Cast: Charlton Heston (Chinese Gordon), Laurence Olivier (The Mahdi), Richard Johnson (Colonel J. D. H. Stewart),

Ralph Richardson (William Gladstone), Alexander Knox (Sir Evelyn Baring), Johnny Sekka (Khaleel), Michael Hordern (Lord Grenville), Zia Mohyeddin (Zobeir Pasha), Marne Maitland (Sheikh Osman), Nigel Green (General Wolseley), Hugh Williams (Lord Hartington), Ralph Michael (Sir Charles Dilke), Douglas Wilmer (Khalifa Abdullah), Edward Underdown (Colonel William Hicks), Peter Arne (Major Kitchener)

Producer: Julian Blaustein; Director: Basil Dearden; Writer: Robert Ardrey; Photographer: Edward Scaife (color); Editor: Fergus McDonell

If the threat of an Islamic jihad seemed of antiquarian interest when this movie was made in 1966, it has become the stuff of today's headlines. Like so many historical movies, *Khartoum* is less an exercise in documentary realism than a fiction based on historical events. The film depicts the clash of two remarkable and charismatic leaders from radically different cultures. In November 1881, Egyptian troops tried to arrest Muhammad Ahmad, a thirty-seven-year-old Muslim leader who had called for a holy war—or jihad—to drive the British and Egyptians from the Sudan. Ahmad drew support because of both his military victories and his audacity in proclaiming himself the Mahdi, a holy guide sent to the faithful by the Prophet Muhammad himself. The Mahdi swept through Sudan, forcing major concessions of territory from the Egyptians. What one does not learn from the film is that the Egyptians had taken over much of Sudan in the 1820s and that the Egyptian government was so corrupt it had only a tenuous claim on the loyalty of its own citizens. In addition to the invasion of the Mahdi, a nationalist coup in Egypt appeared to endanger British access to the Suez Canal.

In November 1883, a detachment of British infantry and camel corpsmen, under the command of Colonel William Hicks, were defeated by the Mahdi's forces. The movie begins with this defeat, followed by Prime Minister Gladstone's wondering "how a rabble of tribesmen armed only with spears, swords, and rocks can destroy a modern army." (The fact that the Brits were outnumbered ten-to-one might have had something to do with it.) At that point, Her Majesty's government calls upon Colonel Charles Gordon to supervise an evacuation of Europeans and Egyptians from Khartoum, the administrative capital of Egyptian-ruled Sudan. A second lieutenant during the Crimean War of the mid-1850s, Gordon had become a legend in England for suppressing the Taiping Rebellion in 1864. (This accounts for his nickname of Chinese Gordon.) As things turned out, Gordon ignored his limited orders in an ill-fated attempt to keep Sudan under British influence. In what appears to be a flight of fancy, scriptwriter Robert Ardrey (who, five years later, would inspire Sam Peckinpah's *Straw Dogs*) indicates that this is what Gladstone hoped would happen but could not admit.

The most glaring historical inaccuracy in the film is a scene depicting a meeting between Gordon and the Mahdi. Although no such encounter took place in real life, its dramatic potential was too much to forego. The picture ends with the Sudanese followers of the Mahdi scaling the walls at Khartoum and overwhelming the city's defenders. Unable to stop the onslaught, Gordon is speared and beheaded. This is seen not just as the death of a single British martyr but as the tragic demise of imperialism itself. Like the defenders of the Alamo, Gordon took on a greater grandeur in death than in life. A final voice-over informs us that "a world without Gordons would return to the sands."

## KING OF THE HILL SEASON ONE

Actually, any season of this marvelous animated series could be included in the hall of fame of political incorrectness; however, I have chosen Season One (the winter and spring of 1997) because it served to introduce the gang from Arlen, Texas, to American television audiences. *King of the Hill* is fundamentally different from both *The Simpsons* and *Family Guy*, each of which is brilliant in its own way. For one thing, *King* is less a cartoon than a totally realistic situation comedy which happens to be animated. In fact, it is far more realistic than most series featuring live actors. Even more importantly, the moral center of the show is solidly conservative and Middle American, simmered with a bit of Texas barbeque (cooked in propane, of course). The satire is usually directed against liberal, New Age culture. When the jibes are turned against the Right, it is almost always done in a gentle, self-deprecatory tone, with none of the nastiness that one discerns in so much that passes for political comedy in today's cutting-edge entertainment.

Episode One: Pilot (January 12, 1997)
Director: Wes Archer; Writers: Mike Judge and Greg Daniels

In the pilot episode, an officious social worker (originally from Los Angeles) suspects Hank Hill of child abuse when young Bobby sports a shiner after being hit in the eye by a baseball during a Little League game. Hank's understandable rage at the social worker only makes him look more guilty. Fortunately, the social worker's superior (who is from Texas) straightens the situation out and sends the twiggy bureaucrat back to the Left Coast where he belongs. (In a bit of priceless visual humor, we see that the intrusive social worker has both arms in some kind of wrap to indicate carpal tunnel syndrome.) In addition to being a funny story in its own right, this episode introduces the major characters in the series. The Hill household consists of Hank and Peggy; their son, Bobby; and Peggy's hapless trailer-trash niece, Luanne. Hank's best friends in the neighborhood are Boomhauer, the womanizing bachelor who speaks in a kind of fast-talking drawl; Bill Dauterive, the hapless divorcé and army barber; and Dale Gribble, a feckless cuckold who is also a lovable right-wing conspiracy nut.

Episode Two: "Square Peg" (January 19, 1997)
Director: Gary McCarver; Writer: Joe Stillman

Hank and Peggy are both traditional enough to be horrified by the prospect of Bobby's taking sex education in the fifth grade. The matter seems to be settled when they refuse to sign the consent form and determine to teach him themselves about the birds and bees. Unfortunately, the education they received from their own parents does not prepare them even to achieve the goal of having Bobby grow up as repressed as they are. In the meantime, Dale has scared off the designated sex-ed teacher with hilariously threatening phone calls, and substitute-teacher-of-the-year Peggy Hill is called into service. Despite her misgivings, Peggy is committed to her job. Doubly upset at the prospect of both his wife and son being engaged in this embarrassing enterprise, Hank takes Bobby to work with him at the local propane store. By the end of the episode, however, he dutifully delivers Bobby to the sex-ed class, where he is the only student with a signed permission slip. (Everyone else heads for a free period at the library.) Dale now directs his threatening (and supposedly anonymous) calls to Peggy, after which he gives her a message for Hank—in his own undisguised voice—concerning their tee time the next day.

Episode Three: "The Order of the Straight Arrow" (February 9, 1997)
Director: Klay Hall; Writer: Cheryl Holliday

This episode focuses on intergenerational male bonding when Hank, Boomhauer, Bill, and Dale take Bobby's scout troop on a wilderness outing. It soon becomes evident, however, that the men are actually using the boys to relive (or reimagine) their own youth. The adults cynically believe that the mystic Indian lore they are feeding the lads is poppycock until Bobby accidentally fells a whooping crane. Rather than admitting to the apparent killing of a creature on the Endangered Species List, Hank and cronies try unsuccessfully to hide the bird and get out of the woods undetected. It is at that point that Bobby uses the Indian lore to revive the bird and get everyone off the hook. The woman who discovers this apparent crime against the environment is a stereotypical tree-hugger with unshaven armpits. This particular segment manages to affirm care for the environment while poking fun at environmentalists.

Episode Four: "Hank's Got the Willies" (February 9, 1997)
Director: Monte Young; Writer: Johnny Hardwick

Hank's adoration of his old guitar causes a potential rift in the family. Emulating a punk-rock celebrity, Bobby commits the sacrilege of playing the sacred instrument with a piece of cheese, while Peggy simply feels neglected. These story lines create a vehicle for a guest appearance by Willie Nelson, who is Hank's musical hero. Both Hank and Willie are from Texas, both play the guitar, and both have had problems with the IRS. Not until Bobby accidentally hits Willie on the head with a golf club, however, does Hank actually meet his idol. Although the narrative is thin and the humor is less pointed than in some of the episodes, this episode is still worth watching. By the end, father and son are reunited when Willie convinces Hank that Bobby is simply trying to be like his obvious hero—Hank Hill. And Peggy melts when she hears Hank play and sing a Buddy Holly–like tribute to her. The closest we get to Willie's own music, however, is a doorbell that plays "On the Road Again" when Hank tries to gain admittance to an estate repossessed by the IRS.

Episode Five: "Luanne's Saga" (February 16, 1997)
Director: Pat Shinagawa; Writer: Paul Lieberstein

Although Hank's narrow urethra has prevented the Hills from having more than one child, Peggy's niece Luanne is a more or less permanent boarder. Raised in a trailer park, she tries valiantly to make it through beauty school and rise above her shoddy upbringing. Her path to the middle class is impeded by the string of losers she has as boyfriends. In this episode, she is dumped by her latest beau, who works as a clerk at the local mall. In an attempt to repair her broken life (and, more importantly, to retrieve his den, where Luanne has slept since moving in), Hank tries to find her a more suitable boyfriend. Instead, he manages inadvertently to get her hooked up with Boomhauer. Although Luanne's background is the object of satire, it is neither mean nor condescending, and she is a genuinely likable character. At one point, Hank remarks that tomorrow is her mother's big day. To that, Luanne innocently replies: "No, her big day is the sentencing. Tomorrow's just the arraignment."

Episode Six: "Hank's Unmentionable Problem" (February 23, 1997)
Director: Adam Kuhlman; Writers: Greg Daniels and Mike Judge

Constipation can easily be the occasion for a lot of cheap toilet jokes. Although this episode contains its share of such humor, we are also made to see Hank's irregularity as a potentially serious medical problem that causes great concern for his wife, even as it produces great embarrassment for Hank. The tone is so perfectly modulated that this tale is neither too vulgar nor too maudlin. As Hank's "unmentionable problem" persists, Peggy finds herself incapable of not mentioning it. Consequently, it becomes known to everyone in town. It is not the constipation itself so much as Hank's embarrassment that provides the humor here. When the problem is finally resolved, we don't know whether it is more a triumph for Hank's physical or mental health. The episode would hardly seem political at all were it not for the fact that Lynne Cheney, celebrated author of lesbian novels, denounced it without ever having seen it. That alone should be recommendation enough.

Episode Seven: "Westie Side Story" (March 2, 1997)
Director: Brian Sheesley; Writers: Jonathan Aibel and Glenn Berger

Multiculturalism enters the block in the person of the new Asian neighbors, Con and Min, and their daughter, Con Jr. When Hank asks them if they are Chinese or Japanese, Con replies that they are Laotian. It's nice that they lived by an ocean, Hank observes, but he still wants to know if they're Chinese or Japanese. In a politically incorrect reversal of expectations, the Laotians turn out to be at least as bigoted as the well-meaning Texans. Con thinks that Hank and his pals are ignorant rednecks, while Min thoughtlessly ridicules Peggy's huge feet and even more thoughtlessly improves upon her recipe for Brown Betty. When Con tries to patch things over by hosting a neighborhood barbeque, a misunderstanding causes Hank and his pals to think that he is cooking and serving dog. Over the following seasons, the clash of cultures between the recent arrivals and the established families will be the source of continuing humor.

Episode Eight: "Shins of the Father" (March 23, 1997)
Director: Martin Archer Jr.; Writers: Alan R. Cohen and Alan Freedland

We see more of Hank's extended family with the introduction of his father, Cotton Hill, an irascible old man who lost his shins "fighting for Texas in World War II." Divorced from Hank's mother, Cotton is now married to a much younger woman who went to kindergarten with Hank. Try as he might, Hank has never been able to live up to his father's expectations. Much to Peggy's consternation, Cotton arrives on horseback for Bobby's birthday party and manages to stay several days past his welcome. During that time, Bobby learns to slap his mother on the rear end and order her to get his dinner. If that isn't bad enough, Cotton keeps Bobby out of school to celebrate Angie Dickinson's birthday. The final straw, however, comes when the old man tries to reenact a male bonding experience by taking his grandson to the Hotel Arlen for his first hooker. Remembering his own humiliation during a similar experience, Hank finally tells his father off. This and subsequent episodes establish Peggy Hill as the avatar of acceptable feminism.

Episode Nine: "Peggy the Boggle Champ" (April 13, 1997)
Director: Chuck Sheetz; Writers: Jonathan Aibel and Glenn Berger

Because of her gift for anagrams, Peggy becomes boggle champion of Arlen, Texas, and wins a spot in the state tournament in Dallas, a town that Hank believes is filled with crack-heads and debutantes—"half of whom play for the Cowboys." Hank and his buddies go along for the ride, thinking that they can skip out of the tournament to attend a mower expo also being held in Dallas. (For $7.50, you can ride the mower that cut the grassy knoll.) This creates a conflict when Peggy expects Hank to be her coach as well as her husband. Things start out badly when the only opponent Peggy can beat is the boggle-playing chicken. After managing to gain some poise and momentum, however, Peggy is matched against the incredibly snooty reigning champion. On the night before the climactic match, Hank only makes things worse by giving Peggy the sort of rough half-time pep talk he recalls getting from his high school football coach when Arlen lost the state championship. Fortunately, everything turns out all right in the end for both the boggle game and the marriage.

Episode Ten: "Keeping up with Our Joneses" (April 27, 1997)
Director: John Rice; Writers: Jonathan Collier and Joe Stillman

In an age when adolescents increasingly experiment with hard drugs, the worst thing that Bobby Hill and Joseph Gribble do is light up a cigarette. Dale responds by giving Joseph a report on smoking prepared by the tobacco industry. Hank figures that he can best discipline Bobby by making him smoke until he throws up. In the process, Bobby gets both sick and hooked, and the second-hand smoke reminds Hank and Peggy of their younger days. (Some charming flashbacks are accompanied by the sound of "What Do You Get When You Fall in Love?") Soon all three members of the Hill family are sneaking smokes until they are reduced to battling each other for the lone remaining cigarette. In one scene, Hank and Peggy return to a restaurant that they used to frequent when they were young smokers, only to discover that the former owner has died a painful death and that the designated smoking room is filled with customers with hacking coughs. Rarely have both the lures and drawbacks of smoking been better depicted.

Episode Eleven: "King of the Ant Hill" (May 4, 1997)
Director: Gary McCarver; Writers: Johnny Hardwick and Paul Lieberstein

Hank's greatest source of aesthetic pride is the appearance of his lawn. But in this, as in so many other areas, his new Asian neighbors threaten to outdo him. When the annual competition comes around, Hank invests a small fortune in some exotic grass that he is certain will win him the award for best lawn. Just to be on the safe side, he also tells Dale not to spray any more chemicals on the yard. This decision backfires, however, when Dale spitefully and secretly dumps a bunch of fire ants on Hank's lawn. Almost overnight, it turns into a desert. After a chastened Dale tries to reverse the damage, only to incur ant bites all over his face and body, the neighbors contribute pieces of their own sod to help restore Hank's lawn. This is the first of many episodes in which the lawn becomes a source of rivalry and intrigue.

Episode Twelve: "Plastic White Female" (May 11, 1997)
Director: Jeff Myers; Writer: David Zuckerman

One of the stock story lines of situation comedy is the one in which an adolescent reaches puberty before his or her parents think that the child is ready. This episode reverses that scenario when Bobby is invited to his first boy-girl party. Although neither Bobby nor Peggy thinks that he is ready for this leap into the abyss, Hank is more than eager to see the lad flash his charms. That fantasy comes to an abrupt end, however, when the Hills discover Bobby playing spin the bottle with one of Luanne's plastic beautician-school heads. (A horrified Hank tells him that there is no state in the country that will allow him to marry a plastic head.) Far from being a pervert, the boy is simply trying to master the moves expected of him in a non-threatening situation. When he bolts from the party, he runs into Con's daughter Connie, who is not allowed to kiss a boy until she is married. They both innocently experiment on each other without quite realizing that they have exchanged their first kiss.

Episode Thirteen: "The Company Man" (December 7, 1997)
Director: Klay Hall; Writer: Jim Dauterive

We see Hank's dedication to the cause of propane and propane accessories when his boss, Buck Strickland, puts him in charge of persuading a new arrival from Boston to open a large account for a subdivision he is building. Unfortunately, the newcomer is afflicted with every conceivable cliché about Texas. Against his own better judgment, Hank dresses and acts the part of a stereotypical cowboy. (The Bostonian persists in calling him "J. R." and complains about the fact that he can't find the theme to *Dallas* on the jukebox in the local diner.) The situation is complicated by the fact that Hank's main competition is a more adept and unscrupulous liar. Although all of the popular misconceptions about Texas are paraded across the screen, the real object of satire in this episode is Yankee credulity. There is also an amusing exchange between Hank and a stripper, who confesses that she never made six figures working at the potato bar.

## THE LEOPARD

1963 (163 minutes) • Historical Drama
Twentieth Century-Fox • Unrated

Cast: Burt Lancaster (Fabrizio Salina), Claudia Cardinale (Angelica Sedara), Alain Delon (Tancredi Falconeri), Paola Stoppa (Don Calogero Sedara), Rina Morelli (Maria Stella), Romolo Valli (Padre Pirrone), Serge Reggiani (Don Francisco Ciccio Tumeo), Terence Hill (Count Cavriaghi)

Producers: Goffredo Lombardo (Producer), Pietro Notarianni (Executive Producer); Director: Luchino Visconti; Writers: Suso Cecchi D'Amico, Enrico Medioli, Pasquale Festa Campanile, Massimo Franciosa, Luchino Visconti (From the novel by Giuseppe Tomasi Di Lampedusa); Photography: Giuseppe Rotunno (Technicolor); Editor: Mario Serandrei

The late Sam Francis once wrote a book about conservatives called *Beautiful Losers* (1993). In a sense, this is the theme of Giuseppe Tomasi di Lampedusa's novel *The Leopard* (1958) and the film that Luchino Visconti made from it. The story is set in 1860, when Giuseppe Garibaldi and his followers were seeking to unite the various sections of Italy into a single nation. The protagonist is Prince Fabrizio Salina of Sicily, a nobleman wary of political and social change but unconvinced that he can stop it. Committed to the notion of appeasement, he believes that allowing a little reform is the best way of keeping most things the same. In contrast, his nephew, Tancredi Falconeri, is an opportunist who initially fights with Garibaldi and later becomes an officer in the army of the first king of Italy, Victor Emmanuel. Although Fabrizio does not follow his nephew's example, he half admires the young man's vitality and sees him as the wave of the future.

The bulk of the film takes place at Donnafugata, Fabrizio's summer residence. The prince is amused and shocked to discover that the most powerful man in the region is Don Calogera Sedara, a wealthy but uncultured landowner who is now mayor of the town. Despite his own vulgarity, Don Calogera's beautiful daughter Angelica would be a prize catch for Tancredi. (It doesn't hurt matters that the two young people are smitten with each other.) Fabrizio has the awkward task of asking for Angelica's hand on his nephew's behalf. (Lampedusa compares the experience to eating a toad.) It turns into a humiliation when he learns how much poorer he is than his former fief Don Calogera.

Fabrizio has already turned down a position as senator in the new united Italian government, suggesting that Don Calogera is a man more suited to the position and the times. In an effort to advance compromise, Fabrizio urged the townspeople to vote in favor of a united Italy. The only man who dared voice his opposition to this plan was the organist at the local church, Don Francisco Ciccio Tumeo. If Tancredi is a shrewd but unprincipled timeserver and Fabrizio a noble anachronism, the feisty Don Ciccio is the sort of patriot who would rather go down fighting than surrender to a cause in which he does not believe. Unfortunately, none of these men represents an effective model of social action.

We see a last elegant gasp of the dying social order in a magnificent ball at Prince Fabrizio's summer palace. It is clear that the middle-aged prince possesses more grace than the young people, who seem to be an example of too much inbreeding. (When Fabrizio gazes upon them, he comments on the inadvisability of cousins' marrying.) Although the novel goes on to depict the prince's death and the wretched life his daughter will lead, such outcomes are only suggested in the movie. (The ball itself constitutes the last hour of this three-hour film.) Despite the fact that Visconti was a Marxist, the point of view of the story is aristocratic. It is therefore an exercise in unrelieved pessimism. If American conservatives often seem obsessed with how to win the next election, their European counterparts are frequently more elegiac—which may account for the fact that this is Robert Novak's favorite movie. As a form of art, the elegy beats the exit poll every time.

## THE LIFE AND DEATH OF COLONEL BLIMP

1943 (163 minutes) • Drama
Archers • Unrated

Cast: Roger Livesey (Clive Candy), Deborah Kerr (Edith Hunter / Barbara Wynne / Angela Cannon), Anton Walbrook (Theo Kretschmar-Schuldorff), James McKechnie (Spud Wilson), Neville Mapp (Stuffy Graves), David Hutcheson (Hoppy), Spencer Trevor (Period Blimp), Roland Culver (Colonel Betteridge), Frith Banbury (Baby-Face Fitzroy)

Producers: Michael Powell, Emeric Pressburger (Producers), Richard Vernon (Assistant Producer); Directors: Michael Powell, Emeric Pressburger; Writers: Michael Powell, Emeric Pressburger; Photographer: Georges Périnal (color); Editor: John Seabourne

By the time this film was made in 1943, the figure of Colonel Blimp was familiar to the British public from a series of cartoons by David Low. A caricature of the pompous and overweight career military officer, Blimp was hardly the image that England wished to project in the midst of World War II. What director Michael Powell has done is to look beneath the caricature and present an affectionate portrait of a flesh-and-blood Blimp—General Clive Candy—during a forty-year career in the British army. Although not jingoistic enough to win the approval of Winston Churchill and the keepers of wartime propaganda, this film presents the traditional British military in a favorable light and raises profound questions about the changing nature of warfare.

The story begins in 1942 with a war game conducted by the British Home Guard. Although the exercise is scheduled to begin at midnight, a young lieutenant on one side begins his offensive immediately on the grounds that the Nazis do not play by gentlemen's rules. Leading his men into the Turkish bath of General Candy's London club, the young officer finds the Blimp-like general red as a boiled lobster and wrapped in a towel. Enraged at the lieutenant's insubordination, Candy explodes: "You laugh at my big belly but you don't know how I got it! You laugh at my [walrus] mustache but you don't know why I grew it!" He then pushes the young pup into the pool, as the camera pans along the surface of the water. At the other end, a young, svelte, and clean-shaven Clive Candy emerges in 1902. This epic film then takes us through the ensuing four decades.

Home from the Boer War, the young Candy uses part of his leave time to travel to Germany to combat rumors of British atrocities against the Africans. (He has been lured there by a letter from a young British governess.) In the process, he fights an inconclusive duel with a young German officer who becomes a lifelong friend. During his recuperation, Clive grows a mustache to conceal a scar he incurred in the duel. (This conflicts with the German habit of flaunting such scars.) When his German adversary falls in love with the British governess, Candy wishes them well and returns home, only to realize too late that he too was in love with the young woman. The rest of his life is spent trying to find her reincarnation in ever younger women. Fifteen years later, during World War I, he finds and marries a young nurse who resembles his long-lost love. In World War II, his wife long since dead, the general again sees his feminine ideal—in a working-class woman who serves as his driver. The roles of all three women are played by a young and radiant Deborah Kerr.

The friendship between Candy and his German friend Theo is a gauge of British-German relations during the early decades of the twentieth century. When he finds Theo in a prisoner-of-war camp during World War I and invites him to dinner, Clive and his British friends assure their guest that the peace terms will be benevolent because "Europe needs a healthy Germany." What no one at the table could have imagined was the Nazi threat. When Theo flees that threat in 1939, he eloquently explains his preference for England and the uniquely evil nature of Nazism. It is clear that the era in which wars were fought by gentlemen according to civilized rules is a thing of the past. Clive Candy and all the other Blimps are magnificent anachronisms. So it is almost anticlimactic when the general is forced into retirement. We cannot help feeling that a better way of life has passed with him.

## THE LITTLE COLONEL

1935 (80 minutes) • Comedy
Twentieth Century-Fox • NR

Cast: Shirley Temple (Miss Lloyd Sherman), Lionel Barrymore (Col. Lloyd), Evelyn Venable (Elizabeth Lloyd Sherman), John Lodge (Jack Sherman), Sidney Blackmer (Swazey), Alden Stephen Chase (Hull), William Burress (Dr. Scott), Frank Darien (Nebler), Robert Warwick (Col. Gray), Hattie McDaniel (Becky "Mom Beck" Porter), Bill Robinson (Walker)

Producer: Buddy G. DeSylva; Director: David Butler; Writer: William M. Conselman (based on the novel by Anne Fellows Johnston); Photographers: Arthur C. Miller, William V. Skall (black and white; last scene in color); Editor: Uncredited

One of the most enduring images of nineteenth-century American culture was that of a curly-haired little blonde girl and a wooly-haired old black man enacting a totally chaste version of racial harmony. This is one of several such images given us by Harriet Beecher Stowe in *Uncle Tom's Cabin*. Because such visions exist primarily in the realm of myth, they embody dreams that defy historical or ideological analysis. Even if Shirley Temple and Bill "Bojangles" Robinson never collaborated in a film version of *Uncle Tom's Cabin*, they helped perpetuate the pairing of the angelic tot and the dusky retainer well into the 1930s. In *The Little Colonel*, in particular, the pair danced their way into immortality. In one unforgettable scene, we see Bojangles tap up and down the staircase of a Southern mansion while making an accompanying trumpet sound with his mouth. Before too long, six-year-old Shirley joins in, to the delight of all. It may not be Little Eva greeting Uncle Tom when he enters Heaven, but it's close.

The story of this film involves the travails of Colonel Lloyd and his family in Kentucky during the 1870s. The old Colonel has become estranged from his beloved daughter after her elopement with a Yankee who bears the same surname as the most hated Union general. Nevertheless, the young couple christen their daughter with the family name (she is Lloyd Sherman). The adoring soldiers at the outpost where the father is stationed subsequently give her the honorary rank of colonel. When papa Jack heads west in pursuit of gold, mother and child take up residence near the old colonel in Kentucky. Much of the film is devoted to the little colonel's efforts to melt the old colonel's heart. As corny and sentimental as the situation may seem, it works for most audiences, if only because of the charm of Shirley as little Lloyd and Lionel Barrymore as her crusty grandfather. By the closing credits, the entire family (including Jack Sherman) are reconciled to each other in a Southern paradise seemingly untouched by the late unpleasantness.

This is the sort of movie that wouldn't be made anymore. Or if it were, it would be as the paranoid fantasy of a politically correct director, preferably black, as even the most righteous whites are no longer trusted to deal ironically with racial themes. What is utterly captivating about this picture is its utter lack of irony. Because of its ingenuous good will, all but the terminally sensitive might want to excuse a few racial anachronisms. These include a scene of Jim Crow humor involving Bojangles and Hattie McDaniel, in her pre–*Gone with the Wind* days, and the inordinate love of watermelon among Shirley's "pickaninny" playmates. These howlers notwithstanding, the larger message of the movie seems to be that we *can* all get along—old and young, North and South, and, yes, even black and white.

## LOOKING FOR COMEDY IN THE MUSLIM WORLD

2005 (98 minutes) • Comedy
Warner Independent Pictures • PG-13

Cast: Albert Brooks (Himself), Penny Marshall (Herself), Fred Dalton Thompson (Himself), Sheetal Sheth (Maya), Jon Tenney (Mark), John Carroll Lynch (Stewart), Amy Ryan (Emily Brooks)

Producers: Stephanie Antosca (Washington, D.C.), Steve Bing, Herb Nanas, Tabrez Noorani (India), JoAnn Perritano (Executive Producer); Director: Albert Brooks; Writer: Albert Brooks; Photographer: Thomas E. Ackerman (color); Editor: Anita Brandt-Burgoyne

One of the many scandals of contemporary Western culture, particularly in the post-9/11 era, is the double standard concerning humor directed at the Muslim world. For the most part, the other major religions of the planet are fair game for even the most virulent ridicule. (This is particularly true of Christianity.) But try to poke a little fun at our Islamic neighbors, and all hell breaks loose. Salman Rushdie discovered this when he published *The Satanic Verses* in 1989, as did much of Europe when Danish cartoonists drew some dopey caricatures of the Prophet Muhammad in 2006. Even more objectionable than the behavior of the Muslims is the craven cowardice shown by the power players in what passes for our own civilization. Caving in to fear of jihadists, the executives at Sony Pictures backed out of an agreement to distribute Albert Brooks's *Looking for Comedy in the Muslim World* because of concerns over the title. After Brooks refused to change the title, his film was finally released by Warner Independent Pictures and suffered the minimal exposure and financial losses to which so many independent films are subjected.

The premise of this movie is intriguing. In an effort to learn more about the Islamic mind, the U.S. government commissions Brooks, who plays himself, to travel to the Far East to determine what Muslims think is funny. (The chairman of the commission is the actor-politician and future presidential candidate Fred Dalton Thompson, who also plays himself.) The government seems to have chosen Brooks primarily because their first choices were all working. He is dispatched, with minimal support and virtually no direction, to India—an overwhelmingly *Hindu* country. When his man-on-the-street interviews result in hostile or non-sequitur responses, Brooks hires an auditorium in which to try out some of his own material—all of which bombs. Because he cannot secure a visa to enter the predominantly Muslim country of Pakistan, he is forced to make an illegal border crossing in the dead of night to meet with some prospective Pakistani comedians. His act goes over much better here, primarily because Brooks and his audience are both stoned on some exotic weed. The only career opportunity that opens up on his trip is an offer by Al Jazeera to star in *That Darn Jew*, a sitcom about a Jew living among Muslims, which Brooks rejects.

If much of the joke of this film is on the Islamic world, it is also on the fecklessness of government bureaucracy. Whatever inspired plausibility there may have been in Brooks's mission is foiled by inept execution. Fortunately, Brooks is shrewd enough to make himself part of the joke. In the opening scene, Penny Marshall turns him down for the Jimmy Stewart role in a remake of *Harvey*, and frequent references are made to his most recent job as the father's voice in *Finding Nemo* (2003). Moreover, his disastrous performance in the comedy concert in India becomes hilarious by virtue of its failure. (Few comedians would take that risk.) At one point, Albert even wonders if the government has mistaken him for *Mel* Brooks. Finally, there are several scenes of subtle but devastating humor. At one point, Albert and his cohorts walk right by the Taj Mahal without even noticing this monument to the culture they are purporting to understand. Even earlier in the film, we pass an office full of women at telephones in a building in India. "State Farm Insurance," one of them says. "How may I direct your call?"

## LORD OF THE FLIES

1963 (90 minutes) • Drama
Two Arts (UK) • Unrated

Cast: James Aubrey (Ralph), Tom Chapin (Jack), Hugh Edwards (Piggy), Roger Elwin (Roger), Tom Gaman (Simon), Surtees Twins (Sam and Eric), Roger Allan (Piers), David Brunjes (Donald), Peter Davy (Peter), Kent Fletcher (Percival)

Producer: Lewis Allen; Director: Peter Brook; Writer: Peter Brook (based on the novel by William Golding); Photographer: Tom Hollyman (black and white); Editors: Peter Brook, Gerald Feil, Jean-Claude Lubthansky

One way of measuring cultures of different locales and different ages is to compare their view of children. The doctrine of Original Sin, shared by many Christians and Jews, holds that human beings are born with the taint of Adam and can be saved only through supernatural grace. Adherents of other religions and many secularists regard children as barbarians who can be molded into civilized adults only through the most rigorous training. Such essentially pessimistic views contrast with the Romantic notion that we come into the world innocent and are actually corrupted by civilization. Even those who will not go quite that far are tempted to idealize children and childhood. Did not Jesus himself say, "Of such is the Kingdom of Heaven"?

With the advent of Freudian psychology, however, the Romantic adoration of children has been replaced by a renewed appreciation of the darker aspects of their personalities. Near the dawn of the twentieth century, Henry James's *Turn of the Screw* (1898) featured two seemingly angelic children who turn out to be demonic. Vladimir Nabokov's scandalous best-seller *Lolita* (1955) depicts a barely pubescent girl as the temptress of a middle-aged man. And such popular horror films as *Village of the Damned* (1960, 1995), *The Exorcist* (1973), and *The Omen* (1976, 2006) derive much of their shock value from their depiction of evil children. But perhaps the most memorable of such portrayals is in William Golding's novel *Lord of the Flies* (1954), which has been the source of two movies, the first and better of which was directed by Peter Brook in 1963.

The film begins with a plane full of wealthy English schoolboys fleeing from an unspecified nuclear war. When the plane crashes on a desert island, the adults on board perish, but forty boys survive to create their own provisional civilization while awaiting rescue. It is not long before the lads split into two groups under two leaders with contrasting views of society. Jack leads a band of choirboys who quickly revert to a kind of tribal savagery. In contrast stand the more rational Ralph (son of a British naval officer) and his bespectacled pal Piggy.

The dominance of the savages might well suggest something about human nature unimproved. (It certainly calls into question Rousseau's concept of the "noble savage.") Because the boys are rescued by a military man at the end of the film, we do not see this symbolic conflict played out to its logical conclusion. One might infer that the rescue represents the triumph of adult rationality. The critic for *DVD Times* reminds us, however, that the officer is "on a manhunt mission, seeking out the enemy." Thus the larger society, while appearing "to be more civilised, is actually still bogged down by other more covert forms of savagery that it pretends to distance itself from." (The fact that "lord of the flies" itself is a literal translation of "Beelzebub," one of the biblical names for the devil, may suggest where Golding comes down on this issue.) Filmed in stark black and white with an amateur cast, this is a harrowing film.

## A MAN FOR ALL SEASONS

1966 (120 minutes) • Historical Drama
Columbia • Unrated

Cast: Paul Scofield (Sir Thomas More), Wendy Hiller (Alice More), Leo McKern (Thomas Cromwell), Robert Shaw (King Henry VIII), Orson Welles (Cardinal Wolsey), Susannah York (Margaret More), Nigel Davenport (Duke of Norfolk), John Hurt (Richard Rich), Corin Redgrave (William Roper, the Younger), Colin Blakeley (Matthew), Cyril Luckham (Archbishop Cranmer), Jack Gwillim (Chief Justice), Vanessa Redgrave (Anne Boleyn)

Producers: Fred Zinnemann (Producer), William N. Graf (Executive Producer); Director: Fred Zinnemann; Writer: Robert Bolt (based on his play); Photographer: Ted Moore (color); Editor: Ralph Kemplen

Few terms have been so promiscuously overused as "Renaissance Man." The phrase is meant to designate someone so learned that he knows everything there is to know—or comes so close that it isn't worth quibbling over the difference. Thomas More (1478–1535) was such an individual. He was a statesman, a lawyer, a lay theologian, a writer of considerable distinction, and an intellectual of astonishing breadth. He was, indeed, "a man for all seasons." What is most impressive about More, however, was his intellectual seriousness. Not only did he live for ideas, he finally died for them when he refused to concede that Henry VIII, not the pope, was head of the church in England. Having argued vigorously for his faith against Protestants such as William Tyndale, More was willing to stand up to his king when Henry sought to annul his marriage with Catherine of Aragon and wed Anne Boleyn in a continuing attempt to produce a male heir. More went from being the most trusted and powerful political figure in England to being an executed criminal. In 1931, he was canonized as a saint by the Roman Catholic Church.

The character of Thomas More in both the stage and film versions of *A Man for All Seasons* is a figure not so much of historical scholarship as of the historical imagination. In the nearly fifty years since the play was written, historical revisionists have questioned Bolt's image of More as a man of moderation and broad human sympathy. His religious commitment occasionally manifested itself in what might be taken as sadistic glee in the torture and execution of heretics. Far from protecting the purity of the English church against a priapic king wishing to rid himself of a queen too long on the vine, More was fighting a rearguard action doomed to failure. After centuries of strife with Rome, the majority of English believers had already effected a reformation of sorts. One of the bloodiest periods of English history ensued when Catherine of Aragon's daughter, Queen Mary, tried to reinstitute Roman Catholicism by force. Finally, one cannot be certain that the pope wouldn't have annulled the sonless marriage of Henry and Catherine were he not cornered by Catherine's nephew at the time.

But revisionism aside, the Thomas More whom Robert Bolt recreated and Paul Scofield brought brilliantly to life is a man for *our* season. Certainly by the 1960s the Western world was suffering from a crisis of confidence. William Butler Yeats had prophesied this crisis when he wrote in "The Second Coming" (1920) of a time when "The best lack all conviction, while the worst / Are full of passionate intensity." Whatever the substantive merits of Vatican II, many loyal communicants were beginning to wonder if the Catholic Church itself even knew what it believed any longer. In such a time, the sanctity of Thomas More was not only useful but essential. He was, in the words of that great Anglican Samuel Johnson, "the person of the greatest virtue these islands ever produced."

## METROPOLITAN

1990 (98 Minutes) • Romantic Comedy
New Line Cinema • PG-13

Cast: Carolyn Farina (Audrey Rouget), Edward Clements (Tom Townsend), Chris Eigeman (Nick Smith), Taylor Nichols (Charlie Black), Allison Parisi (Jane Clark), Dylan Hundley (Sally Fowler), Isabel Gillies (Cynthia McLean), Bryan Leder (Fred Neff), Will Kempe (Rick Von Sloneker), Ellia Thompson (Serena Slocum), Stephen Uys (Victor Lemley), Alice Connorton (Mrs. Townsend), Linda Gillies (Mrs. Rouget), John Lynch (Allen Green)

Producers: Whit Stillman (Producer), Brian Greenbaum (Line Producer), Peter Wentworth (Coproducer); Director: Whit Stillman; Writer: Whit Stillman; Photographer: John Thomas (color); Editor: Christopher Tellefsen

The social class depicted in Whit Stillman's debut film, *Metropolitan*, was a staple of American fiction one hundred or even seventy years earlier. The old-money aristocrats of Manhattan and Long Island populated the novels of Edith Wharton and F. Scott Fitzgerald. Even in Wharton's time, however, this class was beginning to die out or at least to be less interesting to the rest of the American population. By the end of the twentieth century, there is the feeling that this may be the last debutante season. Although this may not have the elegiac resonance of the passing of the Old South or the disappearance of an immigrant culture, Stillman treats it with wit and seriousness. One is reminded of Joan Didion's quip: "Some of us are not Jews. Neither are some of us Southerners, nor children of the Iroquois, nor the inheritors of any other notably dark and bloodied ground. Some of us are even Episcopalians."

*Metropolitan* begins when a young man named Tom Townsend shares a cab with some debutantes and their escorts. Although he is not part of their circle (even his tuxedo is rented), he begins attending their parties because of a shortage of male escorts. Like Lawrence Selden in Wharton's *House of Mirth* (1905), Townsend is an outsider who smugly critiques the aristocracy while secretly enjoying their company. Although he is an admirer of the American social critic Thorstein Veblen and the French socialist Charles Fourier, Townsend was well-heeled until his caddish father took away the trust fund he had been relying on. He also discovers that his reservations about his new circle of friends are fully matched by their reservations about themselves.

Tom discovers that his old flame, Serena Slocum, is well known to his new acquaintances and soon reunites with her. Although some of the passion is still there, Tom can now discern Serena's basic shallowness and their essential incompatibility. He has also begun what seems to be a platonic relationship with an emotionally insecure debutante named Audrey Rouget. A former classmate of Serena, Audrey has read Tom's letters and become fascinated with this stranger. When they come to know each other, much of their conversation is devoted to a discussion of Jane Austen, whose work Audrey knows and reveres. Tom's only familiarity with the novelist comes secondhand through reading Lionel Trilling's criticism.

Charlie, the philosopher of the group, refers to himself and his friends as the urban haute bourgeoisie. Although this is a cynical reference, Charlie also asserts: "The term 'bourgeois' has almost always been one of contempt. Yet it is precisely the bourgeoisie which is responsible for nearly everything good which has happened in our civilization over the past four centuries." It is significant that the one unadulterated villain in the picture is a member of the titled aristocracy—Baron Rick Von Sloneker. The film ends with Charlie and Tom taking a long and expensive cab ride out to Von Sloneker's home in Southampton in a noble effort to rescue Audrey from the baron's clutches. As annoying as the young man might be, it turns out that he poses no threat to Audrey. The movie closes with Charlie, Tom, and Audrey trying to hitchhike back to Manhattan. Filled with quotable lines and trenchant observations, *Metropolitan* gives us an inside glimpse of the former ruling class in the process of extinction.

## A MIGHTY WIND

2003 (87 minutes) • Comedy
Castle Rock Entertainment • PG-13

Cast: Christopher Guest (Alan Barrows), Michael McKean (Jerry Palter), Harry Shearer (Mark Shubb), Eugene Levy (Mitch Cohen), Catherine O'Hara (Mickey Crabbe), Jane Lynch (Laurie Bohner), John Michael Higgins (Terry Bohner), Ed Begley Jr. (Lars Olfen), Bob Balaban (Jonathan Steinbloom), Jennifer Coolidge (Amber Cole), Paul Dooley (George Menschell), Michael Hitchcock (Lawrence E. Turpin), Don Lake (Elliot Steinbloom), Larry Miller (Wally Fenton), Jim Piddock (Leonard Crabbe), Parker Posey (Sissy Knox), Fred Willard (Mike LaFontaine).

Producers: Donna E. Bloom, Karen Murphy; Director: Christopher Guest; Writers: Christopher Guest, Eugene Levy; Photographer: Arlene Donnelly Nelson (color); Editor: Robert Leighton

By now, the Christopher Guest "mockumentary" (or, in this case, just straight satire) has become a familiar film genre. Employing a serious tone and many of the same actors, Guest's movies craft droll parodies of some vulnerable aspect of modern life. In *Waiting for Guffman* (1997), the target was community theater; in *Best in Show* (2000), it was the dog-show circuit. *A Mighty Wind* takes on one aspect of the folk-music scene of the sixties. When a veteran promoter dies, his son sponsors a reunion of (mostly disbanded) folk groups as a posthumous tribute.

The story revolves around three groups—the annoyingly upbeat New Main Street Singers (Lynch, Higgins, Posey, Dooley, and five others); the more traditional Folksmen (Guest, Shearer, and McKean); and the duo Mitch and Mickey (Levy and O'Hara), whose greatest hit was the love ballad "A Kiss at the End of the Rainbow." (The song was nominated for an Academy Award and performed at the Oscar ceremonies by Levy and O'Hara.) For all these years, it has been unclear to fans—and perhaps to the singers themselves—how much genuine romance was implicit in the song. While the world waits to see if the two will kiss at the end of the song, the tension heightens as Mitch is missing right up to the moment that the act is scheduled to go on.

Although Levy threatens to steal the show as the neurotic Mitch, this is generally an ensemble effort. In fact, the performance is so smooth and the tone so understated that the film rewards repeated viewings to catch jokes that one might have missed the first couple of times through. The soundtrack album is also particularly helpful in catching some of the subtler nuances of the satire. Despite the originality of the new music, it bears an uncanny resemblance to the old in both sound and sense. (One suspects, for example that "Blowin' in the Wind" inspired the title song—"There's a mighty wind a blowin', it's blowin' you and me.") With this sort of material, anything less than a deadpan delivery would have spoiled the effect.

One of the reasons that the folk scene lends itself to satire is the self-importance of some of the artists and their fans. (One thinks of Country Joe and the Fish exhorting the huddled masses at Woodstock to sing louder "if you want to end the war.") Although artists such as Bob Dylan, Joan Baez, and Peter, Paul, and Mary were part of the political ambience of the sixties, their actual impact on world events may have been less than was assumed at the time. Surprisingly, Guest steers clear of the politicized folkies to concentrate on the sort of feel-good acts exemplified by the Kingston Trio. If this makes for less obvious laughs, they are nevertheless well-earned. Given the way that popular entertainment reflexively panders to the tastes and nostalgia of the baby boomers, *A Mighty Wind* is a refreshing (and politically incorrect) change of pace. One can only wish that it had been even bolder.

## THE MOUSE THAT ROARED

1959 (83 minutes) • Comedy
Open Road • Unrated

Cast: Peter Sellers (Tully Bascombe, Grand Duchess Gloriana XII, Prime Minister Count Mountjoy), Jean Seberg (Helen), David Kossoff (Professor Kokintz), William Hartnell (Will), Timothy Bateson (Roger), MacDonald Parke (Snippet), Monte Landis (Cobbley), Leo McKern (Benter), Harold Kasket (Pedro), Colin Gordon (BBC Announcer)

Producers: Jon Penington, Walter Shenson; Director: Jack Arnold; Writers: Roger MacDougall, Stanley Mann (based on the novel *The Wrath of the Grapes* by Leonard Wibberley); Photographer: John Wilcox (Eastmancolor); Editor: Raymond Poulton

Although Peter Sellers was already a major star in England, *The Mouse That Roared* was his breakthrough international movie. Playing multiple comedic roles of both genders, he was following in the tradition of Alec Guinness. Starting with a one-joke comedic premise, this film manages to paint a wickedly funny (and generally nontendentious) picture of international relations at the height of the Cold War. The story begins when the world's smallest nation, the Grand Duchy of Fenwick, is threatened with economic ruin because the fine wine that is its sole export has been copied by a large American company. After letters to the U.S. State Department go unanswered, the prime minister of Grand Fenwick comes up with the brilliant idea of declaring war on the United States. Perhaps remembering the Marshall Plan, he expects that certain defeat will bring with it massive foreign aid. When Grand Fenwick dispatches an army of twenty soldiers armed with bows and arrows, things really start to get weird.

When the army of Grand Fenwick arrives in New York, the city is in the midst of one of the many air-raid drills common to the era. Hence, the streets are deserted, and there is no one to surrender to. Led by the hapless Tully Bascombe, the intrepid Fenwickians stumble upon the laboratory of the eccentric scientist who is designing the next wonder weapon. (Perhaps in an allusion to Orson Welles's historic 1938 broadcast of *The War of the Worlds*, the few ordinary New Yorkers still on the street assume that they have been invaded by aliens.) Bringing the scientist, his daughter, the bomb, and several New York policemen back to Grand Fenwick, the army has won an unexpected and completely unwelcome victory. This sparks an international incident and some dated humor that seems to anticipate *Dr. Strangelove.*

At a time when the United States was lavishing foreign aid on many ungrateful countries, the idea that a nation could advance its interests by provoking war with America seemed diabolically logical. Grand Fenwick itself is a marvelously anachronistic duchy belonging more to the Middle Ages than to the modern world. It is a stroke of satiric genius that the inept Fenwickians should accidentally win a war and capture the bomb in the midst of a high-tech arms race between the world's superpowers. (This absurdity takes on surprising urgency in an age when Third World terrorists pose the primary threat to civilization.) Finally, the genius of Peter Sellers makes what might otherwise have been a charming period piece into a film classic.

## THE MUSIC MAN

1962 (151 minutes) • Musical
Warner Brothers • Unrated

Cast: Robert Preston (Professor Harold Hill), Shirley Jones (Marian Paroo), Buddy Hackett (Marcellus Washburn), Hermione Gingold (Eulalie Mackechnie Shinn), Paul Ford (Mayor Shinn), The Town Council (The Buffalo Bills), Pert Kelton (Mrs. Paroo), Ronny Howard (Winthrop Paroo)

Producer: Morton Da Costa; Director: Morton Da Costa; Writer: Marion Hargrove (based on the musical by Meredith Willson); Photographer: Robert Burks (Technirama and Technicolor); Editor: William Ziegler

There is no consensus concerning the greatest American musical. Some would nominate Jerome Kern's *Show Boat* (1927) for that honor. Several works by Rodgers and Hammerstein would have to be in the running. So too would

George Gershwin's *Porgy and Bess* (1935). In my judgment, however, the most American of all musicals is Meredith Willson's *The Music Man*. This show, which was a phenomenal success when it opened on Broadway in 1958, was brought to the screen essentially intact in 1962.

Set in Iowa in the early years of the twentieth century, it is a tribute to the American small town. In the literature of the adversary culture, the small town is an oppressive and stultifying place with a name such as Winesburg, Ohio, or Gopher Prairie, Minnesota. Although Willson's River City, Iowa, may share some of the narrow-mindedness of these municipalities, even its faults seem endearing. Because he is one of them, Willson can poke fun at these rubes without ever really ridiculing them. Moreover, the array of songs in the show is breathtaking in both quality and simplicity. From barbershop-quartet numbers (performed by the incomparable Buffalo Bills) to choral chants to the classic love song "Till There Was You," *The Music Man* has more memorable tunes than any show I can think of. And I haven't even mentioned Robert Preston's pool-table monologue and the show-stopping "Seventy-Six Trombones."

The protagonist of the tale is Professor Harold Hill, a traveling salesman who cons the residents of small towns into purchasing instruments and uniforms for a boys' band, which he promises to direct. Not knowing a note of music, he skips town before his unsuspecting customers know what he is up to. In River City, however, his scheme is delayed by his infatuation with the town librarian, Marian Paroo. Their relationship is the typical romance of the Good Bad Boy and the Good Good Girl. He turns out to be not nearly as bad as he appears, nor she nearly so prim. His seemingly self-serving lies excite a previously moribund community, in particular bringing Marian's withdrawn younger brother Winthrop out of his shell. As things turn out, the sight of their sons wearing handsome uniforms and playing shiny instruments causes the proud parents to ignore the fact that no actual music is being played. Hill is tamed but wins the girl of his dreams, just as Marian herself has found her special someone. And everyone lives happily ever after.

This may well be a sentimental cornball story. But it works precisely because it refuses to take itself too seriously. The wit of the lyrics and dialogue makes *The Music Man* a particularly winning celebration of middle-class American values. By the early twentieth century, the traveling salesman was one of the figures vying to replace the frontiersman and the cowboy as the isolated American hero. In first fulfilling and then relinquishing that role, Harold Hill affirms the value of community. It is surely significant that he does so in the cultural heartland of the American nation.

## NASHVILLE

1975 (159 minutes) • Social Satire
Paramount • R

Cast: Henry Gibson (Haven Hamilton), Barbara Baxley (Lady Pearl), Ronee Blakley (Barbara Jean), Allen Garfield (Barnett), Ned Beatty (Delbert Reese), Lily Tomlin (Linnea Reese), Karen Black (Connie White), Timothy Brown (Tommy Brown), Michael Murphy (John Triplette), Gwen Welles (Sueleen Gay), Robert DoQui (Wade), Keenan Wynn (Mr. Green), Shelley Duvall (L. A. Joan), Scott Glenn (Pfc. Glenn Kelly), Keith Carradine (Tom Frank), Geraldine Chaplin (Opal), Barbara Harris (Albuquerque), David Hayward (Kenny Fraiser), Jeff Goldblum (Tricycle Man), Elliot Gould (Himself), Julie Christie (Herself)

Producer: Robert Altman; Director: Robert Altman; Writer: Joan Tewkesbury; Photographer: Paul Lohmann; Editors: Sidney Levin, Dennis M. Hill

By the mid-1970s, Nashville had become a microcosm of America. The political entity known as the Metropolitan Government of Nashville and Davidson County consisted of urban, suburban, and rural areas. Country music, which had long been a provincial taste, was drawing enthusiastic audiences worldwide. The Grand Ole Opry was even moving out of the historic Ryman Auditorium in downtown Nashville into a state-of-the-art facility at a theme park located on the outskirts of the city. Small-town charm was running up against big-city problems. (The first unmistakable sign was the brutal murder of banjo-picker David Stringbean Akeman and his wife Estelle in the fall of 1973.) The city's modest skyline was celebrated in the title of an album by none other than Bob Dylan. With Vanderbilt University located on Twenty-First Avenue and the bulk of the recording studios a few blocks away on Sixteenth Avenue, the elite and popular cultures of the American South existed almost literally side by side.

In the summer of 1974, the genius film director Robert Altman and his crew took Nashville by storm. With an ensemble cast of twenty-four characters, Altman shows us the various levels of life in Nashville and America. Haven Hamilton (a character played by Henry Gibson, whose look and sound seem to be modeled on Hank Snow) opens the film recording a sappy Bicentennial song. Increasingly irritated by the studio piano player, he finally stops the session and tells the young man to get a haircut as he stomps out of the room. One of the themes running through this movie is the clash between country's old guard and the scruffy young folk-rock singers who have made Nashville their new mecca. The latter group is epitomized by a particularly hedonistic lout named Tom Frank (played by Keith Carradine), who spends most of the movie bedding women and listening to tapes of his own music.

Barbara Jean, the reigning queen of country music (played by Ronee Blakley, she resembles Loretta Lynn), arrives at the Nashville airport after spending some time at a burn clinic and immediately collapses in front of her adoring public. Once out of the hospital, she suffers a mental breakdown of sorts in a performance at Opryland. To make it up to her fans, her husband/manager promises that she will perform free at a Nashville park the following day. When she does, she is shot by a demented loner of the sort who stalked American political figures in the sixties and who would gun down John Lennon only a few years later. If the Barbara Jean story is the main plot of the film, a dozen equally interesting subplots intersect with each other as the characters continually cross each other's paths in a fugue-like harmony.

In the midst of this organized chaos, we follow a slick organizer for an insurgent presidential candidate—Hal Philip Walker of the Replacement Party. Walker, who is nothing more than a voice from a sound truck, poses as the quintessential outsider, spouting empty populist rhetoric. (At the time, he reminded observers of Jimmy Carter and George Wallace but now seems even more eerily prophetic of Ross Perot.) Walker may well be the perfect leader for the country depicted in this film. When Barbara Jean is shot, Haven Hamilton declares in anguish: "This isn't Dallas. This is Nashville." Unfortunately, Nashville has become America writ large.

## THE NATIVITY STORY

2006 (101 minutes) • Biblical Drama
New Line Cinema • PG

Cast: Keisha Castle-Hughes (Mary), Oscar Isaac (Joseph), Hiam Abbass (Anna), Shaun Toub (Joaquim), Ciarán Hinds (Herod), Shohreh Aghdashloo (Elizabeth), Stanley Townsend (Zechariah), Alexander Siddig (The Angel Gabriel), Nadim Sawalha (Melchior), Eriq Ebouaney (Balthasar), Stefan Kalipha (Gaspar), Alessandro Giuggioli (Antipas), Farida Ouchani (Ruth), Said Amadis (Tero), Maria Giovanna Donzelli (Mary's friend)

Producers: Marty Bowen, Wyck Godfrey (Producers), Cale Boyter, Toby Emmerich, Catherine Hardwicke, Mike Rich, Tim Van Rellim (Executive Producers), Michael Disco, Judd Funk (Co–Executive Producers), Enzo Sisti (Line Producer, Italy); Director: Catherine Hardwicke; Writer: Mike Rich; Photographer: Elliot Davis (color); Editors: Robert K. Lambert, Stuart Levy

This film may well be the prototype of what the biblical epic of years past has become in the twenty-first century. At 101 minutes, it is less than half the length of some earlier blockbusters, and there are no recognizable names in the cast. Although Hollywood may have been trying to capitalize on the surprise popularity of Mel Gibson's *The Passion of the Christ* two years earlier, there is nothing particularly controversial or unusual about *The Nativity Story*. The tale is so old and well-known that it would have been difficult for any storyteller to breathe new life into it. (In my judgment, the last artist to do so was Henry Van Dyke in his magnificent *Story of the Other Wise Man*, which was published in 1899.) Of course, if the alternative was to make *The Last Temptation of the Virgin Mary*, director Catherine Hardwicke has chosen the path of prudence in giving us an inoffensively pious rendering of the most familiar story ever told.

Perhaps the most interesting character in this film is Mary's husband Joseph. The Christian tradition has never known quite what to do with this necessary but awkward figure. If we adhere to the Catholic doctrine of Mary's perpetual virginity, Joseph becomes the most famous cuckold in history. As the movie makes clear, it was necessary for him to vouch for Mary's integrity to keep her from severe punishment and a premature end to her son's salvific mission. The fact that an angel fills him in on what is to happen may enlighten him intellectually without alleviating the ambivalence of his position.

To her credit, Hardwicke does not take the easy way out and make Joseph an impotent old man who will obligingly shuffle off his mortal coil during Jesus's adolescence. Although the marriage is arranged, he does not seem to be more than ten years older than his teenage bride. As Stephanie Zacharek notes, the movie "brings these characters, so often portrayed as larger than life, down to human scale." Indeed, we see some human-scale heroics when the holy couple ford a stream on their journey. A symbolically portentous snake (perhaps having slithered over from the set of Mel Gibson's picture) spooks Mary's donkey, who tosses the BVM into the water. Joseph grabs the snake and tosses it away before rescuing his wife (and all humanity) in the nick of time.

The film dwells so long on the trip to Bethlehem that the events of Christmas Eve seem rushed. For example, we see a single angel (not the Heavenly Host) make his announcement to the shepherds but do not see the shepherds at the stable. Perhaps Hardwicke did not want to upstage the wise men with their expensive gifts and wry commentary. What made Van Dyke's story (and Yeats's poem "The Magi") so compelling was the way in which it brought both the nativity and the crucifixion together as part of a single story. There is a hint of this when we see some crucified prisoners early in the film, but the point is allowed to drop. Not even the slaughter of the innocents serves to remind us emphatically enough that gentle Jesus, meek and mild, came not to bring peace but a sword. When we see Mary and Joseph and the babe heading off to Egypt ahead of Herod's holocaust, we half expect to hear a jolly old elf proclaim: "Happy Christmas to all, and to all a good night."

## OLEANNA

1994 (89 minutes) • Drama
Bay Kinescope/Channel Four Films/Samuel Goldwyn Company • R

Cast: William H. Macy (John), Debra Eisenstadt (Carol), Diego Pineda (Quarterback), Scott Zigler (Clerk in Copy Shop)

Producers: Sarah Green, Patricia Wolff; Director: David Mamet; Writer: David Mamet; Photographer: Andrzej Sekula (color); Editor: Barbara Tulliver

Judging from the reaction of audiences and critics alike, David Mamet's *Oleanna* is a drama whose meaning lies very much in the eye of the beholder. The play was originally produced in 1992, not long after Anita Hill had raised charges of sexual harassment against Clarence Thomas when he was nominated for a seat on the Supreme Court. Those sympathetic to Hill regarded her as the victim of an overbearing male employer, while Thomas's advocates believed that he was being smeared by the lies of an emotionally unstable accuser. In Mamet's play, the principal characters are a college professor, John, and a female student, Carol, who is failing his class. The action of the play takes place in his office, as John seems to offer Carol counsel and advice. Rightly or wrongly (depending on one's perspective), she interprets his behavior as an inappropriate assertion of his professorial power. At the urging of a feminist support group, she brings charges of sexual harassment against him at the very time that he is being considered for academic tenure.

*Oleanna* was the first of his own plays that Mamet directed on film. Perhaps because it was a two-person drama, critics thought that it was less a movie than a photographed play. For that reason, the film leaves the audience with some of the same questions as the stage play. What, for example, does the title mean? In the published version of the play, Mamet includes the following epigraph from a Norwegian folk song:

Oh, to be in Oleanna,
That's where I would rather be.
Than be bound in Norway
And drag the chains of slavery.

Oleanna was a nineteenth-century utopian community whose agricultural objectives failed because of its rocky and infertile soil. The critic Brenda Murphy surmises that, for Mamet, academia is meant to be a similarly failed utopia. John is unfulfilled as a teacher, and Carol is unenlightened as a student.

Although feminists tend to be sympathetic with Carol, men in the audience have been known to cheer for John when he loses control of himself and resorts to physical violence at the end of the play. In the highly charged atmosphere of political correctness, the mere accusation of sexual harassment is enough to cast a cloud over one's reputation. For men who have had to live in this new reality, John seems to be an innocent victim. His ambiguous behavior has led to the loss of both his job and his dreams for the future. In contrast, Carol's behavior appears to be the ploy of an unsuccessful student. However simplistic such a reading might seem, it surely accounts for much of the power and popularity of this drama on both stage and screen.

## ON THE WATERFRONT

1954 (107 minutes) • Drama
Columbia • Unrated

Cast: Marlon Brando (Terry Malloy), Karl Malden (Father Barry), Lee J. Cobb ("Johnny Friendly"), Rod Steiger (Charley Malloy), Pat Henning ("Kayo" Dugan), Leif Erickson (Inspector Glover), James Westerfield (Big Mac), Tony Galento ("Truck" Jarotta), Tami Mauriello (Tullio A. Rodelli), John Hamilton (Pop Doyle), John Heldabrand (Mutt), Rudy Bond (Moose), Don Blackman (Luke), Arthur Keegan (Jimmy Collins), Abe Simon (Barney), Eva Marie Saint (Edie Doyle)

Producer: Sam Spiegel; Director: Elia Kazan; Writer: Budd Schulberg; Photographer: Boris Kaufman (black and white); Editor: Gene Milford

At a time when Hollywood was spawning Technicolor extravaganzas in a desperate attempt to compete with television, *On the Waterfront,* a gritty black-and-white film, won nine Academy Awards—including ones for best picture, best director, best screenplay, best actor (Brando) and best actress (Saint). This was an era when a Senate committee chaired by Estes Kefauver was exposing corruption in various aspects of American life. Although the story the movie tells is fictional, it is based on a series of magazine articles by Malcolm Johnson. The character of Father Barry was inspired by a real priest—Father John Corriden—while several of the other roles are composites of actual people. Because of its documentary realism, the film could be viewed as an example of cinematic muckraking. It has survived for over half a century, however, because of more enduring aesthetic qualities.

Never before had a picture featured so many alumni of New York's famed Actor's Studio. Kazan, Brando, Malden, Cobb, and Steiger were all adherents of the introspective Stanislavski method, which was replacing the more histrionic style associated with earlier periods in the theater. Although Brando was clearly first among equals, this movie was not considered a star vehicle. (Several uncredited actors—Fred Gwynne, Martin Balsam, and Pat Hingle—launched distinguished careers in this film.) Even the musical score, which resulted in an Academy Award nomination for a rising young composer named Leonard Bernstein, was fitting if unobtrusive. Unlike many of the film noir classics of the era, which have had to be rediscovered, *On the Waterfront* has never fallen out of favor with critics or audiences.

The story follows Terry Malloy, an ex-boxer who owes his job on the waterfront to his close personal ties with the mobster Johnny Friendly. Terry begins to feel a twinge of conscience when Friendly uses him to set up what turns out to be a deadly confrontation with Joey Doyle, a longshoreman who has given testimony to the crime commission. Malloy's sense of guilt mounts as he begins a romance with Joey's sister Edie. Meanwhile, the crusading Father Barry encourages the men on the waterfront to stand up and speak out for justice. When his brother Charley is murdered by Friendly's thugs, Terry decides to tell the crime commission everything he knows. Although this earns him a brutal beating, Terry picks himself up and leads a throng of fellow longshoremen onto the pier as the movie closes. The triumphalism of this ending is perhaps undercut by the ambiguity of Terry's situation and the very real threat that Friendly and his mob continue to pose.

Politically, *On the Waterfront* has always been considered a controversial film because both Kazan and Schulberg gave friendly testimony to the House Committee on Un-American Activities during the time of the Hollywood blacklist. Both men were disillusioned former Communists who saw nothing wrong with denouncing the perfidy of Stalinism. Neither was ever forgiven by surviving members of the hard Left and revisionist historians, who will go to any length to romanticize the Hollywood Communists. Although Schulberg has always denied that *On the Waterfront* was a metaphorical apologia for his appearance before HUAC, Kazan was more ambivalent about this issue until the day he died. Whatever their intentions, the critical community has chosen to read the message of this film through the lives of its director and writer. (Brando was so convinced of the connection that he refused the lead role in the movie until he was persuaded by his psychiatrist to take it.) If nothing else, that widespread interpretation earns this picture an honored place in the pantheon of political incorrectness.

## THE OUTLAW JOSEY WALES

1976 (135 minutes) • Western
Warner Brothers • PG

Cast: Clint Eastwood (Josey Wales), Chief Dan George (Lone Watie), Sondra Locke (Laura Lee), Bill McKinney (Terrill), John Vernon (Fletcher), Paula Trueman (Grandma Sarah), Sam Bottoms (Jamie), Geraldine Kearns (Little Moonlight), Will Sampson (Ten Bears), Woodrow Parfrey (Carpetbagger)

Producer: Robert Daley; Director: Clint Eastwood; Writers: Phil Kaufman, Sonia Chernus (based on Forrest Carter's novel *Gone to Texas*); Photographer: Bruce Surtees (color); Editor: Ferris Webster

*The Outlaw Josey Wales* was the fifth film directed by Clint Eastwood. Although he has cast himself in a familiar Western role, the critic Laurence F. Knapp has argued that this movie owes less to the pictures Eastwood made with Sergio Leone than to the classic Hollywood films of John Ford and Howard Hawks. Beginning as a lone figure bereft of family, Josey Wales eventually attracts an assortment of followers who are physically dependent on him, even as he relies on them for reintegration into the human community. Although the film is set in the aftermath of the War Between the States, it has been read as a parable of the more recent conflict in Vietnam.

The movie begins when Union vigilantes murder Wales's wife and son and burn his farm. Shortly thereafter, Josey, a Missouri farmer, joins a band of Confederates who have not yet surrendered. Even when their leader (Fletcher) eventually realizes the futility of the fight and negotiates what purports to be an amnesty, Wales is the lone holdout. Much to Fletcher's distress, the deal turns out to be a trap in which the surrendering rebels are mercilessly gunned down. Seeing what has happened, Josey commandeers a Gatling gun and single-handedly wreaks vengeance on a sizeable number of the hated "blue bellies" before he and a young companion escape.

Because Josey's young friend, Jamie, is badly wounded, he does not last for very long. (As Josey notes later in the film, "before I get to liking someone, they ain't around long.") Despite the price on his head, Wales is never able to travel unencumbered for long. He soon meets up with the Indian Lone Watie, who despises the federal government for the loss of his family on the Trail of Tears. Shortly thereafter, Josey rescues Little Moonlight, an Indian girl who has been virtually enslaved by the tyrannical owner of a trading post. Later the group expands to include Grandma Sarah and Laura Lee, two women who have survived an attack by Comancheros. If Josey Wales has lost his biological family, he seems to have a knack for picking up strays wherever he roams.

Although this ad hoc family finds a kind of refuge in a ranch owned by Grandma Sarah's son, they are still plagued by Indians, who claim the land, and by bounty hunters eager to capture or kill the legendary Josey Wales. Josey makes peace with the Comancheros when he confronts their chief, Ten Bears, with the following proposition:

> I came here to die with you or live with you. Dying ain't so hard for men like you and me. It's living that's hard when all you've ever cared about has been butchered or raped. Governments don't live together, people live together. With governments you don't always get a fair word or a fair fight. Well I've come here to give you either one or get either one from you. I came here like this so you know my word of death is true and that my word of life is then true. The bear lives here, the wolf, the antelope, the Comanche. So will we.

The bounty hunters are repulsed in a gunfight in which Josey's newfound family actually scores more kills than he does himself.

The film concludes with Wales (again on the run and living under the pseudonym of "Mr. Wilson") encountering his old nemesis Fletcher in a dusty Western town. Although the two recognize each other, Fletcher has already indicated his willingness to believe that Wales has escaped to Mexico. When Josey asks him what he would do if he ever found his prey, Fletcher replies: "I think I'll try to tell him that the war is over." "I reckon so," Wales responds. "I guess we all died a little in that damn war." As Josey rides off into the sunset, apparently a free man, one can only hope that he will return to his new family and begin life over again.

## THE PASSION OF JOAN OF ARC

1928 (77 minutes) • Historical Drama
Societe Generale des Films • Unrated

Cast: Renee Maria Falconetti (Joan), Eugene Silvain (Bishop Pierre Cauchon), Andre Berley (Jean d'Estivet), Maurice Schutz (Nicolas Loyseleur), Antonin Artaud (Jean Massieu), Jean d'Yd (Guillaume Evrard), Louis Ravet (Jean Beaupère), Armand Lurville (Judge), Jacques Arnna (Judge), Alexandre Mihalesco (Judge), Léon Larive (Judge)

Producer: Carl Theodor Dreyer; Director: Carl Theodor Dreyer; Writers: Joseph Delteil, Carl Theodor Dreyer; Photographer: Rudolph Maté (black and white); Editors: Marguerite Beauge, Carl Theodor Dreyer

For nearly seven hundred years, Joan of Arc (1412–31) has been a figure of endless intrigue for both the historical and the literary imagination. By 1871, she had been the subject of more than twenty-five hundred publications, including Shakespeare's *Henry VI*, a drama by Schiller, an epic by Voltaire, and a fictionalized autobiography by Mark Twain. An illiterate peasant girl who claimed to hear voices from St. Margaret, St. Catherine, and St. Michael, Joan presented herself at the court of the dauphin—Charles VII, the hereditary king of France—and urged him to allow her to defend the city of Orleans, which the English had held under siege for months. Under her command,

French soldiers lifted the siege and proceeded to rout the English at Patay. Pushing on to a victory at Reims, Joan saw Charles crowned king. At this point, the cautious dauphin made a treaty with the Burgundians. Against his advice, Joan fought both the Burgundians and the British at Compiegne, where she was captured. Subsequently tried by an ecclesiastical court at the University of Paris, Joan was condemned as a heretic and sorcerer. Although she was burned at the stake in 1431, her reputation has stood the test of time, leading to her canonization by the Roman Church in 1920.

Joan's story has been the subject of at least four films, the first and greatest of which is Carl Dreyer's *The Passion of Joan of Arc*. For many years, it was thought that the print of this movie had been lost or destroyed. Then, in 1981, a copy was found in a closet in a mental asylum in Oslo, strangely enough, thus enabling the viewing public to see this legendary film as it was first shown in 1928. The title role is played by Renee Maria Falconetti in her only screen appearance. Falconetti was a stage comedienne when Dreyer discovered her and determined that her expressive face was precisely what he was looking for in Joan of Arc.

Other dramatizations of Joan's story include her military and diplomatic triumphs. Dreyer, however, chooses to concentrate exclusively on her martyrdom. The "action" consists of her trial and subsequent execution, with most of the dialogue taken from actual transcripts of her interrogation. The words, however, are beside the point. The tale is told visually in a succession of close-up shots of the maid and her accusers. (The scholar David Bordwell notes that "of the film's over 1,500 cuts, fewer than 30 carry a single figure or object over from one shot to another.") The emotional intensity of this technique makes watching Dreyer's film a harrowing experience.

The meaning of the picture is expressed in its title. Joan's "passion," like that of Christ, consists of terrible physical and mental anguish, all of which we see in Falconetti's face. (Pauline Kael said that "it may be the finest performance ever recorded on film.") Such commitment and heroism may not be entirely foreign to our time, but there are very few individuals in any age who would allow themselves to be burned alive in defense of a religious vision. When we see examples of this kind of dedication in the Middle East, it is profoundly unsettling. What then are we to make of the fact that Joan is one of our own? All evil may be fanatical, but not all fanatics are evil.

## PHARAOH'S ARMY

1995 (Ninety minutes) • Historical Drama
Cicada • PG-13

Cast: Chris Cooper (Captain John Hull Abston), Patricia Clarkson (Sarah Anders), Kris Kristofferson (Preacher), Robert Joy (Chicago), Richard Tyson (Rodie), Frank Clem (Neely), Huckleberry Fox (Newt), Will Lucas (Boy), Mac Miles (Israel), Robert E. Simpson (Narrator)

Producers: Robby Henson, Doug Lodato; Director: Robby Henson; Writer: Robby Henson; Editor: Robby Henson

The Negro spiritual "Go Down, Moses" establishes a metaphorical parallel between the condition of the Hebrew slaves in Old Testament Egypt and that of the African chattel in nineteenth-century America. No one, however, owns a copyright on biblical analogies. In this film, it is the Yankee army that is equated with Pharaoh and the Confederate South with the people who are seeking deliverance. The story, which is set in wartime Kentucky, is recollected by an old man in the 1940s. When he was a boy, Union sympathizers had dug up the grave of his infant sister because their father was away fighting for the Confederacy. Although the young girl has been reburied nearer to home, her mother (Sarah Anders) is naturally embittered when a group of Yankee soldiers arrive at her doorstep demanding food and lodging.

The drama becomes more complex when the commanding Yankee officer (Captain John Hull Abston) turns out to be a relatively decent human being. As a measure of civility develops between the captain and Sarah, his men take it for a blossoming romance. (The Yankees are forced to remain longer than expected with the Anders family when one of them is seriously injured in a mishap on the farm.) The hostility of a soldier whose brother was killed by Confederates so poisons the atmosphere that the Anders boy guns him down as the Yankees prepare to leave with the family's livestock in tow. Sarah protects the boy by swearing that he was with her the entire time. Even though he strongly suspects that this is not true, the captain simply buries his dead underling and leaves. Not surprisingly, Sarah and her son dig up the Yankee corpse and let it float down the creek.

The larger ideological issues of the period are hardly mentioned. (The captain does confess that he joined the Union Army when he saw the wounds on a runaway slave.) Neither the Anders family nor anyone in this backwoods community is wealthy enough to have owned slaves. One must surmise that they have cast their lot with the Confederacy out of nothing more abstract than tribal loyalty. But that sentiment is strong enough to have shaped our subsequent view of American history.

The fact that this story was told to the noted folklorist Harry Caudill in 1941 not only supports its authenticity, it also reminds us of how recent the War Between the States actually was. In the year that America entered World War II, there were still people around who remembered that earlier conflict. And judging from the more recent battle over Confederate symbols, plenty of people were still willing to re-fight the war when *Pharaoh's Army* was made in 1995. Although the story is told from a Southern point of view, there is enough generosity and spite on both sides to keep *Pharaoh's Army* from being a simplistic morality play. It is finally an unsentimental look at antagonisms too deeply rooted to be dislodged by individual acts of goodwill. Those who ask why we can't all just get along will find a powerful answer in this picture.

## PLACES IN THE HEART

1984 (112 minutes) • Drama
Tri Star • PG

Cast: Sally Field (Edna Spalding), Danny Glover (Moze), John Malkovich (Mr. Will), Ed Harris (Wayne Lomax), Lindsay Crouse (Margaret Lomax), Amy Madigan (Viola Kelsey), Yankton Hatten (Frank Spalding), Gennie James (Possum Spalding), Lane Smith (Albert Denby), Terry O'Quinn (Buddy Kelsey), Bert Remsen (Tee Tot Hightower), Ray Baker (Royce Spalding), Jay Patterson (W. E. Simmons), Toni Hudson (Ermine), De'voreaux White (Wylie)

Producers: Arlene Donovan (Producer), Michael Hausman (Executive Producer); Director: Robert Benton; Writer:

Robert Benson; Photographer: Néstor Almendros (color); Editor: Carol Littleton

This film is set on a Texas farm during the Depression. It begins with a nuclear family—father mother, and two children—sitting around the supper table. The father, who also moonlights as sheriff, is called away when a black adolescent gets drunk and begins firing a gun down at the railroad tracks. The youth accidentally discharges his weapon into the sheriff, who dies instantly. After some townspeople conduct the predictable lynching, the sheriff's widow, Edna Spalding, resolves to stay on the place and farm cotton despite falling prices and her own lack of experience. She is assisted by a black tramp named Moze, who stops by her house looking for work and insists that he is just the man to bring in the crop. Shortly thereafter, the local banker suggests that Edna could help her financial situation by taking in his blind relative, Mr. Will, as a boarder. This is the main, but not the only, story of *Places in the Heart.*

Roger Ebert is probably right when he argues that the narrative drive of the main plot is weakened by the largely extraneous story of Edna's sister and her philandering brother-in-law. The only thematic justification would seem to be the contrast between Edna's stable family, ripped apart by violence, and her sister's dysfunctional home. Even the odd assortment of adults who find lodging under Edna's roof form a closer bond than her brother-in-law is able to find with either his wife or his mistress. But Ebert is surely correct when he says, "We learn just enough about the other characters to suspect that there might be a movie in their stories—but not this one."

Against all odds, Edna, Moze, the children, and a group of black hired hands harvest the cotton. Edna sells the crop and saves the farm. It is an inspiring and heartwarming story of the Hallmark variety. But it does not end there. Just as we think that the racist vigilantes who lynched her husband's killer are willing to ignore the fact that a black man lives on Edna's place, a group of hooded Klansmen appear from nowhere to terrorize Moze. Taking the hint, he moves on down the road with Edna's sincere gratitude for what he has done. What will happen next year is left to the imagination.

This minor but heroic triumph of human decency affirms family values within an agrarian setting. It is also a celebration of religion—both in the practical churchgoing sense of the term and at a more spiritual level as well. The visionary final scene of the film is so stunning that it threatens to overwhelm the preceding story. We see a church service in which all of the characters of the film take communion together. The divisions that had previously separated individuals and races, and even the living from the dead, are obliterated. Although we appear to be in a country church, the scene suggests that we are seeing Heaven itself, as the film closes with the sheriff passing the grape juice to his killer. Although there may be no direct influence, this scene reminds me of Martin Luther King Jr.'s dream, in which the children of slaves and those of slaveowners gather around the table of brotherhood. This is a story that includes race and a good deal more.

## THE PLAYER

1992 (123 minutes) • Comedy/Drama
Fine Line Features • R

Cast: Tim Robbins (Griffin Mill), Greta Scacchi (June Gudmundsdottir), Fred Ward (Walter Stuckel), Whoopi Goldberg (Detective Avery), Peter Gallagher (Larry Levy), Dean Stockwell (Andy Civella), Sydney Pollack (Dick Mellon), Dina Merrill (Celia)

Producers: David Brown, Michael Tolkin, Nick Wechsler; Director: Robert Altman; Writer: Michael Tolkin (Based on his novel); Photographer: Jean Lépine (color); Editor: Geraldine Peroni

The anti-Hollywood novel has been a thriving subgenre of American literature since at least the 1930s. Anti-Hollywood films, however, are of a more recent vintage. (The first one of note was probably Billy Wilder's *Sunset Boulevard* [1950].) And even these tend to focus on a past era in the film industry. Robert Altman's *The Player* is therefore unusual in satirizing contemporary Hollywood. Even if Altman is showing a measure of personal spite at the town that lionized him in the '70s only to exile him in the '80s, *The Player* is far more than a personal vendetta. Although not quite another *Nashville* (what American film is?), this movie has found an effective synecdoche for much that is vulgar and meretricious in American life.

The protagonist, Griffin Mill, is vice president of a major Hollywood studio. His job consists of listening to writers pitch story ideas. Because only about a dozen of the thousands of pitches he hears ever make it to the screen, he must disappoint countless writers over the course of a year. (At that, Griffin does not have the authority to "green light" a project, only to pass it up the chain of command.) The story begins when one such writer begins sending him threatening and anonymous postcards. Alarmed by the stream of threats, Griffin identifies a likely suspect, tracks him down, and tries to mollify him. A scuffle ensues, in which Griffin accidentally kills the writer, who turns out not to have been the predator after all. His successful attempts to evade capture merge with Altman's portrait of Hollywood, in what resembles a collaboration of Raymond Chandler and Nathanael West.

The film itself opens with a long continuous tracking shot on a Hollywood studio lot. This sets not only the scene but also the mood of the picture. We hear the names of directors, movies, and performers both past and present. In addition, the film manages to include cameo appearances by nearly seventy Hollywood personalities portraying themselves. (One story idea that the writer considers "too serious" to involve bankable stars is finally made with Julia Roberts and Bruce Willis.) If the older satires of Hollywood depicted Tinseltown as a corruption of the American Dream, what we see here is a caricature of the vacuousness of corporate America. This is only enhanced by the celebrity that magnifies the self-importance of the people who live and work in Hollywood.

At first glance, one wonders how such a brutal portrayal of the contemporary film industry could have been made by that industry itself. Did Altman trick Hollywood in the same way that the Hal Philip Walker campaign tricked the denizens of Nashville? The answer, I suspect, is even more cynical. If our national dream factory is an intellectual and moral cesspool, what does that say about the millions of Americans who idolize the dream merchants? *The Player* shows us how a man of no talent, intelligence, or ethics can literally get away with murder. But, even worse, it shows us a town and a country in which such things can happen.

## PRIMARY COLORS

1998 (135 minutes) • Political Satire
Universal • R

Cast: John Travolta (Governor Jack Stanton), Emma Thompson (Susan Stanton), Billy Bob Thornton (Richard Jemmons), Adrian Lester (Henry Burton), Kathy Bates (Libby Holden), Maura Tierney (Daisy), Larry Hagman (Governor Fred Picker), Paul Guilfoyle (Howard Ferguson), Caroline Aaron (Lucille Kaufman), Rebecca Walker (March Cunningham)

Producer: Mike Nichols; Director: Mike Nichols; Writer: Elaine May (based on the novel *Primary Colors* by Anonymous [Joe Klein]; Photographer: Michael Ballhaus (color); Editor: Arthur Schmidt

In 1996, as President Bill Clinton was preparing to run for reelection, the political world was rocked by a novel that everyone recognized as a fictionalized account of Clinton's 1992 campaign. Because the author used the pseudonym "Anonymous," a guessing game ensued concerning his true identity. Eventually veteran journalist Joe Klein confessed to having written this roman à clef, which was subsequently made into a movie that does more than merely lampoon our libidinous forty-second president.

Among other things, the film *Primary Colors* reminds us why its director, Mike Nichols, and screenwriter, Elaine May, constituted one of the most brilliant comedy teams in America in the early 1960s. They are able to evoke laughter with intelligent humor that never forces the issue. And John Travolta is particularly good as the Clintonesque Jack Stanton. Beginning with his comeback role in *Pulp Fiction* (1994), Travolta has made the transition from youthful sex star to one of our finest middle-aged character actors. The supporting cast (including Emma Thompson as Stanton's cold-blooded and long-suffering wife Susan; Billy Bob Thornton as a redneck political advisor reminiscent of James Carville; and Kathy Bates as Libby Holden, the campaign's idealistic but mentally unbalanced head of damage control) are all excellent.

The narrator and moral center of the film is Henry Burton, a young black man who is the grandson of a legendary civil-rights leader. Henry signs on with the Stanton campaign because he believes that the Southern governor is sincere in his commitment to progressive change. Like Clinton, Stanton is hit with revelations of philandering and draft dodging. Unlike less brazen candidates, he weathers these storms with even more dissimulation (including an appearance with his wife on *60 Minutes*, which mirrors the shameless exhibition of the Clintons on Super Bowl Sunday 1992). Stanton dodges the charge that he has impregnated a seventeen-year-old black girl by surreptitiously submitting his uncle's DNA to a bogus pregnancy test. The final straw for both Libby Holden and Henry Burton comes when Stanton blackmails a rival with evidence of past cocaine use and a homosexual dalliance with his supplier. (Apparently, the Stantons are supposed to be too ethical for such tactics.) Although the distraught Libby takes her own life, Henry simply quits the campaign to play another day. In the final scene of the picture, he is shaking hands with President Stanton at the inaugural ball.

The satire of *Primary Colors* would not have been nearly as effective had it been the work of a partisan Republican. Except for his self-serving prevarications, the film separates Stanton's personal weaknesses from his political philosophy. By now we know that, for all their protestations about family values, Republicans are no more apt than Democrats to keep their pants zipped. Whether the culprit be John F. Kennedy, Martin Luther King Jr., or Bill Clinton, unprincipled liberals are inclined to look the other way in order to advance their ideological agenda. But so too are unprincipled conservatives. As a result, *Primary Colors* provides more than cheap gratification for viewers on the Right. It is an occasion for soul-searching for hypocrites of every political stripe.

## THE PRODUCERS

1968 (88 minutes) • Comedy
MGM • Unrated

Cast: Zero Mostel (Max Bialystock), Gene Wilder (Leo Bloom), Kenneth Mars (Franz Liebkind), Estelle Winword ("Hold Me, Touch Me"), Renée Taylor (Eva Braun), Christopher Hewett (Roger De Bris), Lee Meredith (Ulla), Andréas Voutsinas (Carmen Ghia), Dick Shawn (Lorenzo St. Dubois)

Producers: Sidney Glazier (Producer), Jack Grossberg (Associate Producer); Director: Mel Brooks; Writer: Mel

Brooks; Photographer: Joseph F. Coffey (Pathécolor); Editor: Ralph Rosenblum

In his first motion picture (which ranks eleventh in the American Film Institute's list of the one hundred funniest American movies), Mel Brooks commits what seems the ultimate act of bad taste in constructing a comedy around the figure of Adolph Hitler. It is true that Charlie Chaplin had lampooned Hitler in *The Great Dictator* (1940), and Nazi guards had been the butt of jokes in both the film *Stalag 17* (1952) and the television series *Hogan's Heroes*. But in all of these previous comedies, the anti-Nazi side had emerged triumphant. In *The Producers*, everyone seems to be the object of derision, and no one triumphs. In fact, the two Jewish protagonists of the film end up in jail. Max Bialystock is a hapless Broadway producer who manages to stay marginally afloat by selling shares in his failed productions to aging women. In order to maintain this scam, however, he is required to bed the hags. The plot thickens when Max hooks up with a young accountant named Leo Bloom, who convinces him that he can make a fortune in tax losses by launching a play that is guaranteed to be a monumental flop.

Max and Leo are certain that they have found the worst play imaginable in a work called *Springtime for Hitler* by a young German who still romanticizes the führer. As insurance against an accidental success (or a mere marginal failure), the producers engage a moronic drag queen to direct the show and a mindless hippie named Lorenzo St. Du Bois (LSD) to play the lead role. In a perverse twist of fate, the audience (after some initial apprehension) greets *Springtime for Hitler* as wonderfully camp entertainment. As Maurice Yacowar observes: "Bialystock's expensive lesson is that there is no moral absolute that he can confidently offend, either on Broadway or in Western Civilization (As We Know It). There is no sure distinction between Right and Wrong in his society's ethics, even for the hardy criminal spirit who wishes to pursue the Wrong. So what he thought would upset his audience pleased them immensely."

Like so many great works of popular art, *The Producers* has thrived in different genres. It was transformed into a hit Broadway play, which then became the basis for a second motion picture. It is doubtful that anyone other than a Jewish comedian of the stature of Mel Brooks would have dared to bring such controversial material to the screen. Certainly by 1969, earnest denunciations of the Third Reich had all begun to sound the same. So Brooks argued that "you can bring down totalitarian governments faster by using ridicule than you can with invective." Whether or not that is literally true, ridicule is the only weapon a satirist has. (In addition to Hitler, the counterculture, American tax laws, and Broadway itself come in for their share of knocks.) Roger Ebert remembers seeing a woman accost Mel Brooks shortly after the original version of *The Producers* was released. When she accused him of having produced a vulgar movie, Brooks replied: "Madam, my film rises below vulgarity."

## THE QUEEN

2006 (97 minutes) • Historical Drama
Miramax • PG-13

Cast: Helen Mirren (Elizabeth II), Michael Sheen (Tony Blair), James Cromwell (Prince Philip), Sylvia Syms (Queen Mother), Paul Barrett (Trevor Rees-Jones), Helen McCrory (Cherie Blair), Alex Jennings (Prince Charles)

Producers: Andy Harries, Christine Langan, Tracey Seaward (Producers), Francois Ivernel, Cameron McCracken, Scott Rudin (Executive Producers); Director: Stephen Frears; Writer: Peter Morgan; Photographer: Affonso Beato (color); Editor: Lucia Zucchetti

This film is about the way in which two very different personalities confronted what began as a private misfortune (I hesitate to misuse the word "tragedy") but soon became a public crisis. In August 1997, Diana, former Princess of Wales, was killed in a car wreck in Paris while she and her current boyfriend, Dodi Fayed, were pursued by crazed paparazzi. What followed was an immense outpouring of grief for this beautiful and popular young woman. During the week leading up to Diana's funeral, Queen Elizabeth II had to decide how to react publicly to her death. The queen's initial response was to follow protocol and take a low-key approach to the passing of a woman who was no longer a member of the royal family. The newly elected prime minister, Tony Blair, realized that this stance was so deeply unpopular with the British people that it threatened the survival of the monarchy itself. Much of the film consists of Blair convincing the queen that it is in her own best interest to bow to public pressure. In the process, Blair develops an appreciation for the extraordinary monarch he serves.

When the queen first meets Blair after his election, she says: "Mr. Blair, you are my tenth prime minister. The first was Winston Churchill." In addition to breaking the ice, this statement reminds us of the historical continuity represented by the monarchy. In 2002, Elizabeth celebrated fifty years on the throne and seems to be closing in on the sixty-four-year record of her great-grandmother Victoria. It goes without saying that she and Diana represent different generations and different ways of looking at the world. Much of the media coverage of Diana's death and funeral put Elizabeth in an unfavorable light. This captivating film goes a long way toward redressing the balance.

All her life, the queen had devoted herself to a vision of public duty. Her father, George VI, had not wanted to be king but had been forced into the position when his brother, Edward VIII, abdicated his throne to marry an American divorcée. (Cynics point out that the imminence of World War II made it an opportune time to jump ship.) So Prince Bertie became George VI at a time of great national and international crisis. He and his family refused to leave London, even as Hitler was dropping bombs on the city. For her part, Princess Elizabeth drove an ambulance and rolled bandages for the war effort. Although she lent her name to some worthy causes, Diana was best known for getting her picture taken and for screwing her riding instructor. But then, with a husband such as Charles, few people blamed her.

It is to Elizabeth's credit that she showed as much flexibility as she did while bucking a lifetime of tradition and the counsel of her even more conservative husband, Price Philip. (Philip's reaction to hearing that Elton John will be singing at Westminster Abbey helps to crystallize the conflict of cultures.) Helen Mirren's Academy Award–winning portrayal of the title character makes a distant public figure come alive as a complex human being. Whatever else may be said of her, Elizabeth II is the last world leader from what may be the most remarkable generation of the twentieth century.

## RAMBLING ROSE

1991 (112 minutes) • Comedy/Drama
Seven Arts • R

Cast: Laura Dern (Rose), Robert Duvall (Daddy), Diane Ladd (Mother), Lukas Haas (Buddy), John Heard (Buddy as an adult), Kevin Conway (Dr. Martinson), Robert John Burke (Dave Wilkie)

Producers: Renny Harlin (Producer), Mario Kassar, Edgar J. Scherick (Executive Producers); Director: Martha Coolidge; Writer: Calder Willingham (based on his novel); Photographer: Johnny E. Jensen (color); Editor: Steve Cohen

The situation in *Rambling Rose* is not unusual for a Hollywood movie. A young woman who is the very embodiment of sensuality comes to board with a straitlaced Southern family. The clash of values, though not the outcome, is predictable. The bulk of the story is rendered through the memory of Buddy Hillyer, who was thirteen years old when Rose arrived at his family home in 1935. Because the Depression is in full force, an adolescent girl with neither a family nor a marketable skill has few options. Although she functions as a domestic servant for the Hillyers, Rose is more like a troublesome family member. She shows her gratitude to Daddy Hillyer in the only way she knows how—by trying to seduce him. Daddy is ethical enough to resist temptation but charitable enough not to send the borderline nympho packing. (He may have inadvertently led her on by saying, "I swear to God, you're as graceful as a capital letter S. You'll give a glow and shine to these old walls.") In the meantime, Buddy uses Rose as his introduction to puberty, although he appears not to have gone beyond some preliminary looking and touching.

Buddy's mother (and Daddy's wife) is a graduate student in history at Columbia University who is writing her thesis on some unspecified topic. Although it is not clear how much she knows about the havoc that Rose is raising under her nose, she turns out to be one of the girl's staunchest defenders. It is not that the family approves of Rose's late-night trysts and her bumbling run-ins with the law. But their compassion always trumps their censure. When an apparent pregnancy turns out to be an ovarian cyst, the local doctor thinks that a full hysterectomy will take care of that problem and Rose's wanton sexuality in one fell swoop. Although Daddy seems to be taken in by his arguments, Mother refuses to approve the operation. This enables Rose to find a home, if not happiness, as the wife of a local cop.

The story is framed in the 1970s—after both Mother Hillyer and Rose have died. Because Buddy and Daddy reveal nothing of importance to each other or to us, John Simon is surely right to find the frame distracting. (The film is elegiac enough without it.) The underappreciated Southern writer Calder Willingham has based the script for this movie on his own novel. He finds enough local color to evoke time and place without the usual Hollywood clichés about the South. In the hands of, say, Tennessee Williams or one of his lesser clones, Daddy (and probably Buddy as well) would have been compromised by Rose. The girl would have created a scandal and then been victimized by the repressed hypocrites of the town. She would almost certainly have been subjected to a therapeutic sexual mutilation. The fact that genuine goodness triumphs in this film is nothing short of amazing.

## RED DAWN

1984 (114 minutes) • Action Drama
United Artists/Valkyrie Films • PG-13

Cast: Patrick Swayze (Jed Eckert), C. Thomas Howell (Robert Morris), Lea Thompson (Erica), Charlie Sheen (Matt Eckert), Darren Dalton (Daryl Bates), Jennifer Grey (Toni), Brad Savage (Danny), Doug Toby (Aarvark), Ben Johnson (Mr. Mason), Harry Dean Stanton (Tom Eckert), Ron O'Neal (Colonel Ernesto Bella), William Smith (Col. Strelnikov), Vladek Sheybal (General Bratchenko), Powers Boothe (Lt. Col. Andrew Tanner), Frank McRae (Mr. Teasdale), Roy Jenson (Samuel Morris), Pepe Serna (Aardvark's father), Lane Smith (Mayor Bates)

Producers: Buzz Feitshans (Producer), Barry Beckerman (Executive Producer); Director: John Milius; Writers: John Milius, Kevin Reynolds; Photographer: Ric Waite (color); Editor: Thom Noble

John Milius was among a group of young filmmakers who studied at the University of Southern California in the late 1960s and then began revolutionizing

Hollywood in the following decade. (Others in this contingent included Steven Spielberg, George Lucas, Francis Ford Coppola, and Robert Zemeckis.) Milius made some uncredited contributions to the script of *Dirty Harry* in 1971 and then received his first solo screenwriting credit on John Huston's *The Life and Times of Judge Roy Bean* in 1972. The following year, he directed his first commercial Hollywood film, *Dillinger*. He was also cowriter of Coppola's epic Vietnam film *Apocalypse Now*. Milius is probably the only political conservative among the so-called USC mafia. Nowhere is this fact more evident than in *Red Dawn*. At a time when liberal Hollywood was toasting the Sandinistas, Milius offered a nightmare vision of a Communist invasion of the United States by Soviet troops and their Latin American proxies. The film was also an early showcase for both Patrick Swayze and Charlie Sheen and includes an effective performance by the underrated Powers Boothe.

The picture opens with a shot of a fairly typical high school class in America's heartland. In a truly chilling scene, paratroopers start descending on the football field outside the window. (This invasion of conventional forces is meant to refute the notion that nuclear deterrence was all that was needed to keep the Commies at bay.) Just as the NRA had predicted, the invaders start rounding up registered gun owners. The U.S.'s only remaining means of defense consists of guerilla forces, including a band of intrepid high school warriors who call themselves the Wolverines. In addition to garden-variety anticommunists, this movie also appealed to survivalists and militia members, two groups generally scorned by the Hollywood elite. *Red Dawn*, however, aspired to be more than a mere action flick or an appeal to blue-collar audiences. The fact that Milius can imagine circumstances under which armed resistance might be justified does not make him a war lover. If anything, it can be argued that those who ignored the Communist threat or underestimated the enemy were the ones who made war more likely.

In an interview with the critic Nat Segaloff, Milius said that he wanted to show that World War III would be unwinnable and to demonstrate "the desperate futility of war." "At the end of the movie," Milius observes, "in spite of all the heroism and valor, and the reasons and revenges on both sides, all that's left to remember these fighters is a lonely plaque on some desolate battlefield that nobody visits anymore." There is almost a sense in which both sides walk the fine line between humanity and inhumanity. The Wolverines end up shooting prisoners in reprisal for their own friends and kin who have been killed. And yet, in one particularly powerful scene, the Cuban commander lets Jed carry off the body of his wounded brother. At the end, the film is deliberately unclear about which side has prevailed.

## RED RIVER

1948 (125 minutes) • Western
United Artists • Unrated

Cast: John Wayne (Tom Dunson), Montgomery Clift (Matthew Garth), Joanne Dru (Tess Millay), Walter Brennan (Groot Nadine), Coleen Gray (Fen), John Ireland (Cherry Valance), Noah Beery Jr. (Buster McGee), Harry Carey (Mr. Melville), Harry Carey Jr. (Dan Latimer), Paul Fix (Teeler Yacey)

Producer: Howard Hawks; Director: Howard Hawks; Writers: Borden Chase, Charles Schnee (based on the novel *The Chisholm Trail* by Borden Chase); Photographer: Russell Harlan (black and white); Editor: Christian Nyby

Like *The Man Who Shot Liberty Valance*, *My Darling Clementine* (1946), *Shane* (1953), and other classic Western films, *Red River* deals with the conflict between the individual and the community. The film opens when Tom Dunson and his sidekick Groot leave a wagon train heading west in order to seek their fortune near the Red River in Texas. As soon as they depart, Indians attack the wagon train and kill nearly everyone aboard. Not long thereafter, Dunson and Groot encounter young Matthew Garth, one of the few survivors of the massacre. He becomes Dunson's partner and adopted son, and together they form a cattle ranch on land that Dunson arbitrarily seizes from a much larger claim bequeathed to a local Mexican by the Spanish government. In essence, Dunson is a man who makes his own rules and then enforces them with legalistic rigidity.

Although the wagon train might have been lost even if Dunson had stayed, his departure clearly dooms Fen, the girl he leaves behind. Despite her pleas to go with him, Dunson travels only with Groot, apparently believing that a woman would slow him down. Promising that they will be reunited at some point in the future, he slips a snake bracelet on her wrist. The next time he sees it, it is on an Indian he has just killed. Rather than finding another woman to replace the one he has abandoned, Dunson is increasingly given to empire building and, finally, to isolation. As the film critic Robert Sklar points out, Dunson should realize his need for the feminine when an Indian attack spares his bull but kills both his cows. He is prevented from building a herd until Matthew shows up with a cow of his own. This becomes the material basis of their bonding.

After enough years have passed for Matthew to grow to manhood and for the herd to expand, the cash-poor Dunson decides to drive his cattle north to sell them. Having settled on a plan and a route, Dunson will not be swayed by either circumstance or the counsel of wiser men. As men begin to desert his camp, Dunson becomes even harsher—to the point of jeopardizing the entire enterprise. In order to save the herd and the men (and perhaps Dunson himself), Matthew and Groot disarm Dunson and take control of the cattle drive. Although they intend to deliver the proceeds to Dunson, their mutiny so infuriates him that their lives are endangered should he ever catch up with them. This almost happens when Garth delays the cattle drive to rescue a wagon train besieged by Indians. He quickly falls in love with a woman named Tess Millay and gives her the bracelet that had once belonged to Fen but is now his. Finally making it to Abilene, Garth sells the cattle for a good price. Meanwhile, Dunson has come upon the wagon train and heard Tess's story. Rather than repeating his earlier mistake with Fen, he agrees to take her along as he follows Matthew's trail. When Matthew refuses to engage in a gunfight with his foster father, a slapstick brawl ensues. Sensing the latent affection between the two men, Tess serves as peacemaker. Dunson incorporates Matthew's brand into his own and suggests that the two young people marry. As M. E. Bradford notes: "Dunson has entered the corporate life, even though the heroic life was his way of getting there."

## THE RIGHT STUFF

1983 (192 minutes) • Historical Drama
Ladd • PG

Cast: Sam Shepard (Chuck Yeager), Ed Harris (John Glenn), Dennis Quaid (Gordon Cooper), Scott Glenn

(Alan Shepard), Fred Ward (Gus Grissom), Barbara Hershey (Glennis Yeager), Kim Stanley (Pancho Barnes), Veronica Cartwright (Betty Grissom), Pamela Reed (Trudy Cooper), Scott Paulin (Deke Slayton), Recruiter (Jeff Goldblum), Recruiter (Harry Shearer)

Producers: Irwin Winkler, Robert Chartoff; Director: Philip Kaufman; Writer: Philip Kaufman (based on the book by Tom Wolfe); Photographer: Caleb Deschanel (Technicolor); Editors: Glenn Farr, Lisa Fruchtman, Stephen A. Rotter, Tom Rolf, Douglas Stewart

Phillip Kaufman's *The Right Stuff* is a magnificent cinematic adaptation of one of the great books of our time. In 1978, when American culture was languishing in malaise over the twin disasters of Vietnam and Watergate, Tom Wolfe published a nonfiction novel celebrating two groups of military heroes clearly unfashionable to the elite audiences who had been mesmerized a decade earlier by his psychedelic narrative *The Electric Kool-Aid Acid Test* (1968). The test pilots of the late 1940s—a breed exemplified by Chuck Yeager, who broke the sound barrier—labored in anonymity at a desert air base in California. In contrast, the Mercury astronauts, who were selected to make the first manned space flights for the United States, became media-made celebrities.

The one characteristic connecting both groups was a combination of reckless courage and technical competence that Wolfe dubs the "right stuff." Most of the test pilots and astronauts are depicted as mavericks who love their country and their vocation but ridicule the bureaucracy and cupidity that pervades the world outside their close-knit fraternity. The notable exception would seem to be super-clean John Glenn, who admonishes his fellow astronauts to curtail their blatant womanizing to protect public support for the space project. Nevertheless, Glenn shows his own streak of independence by using the threat of media exposure to force the scientists controlling the space program to make changes to the liking of the pilots. And, in a heroic display of marital affection and political courage, he tells his wife (who is understandably shy because of a speech defect) that she does not have to subject herself to the public intrusion of her home by Vice President Johnson and the TV networks.

Kaufman does a splendid job capturing the many affinities and differences between essentially two different casts of characters. In the next-to-last scene in the film, we see Yeager anonymously setting a new airborne altitude record in dusty California while the Mercury Seven astronauts are feted by a packed house in the Houston Astrodome and a flamenco dance by the aging stripper Sally Rand. After Yeager has been forced to bail out of his plane, it is not immediately clear whether he has survived. Significantly, when one of the two members of the rescue mission asks if a man is emerging from the smoke and rubble, his companion says, "You're damn right, there is." In what may be a deliberately anticlimactic closing scene, the final Mercury astronaut (Gordon Cooper) is awakened after having fallen asleep in his spacecraft while waiting to take off. (As both the book and movie suggest, one can't get much calmer and cooler than that.) Cooper was the last American astronaut to fly alone.

Although the film cannot duplicate Wolfe's riveting prose style, interior monologues, and historical perspective, the visual effects are stunning. (One can only regret that this picture was made before IMAX.) Kaufman also maintains the spirit of insouciant American individualism that pervades the book. Nominated for eight Academy Awards and winning four (best film editing, best score, best sound, and best sound effects editing), *The Right Stuff* was one of the most honored films of the year. By 1983, America was well into the Reagan era, and the vision of the country that might have seemed anachronistic when Wolfe published his book five years earlier appeared more relevant than ever. (John Glenn, in 1983 a senator from Ohio, was even preparing to run for the Democratic presidential nomination.) The Soviets were still our adversaries, and control of outer space was still on the national agenda. One might well discern a cultural divide between those who called the Strategic Defense Initiative "Star Wars" and those who saw it as an example of the "right stuff."

## SEPARATE BUT EQUAL

1991 (194 minutes) • Historical Drama
Republic Pictures (TV Movie) • Unrated

Cast: Sidney Poitier (Thurgood Marshall), Burt Lancaster (John W. Davis), Richard Kiley (Earl Warren), Cleavon Little (Robert L. Carter), Gloria Foster (Buster Marshall), John McMartin (Gov. James F. Byrnes), Graham Beckel (Josiah C. Tulley,) Ed Hall (The Rev. J. A. Delaine), Lynne

Thigpen (Ruth Alice Stovall), Macon McCalman (W. B. Springer), Randle Mell (Charles L. Black Jr.), Cheryl Lynn Bruce (Gladys Hampton), Tommy Hollis (Harry Briggs, Sr.), John Rothman (Jack Greenberg)

Executive Producers: George Stevens Jr. Stan Margulies; Director: George Stevens Jr.; Writer: George Stevens Jr.; Photographer: Nic Knowland (color); Editor: John W. Wheeler

In 1950, Thurgood Marshall argued before the U.S. Supreme Court that the segregation of public schools violated the equal protection clause of the Fourteenth Amendment to the Constitution. This made-for-TV movie does an excellent job of presenting both the human and legal dimensions of this historic controversy. It begins with the situation of a segregated black school in Clarendon County, South Carolina. The scene in which a black student, who must walk five miles each way to school, is passed on the road by several school buses dramatizes the actual inequality of the separate-but-equal doctrine. When the principal of the black school is rebuffed in his attempt to obtain even one bus for his students, Marshall and the NAACP Legal Defense Fund file suit. Although their main objective is simply to obtain the equal facilities promised by law, they also make the ancillary argument that segregation by race is inherently a denial of equal protection. When a liberal white judge chooses to focus on that basic principle, the NAACP is forced to abandon its gradualist approach and focus on an all-or-nothing constitutional argument.

Many who now hail the outcome of that case are probably unaware of how tenuous the situation seemed at the time. Marshall was arguing against legislative history (the same Congress that ratified the Fourteenth Amendment established segregated public schools in Washington, D.C.) and an almost sixty-year-old precedent in which the Supreme Court had established the validity of the separate-but-equal principle in the decision of *Plessy v. Ferguson* (1896). Moreover, a majority of the Supreme Court, under the indecisive leadership of Chief Justice Fred Vinson, seemed reluctant to upset established precedent and unleash a probable social revolution in the South. Finally, the attorney for the defense was John W. Davis, universally recognized as one of the ablest lawyers of the twentieth century. Many within the black community believed that the NAACP had stumbled into an unwinnable case that would prove to be a severe setback to the cause of civil rights.

Because of deep divisions on the court, Vinson kept this case on the back-burner for three years. His sudden death gave the new president, Dwight Eisenhower, an opportunity to appoint a new chief justice. His pick was California governor Earl Warren, a man with no previous judicial experience. Because Eisenhower, as general, had opposed full integration of the armed forces and Warren, as attorney general of California, had overseen the internment of Japanese Americans during World War II, the prospects for an NAACP victory seemed even more hopeless. But a lifetime appointment to the Supreme Court has a way of changing one's perspective. Warren became convinced of the moral imperative of desegregation and used his considerable political skills to orchestrate a unanimous verdict.

The film's celebration of the Supreme Court's decision was to be expected. What lifts this drama from the level of caricature is a surprisingly fair treatment of the other side of the case. Lancaster gives a compelling performance as John W. Davis. Furthermore, it is clear that Warren's position on desegregation was based on moral and political considerations for which he constructed a fig leaf of constitutional justification. In the 1960s, he would use this same judicial philosophy to steer a far more liberal court to decisions that have proved to be historically more controversial than the one apotheosized in *Separate But Equal.*

## SHANE

1953 (118 minutes) • Western
Paramount • Unrated

Cast: Alan Ladd (Shane), Jean Arthur (Marian Starrett), Van Heflin (Joe Starrett), Brandon de Wilde (Joey), Jack Palance (Wilson), Ben Johnson (Chris), Edgar Buchanan (Lewis), Emile Meyer (Ryker), Elisha Cook Jr. (Torrey), Douglas Spencer (Shipstead)

Producer: George Stevens; Director: George Stevens; Writers: A. B. Guthrie Jr., Jack Sher (based on the novel by Jack Schaefer); Photographer: Loyal Griggs (Technicolor); Editors: William Hornbeck, Tom McAdoo

Like so many Westerns, *Shane* focuses on the conflict between the rancher and the small farmer. These two classes of settlers represent different periods in the development of the frontier. Although the rancher has a historically prior claim, he was preceded by the Indian-fighter and the mountain man, who themselves displaced the original inhabitants. If there is room enough for everyone in the West, then the rancher must acknowledge the moral claim of the farmer. This film concerns the efforts of one family to withstand the intimidation of a local cattle baron. The action begins when a stranger named Shane rides onto the farm of Joe and Marian Starrett and asks for water for himself and his horse. After being invited to supper and to stay the night, Shane becomes a hired hand on the farm and a virtual member of the family. Although we know very little about his background, it soon becomes clear that Shane is a former gunfighter.

Relatively early in the movie, Shane makes a trip to the town's combined general store and saloon to exchange his buckskins for work clothes, pick up provisions for his employer, and purchase a bottle of soda pop for young Joey Starrett. When he refuses to defend himself against the taunts and abuse of the cattle baron's hired men, Starrett's neighbors conclude that Shane is either a coward or a weakling. A few days later, Shane redeems his honor when he and Joe get the best of the cowhands in a fistfight in the same location. Not to be outdone, the cattle baron brings in a hired gunslinger named Wilson to dispose of Shane. His first victim, however, is a hot-blooded Southerner who draws on Wilson when the gunslinger insults several heroes of the Confederacy. Although this killing is enough to encourage most of the other farmers to pack up, Joe Starrett persuades them that they have an obligation to stay. Shane, however, realizes that Joe is no match for Wilson. To protect his friend, Shane knocks Joe unconscious when he is preparing to go into town and face the gunslinger himself. Shane straps his six-shooter on, dispatches Wilson and several cohorts, and then rides back into the anonymity from which he came.

Unlike Tom Dunson in *Red River*, Shane is never incorporated into any community. There are suggestions early in the film that he wants to leave his past behind him, and he seems to have a salutary effect on each member of the Starrett family. He becomes an essential male companion for Joe, a role model for Joey, and a kind of platonic lover to Marian. But there is a potential danger in these benefits, especially for the wife and son. As M. E. Bradford points out: "No respectable woman can have two husbands or a brother that is not her blood kin; and no boy can have two fathers, at least not at the same time."

Even if he were to remain alone in the community, Shane might very well have become a pathetic anachronism such as Tom Doniphon in John Ford's *The Man Who Shot Liberty Valance* and Scratchy Wilson in Stephen Crane's "The Bride Comes to Yellow Sky." Instead, he must ride out of town, as the critic Lloyd Baugh has noted, into the *rising* sun.

## SULLIVAN'S TRAVELS

1941 (91 minutes) • Comedy
Paramount • Unrated

Cast: Joel McCrea (John L. Sullivan), Veronica Lake (The Girl), Robert Warwick (Mr. Lebrand), William Demarest (Mr. Jones), Franklin Pangborn (Mr. Casalsis), Peter Hall (Mr. Hadrian), Byron Foulger (Mr. Valdelle), Margaret Hayes (Secretary), Robert Grieg (Sullivan's Butler), Eric Blore (Sullivan's Valet).

Producer: Paul Jones; Director: Preston Sturges; Writer: Preston Sturges; Photographer: John Seitz (black and white); Editor: Stuart Gilmore.

During the 1930s and 1940s, Preston Sturges brought an unusual degree of wit and erudition to American movies. Although he directed only thirteen films, seven (all made between 1939 and 1942) are considered classics. Of these, four were voted by the American Film Institute to be among the one hundred funniest American movies. The highest-rated (#39) was *Sullivan's Travels*. Made in 1941, when the Great Depression was still a painful memory for most Americans, this film provides a sardonic look at Hollywood and a critique of social consciousness that reflects more genuine social conscience than most movies explicitly in that genre.

The film opens with a shot of two men fighting on the roof of a boxcar. When "The End" flashes across the screen, we realize that we have been watching a film-within-a film screened by the successful Hollywood director John L. Sullivan. (Why he has the same name as the great bare-knuckled fighter is anyone's guess.) Although Sullivan is best known for his comedies, his ambition is to direct a film of social significance. To this end, he plans to go on the road posing as a hobo to learn what life is like among the poor. Although the studio tries to follow him to protect a valuable human property, Sully ditches them. Unfortunately, he also manages to hitch a ride that takes him right back to Hollywood. There he meets a beautiful blonde girl who insists on joining him on the road.

After a couple weeks of deprivation, Sully decides to call a halt to his experiment and return to Hollywood. (By this point, he and the girl have fallen in love.) His final gesture is to pass out a thousand dollars' worth of five-dollar bills to the bums hanging around the railroad tracks. One of his greedier beneficiaries knocks him over the head, steals his identification, and throws him in a railroad car. When trying to grab money that has blown onto the railroad tracks, the bum is run over by a train and is mistaken for Sullivan. In the meantime, Sully, who suffers from amnesia because of the knock on his head, gets in a brawl with a railroad official who mistakes him for a bum. At this point, he is sentenced to six years in a prison camp, where he works on a chain gang, gets put in solitary confinement, and suffers the continuing pains of the proletariat rather than the temporary ones of the dilettante. In a stroke of genius, he "confesses" to the murder of John L. Sullivan, thus getting his picture and his true identity in the papers.

While still a prisoner, however, Sully and several of his fellow inmates are allowed to attend a black church to view a Disney cartoon. When he witnesses the spontaneous laughter this evokes, he realizes that his comedies have probably done more human good than any amount of agitprop he might make with pretentious titles such as *O Brother, Where Art Thou?* "There's a lot to be said for making people laugh," he says. "Did you know that's all some people have? It isn't much . . . but it's better than nothing in this cockeyed caravan."

## THE TAMING OF THE SHREW

1967 (122 minutes) • Romantic Comedy
Columbia • PG

Cast: Elizabeth Taylor (Katharina), Richard Burton (Petrucio), Michael York (Lucentio), Cyril Cusack (Grumio), Michael Hordern (Baptista), Alfred Lynch (Tranio),

Alan Webb (Gremio), Giancarlo Cobelli (Priest), Vernon Dobtcheff (Pedant), Ken Parry (Tailor), Anthony Gardner (Haberdasher), Natasha Pyne (Bianca), Victor Spinetti (Hortensio), Roy Holder (Biondello), Mark Dignam (Vincentio), Bice Valori (Widow)

Producers: Franco Zeffirelli, Richard Burton, Elizabeth Taylor (Producers), Richard McWhorter (Executive Producer); Director: Franco Zefferelli; Writers: William Shakespeare, Franco Zeffirelli; Photographer: Oswald Morris (color); Editor: Peter Taylor

It has become a cliché of Shakespearean criticism that the immortal Bard has remained "relevant" by meaning something new to each generation. To appreciate the impact of Franco Zeffirelli's version of *The Taming of the Shrew*, it is necessary to understand both the nature of sexual politics in America and the status of Richard Burton and Elizabeth Taylor as international celebrities in the late 1960s. This was the time when feminism was becoming a major topic of cultural discussion. Betty Friedan's *Feminine Mystique* (1964) had reminded desperate housewives of all they were missing in their subjugation to patriarchal norms. In the intellectual realm, writers such as Germaine Greer and Kate Millet were exposing the biases of high culture, even as young women were burning their bras and beginning to read Gloria Steinem's *Ms.* magazine. As the saying went: "A woman without a man is like a fish without a bicycle."

Anyone who would laugh at such a joke probably would not have found Shakespeare's misogynistic humor very funny. At the same time, Burton and Taylor were accomplished actors whose public personae seemed to transcend their screen roles. In an era when talentless nonentities such as Paris Hilton and Britney Spears are called "pop culture icons" by people too ignorant to know the definition of the term "icon," it is well to remind oneself of a time when gifted performers such as Burton and Taylor were also the biggest stars. This inevitably meant that viewers of, say, *Who's Afraid of Virginia Woolf?* (1966) would see not only brilliant individual performances but also a hint of the offscreen chemistry between the Burtons. This was certainly true of *The Taming of the Shrew.*

Shakespeare's classic comedy is a tale of two sisters. Bianca, the younger, is sweet-tempered and besieged by suitors. According to custom, however, she cannot marry until her older sister, the shrewish Katharina, is wed. Fortunately, one of Bianca's admirers finds a man who is willing to court Katharina for her substantial dowry. Having earned her father's consent, Petruchio must now mold his bride into an obedient wife. Although he does not beat her, he subjects her to what today would be considered acts of mental cruelty. This involves showing up late and shabbily dressed for the wedding ceremony, throwing out perfectly good food at his own home on the specious grounds that it is badly cooked, and finally forcing her to agree to palpable nonsense simply to humor him. By the final scene, Katharina has been transformed from a shrew into the most compliant wife in the play.

The standard antifeminist reading would hold that this is simply the way that men must deal with women and that this is what women secretly want. Another interpretation might be that Petruchio and Katharina are two passionate individuals who are ideally suited to one another. Having finally met her match in Petruchio, the former shrew is willing to play the role of the submissive wife. Even if the actual marriage of the Burtons did not follow that script, moviegoers around the world were more than willing to believe it had.

## TENDER MERCIES

1983 (92 minutes) • Drama
Universal • PG

Cast: Robert Duvall (Mac Sledge), Tess Harper (Rosa Lee), Betty Buckley (Dixie), Wilford Brimley (Harry), Ellen Barkin (Sue Anne), Allan Hubbard (Sonny), Lenny von Dohlen (Robert), Norman Bennett (The Reverend Hotchkiss)

Producer: Philip S. Hobel; Director: Bruce Beresford; Writer: Horton Foote; Photographer: Russell Boyd (color); Editor: William Anderson

Country-and-western music made its debut in the American cinema when Jimmie Rodgers appeared in a ten-minute short called *The Singing Brakeman* in 1930. In the following decades, hillbilly performers such as Roy Acuff and Ernest Tubb supplemented their concert appearances with formulaic B pictures, while cowboy singers such as Gene Autry and Roy Rogers came to be known primarily for their appearances on screen. None of these films, however, aspired to the level of mainstream entertainment, much less high art. With the exception of Robert Altman's *Nashville*, it was not until the 1980s, when country music had broken out of the entertainment ghetto, that films such as *Coal Miner's Daughter* (1980) and *Honky Tonk Man* (1983) began depicting the lives of country performers with sensitivity and seriousness.

For several reasons, *Tender Mercies* is probably the best of such films. Although country music (of the hardcore variety, before country was cool) gives the picture a specific social texture, the focus here is not so much the music scene as the human drama itself. Mac Sledge is an alcoholic drifter who used to be a country music star and still remains a legend in the eyes of a few devoted fans. Stranded at a motel and filling station in a desolate section of Texas, he signs on as a handyman to pay off his bills and try to get his life back on track.

Mac eventually marries the motel owner, Rosa Lee, and adopts her boy Sonny. (The lad's father was killed in Vietnam.) The past, however, continues to haunt Mac. A local band that idolizes him coaxes him to unpack some songs he has written while in retirement. Meanwhile, his former wife, Dixie Scott (who looks like Loretta Lynn and sounds like Dolly Parton), experiences both the pleasures and perils of success by singing songs that Mac has written for her. Remembering his violent alcoholic behavior, Dixie hates Mac and tries to prevent any contact between him and their adolescent daughter, Sue Anne. Toward the end of this short film, Sue Anne elopes with a considerably older member of her mother's band and is killed in an automobile accident somewhere in Louisiana. *Tender Mercies* ends with Mac and Sonny tossing a football in an act of male bonding. If the story line seems sparse, it is because this is not a plot-driven picture. Character, mood, and theme predominate. Such an approach requires superior talent, which fortunately is in abundant supply in the persons of screenwriter Horton Foote, director Bruce Beresford, star Robert Duvall, and an excellent supporting cast.

Typically, the white working class of the American South and Southwest are objects of ridicule, when they are not ignored altogether. *Tender Mercies* even treats fundamentalist religion as a positive force. It may be that the Texan Horton Foote is close enough to the film's milieu and the Australian Bruce Beresford far enough removed from it to provide proper balance. One suspects, however, that the real auteur of this picture is Robert Duvall, who won a well-deserved Academy Award as best actor for his portrayal of Mac Sledge.

## THE TERMINAL

2004 (128 minutes) • Comedy
Dream Works • PG-13

Cast: Tom Hanks (Viktor Navorski), Catherine Zeta-Jones (Amelia Warren), Stanley Tucci (Frank Dixon), Chi McBride (Mulroy), Diego Luna (Enrique Cruz), Barry Shabaka Henley (Thurman), Kumar Pallana (Gupta Rajan), Zoe Saldana (Torres), Eddie Jones (Salchak), Jude Ciccolella (Karl Iverson), Benny Golson (as himself)

Producers: Laurie MacDonald, Walter F. Parkes, Steven Spielberg (Producers), Jason Hoffs, Andrew Niccol, Patricia Whitcher (Executive Producers), Sergio Mimica-Gezzan (Coproducers); Director: Steven Spielberg; Writers: Andrew Niccol, Sacha Gervasi, Jeff Nathanson; Photography: Janusz Kaminski (color); Editor: Michael Kahn

In this day and age, any movie that lampoons airport security is bound to appeal to millions of passengers who have been subjected to needless harassment by officious bureaucrats. *The Terminal*, however, works like a pre-9/11 story, in which the airport is more a metaphor than a target. Tom Hanks portrays an Eastern European traveler named Viktor Navorski who has the misfortune to arrive at JFK Airport at the same time that the government of his native country is overthrown by a coup. Because the United States government has not yet recognized the new government, Viktor is a man without a country. His current visa is invalid, and no new one can yet be issued. The man due to be appointed security director of the airport is intent on protecting his career by adhering strictly to regulations. (Viktor complicates the situation by ingenuously refusing to take advantage of several opportunities to escape.) As a result, Viktor remains in the airport for nine months.

Much of the film consists of a series of situation comedies involving Viktor's relations with others in the terminal. He befriends Amelia, a befuddled flight attendant played by Catherine Zeta-Jones. Having spent half her life working for the airline and now finding herself trapped in an adulterous affair with a man who sees her as a one-night stand, Amelia discovers a soulmate in Viktor. For his part, Viktor faithfully brings the wrong form to a pretty young airline official every day. Seeing Viktor's friendly relationship with the young woman, a shy maintenance worker who is secretly in love with her pumps Viktor for information about her likes and dislikes. At the same time, Viktor and a janitor from India strike up a warm relationship. (An illegal alien who is fleeing an extortion racket in his own country, the janitor admires Viktor's ingenuity in helping an international passenger smuggle lifesaving medicine past airline security.) Although this situation might remind one of the absurdism of Beckett or Ionesco, there is a genuine sense of community among these deracinated people connected only by an impersonal airline terminal.

This film strikes one as a change of pace for both Steven Spielberg and Tom Hanks. Had it been made forty years earlier, one could easily imagine Peter Sellers playing Viktor, the security chief, and the Indian janitor. The ending, however, is neither bleak (as in *Dr. Strangelove*) nor enigmatic (as in *Being There*). Viktor has come to America to complete his late father's collection of autographs from his favorite jazz artists. At the end of the film, Viktor's airport friends manage to get him out of the terminal—with the acquiescence of the security chief. Collecting his final autograph (from Benny Golson), he announces his intention to return home. If there is a message here, it would seem to be that the human spirit can finally triumph over even the most mindless bureaucracy. Keep that in mind the next time a security guard randomly strip-searches your eighty-year-old grandmother.

## THANK YOU FOR SMOKING

2005 (92 minutes) • Comedy
Room Nine Entertainment • R

Cast: Aaron Eckhart (Nick Naylor), Maria Bello (Polly Bailey), Cameron Bright (Joey Naylor), Adam Brody (Jack), Sam Elliott (Lorne Lutch), Katie Holmes (Heather Holloway), David Koechner (Bobby Jay Bliss), Rob Lowe (Jeff

Megall), William H. Macy (Sen. Ortolan K. Finistirre), J. K. Simmons (Budd "B. R." Rohrabacher), Robert Duvall (Doak "The Captain" Boykin)

Producer: Eveleen Bandy, David O. Sacks (Producers); Michael Beugg, Alessandro Camon, Max Levchin, Elon Musk, Edward R. Pressman, John Schmidt, Peter A. Thiel, Mark Woolway (Executive Producers); David Bloomfield (Co–Executive Producer); Stephen Belafonte (Assistant Producer); Director: Jason Reitman; Writer: Jason Reitman (from a novel by Christopher Buckley); Photographer: Jim Whitaker (color); Editor: Dana E. Glauberman

Andrew Sarris had it right when he said of *Thank You for Smoking*: "[W]hat makes the movie curiously timely is its emphasis on the process of spin as opposed to the moral content of what is being spun." In the twelve years it took to get Christopher Buckley's 1994 novel on the screen, the political wars over tobacco had been considerably defused by historic court rulings against the tobacco companies. However, influence-peddling scandals of a different kind (involving Rep. Duke Cunningham, Jack Abramoff, and others) continued to dominate the headlines. Those looking for a simple trashing of big tobacco—no matter how inviting the target—will have to settle for a more narrowly based satire. The principal character, Nick Naylor, is a facile and amoral spokesman for the Academy of Tobacco Studies, a transparent think tank sponsored by the tobacco industry. His two closest friends in Washington are lobbyists for the alcohol and gun interests. They call themselves the MOD (Merchants of Death) Squad and privately brag about the number of deaths for which they are responsible. Naylor is both a likeable fellow and a devoted single father; however, his hubris gets the best of him when he allows himself to be seduced by an equally amoral female reporter, who blows his cover.

The film is filled with memorable scenes. One that played frequently in television promos shows Nick giving his sales pitch to his son's grade school class on career day. As the film progresses, one suspects that one of its sources was Orwell's classic essay "Politics and the English Language." (The alcohol flack sits on the Moderation Council.) In a ploy that seemed outlandish when the novel was published in 1994 but prophetic today, Nick suggests that the tobacco industry sponsor a campaign against underage smoking. He surmises that this will produce good press while exerting reverse psychology on the young. If his campaign to bribe bankable stars into lighting up on screen seems unspeakably cynical, at least he is not as ham-fisted as the opposition, which replaces images of cigarettes with coffee and the like in historical images. Nick even argues that the righteous Vermont senator who leads the antitobacco forces is doing great harm to the nation's arteries by hocking his home state's cheddar cheese.

Because Buckley and director Jason Reitman poke fun at the puritanical excesses of the antismoking zealots, this film is far more than a heavy-handed indictment of corporate greed. In fact, the business and political interests finally seem engaged in a high-stakes contest in which each needs the other to exist. In the greatest of satires, however, at least an implied moral center can be discerned. If all of the characters depicted are scoundrels of one sort or another, there is no standard against which to judge them other than their own absurdity. Fortunately, that is more than enough to produce entertaining and enlightening cinema.

## THREE COLORS TRILOGY

Following the triumph of his series of films on the Ten Commandments, Krzysztof Kieslowski produced a trilogy of pictures based on the colors of the French flag. Although blue, white, and red are also the colors of several other national flags (including the British and American), they stand for particular ideals within the French scheme of things. Kieslowski, however, is less interested in making political—or at least ideological—points than in exploring the way in which these ideals are experienced by individual people in the existential crises of their lives. In discussing these films, Marek Haltof writes: "This is not so much a trilogy about liberty, equality, and fraternity but, as Tony Ryans has said, 'a trilogy about love in the 1990s.' Other critics describe it differently, for example a trilogy about fate or 'a trilogy preoccupied with themes of death, loss, and trauma.'" Kieslowski has candidly admitted that "if a different country had provided the finance—Germany, for instance—and I had made it as a German film, then yellow would have taken the place of blue and one would have had 'yellow, red, and black.'"

## BLUE

1993 (98 minutes) • Drama
CAB Productions • R

Cast: Juliette Binoche (Julie Vignon), Benoît Régent (Olivier), Florence Pernel (Sandrine), Charlotte Véry (Lucille), Hélène Vincent (Journalist), Emmanuelle Riva (Julie's Mother), Philippe Volter (Real Estate Agent), Claude Duneton (Doctor), Hugues Quester (Patrice), Jacek Ostaszewski (Flautist), Florence Vignon (Copyist), Yann Trégouët (Antoine), Zbigniew Zamachowski (Karol Karol), Julie Delpy (Dominique), Isabelle Sadoyan (Maid), Pierre Forget (Gardener)

Producer: Marin Karmitz; Director: Krzysztof Kieslowski; Writers: Krzysztof Kieslowski, Krzysztof Piesiewicz, Agnieszka Holland, Edward Zebrowski, Slawomir Idziak; Photographer: Slawomir Idziak (color); Editor: Jacques Witta

This film follows a woman who mistakenly seeks freedom by cutting herself off from her past. *Blue* opens with an automobile wreck that kills a famous French composer named Patrice and his small daughter. Patrice's wife Julie, who is the only survivor of the wreck, learns of these deaths while recovering in the hospital. When her attempt at suicide fails, she leaves the hospital and tries to begin a new life by selling or giving away her possessions. ("I don't want any belongings, any memories," she says. "No friends, no love. Those are all traps.") She even destroys Patrice's remaining compositions, including the unfinished "Concerto for the Unification of Europe." When she secretly moves to an apartment in another section of Paris, the only memento she allows herself is a blue chandelier that had previously belonged to her daughter. Before making this move, she invites her husband's collaborator, Olivier, to her mansion and makes love to him. She then dismisses him, saying: "I appreciate what you did for me. But you see, I'm like any other woman. I sweat, I cough, I have cavities. You won't miss me."

Alone in her new apartment, Julie sees a fight break out underneath her window but has neither the energy nor the concern to do anything about it. When she briefly steps out of the apartment, the door blows closed, and she is left to spend the night in the hallway, where she is forced to witness her neighbors' indiscretions. Julie unwittingly endears herself to one such neighbor, a stripper named Lucille, when she refuses to sign a petition to have the woman evicted. Later, Julie is accosted by a witness to her accident, who tries to return a necklace he found at the scene of the wreck. (Still trying to cut herself off from the past, she tells him he can keep it.) Not long thereafter, she visits her mother, who is effectively removed from reality—both past and present—by Alzheimer's disease or some other form of senility. On the television in the mother's room we see bungee jumpers enacting a physical simulation of freedom.

Olivier eventually finds Julie in her new abode and persuades her to help him finish Patrice's concerto, a copy of which he has saved. (There are unconfirmed rumors that Julie was the real author of her husband's works.) She then discovers that Patrice had kept a mistress. Consumed with curiosity, she tracks the woman down at her job in the law courts, only to discover that she is pregnant with Patrice's child. The past, which is not what Julie imagined it to be, places unsuspected obligations on the future. Realizing that freedom is to be found only by fully engaging oneself with the past rather than fleeing from it, she turns her mansion over to mother and child. It is significant that the text for the concerto she and Olivier are finishing is the thirteenth chapter of Paul's Epistle to the Corinthians, which begins: "Though I speak with the tongue of angels, if I have not love, I am become as hollow brass." This would also appear to be the text for Kieslowski's film and the basis of any true conception of freedom.

## WHITE

1994 (92 minutes) • Drama
CAB Productions • R

Cast: Zbigniew Zamachowski (Karol Karol), Julie Delpy (Dominique Vidal), Janusz Gajos (Mikolaj), Jerzy Stuhr (Jurek), Cezary Pazura (Businessman), Grzegorz Warchol (Businessman), Jerzy Nowak (Farmer), Aleksander Bardini (Lawyer), Jerzy Trela (Karol's Driver), Cezary Harasimowicz (Police Officer), Michel Lisowski (Interpreter), Marzena Trybala (Real Estate Agent), Teresa Budzisz-Krzyzanowska (Ms. Jadwiga)

Producer: Marin Karmitz; Director: Krzysztof Kieslowki; Writers: Krzysztof Kieslowski, Krzysztof Piesiewicz; Photographer: Edward Klosinski (color); Editor: Urszula Lesiak

White, the blandest of colors, stands for equality—the most problematic of the three French ideals. The protagonist of this film is a feckless Polish hairdresser named Karol. He is living in Paris, where he is married to a beautiful French woman named Dominique. Enraged by her husband's impotence, Dominique divorces Karol and leaves him penniless by canceling their credit cards and closing their bank accounts. Reduced to humming old Polish songs on a comb in the subway, Karol runs into a fellow Pole named Mikolaj, who offers him a chance to make some money and return to Poland. All he has to do is kill a man who no longer wants to live but lacks the nerve to do himself in. Agreeing to this proposition, Karol allows himself to be smuggled into Poland in his friend's trunk. Back in the motherland, the trunk is stolen by crooked baggage handlers, who give Karol a sound thrashing when they discover that he is practically penniless. Bruised and battered, he surveys the snow-covered garbage dump where his attackers have left him and sighs, "Home at last."

Although his brother wants him to return to their hairdressing salon, Karol has set his sights higher. He gets himself a job as a security guard for some shady speculators in Poland's new capitalist economy. Then he buys some farmland that he knows speculators wish to develop and sells it to them at a tidy profit. The man who could seemingly do nothing right in Paris soon becomes a big-time entrepreneur on his home turf. In turn, our pity for him turns into contempt. (Although not primarily known as a satirist, Kieslowski exposes the seamier side of Poland's new economy. Joseph G. Kickasola is probably on target when he argues that "Kieslowski was not really so much a Marxist as he was a smiling version of Aleksandr Solzhenitsyn [on this issue]:

critical of totalitarianism, but pessimistic about the negative effects of materialism inherent in contemporary capitalism.") To his credit, however, Karol doesn't stoop to murder. When he discovers that it is his friend Mikolaj who wishes to die, he shoots him with a blank bullet. Coming that close to death is enough to shock Mikolaj back to his senses and to life.

Intent on getting even with the woman who scorned him, Karol revises his will to make her his heir and then fakes his own death. (An unidentifiable corpse is laid in his grave.) When he spies Dominique weeping at his funeral, Karol is emboldened to show up at her hotel room afterward. On Polish soil and riding high, he is finally able to overcome his erectile dysfunction and satisfy his ex-wife. Not content with this minor triumph, however, Karol has arranged things to make it look as if Dominique murdered him for his money. When she is imprisoned for this "crime," he has finally achieved the hollow equality that comes with revenge. At the end of the film, he looks at her in prison, and she returns his gaze. There is every suggestion that she loves and respects him for this show of brutal strength and will reunite with him when she gets out of the slammer. Without endorsing this sadomasochistic view of human sexuality, Kieslowski leaves us believing that these are two people who truly deserve each other.

## RED

1994 (99 minutes) • Drama
CAB Productions • R

Cast: Iréne Jacob (Valentine), Jean-Louis Trintignant (Judge Joseph Kern), Jean-Pierre Lorit (Auguste), Frédérique Feder (Karin), Samuel L. Bihan (Photographer), Marion Stalens (Vetinary Surgeon), Teco Celio (Barman), Bernard Escalon (Record Dealer), Jean Schlegel (Neighbor), Zbigniew Zamachowski (Karol Karol), Julie Delpy (Dominique), Juliette Binoche (Julie)

Producer: Martin Karmitz; Director: Krzysztof Kieslowski; Writers: Krzysztof Kieslowski, Krzysztof Piesiewicz; Photographer: Piotr Sobocinski (color); Editor: Jacques Witta

A good deal of nonsense has been written about the concept of fraternity, which is symbolized by the color red. Kieslowski, however, realizes that our common humanity is defined as much by what separates us as by what draws us together. (Remember, the first two brothers were Cain and Abel.) The protagonist of the concluding film in the trilogy is Valentine, a model who lives and works in Geneva. Throughout much of the story, she is on the telephone with her jealous boyfriend in England or her heroin-addicted brother back home. One night, she accidentally hits, and slightly injures, a dog with her car. When she tracks down the dog's owner, she discovers a reclusive retired judge who entertains himself by illegally listening in on his neighbors' phone conversations. Simply by being there, Valentine is forced to learn the secrets of total strangers—including a man who is cheating on his family with a homosexual lover and an old woman who manufactures domestic and medical emergencies in order to garner the attention of her adult daughter. At the same time, we follow the activities of Auguste, a law student who lives in the same neighborhood as Valentine.

Because the judge is not particularly interested in getting his dog back, he and Valentine evolve a shared custody of the animal and the puppies she is almost ready to deliver. Despite the judge's irascibility, he and the model develop a kind of father-daughter bond, as he shows considerable insight into her troubles. (He correctly infers that her brother's difficulties stem from his discovery that he has been fathered by someone other than his mother's husband.) For her part, Valentine's influence on the judge prompts him to turn himself in to the law. Meanwhile, Auguste's life seems to follow a pattern set by the judge in his youth decades earlier. Like the judge, Auguste drops a book only to have it miraculously open to a page covered on his exam the next day. And, like the judge, he discovers that his blonde girlfriend (in the judge's case, his wife) has been unfaithful to him. We wonder whether Auguste is the judge's döppelganger or whether the world of this movie is simply filled with more coincidences than a Thomas Hardy novel.

When Valentine calls the private weather service run by Auguste's girlfriend (yet another anonymous telephonic connection), she is assured that the water will be calm on the English Channel. As a result, she decides to travel by ferry to England to visit her boyfriend. (Auguste's inamorata will make the same trip in a yacht with her other lover.) But, as we learned in *Decalogue One*, even the best of scientific predictions can turn out wrong. A severe storm on the channel kills the weather girl and the man she is sleeping with. It also wrecks the ferry boat, killing all but seven of 1,435 passengers. The suvivors are the boat's barman, Julie and Olivier from *Blue*, Karol and Dominique from *White*, and Valentine and Auguste from this film. With the exception of Valentine, we are not certain why these familiar faces are on the boat at this particular time, much less why they are spared. But perhaps the very uncertainty is the point. What binds us together is the same thing that drives us apart—the sheer contingency of the world.

## THE TRIP TO BOUNTIFUL

1985 (108 minutes) • Comedy/Drama
Bountiful Film Pictures • PG

Cast: Geraldine Page (Carrie Watts), John Heard (Ludie Watts), Carlin Glynn (Jessie Mae), Richard Bradford (Sheriff), Rebecca De Mornay (Thelma), Kevin Cooney (Roy)

Producers: Horton Foote, Sterling Van Wagenen (Producers), Sam Grogg, George Yaneff (Executive Producers), Dennis Bishop (Line Producer); Director: Peter Masterson; Writer: Horton Foote; Photographer: Fred Murphy (color); Editor: Jay Freund

Horton Foote's play *The Trip to Bountiful* began in 1953 as a live drama during the golden age of television. Thirty-two years later, it was made into a motion picture for which Geraldine Page won a well-deserved Academy Award for best actress. Set in 1947, the story involves a henpecked man, Ludie Watts; his shrewish wife, Jessie Mae; and his mother, Carrie. Living together in a small apartment, the three get on each other's nerves. Jessie Mae cannot stand Carrie's incessant hymn singing and moody silences. Ludie is frustrated by a lack of money and the absence of children in the family. Carrie's main desire is to make a final trip to her rural hometown of Bountiful before she dies. Thinking such a journey unwise, Ludie and Jessie Mae always manage to foil the old lady's efforts before she is able to get very far. But one morning she manages to elude them. Although there is no longer a bus to Bountiful, Carrie purchases a ticket to a town twelve miles away.

Carrie remembers Bountiful as it was when she was young, not as the ghost town it has become. Despite a heart condition, she believes that all will be well if she can return to this lost paradise and work the land with her own hands. During the course of an all-night bus ride, she makes friends with a sweet young woman who is the very antithesis of her daughter-in-law. The ride affords her the opportunity to reveal details of her earlier life, when she secretly loved a man her father disapproved of, married a husband she admired but did not love, and buried all but one child. When she arrives at the nearest stop to Bountiful, she learns that the last resident of her old hometown (and the woman she planned to stay with) has died the previous day. Rather than dissuade her, this news seems only to strengthen Carrie's resolve. When Ludie and Jessie Mae ascertain her whereabouts, she manages to persuade the local sheriff to take her the twelve miles out to her old home place.

Although everything is smaller and more run-down than she remembers, Carrie nevertheless acts as if she has reentered Eden. When Ludie finally overtakes her, he is forced to recall some events from childhood and to confront the emptiness of his life. Carrie is so pacified by having been able to make the trip she had planned for twenty years that she willingly returns to her son and daughter-in-law's apartment in Houston. Even the vain and irascible Jessie Mae seems a bit more tolerable at the end. If the film forces us to sympathize with Carrie, it is because her religious and agrarian values seem more serious and permanent than Jessie Mae's life of drinking drugstore Cokes, attending movies, and playing bridge. (Ludie is so subservient to his wife that he seems not to have any interests or principles of his own until the end of the picture.) Even if Bountiful is badly misnamed, it is the lost home that all of us seek to reclaim.

## THE VIRGIN SPRING

1960 (88 minutes) • Religious Drama
Svensk Filmindustri • Unrated

Cast: Max von Sydow (Töre), Birgitta Valberg (Märeta), Birgitta Pettersson (Karin), Gunnel Lindblom (Ingeri), Axel Düberg (Herdsman), Tor Isedal (His Mute Brother), Ove Porath (His Small Brother), Allan Edwall (Beggar

Monk), Axel Slangus (Bridge Keeper), Gudrun Brost ( Frida), Oscar Ljung (Simon)

Producers: Ingmar Bergman, Allan Ekelund; Director: Ingmar Bergman; Writer: Ulla Isaksson; Photographer: Sven Nykvist (black and white); Editor: Oscar Rosander

As the lapsed son of a Lutheran clergyman, the acclaimed Swedish director Ingmar Bergman never shied away from challenging religious and ethical themes. Filmed in stark black and white, *The Virgin Spring* is a drama of revenge and redemption set in medieval Scandinavia. The story, as fleshed out by screenwriter Ulla Isaksson, is based on a folk song that tells the story of a haughty young virgin named Karin, who is sent to deliver candles to church on Good Friday. The other girl in the family, a foundling named Ingeri, is disqualified for this task by her obvious pregnancy. The film opens with Ingeri kindling a fire in the kitchen hearth while summoning the pagan god Odin three times. (Even though the country is officially Catholic, the old deities still exert a hold on the popular imagination.) The pious wife of the family, Lady Märeta, displays an un-Christian contempt for her adopted daughter, even as she shamelessly spoils Karin. Not surprisingly, the foundling detests her foster sister.

Decked out in her best clothes, Karin is on her way to the church, accompanied by Ingeri, who seems simply to be along for the ride. When the sisters are briefly separated, the foundling stops at the cottage of an old pagan hunchback while Karin rides deeper into the forest. There she runs into three herdsmen who interrogate her in the manner of the wicked wolf in "Little Red Riding Hood." When the girl inadvertently reveals that she knows that the herdsmen are rustlers, they turn violent—raping, robbing, and killing her. (By this time, Ingeri has caught up with her sister but makes no effort to rescue her.) Later that night, the herdsmen arrive at the home of Karin's father, Sir Töre, where they seek shelter from a storm.

Although Töre and Märeta are concerned about Karin's failure to return home, they do not suspect foul play until one of the herdsmen tries to sell Karin's dress to Märeta, claiming that it belonged to his sister. An enraged Töre kills the three herdsmen. By the time Ingeri leads them to Karin's body and confesses her own complicity in what happened, Töre is stricken with remorse and begs God's mercy for his act of vengeance. As if in answer, the Lord causes a spring of pure water to pour forth from the earth where Karin's body had lain. In an apparent allusion to baptism, Ingeri drinks from the spring.

In order to appreciate the message of this tale, we must not only sympathize with Töre but also realize that he was legally within his rights to take revenge over the wrong done to his family. (Although the issue is never explicitly raised in the film or even implied in the original folk song, the modern viewer might speculate about the extent to which Karin's parents have inadvertently contributed to her fate by the way in which they helped to shape her character.) But in the Christian faith, the demands of mercy trump those of justice. In commenting on the transcendent ending of this film, George Garrett writes: "*The Virgin Spring*, while it speaks darkly to our lives and to these times when terrible crimes are commonplace, when murder and rape and the loss of innocence are routine and scarcely more than statistics, while it speaks to us directly, is also the remarkable story of a good man—a severe and strict man, true, but also a righteous and compassionate one, who overcomes his own just nature in recognizing and repenting his ethical conduct."

## VIVA ZAPATA

1952 (113 minutes) • Historical Drama
Twentieth Century-Fox • Unrated

Cast: Marlon Brando (Emiliano Zapata), Anthony Quinn (Eufemio), Jean Peters (Josefa), Joseph Wiseman (Fernando), Arnold Moss (Don Nacio), Alan Reed (Pancho Villa), Margo (Soldadera), Lou Gilbert (Pablo), Harold Gordon (Madero), Mildred Dunnock (Señora Espejo)

Producer: Darryl F. Zanuck; Director: Elia Kazan; Writer: John Steinbeck; Photographer: Joe MacDonald (black and white); Editor: Barbara McLean

This film can best be described as historical fiction. It plays fast and loose with real events in order to make a larger point. For that reason, it was equally disliked by ardent supporters and avid foes of the Mexican revolutionary Emiliano Zapata. Most other viewers were able to appreciate the picture as a parable about the ambiguities of political power. Made a year after *A Streetcar Named Desire*, *Viva Zapata* was the second film collaboration between Elia Kazan and Marlon Brando. Although the movie received five Academy Award nominations, the only winner was Anthony Quinn for best supporting actor. The story follows peasant Emiliano Zapata, who leads a group of dissident farmers in an appeal to the Mexican dictator Diaz. When Diaz waffles about restoring peasant lands that have been seized by large property owners, Zapata and his followers take the law into their own hands. The film presents Zapata as an agrarian reformer with limited ambition who is thrust into power by the forces of history.

While he is pursuing justice for the small farmers, Zapata also seeks the hand of a middle-class woman named Josefa Espejo. Her father opposes the match on economic and social grounds until Emiliano becomes a prominent general in Madero's revolutionary army. As he gains wealth and power, Zapata is forced to make decisions that challenge his youthful idealism. At one point, he has a young comrade executed for consorting with the enemy. (A bit later, Zapata's hedonistic brother is murdered by the husbands of women he has seduced.) It seems that the more he tries to renounce power, the more fervent his supporters become in their loyalty toward him. This very loyalty finally makes Zapata an unacceptable threat to less scrupulous figures seeking control of the revolution. In desperate need of ammunition, he meets with the treacherous Guajardo, who gives the signal for Zapata to be gunned down in the town plaza. Refusing to believe that he is dead, many of Zapata's followers claim that his spirit is still alive. As the film ends, we see his white horse grazing peacefully on a mountain peak.

By the time they made *Viva Zapata*, both director Elia Kazan and writer John Steinbeck had become disillusioned with the revolutionary Left. Although they both considered themselves social democrats, they were wary of the way in which the Communist Party and other radical groups manipulated naïve progressives for their own sinister motives. Rather than rendering a historically accurate depiction of Zapata as a brutal revolutionary and notorious lecher, Steinbeck and Kazan made him into a Mexican equivalent of the liberal naïf seeking a better world. The fact that he is gunned down obviously represents a personal defeat. But what is most important is the fact that his memory lives on in the hearts of the people. (Toward the end of the film, when his wife is urging him not to walk into what she senses is a trap, Zapata observes: "A strong man makes a weak people. Strong people don't need a strong man.")

Like Tom Joad at the end of the film version of *The Grapes of Wrath*, his spirit is everywhere.

## WAG THE DOG

1997 (105 minutes) • Comedy
Tribeca Productions/Punch Productions • R

Cast: Dustin Hoffman (Stanley Motss), Robert De Niro (Conrad Brean), Anne Heche (Winifred Ames), Denis Leary (Fad King), Willie Nelson (Johnny Dean), Andrea Martin (Liz Butsky), Kirsten Dunst (Tracy Lime), William H. Macy (Mr. Young), Craig T. Nelson (Senator Neal), Suzie Plakson (Grace)

Producers: Jane Rosenthal, Robert De Niro, Barry Levinson; Director: Barry Levinson; Writers: Hilary Henkin, David Mamet (based on the novel *American Hero* by Larry Beinhart); Photographer: Robert Richardson (color); Editor: Stu Linder

*Wag the Dog* is based on what might seem to be a pedestrian comedic premise—that the Washington spin doctor and the Hollywood producer aren't all that different. Viewed a decade after its release, however, this film seems to be one of the most prophetic cinematic satires ever produced. When compared to the histrionics of *Dr. Strangelove*, *Wag the Dog* has an eerie documentary quality. The story is set into motion when the president makes sexual advances to an underage girl (identified only as a "Firefly") during a White House tour. Because it is a mere two weeks prior to the election, a presidential aide hopes that the public can be distracted from the scandal until the chief executive is reelected. At this point, veteran political operative Conrad Brean is put in charge of damage control, and he quickly summons the assistance of Hollywood producer Stanley Motss. These two scoundrels create a simulated war, composed entirely of fraudulent film clips and a public-relations blitz, designed to divert the attention of the American people from the real misbehavior in the White House. The repartee between Brean (Robert De Niro) and Motss (Dustin Hoffman), speaking lines written by Hilary Henkin and David Mamet, reminds one of Preston Sturges at his best.

This film both benefited and suffered from hitting the movie theaters at about the same time the Clinton-Lewinsky scandal broke. Whether or not the bombing raids that Clinton ordered during that time of peril were meant to distract attention from his personal embarrassment is beside the point. Politicians by their very nature try to spin public opinion to their advantage. Will Rogers once said that all he knew was what he read in the newspapers. Tens of millions of contemporary Americans can say that all they know is what they see on cable TV. The Gulf War of 1991 was our first cable war. Although it is hard to believe that an American president would wage a fake war on the screen (or that he could get away with doing so), there is a poetic truth in depicting such a scenario. Because politicians live from one election to the next, no one appears to be concerned with what will happen after the votes are counted.

*Wag the Dog* would seem as badly dated as a rerun of a ten-year-old episode of *Saturday Night Live* if it were no more than a shrewd guess about Bill Clinton's libido—which was itself a scandal waiting to happen. When viewed in light of the second war against Iraq, however, this film walks the uncertain line between fantasy and realism. No matter how sincere its motives may have been, the Bush administration has tried every conceivable sales pitch to make a failed military venture seem both necessary and successful. If the current White House image-makers are not as devious as Brean and Motss, neither are they as ingenious. Had this film been made as an explicit satire of the fiasco in Iraq it almost certainly would have been a heavy-handed partisan diatribe. As it is, it is a deft caricature of bipartisan reality.

## WALKING TALL

1973 (125 minutes) • Action Drama
Bing Crosby Productions • R

Cast: Joe Don Baker (Buford Pusser), Elizabeth Hartman (Pauline Pusser), Gene Evans (Sheriff Al Thurman), Noah Beery Jr. (Grandpa Carl Pusser), Brenda Benet (Luan Paxton), John Brascia (Prentiss Parley), Bruce Glover (Grady

Coker), Arch Johnson (Buel Jaggers), Felton Perry (Obra Eaker), Richard X. Slattery (Arno Purdy), Rosemary Murphy (Callie Hacker), Lynn Borden (Margie Ann), Ed Call (Lutie McVey), Sidney Clute (Sheldon Levine), Douglas Fowley (Judge R. W. Clarke)

Producers: Mort Briskin (Producer), Charles A. Pratt (Executive Producer), Joel Briskin (Assistant Producer); Director: Phil Karlson; Writers: Mort Briskin, Steve Downing; Photographer: Jack A. Marta (color); Editor: Harry W. Gerstad

*Walking Tall* became a surprise hit shortly after its release in 1973. The 1960s had seen an explosion in urban crime, which made movies such as Don Siegel's *Dirty Harry* (1971) cult favorites. Law-abiding people fearing anarchy were looking for strong men who could put the bad guys in their place. This had long been the theme of countless Western movies. By the late '60s and early '70s, it seemed as if the Wild West had become a reality in the streets of our major cities. *Walking Tall* simply shifts the scene to a small town in Tennessee. It is a redneck *Dirty Harry*, based on a true story originally documented on *60 Minutes*. Ads run on the entertainment pages of newspapers around the country said: "When was the last time you stood up and cheered at a movie?"

The hero of the film is Buford Pusser, who decides to retire from a professional wrestling career to settle on a farm back where he grew up. Unfortunately, in his absence the county has been taken over by illegal gambling and prostitution. Because the local sheriff and judge are both on the take, the bad guys are in charge. Buford discovers this the hard way when he and an old high school football buddy stop by one of the gambling dens. When Buford objects to being cheated by the house, he is severely beaten, carved up like a turkey, and left for dead. On top of everything else, his station wagon disappears. When the corrupt sheriff claims that he can do nothing about the incident, Buford takes a big wooden club—and the law—into his own hands. He busts up the gambling establishment, gives several of the malefactors a deserved thrashing, and collects compensation for his winnings, medical bills, and station wagon. Not surprisingly, the sheriff arrests Buford. After winning a jury trial, Buford successfully challenges the sheriff in the next election, only to find that his troubles have just begun.

His first case involves the deaths of eight black men from a batch of moonshine. With the help of his black deputy, Buford puts the moonshiner (also black) out of business. (In his use of the vernacular, back when such things were allowed, Buford breaks down his deputy's initial reluctance to give him needed information by reminding him that the previous sheriff wouldn't have cared about "eight dead niggers.") The clashes between Buford and the forces of evil escalate throughout this action-packed movie until Buford's wife is gunned down in a crossfire. After burying her, he crashes his police car into the gambling den. He is now followed by the townspeople, who drag the furnishings out of the place and demolish them. This is probably one of the scenes that brought approving members of the audience to their feet. Buford Pusser serves as a surrogate for every ordinary person who has dreamed of standing up against injustice. It may not have been what Aristotle had in mind, but this film elicits a definite *katharsis*.

## WE THE LIVING

1942 (174 minutes) • Drama
Scalera (Italy) • Unrated

Cast: Alida Valli (Kira Argounova), Rossano Brazzi (Leo Kovalenski), Fosco Giachetti (Andrei Taganov); Giovanni Grasso (Tishenko), Emilio Cigoli (Pavel Sjerov), Cesarina Gherardi (Comrade Sonja), Mario Pisu (Viktor Dunaev), Guglielmo Sinaz (Morozov), Gero Zambuto (Alexij Argounov), Annibale Betrone (Vassili Dunaev)

Producers: Franco Magli (Production Manager), Giorgio Abkhasi, Andrea Belobodoroff (Production Design); Director: Gofreddo Alessandrini; Writer: Anton Guilio Majano (based on the novel by Ayn Rand); Photographer: Giuseppe Caracciolo (black and white); Editor: Eraldo Da Roma

The woman who was known as "Ayn Rand" was one of the most controversial political thinkers to write during the middle years of the twentieth century. She began her career attacking collectivism in the 1930s, a time when many literary intellectuals were sympathetic to the lure of socialism, and achieved her first great success in 1943 with her best-selling novel *The Fountainhead*. Born Alisa Zinovyevna Rosenbaum in 1905, Rand fled her native Russia for the United States after the Communist Revolution and, by 1927, had headed for Hollywood. A chance encounter with Cecil B. DeMille led to a part as an extra in his classic film *King of Kings* (1927). She later became a script reader and eventually worked her way up to head of the costume department at RKO Studios. Despite her ties with the American film industry and the fact that Warner Brothers made a popular movie version of *The Fountainhead* in 1949, the best film based on her work was an unauthorized adaptation of her novel *We the Living* (1936), which was produced in Italy and released in 1942—ostensibly as Fascist propaganda.

*We the Living* concerns a classic love triangle set in Russia during the 1920s. An independent woman named Kira tries to pursue a degree in engineering in the stultifying atmosphere created by the new Bolshevik regime, even as she falls madly in love with a mysterious Byronic hero named Leo Kovalenski. Meanwhile, an idealistic young Communist official named Andrei Taganov is smitten with Kira. Initially, Kira becomes Andrei's mistress as a means of secretly paying for Leo's treatment in a tuberculosis sanitarium. To complicate matters, Leo becomes corrupt and dissolute while Andrei finds himself increasingly disillusioned with the party. After he discovers that he has been deceived, Andrei nobly sacrifices himself for Kira and her lover. At the end of the film, Kira prepares to leave both Russia and the morally compromised Leo.

Although Mussolini's government initially endorsed this film under the impression that it would be crude anti-Soviet propaganda, Alessandrini's finished product turned out to be a more sweeping attack on totalitarianism in general and, for that reason, precipitated a running battle with the Italian censors. Because of the pirated nature of the movie, Rand herself originally opposed its distribution. When she finally saw and approved the picture, however, she sought intermittently to have it edited and rereleased. This project was initiated but never completed prior to Rand's death in 1982. Finally, in 1988 a nearly three-hour version of *We the Living* (cut from a two-film sequence running approximately four hours) was released with subtitles. The mixed reviews of the picture tend to reflect the ideological views of the critics involved. The film seemed to many to be an over-the-top melodrama from another era (an objection almost never raised against *Casablanca* [1942], in which the enemy was simply and unequivocally Nazism). Still others believed that any opposition to Soviet tyranny was simply an example of the dreaded "Red Scare." Mike McGrady of *Newsday* was probably closer to the mark when he wrote: "Though the setting is vital the film is neither about Russia or communism; it is about any human being whose freedoms have been curtailed by the state."

## WE WERE SOLDIERS

2002 (138 minutes) • Action
Icon • R

Cast: Mel Gibson (Hal Moore), Madeleine Stowe (Julie Moore), Greg Kinnear (Major Bruce Crandall), Sam Elliott (Sgt. Major Basil Plumley), Chris Klein (Lt. Jack Geoghegan), Keri Russell (Barbara Geoghegan), Barry Pepper (Joe Galloway), Duong Don (Lt. Col. Nguyen Huu An), Josh Dougherty (Spec 4 Bob Ouellette), Edwin Morrow (Private Willie Godboldt)

Producers: Bruce Davey, Stephen McEveety, Randall Wallace; Director: Randall Wallace; Writer: Randall Wallace (based on the book *We Were Soldiers Once . . . and Young*, by Joe Galloway and Lt. General Harold Moore); Photographer: Dean Semler (color); Editor: William Hoy

As we saw in chapter 10 with regard to Michael Cimino's *The Deer Hunter*, cinematic depictions of the Vietnam War can be as diverse and conflicted as public attitudes toward the war itself. At least in part because of the left-wing bias of Hollywood, Peter Davis won an Academy Award in 1974 for his technically brilliant but blatantly procommunist documentary *Hearts and Minds*. At the other end of the spectrum (both aesthetically and ideologically), we have John Wayne's *Green Berets* (1968). Between these two extremes, there is considerable room for a balanced and accurate portrayal of America's tragic involvement in Southeast Asia. If neoconservatives are still screaming that we were sold out by the New Left, the paleoconservative position would seem to be that liberal hubris doomed the United States to failure in attempting to wage a limited ground war on terrain that the French had found untenable. With a few notable exceptions, our fighting men did their best in a hopeless situation.

Cinematic depictions of violence have become ever more graphic since Griffith's *The Birth of a Nation* in 1915. If the isolated Russian roulette sequences in *The Deer Hunter* created a metaphorical equivalent for the carnage in Vietnam, Oliver Stone drew upon his experiences in that conflict to render a far more literal portrayal of the same carnage in *Platoon* (1986). In *We Were Soldiers*, Randall Wallace follows suit in dramatizing part of a battle in November 1965 that was the first full-scale engagement between American and North Vietnamese troops. The compilers of *TV Guide's 2004 Film and Video Companion* compare the intensity of this footage to that of "most of *Black Hawk Down* and the first 20 minutes of *Saving Private Ryan*."

The one thing that Wallace does not provide is an ideological context that will give meaning to this gripping violence. When we are away from the battlefield, we are taken into the home lives of the soldiers who are called into service. The story is based on the book *We Were Soldiers Once . . . and Young* (1992) by Joe Galloway and Lieutenant General Harold Moore. In his portrayal of Moore, Mel Gibson comes off as a kind of American Braveheart—a devoutly religious family man who is also dedicated to his country. The Catholic piety evident in *Braveheart* and ubiquitous in *The Passion of the Christ* forms an important part of the background of *We Were Soldiers*. In one scene in a military chapel, Moore comes upon a young soldier he finds in prayer. Moore is finally unable to help the young man resolve the contradiction between worshiping a god of compassion and being a professional killer because it is clear that Moore has not yet resolved it for himself.

The one figure in the film who is a true angel of mercy is Moore's wife, who volunteers to inform the other wives in the neighborhood that their husbands have been killed. One is reminded of the dual lives of the astronauts and their wives in *The Right Stuff*. The point in both films is that the high incidence of violent death is an occupational hazard of military service. It takes not only a special kind of man but also a special kind of woman to live such a life.

## THE WILD RIVER

1960 (105 minutes) • Drama
Twentieth Century-Fox • Unrated

Cast: Montgomery Clift (Chuck Glover), Lee Remick (Carol Garth Baldwin), Jo Van Fleet (Ella Garth), Albert Salmi (Hank Bailey), Jay C. Flippen (Hamilton Garth), James Westerfield (Cal Garth), Barbara Loden (Betty Jackson), Frank Overton (Walter Clark), Malcolm Atterbury (Sy Moore), Big Jeff Bess (Joe John Garth), Bruce Dern (Jack Roper)

Producer: Elia Kazan; Director: Elia Kazan; Writer: Paul Osborn (based on novels by Borden Deal and William Bradford Huie); Photographer: Ellsworth Fredericks (Deluxe color); Editor: William Reynolds

The Tennessee Valley Authority, one of the major reform programs of the New Deal, was widely popular for bringing inexpensive electricity to the rural population of several Southeastern states. Less well known was the fact that families had to be displaced from their ancestral lands to make way for the dams that harnessed the power of the river. In his book on the Tennessee River, the Agrarian poet and essayist Donald Davidson wrote:

> Heath fires would be extinguished that were as old as the Republic itself. Old landmarks would vanish; old graveyards would be obliterated; the ancient mounds of the Indians, which had resisted both the plow of the farmer and the pick of the curiosity seeker, would go under the water. There would be tears and gnashing of teeth, and lawsuits. There might even be feud and bloodshed. Yet these harms inflicted upon a sizable and innocent minority, weighed less in the TVA scales than the benefits that would accrue, in terms of industrial and social engineering, to the nearby or distant majority who sacrificed only tax money.

*The Wild River* portrays the sort of indigenous controversies Davidson describes. As a political liberal, Kazan recognized the social and economic benefits of government programs such as the TVA. That point of view is epitomized in the film by the idealistic bureaucrat Chuck Glover. But Glover's perspective is more than balanced by the fierce rootedness of eighty-year-old Ella Garth, whose family and black retainers have lived on their land for generations. Although there is little doubt that the power and vision of the government will ultimately prevail, Ella's position is presented so sympathetically that the audience is tempted to side with her. Much of the reason for this is Jo Van Fleet's unforgettable portrayal of Ella Garth.

In an apparent attempt to make the film more appealing to younger audiences, Kazan has created a romance between Glover and Mrs. Garth's widowed daughter Carol. What might otherwise have been nothing more than adventitious Hollywood schlock is redeemed by Lee Remick's compelling performance as Carol. If Chuck represents liberal progress and Ella conservative continuity, Carol is caught between these two worldviews. Although she finally sides with Chuck, we sense what has been lost in the process. It is altogether fitting that Ella dies shortly after she is removed from her land.

The mindless worship of technology that sometimes passes for conservatism in the modern era would object to the TVA only because it is a *government* program. As an artist, Kazan is able to appreciate a more fundamental conservative sensibility—one that recognizes the cost of progress. At the same time, he does not romanticize the rural folk. The petty cruelty and racism of some of these people are presented as lamentable facts of life. For a film that deals with profound moral issues, *The Wild River* is remarkably free of tendentious moralizing. One cannot help thinking that the ambiguities of his own political struggles enabled Kazan to see the shades of gray in other contentious areas of American life.

## WITNESS

1985 (112 minutes) • Drama
Paramount • R

Cast: Harrison Ford (John Book), Kelly McGillis (Rachel Lapp), Josef Sommer (Paul Schaeffer), Lukas Haas (Samuel Lapp), Jan Rubes (Eli Lapp), Alexander Godunov (Daniel Hochleitner), Danny Glover (James McFee), Brent Jennings (Elden Carter), Patti LuPone (Elaine), Angus MacInnes (Fergie), Frederick Rolf (Stoltzfus), Viggo Mortensen (Moses Hochleitner), John Garson (Bishop Tchantz), Beverly May (Mrs. Yoder), Ed Crowley (Sheriff)

Producers: Edward S. Feldman (Producer), David Bombyk (Coproducer), Wendy Stites (Associate Producer); Director: Peter Weir; Writers: William Kelley, Pamela Wallace; Photographer: John Seale (color); Editor: (Thom Noble)

In this his first American movie, the gifted Australian director Peter Weir chose a most unusual story to tell. On the surface, this is a murder mystery involving corruption in the Philadelphia police department. The tale takes an unexpected turn, however, when the only witness to the murder is an Amish boy. The lad, Samuel, and his mother, Rachel, are delayed in the train station on their way to Baltimore, where she is to help her sister with her new baby. (Rachel's husband was buried in the opening scene of the film.) After two men kill a third in the restroom of the train station, police detective John Book arrives and takes the lone material witness and his mother into protective custody. At first the boy fails to identify any of the suspects in the police lineup. He then recognizes one of the culprits in a police picture at the station. Book is soon involved in a shootout with the corrupt cops and manages to drive himself, Samuel, and Rachel back to Amish country before collapsing from his wounds. At that point, the murder plot fades temporarily into the background, as *Witness* becomes an affecting love story about two people from very different backgrounds.

Most ordinary Americans know the Amish (if at all) as an insular people who farm the land, travel by horse-and-buggy, and deliberately live an archaic style of life based on strange religious beliefs. This film takes us inside an Amish community. Trapped there by his wounds and his flight from his adversaries, Book is considered a dangerous stranger. He packs a gun in a community noted for its pacifism. He also represents a sensual urban culture in a Spartan agricultural society. Nevertheless, he and Rachel grow steadily attracted to each other—first when they are dancing to a song on his car radio (Sam Cooke's "Wonderful World") and later when he sees her taking an erotic sponge bath. When they finally kiss, the passion seems natural, even anticlimactic. But the idyll is too good to last. After Book survives a successful shootout with the bad guys, who track him down to his hideout, he returns to his world and leaves Rachel and Samuel in theirs.

Films dealing with Amish culture are a rare commodity in Hollywood. (The only other one I can think of is *Kingpin* [1996], which features Randy Quaid as a buffoonish Amish bowling prodigy.) Because the Amish are a small community who do not attend movies, the appeal of the film must lie with non-Amish audiences curious about these quaint people. Unlike so many indigenous Hollywood filmmakers, the Australian Weir treats unconventional religious beliefs and strange social practices with the respect they deserve. Not only do the Amish come out superior to the murdering drug pushers in the Philadelphia P.D., they also seem to live a more attractive life than Book's sexually active sister. In fact, had he not been so set in his ways, one suspects that Book himself might have preferred to remain with his newfound friends and the woman he loves. Many conservatives talk a good game in their critiques of modernity. The Amish walk the walk.

## THE YEAR OF LIVING DANGEROUSLY

1982 (115 minutes) • Drama
MGM • PG

Cast: Mel Gibson (Guy Hamilton), Sigourney Weaver (Jill Bryant), Linda Hunt (Billy Kwan), Michael Murphy (Pete Curtis); Bembol Roco (Kumar); Domingo Landicho (Hortono), Noel Ferrier (Wally O'Sullivan), Paul Sonkkila (Kevin Condon)

Producer: James McElroy; Director: Peter Weir; Writers: David Williamson, Peter Weir, C. J. Koch (based on the novel by Koch); Photographer: Russell Boyd (Panivision, Metrocolor); Editor: Bill Anderson

*The Year of Living Dangerously* was a historic film for the Australian cinema. By the late seventies, such filmmakers as Gillian Armstrong, Bruce Beresford, Philip Noyce, and Fred Schepisi were earning international critical acclaim. Contributing to this talk of a new wave of Australian directors were three pictures by Peter Weir—*Picnic at Hanging Rock* (1975), *The Last Wave* (1977), and *Gallipoli* (1981). Then, in 1982, MGM made *The Year of Living Dangerously* the first Australian film to be fully financed and distributed by a major Hollywood studio. (Weir has worked in the United States ever since.) It was also an early vehicle for the Australian-American actor Mel Gibson, who made his first *Lethal Weapon* movie the following year.

Set in Indonesia in 1965, this film provides an unsentimental perspective on postcolonial politics. Fresh from Vietnam, the Australian journalist Guy Hamilton is assigned to another Asian trouble spot. The charismatic but corrupt dictator Sukarno is trying to hold off challenges from both Communist and right-wing Muslim forces, even as the masses in his country are mired in extreme poverty. Although hardly a starry-eyed idealist, Hamilton is less jaded than the other Western journalists on the scene.

His physical and moral guide to the country is a Chinese-Australian cameraman named Billy Kwan. Billy has the uncanny knack to insinuate himself into rival camps. (Early in the film, he arranges for Hamilton to get a rare interview with the leader of the Communist guerillas.) Although he initially admires Sukarno's political dexterity, Billy is appalled by the squalor of the ordinary people. One of his constant refrains is a line from the Gospel of Luke frequently used by Tolstoy: "What then must we do?" Billy's own response is to provide for a destitute woman and her child. When the child nevertheless dies of malnutrition, an embittered Billy hangs a sign outside his window saying, "Sukarno, *feed* your people." Not surprisingly, Sukarno's agents toss him from the window, leading to a death that is as much suicide as murder.

This film has been criticized for its lack of a clear political focus. But Peter Weir's refusal to provide ideological solutions to the political and economic turmoil of the Third World is refreshing. No lasting good can come from the extremes of the Left or the Right and certainly not from demagogues such as Sukarno. Moreover, the sheer immensity of the problem makes individual acts of charity woefully inadequate. For all of his admirable qualities, Billy is himself an ambiguous character who keeps copious files on his acquaintances and seems obsessed with controlling the lives of others. His major undertaking in this regard is a romance that he engineers between Hamilton and an employee of the British embassy named Jill Bryant. Particularly after Billy's departure from the scene, this romance comes to dominate the movie. Many critics and viewers have found this to be a jarring shift in emphasis. Nevertheless, Linda Hunt (who won an Oscar for Best Supporting Actress in her cross-gendered portrayal of Billy) remains the most memorable presence in the film.

## ZULU

1964 (135 minutes) • Historical Drama
Diamond (UK) • Unrated

Cast: Stanley Baker (Lt. John Chard), Jack Hawkins (The Rev. Otto Witt), Michael Caine (Lt. Gonville Bromhead), Ulla Jacobsson (Margareta Witt), James Booth (Pvt. Henry Hook), Nigel Green (Colour Sgt. Bourne), Ivor Emmanuel (Pvt. Owen), Paul Daneman (Sgt. Maxfield), Glynn Edwards (Cpl. Allen), Neil McCarthy (Pvt. Thomas), Richard Burton (Narrator)

Producers: Stanley Baker, Cy Endfield; Director: Cy Endfield; Writers: John Prebble, Cy Endfield (based on a story by Prebble); Photographer: Stephen Dade (Technirama, Technicolor); Editor: John Jympson

These days one would be hard-pressed to find anyone willing to say a good word about imperialism. In the twentieth century, it was associated with totalitarian maniacs such as Hitler and Stalin. Those countries which colonized "lesser breeds" in the nineteenth century (principally the United States and Great Britain) evolved into societies whose intellectual elite felt it necessary to apologize for their earlier expansionism. (Only among neoconservatives do we find a contemporary thirst for empire.) For that reason, it is hard to imagine a movie such as *Zulu* being made today. Filmed a year before the death of Sir Winston Churchill, this masterwork of the blacklisted American director Cy Endfield can be seen as a sort of swansong for "Rule Britannia"—complete with rousing narration by Richard Burton. Much of the emotional appeal of the picture lies in the fact that 150 British lads put up a gallant and successful defense against 4,000 Zulu on July 4, 1879. (One can't help thinking of Gulliver among the Lilliputians.) As the anonymous reviewer for Epinions.com noted: "It does basically for British pride what the Alamo provides for Anglo Texans, *Saving Private Ryan* for American veterans, and the defense of Helms Deep for the self-esteem of Elves, Hobbits, and the Men of Middle Earth."

The film opens with a couple of Swedish missionaries (the Rev. Otto Witt and his daughter Margareta) witnessing a tribal Zulu ceremony. This moment of multicultural understanding is interrupted by news that other Zulu warriors have wiped out 1,200 Brits at nearby Isandhlwana. The missionaries immediately depart to warn the soldiers at Rorke's Drift that they are likely to be next. Back at the British fortress, we see a class conflict between the commanding officer, Lt. Gonville Bromhead, and his colleague Lt. John Chard. Bromhead is an aristocratic dilettante who has gained his post through family connections, while Chard is primarily an engineer commissioned to build a bridge. Because Chard has been in rank a couple of months longer than Bromhead, he is allowed to assume control of what is clearly a desperate situation. (The crisis is exacerbated by the Rev. Witt, who is not only a drunk, but—worse yet—a pacifist, as if one could expect anything else of a Swede.) Rather than abandon their post, the white warriors (most of whom seem to be Welsh) withstand incessant attack while managing to sing a few rounds of *Men of Harlech*.

Critical reaction to this movie has been remarkably similar to the response to *The Birth of a Nation*—praise for its technical qualities, mixed with condemnation of its cultural politics. But, as with Griffith's epic, the visceral appeal of Endfield's film cannot be totally divorced from its content. Although the racism of *Zulu* is more sophisticated and sublimated, audiences throughout the "advanced" world cannot help empathizing with the embattled Brits against an enemy so alien in appearance that they might as well have come from outer space. Even in anticolonialist films, the black hero invariably seems more a dark-skinned European than a savage. Although this fact does not justify either colonialism or white supremacy, it does suggest the power of tribal loyalty in shaping our responses to a work of art.

# NOTES

## FOREWORD

1. Arthur Schlesinger Jr., *The Vital Center: The Politics of Freedom* (Boston: Houghton-Mifflin, 1949), 1, 31, 45.
2. Ibid., 256.
3. James Davison Hunter, *Culture Wars: The Struggle to Define America* (New York: HarperCollins, 1991), 44.
4. Gerald Gardner, *The Censorship Papers* (New York: Dodd, Mead & Company, 1987), xiii.
5. Schlesinger, *The Vital Center*, 255.

## PROLOGUE: THE VIEW FROM MAIN STREET

1. Ben Stein, *The View from Sunset Boulevard: America as Brought to You by the People Who Make Television* (New York: Basic Books, 1979), 135. (For a differing view of the political climate in Hollywood, see Steven Sailer, "Left Coast's Right Turn," *American Conservative*, June 20, 2005: 7–10.) The son of economist Herb Stein, Ben worked in the Nixon White House and remembers weeping when our thirty-seventh president resigned his office in August 1974. Interestingly enough, he has also worked with producer Norman Lear, creator of *All in the Family* and founder of the liberal People for the American Way. When Stein was getting ready to publish *The View from Sunset Boulevard*, his friend John Gregory Dunne warned him that doing so might damage his career. Although there is no way of knowing what rewards he might have reaped had the book not appeared, Stein has gone on to

play supporting roles in more than a dozen movies, including *Casper, The Mask, My Girl 2, Dave,* and *Ghostbusters 2*. He is perhaps best remembered, however, for his characterization of a pedantic high school teacher lecturing his class on the Smoot-Hawley Tariff Act in *Ferris Bueller's Day Off.*

2. Richard Schickel, "No Method to His Madness," in *Hollywood's America: United States History Through Its Films*, third edition, eds. Steven Mintz and Randy Roberts (St. James, New York: Brandywine Press, 2001), 309–19.

3. See Medved's autobiography *Right Turns: Unconventional Lessons from a Controversial Life* (New York: Crown Forum, 2004).

4. Leslie Fiedler in conversation.

5. Tom Dardis, *Some Time in the Sun* (New York: Scribner's, 1976), 8.

6. Michael Medved, *Hollywood vs. America* (New York: HarperCollins, 1992), 292.

7. See ibid., 280–85.

8. See Ronald and Allis Radosh, *Red Star over Hollywood: The Film Colony's Long Romance with the Left* (San Francisco: Encounter Books, 2005), 89–90.

9. See Robert Mayhew, *Ayn Rand and The Song of Russia: Communism and Anti-Communism in 1940s Hollywood* (Lanham, Maryland: Scarecrow Press, 2005), 36–38.

10. Radosh and Radosh, *Red Star over Hollywood*, 100. Ellipsis in original.

11. Ibid., 103. Dwight Macdonald, "Critics Hit 'Submission to Moscow,'" *New Leader* (May 8, 1943): 2.

12. See Robert Vaughan, *Only Victims: A Study of Show Business Blacklisting* (New York: Limelight, 1972).

13. Milton Friedman, *Capitalism and Freedom* (Chicago: University of Chicago Press, 1962), 20.

14. For a brief survey of films denouncing the blacklist, see Radosh and Radosh, *Red Star over Hollywood*, 243–47. For a contemporaneous account of the Kazan controversy, see Jonathan Ellis, "Letter from Los Angeles: On the Celebrity Waterfront," *Chronicles: A Magazine of American Culture* (July 1999): 36–37.

15. Leonard J. Leff, "David Selznick's *Gone With the Wind* and 'The Negro Problem,'" *Georgia Review* 38 (Spring 1984): 151.

16. Bill Kauffman, "The Hollywood Ten(nessean)," *Chronicles: A Magazine of American Culture* (October 1998): 40.

17. See, for example, Melvin B. Tolson's "*Gone With the Wind* Is More Dangerous than *Birth of a Nation*," in *American Movie Critics: An Anthology from the Sixties until Now*, ed. Philip Lopate (New York: Library of America, 2006), 140–44.

## ONE: RIDE TO THE RESCUE (*THE BIRTH OF A NATION*)

1. David Mulroy, "Politics and Great Books," *South Carolina Review* 29 (Spring 1997): 165–67.

2. William Drew, "PC Madness in Hollywood," *Heterodoxy* (January 2000): 8.

3. For a discussion of the theme of interracial rape in *The Clansman* and *The Birth*

*of a Nation*, see Leslie Fiedler, *What Was Literature?: Class Culture and Mass Society* (New York: Simon & Schuster, 1982), 179–95.
4. Richard Schickel, *D. W. Griffith: An American Life* (New York: Simon & Schuster, 1984), 76.
5. Thomas Dixon Jr., *The Clansman: A Romance of the Ku Klux Klan* (Lexington, KY: University Press of Kentucky, 1970 [1905]).
6. Raymond A. Cook, *Thomas Dixon* (New York: Twayne, 1974), 102.
7. Schickel, *D. W. Griffith: An American Life*, 213.
8. The most complete version of *The Birth of a Nation* currently available on VHS was released by Video Yesteryear in 1996.
9. There have been several film versions of *Uncle Tom's Cabin*, beginning in 1909 with a production by Edwin S. Porter (whose picture *The Great Train Robbery* [1903] was the first movie to tell a story). Porter's *Uncle Tom's Cabin* was the first novel to be turned into a screenplay and the first film with subtitles. In 1927, a major Hollywood production of Stowe's novel was brought out at the cost of $2 million—a considerable sum at the time. See Thomas F. Gossett, *Uncle Tom's Cabin and American Culture* (Dallas: Southern Methodist University Press, 1985), 383–85.
10. Fiedler, *What Was Literature?* 193.
11. Ibid., 194.
12. John Greenleaf Whittier, *John Greenleaf Whittier's Poetry: An Appraisal and a Selection*, ed. Robert Penn Warren (Minneapolis: University of Minnesota Press, 1971), 140–42.
13. See, for example, Thomas J. DiLorenzo, *The Real Lincoln: A New Look at Abraham Lincoln: His Agenda, and an Unnecessary War* (New York: Prima, 2002).

## TWO: THE BOURGEOIS SENTIMENTALITY OF *GONE WITH THE WIND*

1. "Democratic Culture," transcript of "Firing Line," November 15, 1974 (Columbia, SC: Southern Educational Communications Association, 1974), 4.
2. George F. Will, "Gone With the Wind, Indeed," *Washington Post*, June 25, 2006, B7.
3. Margaret Mitchell, *Gone With the Wind* (New York: Avon, 1973 [1936]), 662.
4. Ibid., 147–48.
5. Leslie Fiedler, *What Was Literature?: Class Culture and Mass Society* (New York: Simon & Schuster, 1982), 197.
6. The figures of the Good Bad Boy and Good Bad Girl (as well as the Good Good Boy and the Good Good Girl) are discussed at length in Leslie Fiedler's "The Eye of Innocence: Some Notes on the Role of the Child in Literature," *The Collected Essays of Leslie Fiedler*, vol. 1 (New York: Stein & Day, 1971), 471–511.
7. Mitchell, *Gone With the Wind*, 1004.
8. Ibid., 209–10, 517.
9. James Boatwright, "Reconsideration: Totin' de Weary Load," in Richard Harwell, ed., *Gone With the Wind as Book and Film* (Columbia, SC: University of South Carolina Press, 1992), 211–17.

10. Mitchell, *Gone With the Wind*, 999.
11. Ibid., 1024.

## THREE: WHAT A BEAUTIFUL DAY! (*SONG OF THE SOUTH*)

1. Walker's essay ("The Dummy in the Window"), which includes Julia Collier Harris's cited quotations from Joseph Addison Turner and Joel Chandler Harris, can be found in *Living by the Word: Selected Writings 1973–1987* (New York: Harcourt Brace Jovanovich, 1988), 25–32.
2. Although *Song of the South* is available on VHS and DVD, the only retailers I know who stock it are the League of the South store in Abbeville, South Carolina, and Dixie Republic in Travelers Rest, South Carolina. In her story "Nineteen Fifty-Five," Walker has written a fictionalized account of an Elvis Presley-type rock 'n roll singer who rips off the black man's music for fun and profit. Alice Walker, *You Can't Keep a Good Woman Down* (New York: Harcourt, Brace, Jovanovich, 1981), 3–20. For a fuller discussion of racial objections to *Song of the South*, see Karl F. Cohen, *Forbidden Animation: Censored Cartoons and Blacklisted Animators in America* (Jefferson, NC: McFarland, 1998), 60–70.
3. Louis D. Rubin Jr., "Uncle Remus and the Ubiquitous Rabbit," in *William Elliott Shoots a Bear: Essays on the Southern Literary Imagination* (Baton Rouge, LA: Louisiana State University Press, 1975), 89–90.
4. See ibid., 90–91.
5. Paul M. Gaston, *The New South Creed: A Study in Southern Mythmaking* (New York: Knopf, 1970), 181–82. Rubin, *William Elliott Shoots a Bear*, 85.
6. Kenneth S. Lynn, *Mark Twain and Southwestern Humor* (Boston: Little, Brown, 1959), 242. The bonding of white and colored men is a recurring motif in American literature and popular culture. See Leslie Fiedler, "Come Back to the Raft Ag'in, Huck Honey!" in *The New Fiedler Reader* (Amherst, NY: Prometheus, 1999), 3–12.
7. Leonard Maltin, *The Disney Films* (New York: Crown, 1973), 1.
8. Ibid., 77.
9. See Peggy A. Russo, "Uncle Walt's Uncle Remus: Disney's Distortion of Harris's Hero," *Southern Literary Journal* 25 (Fall 1992): 28. See also Walter M. Brasch, *Brer Rabbit, Uncle Remus and the "Cornfield Journalist": The Tale of Joel Chandler Harris* (Macon, GA: Mercer University Press, 2000), 289.
10. See Russo, "Uncle Walt's Uncle Remus," 28–29.
11. Ibid., 29.
12. June Jordan, "A Truly Bad Rabbit," *New York Times Book Review*, May 17, 1987, 32.
13. Jason Sperb, "'Take a Frown, Turn It Upside Down': Splash Mountain, Walt Disney World, and the Cultural De-rac[e]ination of Disney's *Song of the South*," *Journal of Popular Culture* 38 (2005): 933.
14. Jason Isaac Mauro, "Disney's Splash Mountain: Death Anxiety, the Tar Baby, and the Rituals of Violence," *Children's Literature Association Quarterly* 22 (1977): 116.

15. Donald Davidson, *Still Rebels, Still Yankees and Other Essays* (Baton Rouge: Louisiana State University Press, 1972), 223. The letter from Davidson to Warren, dated March 17, 1930, is contained in the Fugitive Collection of the Jean and Alexander Heard Library at Vanderbilt University.
16. Lucinda Hardwick Mackethan, *The Dream of Arcady: Place and Time in Southern Literature* (Baton Rouge, LA: Louisiana State University Press, 1980), 81.
17. Joel Chandler Harris, *Nights with Uncle Remus* (Boston: J. R. Osgood, 1883), 51.
18. Joel Chandler Harris, *Uncle Remus and His Friends: Old Plantation Stories, Songs, and Ballads, with Sketches of Negro Character* (Boston: Houghton Mifflin, 1892), 130.
19. R. Bruce Bickley Jr., *Joel Chandler Harris* (Athens, GA: University of Georgia Press, 1987), 94.

## FOUR: THE KEEPER OF OUR CONSCIENCE (*INTRUDER IN THE DUST*)

1. Malcolm Cowley, "William Faulkner's Nation," *New Republic* (October 18, 1948): 21–22. Elizabeth Hardwick, "Faulkner and the South Today," *Partisan Review* 15 (1948): 1130–35. Edmund Wilson, "William Faulkner's Reply to the Civil-Rights Program," *New Yorker* (October 23, 1948): 120–21, 125–28.
2. Cleanth Brooks, *The Well Wrought Urn: Studies in the Structure of Poetry* (New York: Reynal and Hitchcock, 1947), 229. Cleanth Brooks, *William Faulkner: The Yoknapatawpha Country* (New Haven, CT: Yale University Press, 1963), 288.
3. Robert Scholes and Robert Kellogg, *The Nature of Narrative* (New York: Oxford University Press, 1966), 261–62.
4. William Faulkner, *Intruder in the Dust* (New York: Random House, 1948), 18, italics in original.
5. Faulkner, *Intruder in the Dust*, 19. Malcolm X, *The Autobiography of Malcolm X*, with the assistance of Alex Haley (New York: Grove Press, 1965), 2.
6. Faulkner, *Intruder in the Dust*, 89.
7. Arthur Mizener, "The Thin, Intelligent Face of American Fiction," *Kenyon Review* 17 (1955): 517. Edmund L. Volpe, *A Reader's Guide to William Faulkner* (New York: Farrar, Straus, 1964), 259.
8. William Faulkner, *Selected Letters*, ed. Joseph Blotner (New York: Random House, 1977), 122. Leslie Fiedler, *The Collected Essays of Leslie Fiedler*, vol. 1 (New York: Stein & Day, 1971), 332. See Joseph Blotner, *Faulkner: A Biography* (New York: Random House, 1974), 1252.
9. See Regina K. Fadiman, *Faulkner's* Intruder in the Dust*: Novel into Film* (Knoxville, TN: University of Tennessee Press, 1978), 9.
10. See Brooks, *William Faulkner*, 280.
11. Pauline Kael, *Kiss Kiss Bang Bang* (Boston: Little, Brown, 1968), 284.
12. E. Pauline Degenfelder, "The Film Adaptation of Faulkner's *Intruder in the Dust*," *Literature / Film Quarterly* 1 (Spring 1973): 138.
13. For Maddow's screenplay, see Fadiman, 95–303. For a discussion of Schary's role in shaping the ending of the film, see Gene D. Phillips, *Fiction, Film, and*

*Faulkner: The Art of Adaptation* (Knoxville, TN: University of Tennessee Press, 1988), 94–95.

## FIVE: RACING FOR GLORY (*BEN-HUR*)

1. Lee Scott Theisen, "'My God, Did I Set All of This in Motion?' General Lew Wallace and *Ben-Hur*," *Journal of Popular Culture* 18.2 (1984), 35. *Ben-Hur* was eventually outsold by *Gone With the Wind*.
2. See Paul Gutjahr, "'To the Heart of Solid Puritans': Historicizing the Popularity of *Ben-Hur*," *Mosaic* 26:3 (Summer 1993), 53–67.
3. Lew Wallace, *Lew Wallace: An Autobiography* (New York: Harper & Brothers, 1906).
4. "Ben-Hur." *General Lew Wallace Study and Museum*. September 9, 2006, http://www.ben-hur.com/benhur.html.
5. Theisen, *Journal of Popular Culture*, 37.
6. See Ted Hovet Jr., "The Case of Kalem's *Ben-Hur* (1907) and the Transformation of Cinema," *Quarterly Review of Film and Video* 18:3 (2001), 283–94.
7. Marcia L. Pentz-Harris, Linda Seger, and R. Barton Palmer, "Screening Male Sentimental Power in *Ben-Hur*," in *Nineteenth-Century American Fiction on Screen* (Cambridge: Cambridge University Press, 2006), 131.
8. Quoted in Bruce Babington and William Peter Evans, *Biblical Epics: Sacred Narrative in the Hollywood Cinema* (Manchester: Manchester University Press, 1993), 121.
9. Melani McAlister, "'Benevolent Supremacy': Biblical Epic Films, Suez, and the Cultural Politics of U.S. Power," Macmillan Center Working Paper Database <http://research.yale.edu/ycias/database/files/MESV5 6.pdf#search=%22biblical%20epic%20films%22>. Just as remarkable as this statistic is the fact that, after John Huston's *The Bible* in 1966, Hollywood simply stopped making such pictures. There were epic war films, science-fiction chronicles, and even a worshipful dramatization of the life of Mahatma Gandhi, but movies dealing reverently with the holy writ of Christians and Jews virtually disappeared from the big screen.
10. Ibid.
11. Ibid.
12. Leslie Fiedler, *Love and Death in the American Novel*, rev. ed. (New York: Stein & Day, 1966), 54.
13. Robert K. Johnston, "*The Passion* as Dynamic Icon: A Theological Reflection," in *Re-Viewing* The Passion*: Mel Gibson's Film and Its Critics*, ed. S. Brent Plate (New York: Palgrave, 2004), 56.
14. Pentz-Harris et al., "Screening Male Sentimental Power in *Ben-Hur*," 178.
15. For the comments about Tennessee Williams, see Gore Vidal, "Immortal Bird," *New York Review of Books*, June 13, 1985, 10. Pentz-Harris et al., "Screening Male Sentimental Power in *Ben-Hur*," 133.
16. "Who Really Makes a Film, the Writer or the Director?" *Washington Star*, November 21, 1976, sec. G-I, 8. When Vidal mentioned his idea for a homoerotic

subtext to William Wyler, the director responded: "Gore, this is *Ben Hur. Ben Hur!*: '*A Tale of the Christ*' or whatever that subtitle is. You can't do this with *Ben Hur.*" But when Vidal assured him that the theme would only be implied, Wyler assented to the idea. "We'd inherited a javelin-throwing contest between Ben Hur and Messala [from an earlier script]," Vidal explains in his memoir *Palimpsest*. "This was supposed to symbolize the contest between Zionists and Roman overlords. It could also, as easily, represent male sexuality either in contest or in collusion. . . . I explained how, when Ben Hur refuses to join Messala in supporting the Roman occupation, one could see in Messala's face that the issue was not politics but thwarted love." Gore Vidal, *Palimpsest: A Memoir* (New York: Random House, 1995), 305.

## SIX: CACTUS ROSE (*THE MAN WHO SHOT LIBERTY VALANCE*)

1. For the comments by Weiler, Gill, and Crowther, see Joseph McBride, *Searching for John Ford: A Life* (New York: St. Martin's, 2001), 624–25. Judith Crist is cited in Tag Gallagher, *John Ford: The Man and His Films* (Berkeley, CA: University of California Press), 186, 402.
2. Andrew Sarris, "Cactus Rosebud or *The Man Who Shot Liberty Valance*," *Film Culture* 25 (Summer 1962): 15. For the observations of Bogdanovich and the British reviewers, see McBride, *Searching for John Ford*, 625.
3. For a brief overview of Ford's career, see Andrew Sarris, *The American Cinema: Directors and Directions 1929–1968* (New York: Dutton, 1968): 43–49.
4. Although some critics balk at Ford's comparing himself to Maupassant and at the notion that *Stagecoach* is a "ship of fools" tale, a convincing argument for both propositions is made by Garry Wills in *John Wayne's America: The Politics of Celebrity* (New York: Simon & Schuster, 1977), 81–83.
5. Ibid., 261.
6. For a discussion of the issue of miscegenation in Cooper's *Last of the Mohicans*, see Leslie Fiedler, *Love and Death in the American Novel*, rev. ed. (New York: Stein & Day, 1966), 207–8.
7. Stephen Crane, *The Open Boat and Other Stories* (New York: Dover, 1991), 85.
8. Ibid., 88.
9. Ibid., 85
10. M. E. Bradford, *Remembering Who We Are: Observations of a Southern Conservative* (Athens, GA: University of Georgia Press, 1985), 136.
11. See Frederick Jackson Turner, *The Frontier in American History* (New York: Holt, 1920). The reference to "petticoat government" comes in Irving's "Rip Van Winkle" (1828).
12. At the beginning of *The Glass Menagerie* the narrator, Tom, says, "The play is memory. Being a memory play, it is dimly lighted, it is sentimental, it is not realistic." Tennessee Williams, *The Glass Menagerie* (New York: New Directions, 1945), 23.

13. Dorothy M. Johnson, "The Man Who Shot Liberty Valance," in *Fiction 100*, 5th ed., ed. James F. Pickering (New York: Macmillan, 1988), 799–809.
14. Wills, *John Wayne's America*, 267.
15. Sarris, "Cactus Rosebud," 14.
16. Peter Stowell, for example, writes: "Metaphorically speaking, this is the same stage that delivered Clementine in *My Darling Clementine* to Tombstone and transported that odd band of travelers from Tonto to Lordsburg in *Stagecoach.*" Peter Stowell, *John Ford* (Boston: Twayne, 1986), 109. Tag Gallagher also notes that it "looks like the vehicle used in *Stagecoach* in 1939" (Gallagher, *John Ford*, 388).
17. In "Cactus Rosebud," Andrew Sarris refers to Devine as "Ford's broad-beamed Falstaff" (14) and remarks that "there is some glory in just growing old and remembering through the thick haze of illusion" (15).
18. In Jack Schaefer's *Shane* (1949), we also see a conflict of cultures between the small farmers and the cattle barons.
19. Gallagher, *John Ford*, 400.
20. Cheyney Ryan, "Print the Legend: Violence and Recognition in *The Man Who Shot Liberty Valance*," in *Legal Realism: Movies as Legal Texts*, ed. John Denvir (Urbana, IL: University of Illinois Press, 1996), 25.
21. David F. Courson, "John Ford's Wilderness: *The Man Who Shot Liberty Valance*," *Sight and Sound* 47 (Autumn 1978): 238.
22. Ryan, "Print the Legend," 34.
23. Ibid., 39–40.

## SEVEN: THE UNIVERSAL SOLDIER (PATTON)

1. See Norman Podhoretz, *The Present Danger: Do We Have the Will to Reverse the Decline in American Power?* (New York: Simon & Schuster, 1980), 62–63.
2. The right-wing Japanese novelist Yukio Mishima tried to revive a vision of imperial Japan during the 1960s. This effort, however, led to nothing more than a brief takeover of a military installation, which provided the setting for Mishima's own histrionic suicide.
3. Joseph C. Carter and Michael S. Finer, "A Survey of Leadership: Stonewall Jackson and George S. Patton," *Infantry Magazine* (January–February 2004).
4. Thomas G. West, *In the Mind's Eye: Visual Thinkers, Gifted People with Dyslexia and Other Learning Difficulties, Computer Images, and the Ironies of Creativity* (Amherst, NY: Prometheus, 1997), 19.
5. Carlo D'Este, *Patton: A Genius for War* (New York: HarperCollins, 1995), 130–36.
6. "George Smith Patton, Jr.," 2nd Infantry Division Living History Society, www.2ndinfdiv.com.
7. John J. Pullen, "'You will be afraid': next to Winston Churchill, Gen. George Patton gave the war's most memorable speeches. But nobody knew quite what he said—until now." *American Heritage* 56:3 (June–July 2005), 26.

8. Ibid.
9. Carmine A. Prioli, "The Poetry of General George S. Patton, Jr.," *Journal of American Culture* 8:4 (Winter 1985): 81, 82.
10. X. J. Kennedy, "Meter-Rattling," *Sewanee Review* 102 (Winter 1994): 152.
11. D'Este, *Patton*, 328.
12. Ibid., 533–55.
13. Francis Ford Coppola and Edmund H. North, *Patton*, shooting script, February 1, 1969, 147.
14. Ibid., 154, 155.

## EIGHT: FIXING SIN (*A CLOCKWORK ORANGE*)

1. See Stuart Y. MacDougal, ed., *Stanley Kubrick's* A Clockwork Orange (Cambridge: Cambridge University Press, 2003), 138.
2. Burgess remained attracted enough to the figure of Christ to write the script for the acclaimed television miniseries *Jesus of Nazareth* (1977).
3. Martin Green, *Yeats's Blessing on Von Hugel* (London: Longmans, 1967), 74.
4. Flannery O'Connor, *Mystery and Manners* (New York: Farrar, Straus & Giroux, 1969), 34. D. Keith Mano, "Reflections of a Christian Pornographer," *Christianity and Literature* 28 (1979), 5, 10.
5. Dostoyevsky makes this point in *Notes from Underground*, when he has his protagonist say: "[E]ven if man were nothing but a piano-key, even if this were proved to him by natural science and mathematics, even then he would not become reasonable, but would purposely do something perverse out of simple ingratitude, simply to gain his point." Fyodor Dostoyevsky, *Notes from Underground* (reprint, New York: Dover, 1992 [1864]), 21.
6. Michel Ciment, *Kubrick: The Definitive Edition*, trans. Gilbert Adair (New York: Faber & Faber, 1980), 158.
7. Norman Kagen, *The Cinema of Stanley Kubrick*, 3rd ed. (New York: Continuum, 2000), 181.
8. Ciment, *Kubrick*, 162–63.
9. Ibid., 163.
10. Ibid. Italics added.

## NINE: THE MORAL VISION OF *STRAW DOGS*

1. Pauline Kael, *Deeper into Movies* (Boston: Little, Brown, 1973), 398.
2. David Weddle, *"If They Move . . . Kill 'Em!": The Life and Times of Sam Peckinpah* (New York: Grove Press, 1994), 393.
3. Louis Garner Simmons, *The Cinema of Sam Peckinpah and the American Western: A Study of the Interrelationship between an Auteur/Director and the Genre in Which He Works,* Ph.D. Thesis, Northwestern University, 1975.

4. Weddle, *If They Move*, 396. See William Murray, "*Playboy* Interview: Sam Peckinpah," *Playboy*, August 1972, 68.
5. For a survey of the critical response to *Straw Dogs* and *A Clockwork Orange* in England, see Charles Barr, "*Straw Dogs, A Clockwork Orange* and the Critics," *Screen: The Journal for the Society for Education in Film and Television* (Summer 1972), 17–31. See also Weddle, *If They Move*, 395.
6. Molly Haskell, *From Reverence to Rape: The Treatment of Women in the Movies* (Baltimore: Penguin, 1974), 363.
7. Doug McKinney, *Sam Peckinpah* (Boston: Twayne, 1979), 117.
8. Michael Bliss, *Justified Lives: Morality and Narrative in the Films of Sam Peckinpah* (Carbondale, IL: Southern Illinois University Press, 1993), 146, 147.
9. McKinney, *Sam Peckinpah*, 18–19.
10. Bliss, *Justified Lives*, 151, Weddle, *If They Move*, 423–24.
11. Bliss, *Justified Lives*, 157.
12. Ibid., 156.
13. Ibid., 162.
14. McKinney, *Sam Peckinpah*, 126.

## TEN: RITES IN CONFLICT (*THE DEER HUNTER*)

1. See Jeremy M. Devine, *Vietnam at 24 Frames a Second: A Critical and Thematic Analysis of over 400 Films about the Vietnam War* (Jefferson, NC: McFarland, 1995), 104.
2. For a comparison of *The Deer Hunter* with James Fenimore Cooper's *The Deer Slayer*, see David Axeen, "Eastern Western," *Film Quarterly* 32:4 (1979), 17; Leonard Quart, "*The Deer Hunter*: The Superman in Vietnam," in *From Hanoi to Hollywood: The Vietnam War in American Film*, eds. Linda Dittmar and Gene Michaud (New Brunswick, NJ: Rutgers University Press, 1990), 159–68; and Colin L. Westerbeck Jr., "Peace with Honor: Cowboys and Viet Cong," *Commonweal*, March 2, 1979, 115–17. For a discussion of Cimino's debt to the Western films of John Ford and Howard Hawks, see Robin Wood, *Hollywood from Vietnam to Reagan . . . and Beyond* (New York: Columbia University Press, 1986), 280–82.
3. Norman Mailer, *Why Are We in Vietnam?* (New York: Putnam, 1967), 208. Ranald Jethroe, who is the narrator as well as the protagonist of Mailer's novel, refers to himself as "D. J." because the rhythms of his voice resemble the patter of a radio disc jockey.
4. RogerEbert.com. March 9, 1979.
5. See Wood, *Hollywood from Vietnam to Reagan*, 283.
6. For the reference to simulated orgasms, see ibid., 292.
7. Ibid., 271.
8. Leslie Fiedler, *Love and Death in the American Novel*, rev. ed. (New York: Stein & Day, 1966), 318. For a fuller discussion of the homoerotic subtext of *The Deer Hunter*, see Wood, *Hollywood from Vietnam to Reagan*, 291–97.

9. Ernest Hemingway, *A Farewell to Arms* (New York: Scribner's, 1995 [1929]), 184–85.
10. Ebert, March 9, 1979.
11. Robert E. Bourdette Jr., "Rereading *The Deer Hunter*: Michael Cimino's Deliberate American Epic," in *America Rediscovered: Critical Essays on Literature and Film of the Vietnam War*, eds. Owen W. Gilman Jr. and Lorrie Smith (New York: Garland, 1990), 182.
12. See Divine, *Vietnam at 24 Frames a Second*, 169, and Wood, *Hollywood from Vietnam to Reagan*, 290.
13. For criticisms of Cimino's depiction of the Vietnam War, see Peter Arnett, "War Reporter Compares *Deer Hunter* to Reality," special to the *Los Angeles Times*, rpt. in the *New Orleans Times-Picayune*, April 13, 1979: 6–7; Albert Auster and Leonard Quart, *How the War Was Remembered: Hollywood and Vietnam* (New York: Praeger, 1988), 56–65; Tom Buckley, "Hollywood's War," *Harper's*, April 1979: 84–88; Pauline Kael, "The God-Bless-America Symphony," *New Yorker*, December 18, 1978: 66–79; Arthur Lubow, "Natty Bumppo Goes to War," *Atlantic Monthly*, April 1979: 95–98. Terry Curtis Fox, John Hellmann, and Leonard Quart comment on the alleged racism in the film's depiction of the Vietnamese. See Fox's "Stalking *The Deer Hunter*," *Film Comment* 15 (1979): 22–25; John Hellmann, "Vietnam and the Hollywood Genre Film," in Michael A. Andregg, ed., *Inventing Vietnam: The War in Film and Television* (Philadelphia: Temple University Press, 1991), 64; and Quart, "Superman in Vietnam," 165–66.

## ELEVEN: THAT'S WHAT FRIENDS ARE FOR (*DRIVING MISS DAISY*)

1. Eliza R. L. McGraw, *Two Covenants: Representations of Southern Jewishness* (Baton Rouge, LA: Louisiana State University Press, 2005), 118.
2. RogerEbert.com. January 12, 1990.
3. James Baldwin, *Notes of a Native Son* (Boston: Beacon, 1955), 72.
4. Leslie Fiedler, *The Collected Essays of Leslie Fiedler*, vol. 2 (New York: Stein & Day, 1971), 167.
5. W. E. B. Du Bois, *The Souls of Black Folk* (Boston: Bedford, 1997 [1903]), 113, 116; McGraw, *Two Covenants*, 141.
6. Du Bois, *The Souls of Black Folk*, 210.
7. This includes the television movie *The Murder of Mary Phegan* (1987), David Mamet's novel *The Old Religion* (1997), and Alfred Uhrey's own musical, *Parade* (1998).
8. McGraw, *Two Covenants*, 116.
9. Alfred Uhrey, *Driving Miss Daisy* (New York: Dramatist Play Service, 1987), 30.
10. Ibid., 20.
11. Ibid., 18.
12. Ibid., 21.

13. Ibid., 24.
14. Ibid., 26.
15. McGraw, *Two Covenants*, 123.
16. Uhrey, *Driving Miss Daisy*, 15.
17. Ibid., 29.
18. Ibid., 34.
19. Ibid., 36.
20. Ibid., 38.
21. McGraw, *Two Covenants*, 130.
22. Ann Du Cille, *Skin Trade* (Cambridge, MA: Harvard University Press, 1996), 110.

## TWELVE: NO GREATER LOVE (*SHADOWLANDS*)

1. Michael Medved, *Hollywood vs. America* (New York: HarperPerennial, 1992), 87. In 2006, Columbia Pictures created a lesser stir with its production of *The Da Vinci Code*, based on Dan Brown's best-selling novel. Picking up on the notion that Christ and Mary Magdalene were lovers and produced a child, this story asks us to believe that, two thousand years later, the sole remaining progeny (played by Audrey Tautou and Tom Hanks) just happen to run into each other. As George McCartney notes: "On the wildly conservative assumption that each of Christ's descendants averaged a fertility-challenged 1.3 children in each of the 57 generations since, say, A.D. 33, the extended Holy Family would number nearly a million today." McCartney, "Leonardo's Little Joke," *Chronicles: A Magazine of American Culture* (August 2006), 55. As it turns out, the secret of Christ's lineage has been kept all these years by the ultraconservative Catholic order Opus Dei, which is depicted as the CIA of the church. This film is just the most recent example of Catholic-bashing in the popular media, with Opus Dei as the designated scapegoat.
2. Ibid., 47–48.
3. Ibid., 42.
4. Ibid., 87.
5. For biographical information concerning Lewis's relationship with Joy Gresham, see A. N. Wilson, *C. S. Lewis: A Biography* (New York: Norton, 1990), 336–41, 365–81; and Kathryn Lindskoog, *Sleuthing C. S. Lewis: More Light in the Shadowlands* (Macon, GA: Mercer University Press, 1994), 142–63.
6. William Nicholson, *Shadowlands* (New York: Penguin, 1990), 2.
7. Ibid., 59, 60.
8. Ibid., 68.
9. Two decades earlier, Edward VIII had abdicated his throne in order to marry an American divorcée.
10. Nicholson, *Shadowlands*, 90.
11. Ibid., 96. Cleanth Brooks, *The Well Wrought Urn: Studies in the Structure of Poetry* (New York: Reynall & Hitchcock, 1947), 229.

12. Wilson, *C. S. Lewis*, 284.
13. C. S. Lewis, *A Grief Observed* (New York: Seabury, 1990), 41.
14. Ibid., 67.
15. Nicholson, *Shadowlands*, 99.
16. C. S. Lewis, *The Four Loves* (New York: Harcourt, 1960), 190–91.

## THIRTEEN: COPPERHEAD CINEMA (*RIDE WITH THE DEVIL* AND *GANGS OF NEW YORK*)

1. H. Arthur Scott Trask, "A Southern *Braveheart*," *Chronicles: A Magazine of American Culture* (October 2000), 50.
2. Daniel Woodrell, *Ride with the Devil* [Originally *Woe to Live On*] (New York: Pocket Books, 1999 [1987]), 54–55.
3. The novel begins when Jake is already riding with the bushwhackers. The domestic prologue is added by Lee.
4. Woodrell, *Ride with the Devil*, 58.
5. This exchange is found in the film but not the novel.
6. Trask, "A Southern *Braveheart*," 51.
7. Andrew O'Hehir, Review of *Ride with the Devil*, *Salon.com*, November 24, 1999.
8. Although the official website for *Ride with the Devil* appears to have been dismantled, this quotation can be accessed on *Rottentomatoes.com*.
9. The screenplay for this film can be found in *Gangs of New York: Making the Movie* (New York: Miramax Books, 2002). For this particular scene, see 160–61.
10. Ibid., 163.
11. Ibid., 206.
12. Ibid., 213.
13. Sean Mattie, "Blood, Justice, and American Citizenship," *Perspectives on Political Science* 32:4 (Fall 2003), 11. *Gangs of New York: Making the Movie*, 167.
14. Ibid., 208. In his review of *Gangs of New York*, Clyde Wilson writes: "It seems that the accepted idea of the gloriously united North trampling out the grapes of slavery and treason is not so sound a picture of the real thing after all." See Wilson, *Defending Dixie: Essays in Southern History and Culture* (Columbia, SC: Foundation for American Education, 2006), 220.
15. Benjamin Justice, "Historical Fiction to Historical Fact: *Gangs of New York* and the Whitewashing of History," *Social Education* 67:4 (May–June 2003).
16. *Gangs of New York*, 241.
17. Iver Bernstein, *The New York City Draft Riots* (New York: Oxford University Press, 1990), 20.
18. Ibid., 144.

## FOURTEEN: THE CAUSE OF US ALL (*GETTYSBURG* AND *GODS AND GENERALS*)

1. Jesse Oxford, "Shaara's March," *Book* (January–February 2003), 62.
2. Mick Martin and Marsha Porter, eds., *DVD and Video Movie Guide 2004* (New York: Ballantine Books, 2003), 427.
3. Michael Shaara, *The Killer Angels* (New York: Random House, 1974), 32.
4. Except where indicated, quotations from *Gettysburg* are taken directly from the captions to the DVD of the film itself. In some cases, I have regularized punctuation.
5. Richard Schickel, review of *Gettysburg, Time* (October 25, 1993), 80. After the war, Longstreet proved himself something of a scalawag by joining both the Republican Party and the Grant administration. At one point in the movie, he even mentions "Ulysses Sam Grant" as one of his good friends from his days in the federal army.
6. Christopher Sharrett, review of *Gods and Generals, Cineaste* 28:3 (Summer 2003), 36.
7. These comments were made on Maltin's TV show "Hot Ticket."
8. George Eliot, *Daniel Deronda* (London: Panther, 1970 [1876]).
9. Ellipsis in original to denote pause. The screenplay for this film can be found in *Gods and Generals: The Illustrated Story of the Epic Civil War Film* (New York: Newmarket Press, 2003). For this particular speech, see 176.
10. Mackubin T. Owens, "War and Memory: *Gods and Generals* as History," *National Review Online* (February 25, 2003), 2.
11. *Gods and Generals*, 175.
12. Ibid., 190.
13. Ibid., 200.
14. Jo Ann Skousen, "A War Too Civil," *Liberty* (June 2003), 44.
15. *Gods and Generals*, 191.
16. Ibid., 201. Bill Kauffman, "The Civil War Returns," *American Enterprise* (March 2003), 22. Kauffman begins his review with the following statement: "Mr. Lincoln said he liked his speeches short and sweet, so here it is: The new Warner Brothers picture *Gods and Generals* is not only the finest movie ever made about the Civil War, it is also the best American historical film. Period" (20).
17. *Gods and Generals*, 183.
18. A few weeks earlier, I had joined a group of protesters from the League of the South at an antiwar rally on the campus of Clemson University. When one onlooker saw us with our red shirts and state sovereignty flags, he asked, "Why are y'all protesting the war?" One of our group responded: "Because this is the same Yankee empire that invaded us back in 1861!" Whether one agrees with this analogy, it is clear that the question of political sovereignty was not settled by the War Between the States.
19. *Gods and Generals*, 197.
20. Edmund Wilson, *Patriotic Gore: Studies in the Literature of the American Civil War* (New York: Oxford University Press, 1962), 434.

## FIFTEEN: BLOOD, SWEAT, AND GRACE (*THE PASSION OF THE CHRIST*)

1. Patrick J. Buchanan, "The Passion and Its Enemies," *American Conservative* (April 26, 2004), 13.
2. Michael Medved, *Right Turns: Unconventional Lessons from a Controversial Life* (New York: Crown Forum, 2004), 404.
3. Among other changes, Medved suggested that Simon of Cyrene be clearly identified as a Jew and that a Roman soldier's reference to "this stinking temple" be changed to "this stinking outpost." Also, he persuaded Gibson not to use the potentially incendiary passage from Mathew 27:25: "Then answered all the people, and said, His blood be on us and on our children."
4. Medved, *Right Turns*, 400.
5. Ibid., 402.
6. George McCartney, "The Crux of the Matter," *Chronicles: A Magazine of American Culture* (May 2004), 47. John Bartunek, *Inside the Passion*: *An Insider's Look at* The Passion of the Christ (West Chester, PA: Ascension Press, 2005), 75.
7. Bartunek, *Inside the Passion*, 53.
8. Ibid, 84.
9. Ibid, 102.
10. Ibid, 117.
11. McCartney, "The Crux of the Matter," 46.
12. Bartunek, *Inside the Passion*, 154.
13. Ibid, 148–49.
14. Karen Jo Torjesen, "The Journey of the Passion Play from Medieval Piety to Contemporary Spirituality," in *After the Passion Is Gone: American Religious Consequences*, eds. J. Shawn Landres and Michael Berenbaum (Walnut Creek, CA: Alta Mira Press, 2004), 97.
15. *Baptist Hymnal* (Nashville: Convention Press, 1956).
16. See, for example, Marvin Perry and Frederick M. Schweitzer, "The Medieval Passion Play Revisited," in *Re-Viewing* The Passion*: Mel Gibson's Film and Its Critics*, ed. S. Brent Plate (New York: Palgrave Macmillan, 2004), 3–19.
17. www.michaelmedved.com.
18. Buchanan, "The Passion and Its Enemies," 16.
19. Ibid., 16.
20. Gibson has publicly apologized and asked forgiveness for his behavior that night. He has admitted to having had a drinking problem as a young man but presumably had been sober for a number of years. Why he fell off the wagon that particular night remains a mystery.
21. Lloyd Baugh, "Imago Christi: Aesthetic and Theological Issues in Jesus Films by Pasolini, Scorsese, and Gibson," in Landres and Berenbaum, *After The Passion Is Gone*, 162–63.
22. Buchanan, "The Passion and Its Enemies," 15.

# INDEX

## A

## C

## D

## G

## K

## L

## M

## N



## O

## Q



## R

## S

## T

## W

## ABOUT THE AUTHORS

MARK ROYDEN WINCHELL is professor of English at Clemson University, where he also directs Clemson's program in the Great Works of Western Civilization. He is the author of books on Joan Didion, William F. Buckley Jr., and neoconservative criticism and of authorized biographies of literary critics Donald Davidson and Leslie Fiedler, among other volumes. During the past quarter century he has published over 120 essays and reviews in such periodicals as *Modern Age*, the *American Conservative*, the *Sewanee Review*, and the *Atlanta Journal-Constitution*.

R. BARTON PALMER is the Calhoun Lemon Professor of Literature at Clemson University, where he also teaches film and screenwriting. He is the author or coauthor of a number of books on film, including *Joel and Ethan Coen*; *Nineteenth-Century American Fiction on Screen*; and *Hollywood's Dark Cinema: The American Film Noir.*